MW00824092

# THE PRINCE OF JOCKEYS

# THE PRINCE
## OF
# JOCKEYS

### The Life of
## ISAAC BURNS MURPHY

## PELLOM McDANIELS III

UNIVERSITY PRESS OF KENTUCKY

Copyright © 2013 by The University Press of Kentucky

Scholarly publisher for the Commonwealth,
serving Bellarmine University, Berea College, Centre College of Kentucky,
Eastern Kentucky University, The Filson Historical Society, Georgetown
College, Kentucky Historical Society, Kentucky State University, Morehead State
University, Murray State University, Northern Kentucky University, Transylvania
University, University of Kentucky, University of Louisville, and Western
Kentucky University.
All rights reserved.

*Editorial and Sales Offices:* The University Press of Kentucky
663 South Limestone Street, Lexington, Kentucky 40508-4008
www.kentuckypress.com

17  16  15  14  13          5  4  3  2  1

*Frontispiece:* Depiction of the great 1890 match race between Salvator and
Tenny (Courtesy of Pellom McDaniels III)

Library of Congress Cataloging-in-Publication Data

McDaniels, Pellom, III.
  The prince of jockeys : the life of Isaac Burns Murphy / Pellom McDaniels III.
    pages cm
  Includes bibliographical references and index.
  ISBN 978-0-8131-4271-5 (hardcover : alk. pbk.) —
  ISBN 978-0-8131-4384-2 (epub) — ISBN 978-0-8131-4385-9 (pdf)
  1. Murphy, Isaac Burns, 1861-1896.  2. Murphy, Isaac Burns, 1861-1896
—Influence.  3. African American jockeys—Biography.  4. Jockeys—United
States—Biography.  5. Jockeys—Kentucky—Biography.  6. Kentucky Derby—
History.  7. Kentucky—Race relations—History—19th century.  I. Title.
  SF336.M784M35 2013
  798.40092'9—dc23
  [B]                                        2013019414

This book is printed on acid-free paper meeting the requirements of the
American National Standard for Permanence in Paper for Printed Library
Materials.

Manufactured in the United States of America.

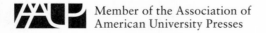

Member of the Association of
American University Presses

A special thank you to the National Endowment for the Humanities, which generously assisted with publication costs.

The National Endowment for the Humanities (NEH) is an independent federal agency created in 1965. It is one of the largest funders of humanities programs in the United States. Because democracy demands wisdom, NEH serves and strengthens our republic by promoting excellence in the humanities and conveying the lessons of history to all Americans.

For Rudolph P. Byrd,
An Elegant Specimen of Manhood

They'll see how beautiful I am
And be ashamed—
I, too, am America.

                    — Langston Hughes

# Contents

*Illustrations follow page 252*

# Introduction

Isaac Burns Murphy was born in the midst of dramatic changes taking place in mid-nineteenth-century America. He lived through the "second American Revolution," which gave people of African descent recognition as citizens, and he died at the end of the same century, when those hard-fought gains were shattered by the adoption of government-sanctioned Jim Crow policies of exclusion. Murphy, one of the most dynamic jockeys of his era, was a casualty of his own success. He lived at a time when former slave turned fiery abolitionist Frederick Douglass and bold yet wise President Abraham Lincoln publicly reproached advocates of the institution of slavery as perpetuators of a "system of brute force that shields itself behind *might*, rather than right."[1] Their vision for a unified nation divorced from the "peculiar institution" encountered resistance from both Northern and Southern whites and European immigrants, whose identities were tied to the notion of a fixed racial hierarchy in which blacks occupied the lowest position.

To most Americans, athleticism is an inherent feature of blackness, directly linked to the mythology of race promoted by the founding fathers in the U.S. Constitution. To say that Murphy was a natural athlete diminishes his life experiences and his decisions, as well as the choices of those individuals who survived through social adaptation and economic opportunism. In his youth, Murphy gained freedom, citizenship, and eventually the right to vote through amendments to the Constitution—a document originally designed to exclude rather than include 4 million people of African descent. He was symbolic of the progress made by African Americans within a generation of the Emancipation Proclamation, the end of the Civil War, and Reconstruction (which, though important, fell short of its promise to fully include African Americans as U.S. citizens). What is more, Murphy represented the potential for blacks to grow into a tremendously powerful body politic, capable of challenging traditional beliefs and Darwinian theories about race and changing the fortunes of those who had previously resided at the bottom of society and whose humanity had been thought nonexistent. For most white men, especially in the South, their imagined position in American society eroded morally, socially, and economically each time an individual of African descent achieved anything that resembled public or private success. This view of race is so entrenched in the white American imagination that it is visible even in the twenty-first century, as evidenced by the public reaction of some government officials to the election of the nation's first African American president, Barack Hussein Obama.

When average Americans think of the Declaration of Independence and the U.S. Constitution, they are not necessarily considering the intersecting contexts within which these documents were written. Nor have they thoroughly examined the lives of the *men* who met and debated the validity of their argument for independence and whose signatures appear on these documents. Yet doing so would reveal important clues about the framers' ideological and personal reasons for endorsing a particular direction for the new nation. Indeed, these paragons of American masculine virtue recognized that the institution of slavery was not sustainable when freedom was the basis of the Revolutionary cause. Still, these men deliberately laid a cornerstone for an American style of democracy that would be hard to extract once the Republic was fully realized. Clearly, the intent was to acquire and defend freedom for some while denying it to others. To most Americans, Thomas Jefferson, James Madison, Samuel Adams, George Washington, and Benjamin Franklin are vaunted heroes from the age of tyranny and oppression.[2] And their collective vision for the nation, written on parchment, is considered not only infallible but also, to those blinded by nationalism and patriotism, divine in both origin and decree.

By design, the Declaration of Independence spoke to the desires and needs of a particular segment of the colonial population, attempting to defend their self-appointed right to exploit their current and future interests in the resource-rich territory of North America.[3] These powerful white men with land, property, and wealth needed protection from King George III and the British government, so they created a social movement to inspire middling and disenfranchised whites, women, Africans, and people of African descent to fight for the primary gain outlined in the Declaration: freedom from oppression and the right to pursue individual happiness. Equally, the U.S. Constitution protected the interests of the same white elite and planter classes who had the most to lose.[4] As examples of American success, prosperity, and manhood, these men represented an American aristocracy, and they were elevated as models of powerful white masculinity. The Constitution simultaneously fixed the status of Africans and their descendants, whose assigned role in American society was based on their blackness and their assumed racial, religious, and cultural inferiority. From these documents evolved the core principle of a uniquely American identity, whereby whiteness would dominate blackness in perpetuity, regardless of the wholesale debunking of quasi-scientific theories related to race.

The tacit use of recognized racial difference was a central feature of the distinctive American credo built on the existential promises of life, liberty, and the pursuit of happiness. Moreover, because race was both a social and a cultural construction used to maintain order in the emerging nation, it would become the bedrock for a privileged white class whose identity was built around fantastical ideas about blackness made popular by fictional accounts of the continent of Africa, religious leaders, and the politically powerful. This race-based orientation had real consequences related to the designation of human beings as human capital, the narrow definition of citizenship, and the challenges of racial assimilation as European immigrants poured into the country during the first half of the nineteenth century. Racialized "others," especially African Americans, were relegated to the margins of society. Over time, the specific cultural and religious differences among people of European descent were erased, as Europeans were amalgamated into an easily accepted whiteness in defense of black competition and empowerment. De-

based and abused, African Americans were used both literally and
figuratively by the majority of whites as an indicator of the latter's
fixed social standing and believed racial superiority. This imagined
position, in turn, influenced political decision making designed to
reinscribe white male power and white privilege. Still, despite its
entrenched position and institutional support, slavery was always a
contested terrain that challenged American interpretations of morality, manly virtue, justice, and the political destiny of the new nation.

By the beginning of the nineteenth century, antislavery advocates, emancipationists, and abolitionists in the commonwealth of
Kentucky began organizing against the perpetuation of slavery. Emboldened by their religious convictions, like-minded Kentuckians
formed the Kentucky Abolition Society in 1808, the same year the
United States banned the importation of African slaves. Led by Baptist preacher David Barrow, members of the society argued that the
system of slavery was "pregnant with moral, national and domestic evils, ruinous to national tranquility, honor and enjoyment, and
[something] which every good man wishes to be abolished."[5] Various
members of Kentucky's growing population, including clergymen,
politicians, and commoners seeking opportunities to own land and
prosper away from the institution of slavery, joined reform-minded
organizations with the concrete objective of dismantling the peculiar institution. Their passionate pleas for moral decency and courageous intervention were acknowledged by many who disapproved
of the use of human chattel as the primary labor force for the developing nation. However, to a majority of slave owners, the simplis-
tic solution of emancipating and educating blacks, with the intent
of creating new citizens who could contribute to the development
of the Republic, was asking too much. To the planter class and the
wealthy elite, the entrenched American tradition of slavery, which
they believed was the most effective method of securing the wealth
and power they desired, was irreversible because it was "nature's design." To proponents of slavery, slaves were private property, similar
to a horse or a carriage; any infringement on a private citizen's ability to pursue life, liberty, and happiness (the American dream), even
if it was related to the ownership of human chattel, was considered

unconstitutional. Slaveholders and their supporters were powerful enough to challenge all efforts to deny them their right to dispossess individuals of African descent of their human rights. And they did.

One of the most prominent slaveholders in Kentucky was Senator Henry Clay, a leading politician and advocate for the colonization of Africa with free blacks from the United States. Clay would become known as the "Great Compromiser" after he negotiated the Missouri Compromise, which admitted Missouri to the union as a slave state in 1821 but prohibited the institution of slavery in the territories north of 36°30' latitude. In an 1827 address to the American Colonization Society, Clay argued that the organization could not "touch the subject of slavery" but could promote the establishment of a colony in Africa for free blacks.[6] Like a majority of slaveholders, he believed the presence of free blacks corrupted the system of slavery by inspiring dissent among those held as human chattel who hoped to claim freedom for themselves. Most of the wealth of the Kentucky elite had been generated by their African American slaves, who provided the muscle needed for gentlemen farmers, merchants, and lawyers to obtain their bounty of good fortune. Besides their slaves, white male Kentuckians prided themselves on their other possessions: land, brick homes, Thoroughbred horses, cattle, and acres of corn, hemp, and tobacco. Still, rallying around calls for Christian decency, the antislavery movement exposed the great hypocrisy at the foundation of the "Great Republic": it prided itself on being a nation of civilized people who valued freedom, yet it maintained the repugnant tradition of owning human beings as property.

Not to be denied their voice, African Americans, both the quasi-freeborn and the self-emancipated, spoke out against the institution of slavery in terms that were easily understood. Gifted writers such as David Walker defined the lives of those held in bondage as a frustrating existence of "wretchedness and endless misery."[7] Enslaved poet George Moses Horton waxed expressively about the "sad disgrace" of slave life and the broken promises of liberty, no doubt referring to those promises found in the Declaration of Independence.[8] Harvard-trained physician Martin Delany argued that his fellow blacks held in bondage were Americans whose "birthright to citizenship" can never "be annulled." What is more, he urged the more powerful members of the race—specifically, urban leaders in Philadelphia and New York—to use their political maturity and assume a stronger position in the growing national debate regarding the "Negro question."[9] By the middle of the nineteenth century, the primary voices opposing the institution of slavery were those of former slaves, who used their publications and public lectures to articulate in detail their experiences as the focus of production and debauchery and to express what it meant to be socially dead in a country where freedom is claimed to be a God-given right.[10] The most compelling narratives came from fugitive slaves such as William Wells Brown, Frederick Douglass, Harriet Jacobs, Henry Bibb, and Solomon Northrup, whose collective experiences excited and accelerated the abolitionist movement that had already been established. Their first-person narratives spoke to the godlessness of the institution and brought attention to the enterprise of human suffering that was supported by the church, the Federal government, and the determined merchants who were benefiting from trade with the South—deemed by many to be the devil's playground, with slave owners as his unholy minions.

In Isaac Murphy's Kentucky, slavery was imagined to be a more benign, less destructive version of what took place down in the Deep South. In reality, the practice was just as brutal and the source of great pain and sorrow for African Americans. Kentucky masters sadistically beat and maimed individuals for the smallest of infractions, and on occasion, a rebellious slave would be murdered to serve as an example to others who might be unwilling to submit to their condition. Although it was not a widespread practice, some Kentucky farmers and planters bred slaves for interstate commerce, selling them to traders transporting new "inventory" to the cotton and sugar plantations in Mississippi, Louisiana, and Texas. Kentucky boasted slave markets fat with merchandise, where the finest slaves could be purchased for a fair price. At auctions, it was common for families to be broken apart and sold for profit, to pay off debts, or just to reduce the amount of "stock" on a farm. Kentucky slave owners even sold their own mixed-race children, born as a re-

sult of the sexual abuse and rape of female slaves in their possession. This type of abuse damaged not only the women whose lives
and bodies were claimed as commodities to be used and discarded.
These reprehensible acts of violence shaped the social and familial
relations between African American men and women, which historians, sociologists, and anthropologists believe are still being affected today.[11] White women also participated in abusing the human
chattel they depended on for the comforts of modern living. The occasional maiming of a mulatto slave child by his or her mistress was
seen as retaliation against a husband's infidelity and revenge against
the black Jezebel who had enticed a weak man in his time of need:
hegemony at work.

More than anything, Kentucky's future prosperity depended
on African American muscle to establish the region's agricultural
and commercial wealth. Working as skilled laborers, field hands,
animal trainers, and grooms, black men were an invaluable source
of productivity on the farms of the Bluegrass State's elite. Numerous
gentlemen farmers invested in stock farms dedicated to the development of sheep, cattle, and horses for the expanding marketplace. As
horse racing became exceedingly important to the landed gentry,
grooms, trainers, and jockeys rose in prestige on Kentucky farms.
This allowed enslaved black men to elevate not only their owners'
status but also their own value on the farm and in slave society. In
generating revenue for their masters, these men created value for
themselves and increased their reputations as quality slaves. This
odd juxtaposition of self-assertion and self-deprecation carried with
it a sense of individual, familial, and community pride.[12] Recognizing their value, these African American men took advantage of
every opportunity to shine, thus ensuring that their future needs
would be met. Indeed, they could almost guarantee themselves and
their families a degree of comfort, based on their ability to succeed
on the oval racetrack. Ironically, like the horses they rode to victory, even the most successful jockeys of the antebellum period were
merely commodities to be bought and sold.

By 1861, African American men were primed to challenge both
the mythological and the legally endorsed notion of their so-called

inherent inferiority.[13] Although it was not the intention of the Lincoln administration to recruit enslaved black men, it became a necessity and then a strategy to unravel the rebel forces from behind enemy lines. Federal encampments and forts became the destiny of African American men and their families in pursuit of freedom and autonomy. Inspired by Douglass's appeal to every able-bodied black male to serve on his own behalf and for their posterity, African American communities rallied around his call to arms. In sending forth their fathers, brothers, and sons to serve in the Union army, African Americans maintained a vested interest in the positive outcome of the war for a unified nation. For black men like Jerry Skillman Burns, Isaac Burns Murphy's father, the ability to serve the Union cause on their own behalf and to control their own labor was central to the creation of a confident and empowered sense of manhood that was directly connected to the promises of freedom and democracy. Significant numbers of African American men from Kentucky did this with the knowledge that their commitment to the Union cause would be rewarded with honor, manhood, self-respect, and, above all, freedom for themselves and their families. This ennobling gift of self-sacrifice would be realized in future generations, which would not have to wear the fetters and feel the shame of slavery. However, the same institution that yoked their ancestors to the inhuman and immoral purposes of white supremacy would continue to have an impact on African Americans' quality of life long after the Civil War and Reconstruction. Although Kentucky was a slave state, its decision not to break from the Federal government (as did the seceding Southern states) affected the lives of blacks as well as whites throughout the Bluegrass region, where slave trading, horse racing, and hard labor for blacks continued during the war. The decision to recruit enslaved African American men for service as soldiers yielded a series of unintended consequences, many of which had social, cultural, political, and economic outcomes that are still very much a part of Kentucky today.

To appreciate the scope of Isaac Burns Murphy's journey from slavery to freedom and his phenomenal rise to prominence and prosperity during the waning years of Reconstruction, one must understand the overlapping and intertwined narratives present in the Kentucky of his youth. By the time he turned fourteen, the horse industry had become an integral part of the developing confidence gained by African Americans in post–Civil War Kentucky, a state that saw tremendous growth in urban black communities for a variety of reasons. To be sure, not all Kentuckians embraced the newly freed people as citizens. The period of Reconstruction was a brutal proposition for African Americans caught in transition from rural to urban living. The violence unleashed by members of the white community in an attempt to resist the sea change brought about by the war, and to maintain social, economic, and political control over the freedmen, was met with equal resistance by African Americans seeking to claim all the rights and privileges the law provided.

Recognizing Murphy's significant link to the past is an important aspect of the exploration of his life and its unique and influential role in African American social, political, cultural, and economic history of the late nineteenth century. In a much larger sense, Murphy can be understood as an integral member of a black renaissance initiated by what Douglass defined as Lincoln's "great movement" to lift the black masses "from the depths of slavery to the heights of liberty and manhood."[14] This great movement inspired and empowered former slaves and their children to strive in all honest, noble endeavors that could provide them a future as well as prove their character to those who considered them inherently inferior. Indeed, through the successful public performance of one person's work, all members of the race could benefit. Although this understanding of an individual's value may have encouraged that portion of the African American community living free from systemic bondage and oppression to strive to become exemplars of the best of society, the reality of their perceived value was ever present in their dealings with white society.

Murphy's work ethic, his relationships with both blacks and whites, his approach to racing horses, and his understanding of the entrenched racism in the Bluegrass region of Kentucky shaped the future of the boy born at the dawn of a new epoch in American history. Still, Murphy had to learn how to express his ideas and his desire for success.

By the 1880s, Murphy was commanding salaries in the tens of thousands of dollars from wealthy breeders and horse-racing enthusiasts seeking the best jockey for their prized Thoroughbreds. Rarely did Murphy disappoint. As the most dominant jockey in America at the time, he epitomized the kind of success black men were capable of in post–Civil War America. Murphy's significance was not necessarily based on his ability to earn more money than politicians, teachers, and bankers. Race tends to complicate scenarios that would otherwise be clear. Murphy's accomplishments made him one of many people of African descent who proved themselves not only worthy of citizenship but also capable of representing the best of the human race. In the post–Civil War South, blacks were rising and outwardly challenging the myths that supported white supremacy and its machinations. Less recognizable than the historical challenges, personal decisions, and choices made by the "folk" was the development of a philosophy of resistance based on self-respect, a virtuous manhood, and a passionate desire for full citizenship. Inspired by the intelligent observations and philosophical writings of Frederick Douglass, Martin Delany, and later journalist Timothy Thomas Fortune, black people were quickly rising above their previous conditions, challenging the notion of white supremacy at its roots by forcing whites as a whole to rethink their self-defined, racially based superiority—a fact that many whites resisted and tried to turn back through reprehensible acts of violence.

Like most biographers and researchers attempting to understand the nature of the people we find compelling, I wish there were more primary sources that clearly depicted Murphy's life experiences both as a child growing up in postbellum Kentucky and as a man of significant influence during the latter part of the nineteenth century. Unfortunately, I was at the mercy of whatever was available in the archives, repositories, and libraries throughout the country. What is more, I wish I could have produced a biography similar in nature to those by Ernest J. Simmons on Anton Chekhov, Henri Troyat on Leo Tolstoy, Hermione Lee on Virginia Woolf, and Larry Jackson and Arnold Rampersad on Ralph Ellison. It is the biographer's job to write in a way that leaves no doubt in readers' minds how our hero would respond to life's changes, but the complexity of African American life and history during slavery does not allow such clarity. Absent Murphy's own account to deconstruct, it is impossible to know all of what he experienced during his lifetime. What I have done in this volume is pull together evidence from all available sources to re-create the social, political, and cultural environments that framed the bulk of Murphy's life.

His is a familiar story that can be read as an example of modern African American masculinity among those of a similar background and life experience. His life was filled with high drama, success, and moments of bravery in the face of oppression and degradation. Somehow, he was able to negotiate the contours of a racist society that held African Americans in contempt as part of its national creed. All the same, to fully understand the significance of Murphy's life, his career as a jockey, and his importance as a black man, it is vital to explore the intersecting historical, social, political, cultural, and economic factors that shaped Murphy's nineteenth-century America, especially in the Bluegrass region of Kentucky. It is important to examine the tangled roots below the surface of what is perceived to be knowable territory and therefore uncontested history.

# PART 1
# *Roots*

# 1

# Into the Bluegrass

Less than a century before Isaac Murphy was born, the institution of slavery was aggressively expanding beyond the borders of the Old Dominion of Virginia into what would eventually become the state of Kentucky. Prior to the Revolutionary War, explorers, frontier families, and land speculators pushed their way into the western boundaries in search of lush, fertile lands where they could cultivate crops, exploit the natural resources, and take advantage of the abundant wild game to feed themselves and their families. A decade after the war for independence, gentlemen farmers, the sons of planters and farmers, and former soldiers followed the trails opened by Native Americans and the first white men to see the world beyond the Appalachian Mountains, migrating to the fertile central Kentucky valley. Along with a desire for wealth and stability, these men and women brought their customs and traditions based on religion, politics, and economics. For the recently liberated colonists, whose American identities were still being shaped with every assertion of their newfound freedom, this westward movement did more than extend their grasp on North America and its natural resources. Westward expansion created a sense of divine right, especially among the upper classes; in Nietzschean terms, this "will to power" extended over everything as they sought to conquer the entire continent as an expression of their uniquely American identities. What is more, through the exploration of western lands, white Americans effectively extended the reach of the peculiar institution of slavery, firmly establishing race as one of the primary factors in the nation's future growth. Still, it would be the U.S. Constitution and its cloaked yet effective language that guaranteed slaveholders' power, accelerating the growth of slavery and justifying its abuses. The impulse of discovery that excited the adventurous spirits of white American men thus affected the lives of those at the foundation of America's social, political, and economic infrastructure: Africans.

Even as white men of the postcolonial period aspired to assert their notions of eminent domain and natural rights, enslaved and free African Americans had a direct impact on the development and expansion of the Republic. African slave labor had been key to the success of the colonies in Virginia, Maryland, South Carolina, and Georgia, creating a surplus of capital that was used to acquire land and more slaves. Those who were financially capable of exploiting the institution of slavery did so with impunity. Decades before the Revolutionary War, African Americans understood that if they were ever going to achieve a real and sustainable sense of freedom, they too would have to fight for their so-called natural rights. Exercising various methods of dissent, Africans and African Americans protested, petitioned, and resorted to violence to challenge the philosophical position of their oppressors, who audaciously claimed and protected liberty for themselves but denied it to those held as human chattel. The 1739 Stono Rebellion near Stono, South Carolina, was one of numerous uprisings against slavery whereby enslaved Africans banded together to extract themselves from their brutal existence or die trying.[1]

Even as the nation began expanding under the leadership President George Washington—whose main agenda was to secure and exercise white men's divine right to live free from tyranny and oppression—both enslaved and free African Americans actively participated in shaping the American discourse on freedom, equality, and citizenship. Although numerically few compared with whites, free blacks were able to take advantage of their positions as merchants, soldiers, guides, scouts, mercenaries, and laborers. These capable men and women envisioned a nation where they owned their own labor as well as their futures. Moreover, these men and women were capable of imagining a world where they controlled their own destinies. As we shall see, in places like Virginia and Kentucky, enslaved and legally free African Americans fought hard to claim their rights to freedom and citizenship, just as the colonists had fought to gain independence from England. In doing so, these men and women of African descent provided a legacy of resistance, dignity, and self-respect that their children and their children's children would draw on in their fight against slavery and their assertion of a right to full citizenship and all that designation entailed.

Although Kentucky did not achieve statehood until 1792, as an undeveloped wilderness with bountiful natural resources, it played a significant role in the outcome of the Revolutionary War and in the overall development of the new nation. The land and its untapped resources were critical factors in the social, political, and economic imaginings of supporters of expansion and the institution of slavery at the end of the eighteenth century. One of the first coordinated explorations of the Ohio River Valley was conducted in 1751 by Christopher Gist, a representative of the Ohio Land Company of Virginia.[2] Gist, along with a party of a few dozen men, traveled deep into the valley to survey the unexplored lands and identify prime locations for future settlements.[3] Coming from Virginia, where enslaved African Americans were the major source of labor, Gist likely brought along one or more bondsmen on his expedition. Though evidence is scarce, there is enough to suggest that African Americans were employed on inland journeys to clear thick forests, to test the security and safety of various land and rock formations, to wade through chest-high waters pulling canoes and flat-bottomed boats, and to search in darkness for shelter and food for their companions and masters.

The most famous of the westward explorations involving enslaved African Americans was led by two Virginians: Captain Meriwether Lewis and Lieutenant William Clark. After the United States purchased the Louisiana Territory from the French on April 30,

1803, President Thomas Jefferson commissioned Lewis and Clark to explore the area west of the Mississippi River to the Pacific Ocean. Covering 8,000 miles between May 14, 1804, and September 23, 1806, the Lewis and Clark Expedition carved out a path from St. Louis, Missouri, to the Oregon coast. It did so with the assistance of Clark's personal slave, York, who had been born in Virginia and raised as part of George Rogers Clark's family. The party of more than thirty explorers left St. Louis and for close to two and a half years navigated the uncharted wilderness and negotiated with native peoples en route to the Northwest Territory.[4] Lewis's and Clark's personal journals and military logs have been heralded by historians as invaluable sources of information about the land features of the Far West, the wildlife, the native peoples and their customs, and the potential growth of the new Republic prior to full-fledged expansion.

The expedition also provided evidence of the capacity of African American men to meet the requirements and challenges of citizenship. Based on Clark's journals, York demonstrated an exceptional capacity for bravery and courage under fire, especially in encounters with native peoples. York's ability with a rifle and his willingness (albeit under his master's direction) to face the dangers of the unknown were important to the expedition's success, and on several occasions he used his sense of leadership to help the explorers achieve their mission of mapping the lands of the West. All this should have served as indisputable proof of his manhood, countering the supposed inherent inferiority of his blackness. It is easy to interpret or even misinterpret York's participation as an equal among the men under the command of Lewis and Clark. However, given the uniqueness of the situation and the expedition's purpose, York's performance should have been a clear indicator that he was deserving of freedom and full citizenship and all the rights and privileges that entailed.

Clark's journals are incomplete in terms of York's experiences; York's voice is absent from the historical narrative.[5] Surely, his encounters with the land and with the native peoples and his sense of his place in the world were different from those of his companions.

His worldview must have been shattered and reconstituted based on his interactions with the attentive Arikaras and Mandan Indians, whose awe at his skin color, his strength, and his storytelling exposed him to the hearts and minds of a people who valued him as an individual and not solely as the property of a white man. Again, we can only speculate, because York did not document his experiences. However, traces of his impact are found throughout the accounts of others. The absence of York's own voice in the recorded narrative leaves us with questions: What were his thoughts about being enslaved? How did he perceive his role in discovering a passage to the Northwest? How did he feel about freedom? Did his faithful service prove detrimental to attaining the freedom he might have thought he deserved? In other words, should he have escaped from slavery when he had the chance in the wilderness, and find shelter with one of the Indian tribes they encountered? Did he try to prove his value and therefore his manhood through his service to the expedition?

By all accounts, York was one of the first African Americans to explore the interior of America, to live among the native peoples and mix his African blood with theirs, and to see the Pacific Ocean. Yet very few chronicles of the Lewis and Clark Expedition recognize him as an American hero, even though he epitomized early-nineteenth-century definitions of American manliness, with one exception: his blackness. York's story parallels that of other blacks in early America, many of whom were central to the nation's development but were relegated to the margins and erased from historical memory in an effort to protect the myth of white supremacy. This void in American history as it relates to the participation of enslaved African Americans in the exploration and settlement of the West is troublesome, to say the least.

European and colonial explorers and surveyors used blacks as wilderness scouts and guides as they probed the western territories beyond the Blue Ridge Mountains and the Cumberland Gap. These descendants of Africans imported as human chattel to work in the fields and industries of colonial America developed valuable skills in tracking and hunting animals over rugged terrain. Well before coordinated surveys and land speculation in the area west of Virginia and east of the Mississippi River, "long hunters" from the established colonies of Virginia and North Carolina tracked and hunted deer, buffalo, and wild turkey and fished rivers swollen with hundreds of varieties of fish.[6] These black men were also utilized as flatboat pilots to navigate the sometimes troublesome waterways beyond the Allegheny Mountains as their owners searched for adventure and resources. Surely, these enslaved African Americans felt some sense of pride in their abilities and were able to extract snatches of freedom for themselves, as well as serve as examples to other blacks. Indeed, for most enslaved African Americans engaged in the drudgery of planting tobacco, rice, and indigo, the prospect of a life away from those patches of dirt and denigration by the overseer must have been appealing.

By the middle of the eighteenth century, tensions increased between the British monarchy and the colonists. The British wanted to control the colonies' rate of expansion, while the colonists were impatient to stake their claims in what they assumed were uninhabited lands. This was problematic, to say the least. First, the lands in the west were not uninhabited; they were the homes and traditional hunting grounds of several indigenous groups, including the Shawnee and Cherokee, both of whom were aware of the colonists' desire to push past the mountains and forests separating their two distinct civilizations. Second, trade agreements between French traders and eastern Indian tribes had been in place since the early seventeenth century, and many of these agreements had been broken through dealings with the English. Third, the aggressive poaching of game on lands considered communal property ultimately became a theater of war between Native Americans and white Americans, the latter taking what they wanted in an effort to gain unlimited access to the resources found in the "Eden of the West."

These violent encounters involving frontiersmen and native peoples in the American backcountry escalated into the French and Indian War, a conflict between England and France linked to the worldwide Seven Years' War. These confrontations set in motion a series of events that would lead to the Revolutionary War, the opening of the Kentucky territory, and the perpetuation and growth of the institution of slavery. As these conflicts among the French, the British, the Native Americans, and the colonists unfolded, the need for able-bodied men increased, and both free and enslaved black men were employed as soldiers, even though it was a "general policy in early America to exclude Negroes from militia service."[7] The tradition of excluding black men from the military was based on the fear of them rebelling against slavery (given the number of slave revolts, such as the 1739 Stono Rebellion) and a reluctance to empower even freeborn blacks who might challenge the notion of inherent black inferiority—the very basis of chattel slavery. Thus, a majority of whites were nervous about arming blacks, even in their own defense. But in 1755 General Edward Braddock of Williamsburg, Virginia, recognized the need to employ all able-bodied men, both black and white, as soldiers. Braddock did not hesitate to arm "mulattoes and free Negroes," whom he felt could be trusted to loyally serve the causes of the colonies.[8] According to one historian, in times of need, the colonists' "fear of slave uprisings" and black rebellion subsided enough to allow the use of blacks as soldiers, albeit on a limited basis.[9] This was one of those times. However, by arming those deemed inferior to defend the interests of the state, including the lucrative trade in human beings, the state was initiating its own demise. The image of the black soldier became a source of inspiration and a symbol of manliness and citizenship for African Americans. This pattern of service would become important to the revolutionary cause, the future civil war over states' rights, the territorial conflicts with the native peoples of the Far West, and well into the twentieth century.

After the defeated French signed the Treaty of Paris in 1763, forcing their withdrawal from lands east of the Mississippi River, south of the Ohio River, and west of the Appalachian Mountains, opportunistic colonial Americans moved quickly to capitalize on the English victory. The diplomatic agreement gave England room for expansion and greater access to exploitable natural resources in the West, most of which were still undiscovered.[10] Unfortunately, the native peoples living in the Ohio River Valley had not agreed to the terms conceded by their French allies, and the French could no longer be depended on to help defend their homes or protect their rights to traditional hunting grounds there. The native peoples initially tried to defend themselves, but after several wars and tens of thousands of lives lost, Native Americans slowly gave up and conceded to the European and American development and exploitation of resources. In the end, the brutality, violence, and determination of white men to do as they pleased, disregarding the traditions and customs of those with a long history and presence in the fertile valley, would win out, leaving a swath of destruction and a legacy of pain.

Historians have succinctly noted the transition from friendly curiosity to hostility between Native Americans and colonists from England, France, and Spain. The new Americans created an environment where skirmishes and wars were inevitable for anyone seeking to settle west of the Allegheny Mountains and deep into the Ohio River Valley.[11] After the Treaty of Paris, King George III wanted these lands reserved for his Native American subjects, whom he mistakenly believed would work for the Crown, collecting furs and other resources for export to England. But King George's desire to control the destiny of his North American empire and the British Proclamation Line of 1763 did little to keep the restless colonists from carving out portions of land for themselves as they gradually moved westward. The increased population in the colonies, the limited resources available, and the gentry's desire to expand its wealth initiated a fever of excitement, and the land hungry slowly eased their way into the hardwood forests and claimed as much land as they could.[12] By the 1770s, British subjects who had fought in the Seven Years' War were desperate to sell their military bounty grants to land speculators for cash or to claim their own pieces of land and set up farms in what was then known as "Kaintuckee" by the Indians and as Fincastle County by Virginians.[13]

Named after the royal governor of Virginia, John Murray, the Fourth Earl of Dunmore and Viscount of Fincastle, Virginia's westernmost county was established in 1772 to handle the increase in population. Much of the county would remain somewhat unexplored and uncultivated by white Americans into the early nineteenth century. From all accounts, colonists from Virginia, Pennsylvania, and North Carolina took advantage of Fincastle County's resources due to their availability and lack of regulation. The absence of law in backwoods territories allowed unlimited hunting to supply food and resources needed for individual and communal survival. Predictably, the early trade in furs, the export of natural resources, and the developing business of land speculation escalated tensions between Indians and whites. The Indians' traditional hunting grounds for deer and wild turkey were disrupted, and buffalo were massacred by the hundreds for their skins and fat-rich humps by wasteful hunters unwilling to carry the entire kill back home.[14] (This form of ecoterrorism would be used in the latter part of the nineteenth century, when the U.S. military killed off the primary sources of food for the Great Plains Indians in an effort to destroy the last vestiges of Native American resistance. In effect, the U.S. military starved Native Americans to force them to acquiesce to the demands of the Great White Father: the president of the United States.) Meanwhile, as Virginia's growing population became restless and more white men began to venture beyond the Allegheny Mountains in search of resources, they brought with them their dreams of power and their African American slaves to help them secure those dreams.

By the spring of 1774, Lord Dunmore, serving his own self-interests, commissioned eager former soldiers from the Indian wars and colonists from Pennsylvania and Virginia to explore Indian lands in the Kaintuckee backcountry. The intent was to survey and sell parts of the region to prominent Virginians such as George Washington and Patrick Henry and to Massachusetts lawyer Samuel Adams—men whose names would resonate loudly in the coming years in the movement against British rule. Led by Pennsylvania-born James Harrod, a party of thirty or more men, including enslaved African Americans, descended the Ohio River into Kaintuckee in search of paradise.[15] After paddling up the Kentucky River and traveling through dense forests and canebrakes, Harrod's party "dispersed into small squads, to select for themselves suitable settlements, and to build on such locations improvement cabins."[16] The first white settlement in Kentucky was established at Harrodsburg on June 16, 1774, by fortune-seeking men who saw the land and its resources as inexhaustible. The relative calm that greeted the party of pioneers was short lived. Native tribes resisted white settlement, challenging the philosophy of eminent domain and white supremacy espoused by explorers and adventurers supported by the white elite. After four months of trying to cultivate crops, the settlement dispersed, and those who survived returned to Pennsylvania to fight in Lord Dunmore's War against the Shawnee and Mingo Indians.

In October 1774 Dunmore sent his Virginia militia to Fort Pitt in Pennsylvania, intending to secure the western lands for future English settlement.[17] Similar to the French and Indian Wars, when "northern and southern colonies were driven to employ colored men" in the war effort, historians believe Dunmore used both free and enslaved African American men who were willing to serve to demonstrate their loyalty to the colonies and to England.[18] An important point is that white men, especially the wealthy, were not as willing to serve. They often sent their able-bodied slaves as replacements for themselves or their sons. Therefore, the traditional restrictions on African Americans serving in the military and possessing guns were lifted to satisfy the needs of the colonies; at the same time, this gave blacks the opportunity to demonstrate their ability to perform as fully vested subjects of the Crown and valuable members of the colonial community. Although he did not totally disregard the concerns of slave owners, Dunmore defended the practice of having black soldiers serve the cause of the British government, calling their support a determining factor in any war that might occur between Britain and the colonists. Still, the very public political debates about freedom and the natural rights of men, and the claims being made by the Americans against the British government, created an environment in which enslaved and freed blacks recognized freedom as a more tangible concept that was within their grasp.

At its roots, the revolutionary cause argued that freedom was a God-given right for which those held in bondage had to fight. Most important, freedom was a cause worth dying for. When the First Continental Congress met in Philadelphia from September 5 to October 26, 1774, Africans and African Americans paid close attention to the resolutions proposed by Thomas Jefferson, Alexander Hamilton, and John Adams. Each argued that the colonists' rights as British subjects suffered due to British laws that denied them the right to representation and the right to life, liberty, and the pursuit of happiness. Ironically, these very men who challenged the sovereign power of the king of England were slaveholders, merchants dependent on the raw materials produced by slaves, or businessmen who benefited directly or indirectly from the labor of blacks held as human chattel. In 1775 a passionate Thomas Paine asked how Americans could "complain so loudly of attempts to enslave them while they hold so many hundreds of thousands in slavery?"[19] The First Continental Congress's struggles over the issue of slavery have been well documented, including Jefferson's attempt to introduce the concept of gradual emancipation into the conversation. This was rejected by a majority of the delegates, who recognized that the world they imagined for themselves was dependent on the labor of enslaved Africans and their descendants.

One year after the initial meeting of the colonial representatives, the Second Continental Congress ratified the second draft of the Declaration of Causes, arguing succinctly that the abuses of the Crown had deprived a free people of their right to representation and had subjected the loyal citizens of England and their posterity to a future of bondage and degradation. As the radicalized colonists rallied to promote the rebellious position of protest and action against England's "Intolerable Acts," their ability to justify the continued denial of rights to blacks became a source of debate.[20] Africans and African Americans adopted the colonists' own language to claim that which had eluded them: freedom from oppression, abuse, and degradation for the benefit of others. By July 4, 1776, the Declaration of Independence not only allowed the colonists to claim freedom and extract themselves from the grips of King George but also became a source of inspiration to blacks, who now understood that it was possible to achieve freedom through revolution.

In December 1776, Virginia was established as one of the original thirteen states, and Kentucky became the official name of that state's westernmost county, erasing the legacy of Lord Dunmore. As

Virginians sought to expand into that western county and establish themselves there as farmers and planters, they realized that a substantial amount of labor would be needed. This, of course, meant the relocation and eventual importation of thousands of Africans. By the end of the Revolutionary War, enslaved African Americans were being brought into Kentucky County by families, overseers, and pioneers. They used this black labor to clear and settle the land, construct homes and storage facilities, build roads, and perform whatever other work was necessary for these former Virginians to establish their roots as Kentuckians.

As the conflict between Britain and America continued to rage, General George Washington succumbed to pressure to open the American army to blacks. In 1777 the commonwealth of Virginia promised freedom to slaves who volunteered to serve as soldiers and fight against the British government in defense of American interests, which included the institution of slavery.[21] Shrugging off their so-called inferiority, African American men defended the political philosophy that "all men are created equal" and are endowed with "certain inalienable rights," and they claimed their freedom through their faithful service. Not be outdone, Lord Dunmore helped liberate enslaved blacks who had served on the side of the British. In 1781 he provided transportation out of New York, Virginia, South Carolina, and Georgia for black Loyalists, sending them to England, Nova Scotia, and Sierra Leone, on the west coast of Africa. Unfortunately, some blacks traveling with their Loyalist masters remained enslaved and were transported to parts of the West Indies, where life was much more difficult than it had been in the North American colonies. On the islands of Jamaica and St. Lucia, enslaved blacks continued to toil in the sugarcane fields and refineries.[22]

Thus, slaves fought on both sides of the war in pursuit of the same outcome: freedom from bondage. Although numerous slaves who served courageously for the American cause were manumitted by their owners or by the government at the end of the war, their blackness was not erasable. The evolving American identity based on racial difference was emerging as an important part of the American credo, which helped define the philosophical language in the Declaration of Independence.

During the Revolutionary War, momentum was building toward mass expansionism, with land-hungry opportunists busily making plans to push through the wilderness and into the West. These men were determined to stake their claims in the "Eden of the West" before anyone else could do so; then they followed James Harrod's example of creating frontier communities to attract white families.[23] In the spring of 1775, Harrod led his party of adventurers and slave laborers back to the central Kentucky settlement he had established a year earlier.[24] There, these resolute men constructed living accommodations and a fort from materials found in the surrounding forest; the fort was necessary to protect themselves from Native American warriors still seeking revenge for English expansion into the western territories and Lord Dunmore's War. The colonial presence in what had been traditional communal hunting grounds created tensions that could be resolved only through bloodshed. The hostile taking of resources by white colonists led to skirmishes and violent confrontations between those trying to expand into the new territory and those trying to protect their land-based traditions and identities.

Harrod's settlement eventually attracted increasing numbers of Virginians eager to travel west and claim their piece of the virgin territory.[25] Many hoped to secure a portion of the bountiful land for themselves and their families. Others came to take full advantage of whatever their wealth could buy them, including the labor necessary to clear the forest and build the required homes that would allow them to assert land claims based on the notion of preoccupancy. By 1777, blacks accounted for about 10 percent of the inhabitants of Harrod's Fort. A majority of these enslaved individuals were males with valuable skills that could be exploited by their owners as they struggled to tame the hostile wilderness. These enslaved men had young families who were most likely the property of the same masters. Of the nearly 200 inhabitants of Harrod's Fort, 19 were of African descent, and all were designated as human chattel.[26]

In the same year Harrod's Fort was established, Daniel Boone, under the direction of Judge Richard Henderson of the Transylvania Land Company, guided a party of settlers through the Cumberland Gap to the Kentucky River and deep into the fertile backcountry. This diverse group of settlers included enslaved blacks who were responsible for carrying provisions, guiding pack mules and hunting dogs, and constructing the rude encampments necessary to explore and eventually settle the wilderness.[27] Like Harrod's, the Boonesborough community used black labor to cultivate, protect, and expand the amount of usable land in the Bluegrass region. In this fertile terrain, Kentucky's future commercial interests in hemp, tobacco, and horses would be developed—three of the state's most important commodities. Nevertheless, in this untamed and hostile environment, white settlers and enslaved blacks became codependent on each other for protection and safety, and each day proved to be a constant negotiation between life and death, the present and the future.

Accounts of black men fighting and dying alongside their white masters to defend their communities against Native American attacks have been largely forgotten. Indeed, the degree of agency claimed by black men, many of whom played integral roles in developing and promoting the heroic frontier narrative, was influential in creating a new mode of American masculinity based on the interaction with the land and its many challenges. Clearly, for some white pioneers seeking to exploit western lands and slave labor, it became necessary to de-emphasize the courageous actions of black men and downplay their demonstrated ability to act independently, which contradicted their status as human chattel. The belief that people of African descent were inferior to whites justified their enslavement and therefore their abuse; it allowed the lowest of immigrants to inflate their own importance and gain access to power, even if it was only imaginary. As growing numbers of Americans from Virginia, North Carolina, and Pennsylvania expanded into Kentucky, Native Americans continued to assault the frontier communities with the goal of turning back efforts to colonize the West and defend their right to use the land as they always had. For the indigenous peoples of the region, white men—and, increasingly, black men—were their enemies.

During this era of exploration and expansion into western Kentucky, enslaved black men contributed to the development of settlements from Boonsborough to Louisville. Given what we know about the brutality of frontier life and the interdependence between slaveholders and their slaves, it is safe to say that many enslaved African Americans fought and died alongside their masters not so much to defend their owners from Indian aggression but to protect themselves. When confronted with the choice to intervene against Indians bent on killing whites or to live another day in pursuit of freedom from bondage, some decided to save their own lives. For example, Adam, a slave owned by William Russell, was traveling with Daniel Boone's son James, five other whites, and another slave named Charles on a mission to retrieve supplies from other settlements. When the group was ambushed by a band of Indians, Adam managed to escape to the river, where he hid under some driftwood. Adam watched as James Boone and young Henry Russell were tortured and killed by one of the Indians they knew. Eventually, Adam worked his way through the woods and returned to his home at the Castle's Wood settlement, where he described the attack in detail to his master and to Boone.[28] Clearly, narratives such as this demonstrate African Americans' ability to serve their own self-interests, regardless of their exclusion from the publicly defined and endorsed ideal of American manhood and masculinity that white men claimed only for themselves.

Within five years of the establishment of the Harrod and Boone settlements, Kentucky became *the* destination for Virginians. Governor Thomas Jefferson proposed to give landless whites access to the rich valley through the Land Act of 1779, which provided settlers with up to 400 acres for a lower fee than that charged to absentee owners or nonresidents. Settlers who made improvements to the land could claim up to 1,000 acres. Unfortunately, the act's flexibility allowed individuals with no intention of occupying the land to build cabins and then sell to migrating settlers or speculators.[29] In the same year the Land Act was instituted, a group of twenty-five frontiersman led by Colonel Robert Patterson journeyed north from Harrodsburg, across the Kentucky River, and through the uninhabited but hostile land to build a garrison to protect the pioneers moving to central Kentucky. To a large degree, their primary objective was to scout out and secure a portion of the fertile valley for themselves, while creating a shelter for those brave enough to venture into the wilderness. The names of these men from Pennsylvania, Virginia, and North Carolina still resonate throughout the Bluegrass region: Simon Kenton, Michael Stoner, John Haggin, John and Levi Todd, John Maxwell, Hugh Shannon, James Masterson, William McConnell, and Isaac Greer. As a gesture of respect for those who had lost their lives on April 19, 1775, at the Battle of Lexington, they chose the name Lexington over the traditional self-aggrandizing practice. The settlement became more than a memorial to those who died in support of the freedom movement being perpetuated by the Continental Congress and its delegates. The name would forever connect the intent of the founding fathers, the institution of slavery, and the perpetuation of white male power as the foundation of America. By 1779, Lexington represented America's capitalist future as well as its ultimate challenge, based on the singular notion that freedom and liberty can be found in the suppression and use of others as a source of profit and power.

With central Kentucky as the focal point of westward migration among those in search of tillable land, financial opportunity, and freedom from tyranny, its waterways and overland dirt roads became swollen with a multitude of hopeful Americans in search of a promised land. Indeed, after the war, news spread of the fertile lands beyond the Blue Hills and the Cumberland Gap. Young white men, excited by the possibility of acquiring land and gaining a foothold in the future development of America and influenced by the twice-told tales of Daniel Boone's wilderness exploits and his heroic hand-to-hand confrontations with so-called savages, sought adventure-filled lives in the backwoods of Kentucky. Early on, narratives of a bountiful and beautiful Far West awaiting the bold and the brave attracted those living in unhappy circumstances. Settlers by the hundreds poured into the Bluegrass region in pursuit of prosperity, bringing with them all their worldly possessions and extended family members. Unfortunately, the lie of universal opportunity would eventually force the naïve and ill prepared to return home to North Carolina, Virginia, and Pennsylvania or to move farther into the wilderness, chasing the elusive dream of independence.

In reality, commoners, displaced Tories "deprived of their lands or otherwise mistreated by overzealous Patriots," poor whites, and immigrants of English, Scots, Scotch-Irish, and German origin were denied access to the choice lands claimed by men of affluence and influence. The wealthy landed gentry, speculators, and individuals with connections in Virginia secured thousands of acres through legal means and forced hundreds of powerless migrants off lands they believed they owned based on "ancient cultivation law" and the concept of "preoccupancy."[30] The Bluegrass region became the primary destination for Virginians who were second sons, gentlemen farmers, and wealthy politicians looking to advance their power through land acquisition. In taking possession of the most fertile land in Kentucky, Virginia's elite classes extended their dominance and control over the developing body politic of America and its social, political, and economic future.[31] The future of Kentucky would be shaped in part by the abundance of land and the need for exploitable labor, reflecting both the inevitable growth of the nation and the development of early capitalism. As we shall see, the wielding of power by the politically connected rather than the morally right, struggles over the definition of citizenship, and limited access to freedom and democracy for those marginalized and abused based on the fiction of race would lead to a "second American Revolution," laying bare the contradictions festering at the country's core.

Woven into this disparate population of white migrants were free and enslaved African American men and women. By the turn of the nineteenth century, more than 40,000 slaves were part of the laboring class, charged with performing a majority of the tasks required to transform the rough and rugged wilderness into paradise personified. This could be accomplished only through the use of black bondmen as human chattel. These individuals—mostly men— were the single most important factor in the Bluegrass region's development. These quasi-Americans underpinned the social, political, and economic ambitions and accomplishments of Old Dominion families who desired to reproduce the Virginia lifestyle they were accustomed to. Clearly, slavery's rapid spread into Kentucky County was based on the movement of these affluent settlers, whose main purpose in acquiring fertile lands in the West was to increase their wealth as well as their social, political, and economic standing in the new Republic. Toward this end, they brought along those who would be the most responsible for carrying out the deed.

In the spring of 1792 these same men struggled with other pioneers over the use of slave labor. In April forty-five elected delegates from the nine counties of the state descended on the township of Danville, thirty-eight miles south of Lexington, for the tenth constitutional convention. By all accounts, the "distinguished citizens" who made up the august body of representatives wielded their power and privilege to influence the outcome of the convention in their favor. Most owned land, cattle, horses, and slaves, and all sought to protect their future investments. The delegates' primary concern was protecting their right to own human chattel, not the ethics of owning human beings, which antislavery advocates considered the more important debate to have. Of the 11,944 African Americans that made up more than 16 percent of Kentucky's 1790 population of 73,077, only 114 were free. Out of 61,133 white inhabitants, more than 22 percent of white landowners held slaves, with concentrations of black bondsmen in Fayette, Woodford, and Jefferson counties.

By June 1792, delegates in favor of the institution of slavery had convened to argue what they believed to be in the best interest of the state, based on the need for inexpensive labor and the so-called natural condition of the Negro. The large landowners and planter classes that had invested heavily in the county's agricultural development sought to benefit financially from their land speculation and the potential productivity of their right to own human property. In support of this right, the state of Virginia granted permission for the new state of Kentucky to be created, with the stipulation that the institution of slavery would not be disturbed. Still, antislavery supporters challenged the morality of the institution and its effect on whites as a whole. Choosing to endorse and perpetuate the bondage of people of African descent was believed to be inconsistent with the principles of Christianity and the intent of the Declaration of Independence. Furthermore, because it promoted idleness in whites, slavery was argued to "sap the foundations of moral, and consequently of political virtue; and virtue is absolutely necessary for happiness and prosperity of free people." To many, the expansion of slavery into the new state of Kentucky and across the continent was like a "building being erected on quicksand, the inhabitants of which can never abide in safety."[32] The prophetic vision of the antislavery advocates would come to pass in subsequent years, as slave insurrections and rebellions increased, taking the lives of both whites and blacks, as the institution expanded throughout the Deep South. Debates over the definition of citizenship, the use of African Americans as labor, and states' rights to choose their own paths to prosperity would divide the country and eventually lead to the Civil War.

The first generation of Kentucky's powerful elite families, with recognizable surnames such as Todd, Breckinridge, Clay, Alexander, and Hunt, would have a significant influence on the state's social, political, cultural, and economic future. All depended on slave labor in some form to build their massive fortunes, which would be passed down from one generation to the next. When prominent Virginia lawyer John Breckinridge decided to move his family to Kentucky, he sent twenty slaves and an overseer out to secure his land claim and construct all the necessary accommodations in preparation for the move. In 1793 the Breckinridge family arrived at their Cabell's Dale plantation near Lexington, where they raised Thoroughbred horses and crops of the local variety.[33] Thomas Jefferson, a personal friend, endorsed Breckinridge's nomination as Kentucky attorney general in 1795. Breckinridge would greatly influence Kentucky's second constitutional convention in 1799, which secured the right of the slaveholding gentry to possess human property without penalty or abuse.[34] Slave labor was central to the development of Kentucky's agricultural and manufacturing industries. The Bluegrass region developed into the state's crown jewel, thanks to the muscle, sweat, and blood of black bondsmen, whose contributions were much more significant than history has recorded. The curving landscape with its fertile fields teeming with livestock, hundreds of farmhouses, and thousands of acres of hemp, flax, wheat, rye, oats, barley, tobacco, and corn generated tremendous capital for the powerful few.

Considered the "Athens of the West" due to its rise as the center of culture, education, and wealth west of the Allegheny Mountains, Lexington also bloomed into one of the most important manufacturing centers for the production and exportation of rope, burlap, and other goods throughout the region and the United States, especially to the South during the cotton boom. Indeed, as suppliers of finished products and raw materials to consumers as far away as New Orleans, New York, and the emerging markets of the Far West, Lexington businessmen and farmers became influential, to say the least. The new state constitution removed any future obstacles to the expansion of slavery and denied free blacks access to the franchise.[35] Plainly, African American slaves were a source of prosperity. They tilled the fields and harvested the crops; they worked in factories, producing goods for the marketplace; and on the racetrack, they provided the means for the white elite to display the quality of horseflesh they owned.

By 1800, the number of blacks in Kentucky had increased to 41,084, or 18 percent of the population. The number of free blacks had also increased, from 114 to 741, since 1790. Even though they had been denied the franchise by the 1799 constitution, black men and their families came to the state looking for the same opportunities sought by European immigrants: land and an opportunity to live free. Kentucky's image as a paradise fat with wild game and fertile soil and as a gateway to the West attracted a range of settlers, from the well-to-do to the subsisting poor. All were determined to pursue the social, political, and economic advancements available to them.

By the turn of the nineteenth century, however, the new nation was still exhausted from the Revolution, and the founding fathers were still struggling with the language intended to shape the country's future. In states such as South Carolina, Georgia, Alabama,

Mississippi, and Louisiana, the domestic slave trade kicked into high gear with Eli Whitney's invention of the cotton gin. Whitney's horse- and hand-driven machinery was capable of cleaning more than 400 times the amount of cotton the average slave could handle. With the demand for raw cotton increasing in the Northern states and in Europe, the demand for slave labor grew as well. Before the 1808 ban on the international slave trade, thousands of Africans were imported into the United States and put to work in the South planting tobacco, rice, and cotton. Others were sold to slave drivers and landowners moving west to the new Kentucky territory, and with the 1821 Missouri Compromise, the institution found another stronghold, increasing the demand for land by the southern slavocracy and the expansion of "King Cotton."

It is more than likely that all of Isaac Burns Murphy's grandparents, black and white, were part of the wave of free and enslaved African and African American emigrants that arrived in Kentucky between 1800 and 1820. On the farms, in the fields, and eventually in the factories, relations between blacks and whites were tested and refined as Kentuckians worked to craft an identity based on their relationship to the land as well as to one another. Sex between blacks and whites was considered taboo, by all accounts, except when white men used their power to gain access to what they wanted—that is, black women.

By 1830, Kentucky's overall population had grown to 687,917. The mass migration of Virginians, North Carolinians, Pennsylvanians, and European immigrants, as well as the enslaved Africans and African Americans brought to clear and work the land, increased the number of people dispersed throughout the state. Some of these new Kentuckians came eagerly, willing to traverse the wilderness in search of paradise; others were forced to travel across the rocky slopes of the Allegheny Mountains into unknown territory, leaving their families behind to meet the challenges awaiting them on the other side as the nation transformed itself into a juggernaut of capitalism.[36] Poor pioneers lived off the land and secured a stake for themselves and their families by taking advantage of the resource-rich woods and waterways of the state. In contrast, the affluent concentrated on expanding agricultural development and increasing their economic prosperity in the Bluegrass region by acquiring the most fertile lands and exploiting black slave labor through the protected institution of slavery.

Indeed, from Maysville to Louisville, farmers, pioneers, and wealthy planters could be found in small communal farm towns, where common folk eked out a living, and in the developing agricultural and urban industrial environments, where the "texture of life of the Negro" was determined by the marketplace and by the whims of a powerful white patriarchy. As the nation continued to grow, so did the need for food and durable goods, and Kentucky became an important factor in that growth. Farmers increased their production of staples such as livestock, wheat, rye, oats, barley, tobacco, and corn. To meet the demands of the growing cotton industry in the Deep South, Kentucky farmers grew hemp, which was used to manufacture cordage and coarse cloth, as well as the rope and bagging materials needed to ship raw cotton to domestic and foreign manufacturers. Kentucky farm products generated immense wealth for those with large landholdings, manufacturing plants, and a workforce capable of harvesting and processing raw products for consumption at home and abroad. There is no doubt that the domestic demand for Kentucky goods and raw products led to the importation of many enslaved African Americans into the state; their numbers peaked at 165,213 in 1830, with bondsmen accounting for 24 percent of the overall population. These men, women, and children provided labor for the large farms and factories throughout the Bluegrass region. Indeed, the blood, sweat, and tears of black labor were at the foundation of all industry and development in Kentucky and in other states where blacks performed the bulk of "domestic drudgery" in the name of freedom, liberty, and democracy.[37] Still, those black slaves who witnessed the birth of American democracy and the maturation of American capitalism became collateral damage of the "New American": a white man whose insatiable appetite for wealth, power, and status could never be satisfied.

As early as 1815, outspoken opponents of slavery began to argue for a program that would abolish the institution, emancipate blacks, and free the United States from the evils associated with human bondage. While progressive groups with good intentions sought to establish colonies in West Africa where slave owners could voluntarily send their emancipated blacks, others wanted to exile free blacks because of the threat they posed to the stability of the institution of slavery, which had proved itself vital, if not necessary, to western expansion and the future of capitalism. For some, sending free blacks out of the country was a way to silence subversive African Americans in the North who undermined the system that slaveholders believed to be their right in the eyes of God and the destiny of the black and white races. Kentucky slaveholders were not among those who refused to part with their human chattel; many endorsed the option of colonizing free blacks in Africa.

One of the most prominent slaveholders in Kentucky, Senator Henry Clay, argued before the American Colonization Society on January 20, 1827, that the "object of the Society was the colonization of the free coloured people, not the slaves, of the country."[38] His position was based on his own interest in maintaining the institution of slavery and the growing popularity of programs and organizations promoting the immediate emancipation of slaves. Brothers Lewis and Arthur Tappan cofounded the American Anti-Slavery Society in 1839 along with fiery abolitionist William Lloyd Garrison, who spoke publicly and wrote frequently about the evils of slavery. In the *Liberator*, Garrison called for the immediate emancipation of slaves in the United States and challenged slaveholders to see that their degradation of human beings was damaging their own souls. In Garrisonian terms, slavery was a sin that guaranteed the highest retribution from God: death of the soul. What is more, Garrison recognized the inevitability of violent rebellion by those who were denied their humanity and saw their freedom as a God-given right.

Free blacks, not to be forgotten, struggled against the colonizationists' push to remove them from the United States. America was as much their country as it was their white counterparts', they argued. Furthermore, free blacks vocalized their resistance to any plan to deny them citizenship in the country of their birth, where their ancestors' spilled blood guaranteed their right to freedom. In 1829 freeborn African American writer David Walker recognized the importance of the moment at hand and published a manifesto, appealing to the black masses to rise up and shape their destiny. Walker writes:

> Do the colonizationists think to send us off without first being reconciled to us? Do they think to bundle us up like brutes and send us off, as they did our brethren of the State of Ohio? Have they not to be reconciled to us, or reconcile us to them, for the cruelties with which they have afflicted our fathers and us? Methinks colonizationists think they have a set of brutes to deal with, sure enough. Do they think to drive us from our country and homes, after having enriched it with our blood and tears, and keep millions of our dear brethren, sunk in the most barbarous wretchedness, to dig up gold and silver for them and their children? Surely, the Americans must think that we are brutes, as some of them have represented us to be. They think that we do not feel for our brethren, whom they are murdering by the inches, but they are dreadfully deceived.[39]

Walker's words resonated with free and enslaved blacks in his home state of North Carolina and other states in the Southeast, as well as in the Northeast, where Garrison and his antislavery associates launched their campaign to abolish slavery.

On August 21, 1831, in Southampton County, Virginia, itinerant slave preacher Nat Turner led a group of armed, self-emancipated black men in an attempt to liberate their fellow bondsmen. Turner's revolt was quickly crushed, but not before he and his men had tortured and killed every white man, woman, and child they encountered.[40] After restoring order, fearful slave owners sold those slaves known to be troublemakers to slave traders, who transported them to the Deep South. Others instituted programs of physical abuse intended to intimidate the slaves and keep them from rebelling. In the end, Garrison's prophetic vision for the future of America and the American South, where enslaved blacks would rise up and claim their humanity through rebellion, violence, and the taking of white lives, was realized.

In the state of Kentucky, free African Americans represented less than 1 percent of the population in 1830: a total of only 4,917 individuals.[41] Although small, this population challenged the institution of slavery as an indelible fact of life for people of African descent as the nation expanded west. The presence of these quasi-free individuals constantly reminded the enslaved of their unnatural state while simultaneously undermining slaveholders' power over their human chattel, especially in urban locations such as Louisville and Lexington. Free African Americans established a sense of citizenship and identity by relying on one another and by working to contribute to the stability of their small communities. Nevertheless, the status of free blacks was a constant debate among the Kentucky legislators of the day.

Slavery is, by design, patriarchal, and in nineteenth-century America it could be useful only within a large agricultural economy. As the needs of Kentucky farmers and manufacturers began to change, slaveholders found themselves with a surplus of workers who still required food, clothing, and shelter. To mitigate the costs of keeping their human chattel, slaveholders hired out or sold off numerous slaves. The slave traders who bought these slaves took them to the Deep South to fill the increasing demand for labor there. As one historian describes the industry, "Negro trading in Kentucky was a constantly growing evil, which had begun with the comparatively innocent buying and selling of slaves by the individual owners to satisfy their own desires."[42]

By the mid-1830s, the practice was more widespread than historians are willing to admit. Gentlemen farmers became slave breeders, buying and participating in the reproduction of human chattel to exploit for the financial rewards.[43] Kentucky slaveholders advertised their "good breeding stock"—girls as young thirteen who were purchased and immediately began having their masters' children. These unions were reminiscent of the raping of African girls and women bound and chained on ships destined for the Caribbean and North and South America during the Middle Passage. Children born from these violent episodes were sold if they survived the voyage. Likewise, the mulatto children born on their master-fathers' farms were kept as additional labor; sold to the highest bidders at slave markets such as Cheapside in Lexington, to be used as domestic help; hired out as factory labor; or sold downriver to Natchez, Mississippi, or New Orleans, Louisiana. In the New Orleans market, wealthy planters, gamblers, and politicians paid high prices for mulatto girls and women, turning them into concubines and courtesans for their own decadent pleasures. With the expansion of "King Cotton" and the need for more slave labor to realize a profit, slave traders also frequented the Bluegrass region in search of new stock, which they found.

In addition to their slaves, the landed gentry were concerned about the breeding of livestock. Short-horn sheep, purebred cattle, and horses could be found on the numerous working farms within the 2,500 square miles surrounding Lexington in Fayette County. Since before the Revolutionary War, the sportsmen of colonial America had shown great interest in horse racing as a form of entertainment and a mass spectator sport. Indeed, throughout the eighteenth century, as the population of colonial America grew and the various towns and cities began to identify as communities, the need for diversions increased. Naturally, the colonists turned to the entertainments they had known in their respective countries of origin: footraces, boxing, cockfighting, bullbaiting, and horse racing. Of these various forms of entertainment, the colonists were especially connected to horse racing as a public contest of skill and bravery, and numerous owners and breeders developed grounds to demonstrate their superior breeding and jockeying know-how.[44] Similar to the turf in England, spectators came from adjoining communities to participate in the public spectacle. Indeed, both gentry and commoner attended the races, where the best horses and jockeys galloped to victory amid the cheering and cursing of a drunken proletariat and a thoroughly entertained planter class.

Similar to the English gentry, Americans, especially those with large farms and plantations in the southern colonies and Kentucky, were determined to improve the horse breeds found in North America.[45] As early as 1787, residents of Lexington were entertained by racing down Main Street, which featured some of the fastest horses bred in Virginia. However, the finest of Thoroughbreds came from the farms of horsemen such as John Breckinridge, William Buford, Henry Clay, Willa Viley, Robert Atchison Alexander, John Wesley Hunt, and Elisha Warfield. Their early Bluegrass breeders, brought from Virginia, set the standard for Kentucky horses and horse racing, rivaling all comers from the Eastern Seaboard and the Deep South. The elite used bloodstock breeding to both improve the quality of animals in North America and create wealth from the sale of stock with strong bloodlines. The Thoroughbred would influence the wealthy to procure the finest horseflesh available, establish jockey clubs, and build grand horse parks to demonstrate their standing.

Moreover, American gentlemen used contests between their horses as public demonstrations of their individual and collective wealth. And similar to their English cousins, the "habit of racing, to test the value of horses by their gaits and speed," became an important aspect of the everyday lives of those who maintained stables and farms dedicated to the turf.[46] Indeed, at the beginning of the nineteenth century, numerous merchants, politicians, and other landholding elites expressed renewed interest in the extravagance of well-bred horses and horse racing. With the nation's expansion west of the Allegheny Mountains, a new generation of bloodstock breeders began to develop animals to compete with their predecessors in the East. One of the most successful was Robert Atchison Alexander.

Alexander was born in 1819 in Woodford County, Kentucky, but was sent to England at age thirteen to attend Trinity College at Cambridge.[47] In 1850, after the death of his father, young Alexander returned to America to claim his inheritance, consisting of land in the Bluegrass region just northwest of Lexington. Using his substantial wealth, most of which was derived from his holdings in Scotland, Alexander quickly acquired more land and began to develop a 3,000-acre farm dedicated to the improvement of native animals.[48] Visitors to his property were awed by the order and economy of the grounds, tended to by a workforce of more than 150 leased African American slaves. The well-manicured, park-like lawns surrounding the main tract of land were divided by rail fences and stone walls constructed by slaves and recently arrived European immigrants. Within the confines of the Alexander home, African Americans worked as servants and cooks, and in the stables they were employed as grooms, trainers, exercise boys, and jockeys. Alexander raised animals of various breeds using stock imported from England, and he sold some of his finest cows, colts, and sheep to farms across the country. For his horses, however, he provided only the best. He built three private one-mile oval tracks: one for Thoroughbreds, one for trotters, and one for hurdle jumpers. To train and groom his beautiful beasts, Alexander employed the finest horsemen available in the Bluegrass: African American men and boys. These enslaved individuals would be vital to the development of horse racing as a national pastime—one that transcended class, ethnicity, race, and religion. Unfortunately, they too were commodities to be bought and sold at the discretion of their owners.

# 2

# America Bourne

On January 6, 1861, near the town of Winchester in Clark County, Kentucky, on the Pleasant Green farm owned by David Tanner, America Murphy gave birth to a baby boy she named Isaac.[1] Or at least this is what we can glean from the little hard evidence that exists. How America came to be on the farm, where exactly she gave birth to her son, who attended her, and whether the boy's father, Jerry Skillman, was present will never be known. What we *do* know is that because of her status as an enslaved black woman, the particulars related to her bringing a child into the world were deemed too unimportant to record—birth certificates were not issued for children born to slaves. Still, when the right questions are asked, the gaps in our knowledge about Isaac Murphy's beginnings become less daunting, and his life unfolds before our eyes.[2]

The lone thread that connects the facts and fictions of Murphy's life is the location of his birth. Kentucky birth records reveal that on January 6, 1861, a nameless black male child was born to a nameless black slave woman who lived on the Tanner farm.[3] Although there is no conclusive evidence that this was baby Isaac and his mother America, it is the only birth listed for the Tanner farm in the years 1860–1861. Thus, the corroborating evidence is strong. In addition, Murphy's 1896 obituary, written by close friend and turf man Llewellyn P. Tarleton, confirms the time and place of the famous jockey's birth. More important, this key shred of evidence provides a window into the past, suggesting the type of environment America Murphy was forced to negotiate daily in an effort to protect her child and herself from the abuses and degradations of slavery, while simultaneously keeping an eye toward the future.

Even 150 years after Isaac Murphy's birth, there is still a veil of curiosity surrounding the early life of one of the most unlikely heroes of the mid- to late nineteenth century. Scholars of African American history, sports, and Southern history share an interest in Murphy, based on his larger-than-life accomplishments on the turf despite the alleged inferiority of people of African descent. Conventional wisdom aside, the institution of slavery was predicated on the ability of the powerful white elite to control an American landscape fat with resources and untapped potential. To do so, the white elite also had to control the lives of blacks, who provided the labor needed to grow America's wealth. Thus, the white majority worked systematically to regulate and manage the narratives associated with people of African descent and their individual and collective histories, especially those that demonstrated blacks' ability to rise above their circumstances. To be born disconnected from one's history—past and present—is one sure way to confuse and alienate an individual's sense of destiny and purpose.

A month after Abraham Lincoln's election as president of the United States and South Carolina's secession from the Union, America Murphy, nearing the end of her pregnancy, may have chanced to think about her fate in the soon to be divided country of strangers. The institution of slavery was a firmly embedded and socially acceptable reality in the Bluegrass region, and black labor had been key to the success of white farmers and manufacturers there. Yet Kentucky would become a major factor in the conflict between the Federal government and the slave states over the states' right to chose their own future with regard to the slavery question: allow slavery to expand into the western territories, or limit it to the states that currently supported the institution. While politicians argued and fought over America's destiny, America Murphy prepared to give birth.

Whether she wanted to bring a new life into the world is not known; whether she saw the world as a sinking ship of despair and degradation or recognized Lincoln's election as the beginning of a wave of change is not detailed in any journal, memoir, or letter. Chances are that she was hopeful, like most in her situation, that she would someday be free and that her child would have a better, freer, more just life. For America Murphy, January 6, 1861, was a day of great hope for herself and for her son's future. Sometime during that day, the dark mulatto woman gave birth to a baby boy in the slave cabin on the Tanner farm, enduring the pain to get what was wanted: a healthy child.

No one can really know, but baby Isaac may have suffered from bouts of pneumonia and other ailments, a consequence of being born during the harsh Kentucky winter. But like his mother, he would have been tough. Like most slave children, baby Isaac would learn to survive from the example set by his mother. America had grown to womanhood within the bowels of slavery. She knew every nasty detail about the institution and its shameless purveyors of unimaginable suffering. She learned about the savagery of whites whose assumed superiority was challenged by willful slaves who audaciously claimed their humanity without fear of death. She saw the anxiety whites felt about blacks' hatred of them and the nightmares they kept to themselves—visions of death at the hands of rebellious slaves determined to right the wrongs of the past. Vulnerable but not helpless, America knew about the debauched decadence of white men's and women's semiprivate lives, as they sought to take whatever they wanted from the weakest among them: the Negro. She knew black people had no rights—this was obvious. And it is possible she was aware of the Supreme Court decision in the Dred Scott case and Chief Justice Roger B. Taney's proclamation to the country's black population—free and enslaved—that they were not entitled to be recognized as citizens under the Constitution of the United States.[4] More than likely, America understood the challenges of free blacks in and around the Bluegrass region as they tried to establish some sense of stability for themselves and their families. Clearly, the pervasive institutional racism woven into the fabric of society prevented any full expression of independence.

But America was smart. She no doubt knew about local abolitionists, the Underground Railroad, and plots among her neighbors to run off into the night with the hope of reaching the Ohio River and the freedom that lay beyond it. Even though they lived on the margins of white society, members of the black community of the Bluegrass region were connected and maintained a connectedness that was unique in every way. Indeed, these invisible people had power, though not in the same sense as white slaveholders or whites in general, who levied life-and-death sentences against human chattel with impunity. The power of those held in bondage was based on an understanding of the nature of white people and their fragile identities built on the myth of white supremacy. Although they were physically limited in their ability to move freely, this invisible community managed to escape the brutality of their lives by using their minds, their individual and collective knowledge, to achieve a specific end. Enslaved African Americans learned to live outside their physical reality through their imaginations, promoting a sense of freedom and a lack of fear of white reprisal or even death. Who can say whether America Murphy plotted to escape and disappear into the wind one day when the Tanners least expected it. She may have been an agent for abolitionists, undetected by her masters, whose naiveté and sense of entitlement left them vulnerable.

Still, by January 1861, America Murphy and her newborn child stood at the edge of a brand-new world where the possibility of freedom had changed the outlook of the "inferior" and the noncitizen. To David Tanner, however, America's newborn baby was a possession like any other, to be used and exploited for his own personal financial benefit. Kentucky farmers, many of whom were from Virginia—the Old Dominion—held on to their economic aspirations and racial attitudes. To men like Tanner, the "natural increase" in slaves represented an investment in human property that could be lucrative, based on the marketplace and the perceived and actual value of slaves. Certainly, the increased demand for slave labor to work in the cotton fields of the Deep South motivated some Kentucky slaveholders to sell their "black brutes" to stock-hungry slave traders and take advantage of the profits available.

Slaveholding farmers took pride in their slaves' ability to produce whatever was needed to sustain daily life. Possessing or hiring out a slave who was a skilled blacksmith, cooper, teamster, or factory or mill hand was essential to numerous Bluegrass slaveholders' sense of identity. Indeed, a farmer's success was not always tied to the crops harvested and sold. Additional income came from the sale of slave labor when there was a lull on the farm, especially during the winter months. Factory workers were needed seasonally to manufacture raw hemp into rope and cord, so it was common for factories to hire slaves for short periods from absentee owners or a sheriff who happened to be in possession of an unclaimed slave. Such transactions could be lucrative for slaveholders, or at least pay for the upkeep of the slave who generated the income.

On Tanner's Clark County farm, each of his slaves contributed their own particular skills and abilities to ensure the success of the planting and harvesting seasons. Like most enslaved African Americans, America Murphy understood the penalty for failing to complete her assigned tasks. On more than a few occasions, Kentucky slaves accused of behavior contrary to that desired by their masters or overseers were "disciplined" within the framework of the law, based on the number of "stripes" (lashes of the whip) an infraction required. On other occasions, enslaved blacks were tortured to death for no other reason than the sadistic pleasure taken by those who applied the whip, the ax, or strategically placed hot coals to elicit the bloodcurdling screams desired.[5]

Still, fear of such abuse did not dissuade enslaved African Americans from rebelling and fighting for their humanity at the cost of their lives. Resistance is the natural outcome of denying people the right to claim that which is natural. In labeling African Americans inferior and subjecting them to reprehensible abuse to satisfy the demented majority, who justified their vicious behavior as discipline, white slaveholders guaranteed their own destruction. To expect anything less than bloodshed was ludicrous, as former slave turned abolitionist Frederick Douglass makes clear. "Slavery," he argues, "is a system of brute force. It shields itself behind might, rather than right. It must be met with its own weapons."[6] In his mind, and to the millions of others held in bondage, the only way to end the suffering was through violence. This was the world America Murphy knew, and it was the world she brought her child into. How she taught him about that world—its challenges and its ideas of civility and humanity—would be shaped by her expectations for him. Indeed, America held her son's future in her hands and in her heart; she would be responsible for guiding his destiny beyond the dark days of slavery.

More than likely, it was America who chose her newborn son's name. There are two viable reasons she might have decided to call him Isaac: a family connection or a biblical connection. Isaac might have been the name of America's grandfather, favorite uncle, or brother. Clearly, the individual would have been someone important to her, someone she would think of each time she reflected on her child and her hopes and dreams for him. Naming her son after a family member would have preserved a connection to America's family's history and therefore given the child a sense of his past. Severing the connection to one's ancestors is like committing social suicide, and enslaved African Americans sought to maintain a tradition of naming that preserved their families' historical narratives and their connections to relatives long passed or separated by distance. One's name provided a sense of family that could not be taken away no matter how far from home one ventured.

Alternatively, America might have taken her son's name from the Bible, in reference to the only son of Abraham and Sarah. It is possible that America had given birth to several other children who had died or been sold. Due to her age (somewhere around thirty) and the circumstances, America may have seen Isaac as a gift from God and chosen his name to reflect her gratitude and joy at being given another chance at motherhood. She invested a great deal of hope in Isaac, for his name is connected to the great things promised to those who are obedient to the will of God. This act of naming would have demonstrated America's faith in her Bible lessons and her willingness to teach her son the meaning and purpose of living a religious life. African Americans' connection to the world through religion provided them with a sense of rootedness. By bestowing such a strong name on her son, along with a knowledge of its biblical implications, America Murphy gave Isaac a sense of purpose and an answer to the question of his destiny.

In Kentucky, children born to enslaved women became field hands, responsible for planting and harvesting the crops; carpenters, whose steady hands built homes and barns; trainers, whose knowledge of animal husbandry helped develop champion bloodstock; jockeys, who rode those champions to victory; and domestic servants, who maintained the households of the wealthy. Indeed, the value of a slave child to its owner was based on the child's future potential as a commodity in the marketplace. These children grew up to be the muscle that built the wealth of Kentucky's first families. This was the world into which Isaac Murphy was born.

Enslaved African Americans organized their lives to create a world of their own, away from the eyes and ears of whites.[7] Within these communities, they experienced full lives, achieved manhood and womanhood, and discussed the world of their masters. Those who worked closest to their masters had an intimate knowledge of white people and their ways, which created windows of opportunity for dissent and rebellion. Whether America Murphy participated in such acts of defiance on the Tanner farm is unknown, but we know she was determined to protect her son and shield him from the worst degradations and abuses perpetrated by those in power. No doubt she hoped and prayed for a better future for her baby boy, one in which freedom was an achievable reality, not some fantastic notion or doomed endeavor that often resulted in the capture of runaways trying to reach the far-off North. With civil war looming, America would maintain a vigil over Isaac to ensure both his survival and her own. He would depend on her, and she would guide his steps toward freedom.

America Murphy had been born into slavery around the time the laws became more deterministic of her future. By 1861, neither she nor Isaac could expect much protection from the laws or traditions that deemed them the property of David Tanner.[8] Still, those who were legally designated human chattel had certain ways to resist the demands of their masters or overseers.[9] Like most enslaved black women, America no doubt understood the value of community and maintained ties to hers in the Bluegrass region. She was likely aware that Lincoln's election represented hope for blacks. Nevertheless, she probably questioned the wisdom of bringing a child into a world where he would be valued similarly to a cow or a horse and could be traded or sold on a whim. As a domestic slave and the mother of a newborn, America would have been concerned about the needs of her infant, his future, and the possibility of his untimely death.[10] If Isaac was going to survive to adulthood, she would have to teach him how to respond appropriately to the systemic abuses of slavery while privately maintaining his dignity and selfhood. In accordance with the principles of the institution of slavery, all children born to enslaved African American women took on the condition of the mother, regardless of the father's status as free or white. Thus, Isaac Murphy was indeed born a slave.[11]

## America Murphy

America Murphy was born around 1831 in Lexington to an enslaved woman named Anne, who was likely of mixed-race ancestry, and to Green Murphy, about whom little is known.[12] America grew to womanhood knowing both her parents and other members of her extended family, many of whom lived in and around the urban center of Lexington. The details of Anne and Green's relationship are unknown. Nevertheless, based on the customs and laws of Kentucky, we know that they would not have been legally married. It is possible that Anne and Green attended the First African Baptist Church, where London Ferrill was minister, and he may have joined the couple as husband and wife.[13] Ferrill conducted marriage ceremonies between slaves that mimicked the peculiarity of their situation: couples were wedded with the understanding that they would be husband and wife until death or distance separated them. It is also possible that Anne and Green maintained a loving relationship and lived in the same home or near each other in Lexington.

We know that Anne was a slave, based on her daughter's designation as human chattel, so the question becomes, what was the status of her father? Was Green Murphy a "native born" white man or a recently immigrated Irishman? Did he own Anne and therefore her children, or was he an enslaved black man who worked as a field hand in one of the surrounding counties? Did he live in Lexington as a hired factory worker, or was he owned by the same master as Anne? Given Kentucky's history of mixed-race children, the prevalence of long-distance marriages, and the widespread use of slave labor in Lexington, the possibilities are endless. What we *do* know about Green Murphy is that he was a bell ringer and town crier for auctions. It is highly plausible that Green announced auctions at Cheapside in Lexington or even stood by as an assistant as his master sold other slaves on the steps of the courthouse or in front of the Fayette County jail. This possibility should not be surprising: slavery is called the *peculiar institution* for a reason. An examination of Lexington directories from the early nineteenth century reveals that no one is listed as serving in the capacity of bell ringer or town crier—an important means of conveying the news of the day. Census data for Fayette and the six surrounding counties do not account for anyone named Green Murphy, which strongly suggests that he was an enslaved black man owned by one of the many white families named Murphy living in Lexington between 1830 and 1860.

An 1891 interview with trainer Eli Jordan suggests that Green Murphy may have been in the business of horses. Jordan claims that the elder Murphy wanted his grandson to become a great jockey like Charles Stewart, Ansel Williamson, and Ed Brown.[14] Among all the white Murphy families living in or around Lexington at the time, only Jeremiah Murphy was directly tied to the horse business; he owned a livery stable on the east side of Mulberry Street between Main and High Streets.[15] In 1834 Jeremiah Murphy sold a tract of land to the Kentucky Horse Association, whose sole purpose was "to improve the breed of horses by encouraging the sports of the turf."[16]

Green Murphy may have come from Fauquier County, Virginia, as a small boy, just as the village of Lexington was beginning to settle and take shape. He may have been hoisted onto the back of one of the blooded horses owned by his master and told to guide the prized beast down Main Street to the finish line at the other end. During the early part of the nineteenth century, when Lexington was young and the Jockey Club was created to regulate racing, Green would have been old enough to understand the value of being a successful jockey in a racially polarized society where blacks had few rights. It is possible that Green Murphy became a fixture in Lexington based on his horsemanship, and he may have hoped to share his love of speed with his children and grandchildren.

America's mother, Anne, may have come to Kentucky at the turn of the nineteenth century as a young girl, traveling across the Cumberland Gap or down the Kentucky River with her owner. She was likely a domestic servant to one of the many urban white slave-holding families. These families participated in the slave trade in the most genteel of ways: purchasing slaves at the Cheapside slave market to hire out to the numerous manufacturing firms in Lexington. As the property of a cosmopolitan Kentuckian, Anne would have been responsible for maintaining the appearance of privilege and entitlement—a façade that was common among Lexington's genteel upper class. Indeed, those who possessed stylish town homes or grand estates understood these to be extensions of their status as members of the bourgeoisie.

As a mulatto woman, Anne would have been the physical representation of the existence of sex across racial boundaries, despite the social taboo.[17] By 1860, 20 percent of the enslaved black population in Kentucky was mulatto. Clearly, this was the result of black women giving birth to children fathered by white men. Indeed, sex between whites and blacks often involved rape and coercion—white men violently asserting their fragile sense of power against black women. Less discussed are the loving relationships between enslaved black women and white men that produced children who were legally defined as slaves due to the principle of children taking on the status of their mothers. Unfortunately, very few narratives of such relationships having happy endings have survived.

Conversely, relationships between black men and white women were not only frowned upon but also illegal in the slave states. Such relationships threatened the stability of slavery in three ways: they undermined the very foundation of slavery, which was that the races were different species of humankind; they challenged the notion of white males' entitlement to sole access to white women's bodies; and they jeopardized the status of whiteness: if black women, enslaved or free, gave birth to black babies even if the father was white, would white women give birth to white babies even if the father was black? Because children took on the status of the mother in Southern society, children born to white women would be born free, even if they were fathered by enslaved black men.[18] The stability of white society hung in the balance.

Lewis Clarke describes the relationship between his enslaved mother and his Scottish immigrant father, who fought at the Battle of Bunker Hill during the Revolutionary War. "My father was from 'beyond the flood,'" he writes, "from Scotland and by trade a weaver. About the year 1800, or before, he came to Kentucky, and married Miss Letitia Campbell, then held as a slave by her dear and affectionate father."[19] Although uncommon, marriages between enslaved black women and white men did occur, especially if the women were near white in complexion. Other narratives of common-law marriages or marriages of convenience between enslaved black women and white men are less romantic, indicative of the changing meaning of race in America in general and Kentucky in particular. The unfortunate outcome of Lewis Clarke's story was all too common. After the death of Letitia's father and the execution of his will, she and her children were not freed, as he had promised; instead, they were disbursed as assets of the estate. Separated from his mother and siblings, the adolescent Lewis was loaned out to members of the Campbell family and forced to negotiate his often brutal surroundings and circumstances with courage and bravery.

To be sure, numerous sexual relationships between black women and white men in the antebellum period were coercive and violent, owing to the simple fact that these women had no rights whatsoever. They did not belong to a protected class; they were not included under the banner of law that shielded white women from sexual exploitation. Black women were often abused without cause or subjected to inhumane cruelty. Black women struggled to find support from white women, who perceived black womanhood as inherently licentious and depraved. White women believed the "Negress" possessed powers to entice and compromise their vulnerable Christian husbands, who were too weak to refuse the advances of such wanton Jezebels. As a black woman, Anne Murphy would have witnessed the consequences of being born black or mulatto in a society that claimed whiteness was as close to godliness as people could get.

It is likely that David Tanner purchased America Murphy when she was a young girl, sometime between 1840 and 1850, to work as a domestic servant on his Clark County farm. She would have been taught as a child to perform the tasks required of her, learning the type of exemplary behavior desired by the Tanner family by watching her mother and other black women serving as "house girls." We know from various slave narratives that white mistresses could be quite abusive, but America's particular experiences in the Tanner household remain a mystery. She would have been up before dawn to prepare breakfast for the Tanner family, clean the dishes, make the beds, and wash clothes. In addition, she may have prepared food for the slaves assigned to the fields and to the stable on the Tanner property.

Similar to his neighbors, Tanner, a transplanted Virginian, used the physical labor of black men and women to clear all traces of wilderness from his land, to cultivate the ground, to plant and harvest the fields, and to transport goods to market. Kentucky farmers took great pride in their ability to produce what they needed to prosper, even though they utilized the muscle of slaves to do so. Slavery made the genteel life possible throughout the Upper and Lower South. Still, enslaved African Americans did not simply accept the status quo. Through an array of public and private actions, bondsmen and -women fought to claim their humanity and their freedom, undermining the institution of slavery at its core.

As a young girl, America would have observed and participated in the bustling life of cosmopolitan Lexington, a city desperate to live up to its potential. However, America had to be aware of both the value placed on her fair skin and the potential life that awaited her, should she be sold and sent down south. Located less than twenty miles from the city of Lexington, the Tanner farm produced agricultural commodities such as hemp, corn, and tobacco. Tanner also raised livestock, including milk cows, sheep, and Thorough-bred horses.[20] As a house girl, America would have seen to the needs of the family, especially Tanner's wife Lydia and his young daughter Julia, who was around the same age as America. As a servant, she would have been trained to cook, clean, sew, and provide companionship for her young mistress. Although this type of job may seem innocuous, it could sometimes be more psychologically damaging than working in the fields under a brutal overseer. Constant demands were placed on adolescent house girls like America, and if they did not perform up to the standards of their mistresses and masters, the consequences could be brutal.

To be sure, America would have been at the mercy of the men on the farm. They may have attempted to coerce her into a sexual relationship or even assault her as a demonstration of their power over her. Prior to 1850, David Tanner may have placed more than a few "rebellious slaves" in the hands of the local jailer, to be auctioned off and "sent down river."[21] Whatever happened in America's life, the available evidence suggests that she learned to negotiate the complex nature of slavery and the ongoing struggle to be free from bondage and abuse. On the Tanner farm, she would have adapted to the family's daily patterns and their comings and goings; she would have listened to their discussions about finances, the politics of the day, the efforts of Kentucky politicians to send free blacks to West Africa, abolitionism, and the pending war between the North and the South.

In 1861, after the birth of baby Isaac, America Murphy's personal life and responsibilities changed, but her role on the farm remained the same. She may have been granted some time to recover from childbirth, but she was probably required to return to her chores within a week's time. Being that Isaac was the only child on the farm and America was unable to care for him because of her duties, she would have left her newborn in the care of an older slave woman also owned by Tanner. Isaac would have spent his earliest years under the watchful eye of this maternal figure who was charged with watching over, feeding, and otherwise tending to the needs of small children while their mothers worked in the fields, the house, or the yard.[22] Once he was old enough, Isaac would be sent to the fields to weed, hoe, and harvest or to perform other tasks on the farm. Subsequently, America would be charged with grooming her son for the rite of passage that marked his transition from boyhood to manhood—albeit more in theory than in practice. Like other slave mothers, America did not want to see her child taken from her without warning and sold without remorse. Nor did she want to see her son whipped as a means of breaking him in. America wanted more for Isaac—more than she had access to—and the pending war between the Federal government and the rebellious slave states gave her hope.

What cannot be overlooked are the enslaved women who chose not to allow their children to live in a world where only heartbreak awaited them. As appalling as it may sound, some women were willing to take the lives of their own children to save them from the horrors of slavery. Cases of infanticide were not common among enslaved women, but there are recorded instances of desperate mothers murdering their children to save them from the hellish existence they themselves had experienced.[23] One such woman was Margaret Garner, who, after a failed attempt to escape to freedom across the Ohio River, took the life of her infant daughter in 1856. An enslaved mother's love was unmatched, but how did she prepare her daughter or son to be raped? At what point did she say it will be all right, just be strong? What kinds of torment haunted the souls of these women? Garner wanted her daughter to be free from the evil she had known; she did not want her daughter to be someone's property, of no greater value than a hog or a horse. She, like most women in her situation, did not know whether or when she would be sold away from her family, whether her newborn would become collateral for a new carriage for her mistress, or whether her child would become the next victim of the slave trader's purpose. Out of love, some enslaved African American mothers took extreme measures to keep their children from abuse, even if it meant destroying the lives they had brought into the world.

By the time Isaac Murphy was born, the world was undergoing great changes, and the promise of freedom for people of African descent became a whisper on the lips of bondsmen. However, they knew enough not to loosen their tongues too quickly, because the fire of rebellion was not yet hot enough. Amid the radical changes taking place across the nation, especially in the Bluegrass, America Murphy prepared to raise her son in a world that did not recognize his humanity.

## Jerry Skillman

With the election of Abraham Lincoln, the so-called black Republican, Americans were preparing for conflict over the institution of slavery. Disagreement over the expansion of slavery and its efficacy as an institution, not the issue of whether slavery was right or wrong, was what threatened to destroy the nation. Nonetheless, the escalating tensions became a beacon of hope to the country's most ardent freedom-seeking inhabitants: enslaved African Americans. Although Kentucky was a slave state and strategically located as a buffer between the North and the South, its loyalties would eventually remain with the Union. The impending war between the Federal government and the Confederate States of America, which refused to yield ground on states' rights and the notion of popular sovereignty, would be a critical event in the lives of America Murphy, her newborn son, and the boy's father, Jerry Skillman.

Born sometime between 1825 and 1840, in a place unknown, Jerry Skillman was likely an enslaved field hand on John Whitney Skillman's farm in Bourbon County, near the town of Levy. Obviously, Skillman's external life was dictated by his position as a slave; as for his dreams and aspirations, we have no way of knowing, since he left no record of his thoughts or ideas. However, we can speculate that he was a man who made choices, many of which were life-and-death decisions. Up until the Civil War, his name does not appear in any public records, so he was not a runaway slave and had not violated any law. Surely, some would identify this as weakness on his part. Why didn't he try to run away? Why didn't he follow in the footsteps of Nat Turner and lead a rebellion against the white men and women who pursued lives of comfort and ease on the backs of blacks? What advantages did he gain by not pursuing freedom in the North?

Historically, we know that enslaved African American men, women, and children were forced to negotiate numerous situations on a daily basis that made it nearly impossible to emancipate themselves from their masters. Physically escaping from the farm may have been the easiest part of running away from slavery. More difficult were the questions that followed: Where to go, and how to get there? How to get resources to survive the trip to the promised land? Who could be trusted? What would life be like after arriving in the North? And what would happen to those left behind? No doubt, the decision to run was complex and linked to factors that cannot be known by the average surveyor of antebellum American history. What is more, we cannot overestimate the power of the human spirit to persevere under the most horrific conditions for the sake of love and family.

As the personal property of J. W. Skillman, Jerry, his brother Charles, and several other enslaved males cultivated the fields, harvested the crops, and processed raw products for the marketplace, including hemp, which Kentuckians of the time called the "nigger crop."[24] The son of a Virginia planter, J. W. Skillman's wealth was based on the real estate he owned, valued at $8,000 in 1850, and his personal property, including nine slaves, worth no less than $10,000.[25] A decade later, the value of his farm property had increased 250 percent to $22,000, and his personal property, which included thirteen slaves, was worth more than $20,000. Of the human chattel owned by Skillman, two of the males were around Jerry's age, thirty to thirty-five. It is possible that several of the thirteen were family members, including Jerry's mother, a number of siblings, and other relatives. Others were likely not blood related, having been purchased at various times as investments. This was not uncommon: Kentucky farmers bought, leased, and traded slaves for different types of work, depending on the season and their needs, such as clearing additional lands or constructing more modern buildings for livestock and storage.

Skillman's financial records show that he took full advantage of the region's most valuable commodity—hemp—to increase his personal wealth, amassing the labor force necessary to generate market surpluses and ensure his success as a farmer. Labor could be acquired, as needed, through leasing agreements between owners or purchases made at the slave market at Cheapside or at the local jail, where slaves held in debt could be bought for a nominal fee. In Kentucky, the system of hiring out workers allowed urban dwellers to take advantage of the demand for labor by purchasing slaves at the slave market and then leasing them to farmers during the harvest and to manufacturing firms in Lexington engaged in the production of rope, bagging, clothes, and other products for export to the South. Although those held in bondage on the Skillman farm likely came to depend on one another and formed some type of familial unit out of necessity and convenience, this cannot be considered a more benign form of slavery. It is possible that Skillman was a breeder, selling children to slave traders who transported them to the South. Regardless of the form it took, the institution of slavery was a tool of oppression with only one desired outcome: to get the most out of human chattel to increase the wealth and social standing of their owners.

By 1860, Jerry was certainly aware of his responsibilities as a member of a large labor force. His ability to be productive increased his value on the Skillman farm, and potentially his own sense of pride. Working alongside as well as under the gaze of whites, African Americans like Jerry gained an intimate knowledge of whites' habits of domination. Jerry and his extended family would have shared information about the white Skillman family, their innermost secrets and their movements, to better navigate their already uncertain existence. Like America Murphy, Jerry would have observed the "frantic terror" and the "agony" that swept over the farm when the disobedient were punished or when the Southern "nigger traders" came to eye new purchases for their coffles.[26]

Even in the more genteel setting of Kentucky, where slavery

was thought to be less abusive, African Americans witnessed the daily brutality of the institution. In this antebellum setting, Jerry Skillman learned how to negotiate his world, achieving a sense of identity as a man despite his circumstances. For Jerry, this would be a temporary state of existence, and the Civil War would be his opportunity to proclaim what he understood all along: that he was a man of bone, liquid, and muscle, just like the white men who claimed dominion over him and his people.

America Murphy and Jerry Skillman may have met during the local county court days, held at the county seats of Paris and Winchester, or at the Cheapside market in Lexington, where farmers came to sell and trade their produce, livestock, and slaves. When they were not serving their owners' needs or otherwise fulfilling their duties, enslaved African Americans were allowed to talk to one another and catch up on the news: who had been sold to whom, and where; who had had a baby; and how runaways relocated in the North were faring. All would have overheard murmurs about the coming war and where white Kentuckians stood with regard to secession by the South. At these mass gatherings, there also would have been discussions about Kentucky-born Republican presidential candidate Abraham Lincoln and his position on the slavery debate.

While moving through the crowd and visiting with friends and relatives, Jerry may have talked in hushed tones with trusted members of the black community about the abolitionist movement or listened as other bondmen discussed the Underground Railroad that ran right through Lexington. They would have reminded one another of the numerous costs of being caught and the rewards of actually achieving freedom. Some of these discussions may have circled around family news: where kin had been sent to work, where they had been sold, or where they were buried. This was one way to maintain and mend family ties in slave communities, especially when distance, deceit, and death were constantly tearing at what bound African Americans together beyond the institution of slavery.

Even with the Civil War looming, Jerry was not dissuaded from pursuing America as his companion. They were both in their thirties, and Jerry would have been attracted to America's strong sense of purpose and resilience, as well as her beauty. The dark mulatto-looking woman had been born and reared in Lexington, within the progressive community of free and enslaved blacks, and her strength would have resonated through small acts of resistance. Jerry, whose muscular body had been conditioned by his occupation as a field hand, was just the type of man America would have wanted in her life. Chances are that something in his manner made him attractive, or perhaps he spoke of freedom in terms that satisfied America's requirements for a potential husband and the father of her children. Who can know for sure? America may have been impressed by Jerry's assured disposition and his work ethic, which guaranteed him certain privileges and opportunities. There was value in being a productive slave on a farm where productivity was essential to the maintenance of stability. Both America and Jerry understood the real and imagined costs of their position as slaves, but they also knew how to use the system to their advantage.

One aspect of the culture of slavery in central Kentucky was the pass system, which permitted certain slaves (usually male) to travel to adjoining counties on business for their owners, visiting family or courting potential partners along the way. Passes also allowed husbands the opportunity to see their wives and children who were living elsewhere. These long-distance, or "abroad," marriages were promoted by slave owners because any children produced could be sold for a profit. Another benefit of such a system was that, by encouraging their female slaves to become involved with black males from other farms in nearby counties, slave owners were expanding the gene pool of their human chattel. Based on this arrangement, Jerry would have been able to visit and court America at the Tanner farm in Clark County. In slaveholding states like Kentucky, especially in communities near urban centers like Lexington, it was common practice for enslaved and free men of color to seek their potential spouses from neighboring farms and plantations.[27]

Still, the institution of slavery dictated that an African American man obtain the consent of his owner, as well as the owner of his prospective wife, before the union could take place. Slave marriages were honored as long as they did not interfere with the spouses' usefulness on their respective farms. Unfortunately, the nature of slavery rarely allowed an extensive courtship period, and slaves sought happiness whenever and wherever it was available. Over the course of weeks or months, America and Jerry would have visited each other before deciding to seek the permission of their respective owners to marry. Unfortunately, there is no record of an official marriage and no narrative of their lives together.[28] Under Kentucky law at the time, it would have been illegal for anyone designated as chattel to be married within the Christian tradition to either another slave or a free person of color.[29] However, based on social customs, they could have "jumped a broom" in the presence of community members to solidify their commitment as husband and wife.[30] This was a common tradition, and most African Americans adhered to it, including Jerry Skillman and his previous wife, Caroline, who had borne him a son, William, three years earlier in an adjoining county.

To consummate their marriage in the eyes of God, Jerry and America would have been allowed to spend time together after the wedding. And depending on the generosity of their masters, they might have been permitted as many as two or three visitations a month. Because their union was an abroad marriage, it is unclear whether Jerry was present at the birth of his son, Isaac. Unless Jerry had been granted a pass from his master to visit the Tanner farm in Clark County, he would have been on the Skillman farm when his son struggled his way into the world. Jerry would have heard the news of his son's birth through the network of individuals traveling the country roads on errands for their owners, conveying bits of information to be passed on to the right people. These networks were important to the survival of both enslaved and free African American communities in mid-nineteenth-century Kentucky, especially in the Bluegrass region, where slavery was a constant source of debate by abolitionists and slavery advocates alike.

## Isaac Murphy's Childhood

By the time Isaac Murphy turned two, he was likely still nursing from his mother's breasts, learning how to communicate his particular needs, and running barefoot on the hard dirt yard of the Tanner farm. Still vulnerable to sickness and disease, the toddler was lucky to have survived past his first birthday. For children born between 1830 and 1860, the mortality rate for enslaved blacks was more than double that for whites. Indeed, death before age five was a common occurrence in slave families. Along with the usual diseases of the day such as pneumonia, influenza, cholera, and diphtheria, enslaved black children died from a lack of proper care and appropriate shelter. What is more, poor nutrition compromised these children's immune systems, stunted their growth, and contributed to other developmental problems.[31] Based on this reality, young Isaac Murphy may have struggled both physically and mentally. He was a child born of circumstances beyond his control.

Still, America was a good mother and did her best to ensure that her child survived. To Kentucky slaveholders, slave children were of greater value once they were able to work in the fields, stables, and kitchens or could be hired out to local farmers and manufacturers. But until they became contributing members of the workforce, black children were vulnerable to abuse from overzealous slaveholders who systematically weeded out the weakest through direct and indirect forms of neglect.

Slave children between the ages of five and ten were often employed in the main household as playmates for their master's children. One of the realities of the culture of slavery in central Kentucky was that these children of different racial, social, cultural, and political status were often half siblings from different mothers: their father's white wife and his black slave women. Beyond the simple pleasures of playing and exploring the world around them, these children were learning how the world functioned and their future roles in it. Often, those slave children assigned as playmates to their young masters would spend their entire lives as their body servants and closest confidants.[32]

Through these innocent interactions, white children learned their place in the world as future masters. This form of social conditioning was at the very heart of slavocracy and black-white power relations. Identity development in the American South during slav-

ery was a constant negotiation between power and purpose. In most
scenarios, black children were conditioned to accept their roles as
subordinate social actors, conscious of their lack of power over anything, including their own lives.

Like a majority of slave mothers, America Murphy took every
opportunity to protect baby Isaac from the ill treatment and cruelty of a society in which blacks had no rights that white men were
bound to respect. Given what we know about the institution of slavery and the spirit of rebellion embedded in the human psyche, there
can be no doubt that America imagined a much sweeter and kind-
er future for the people of her race. She would have worked hard to
shield baby Isaac from the daily trauma of life as a slave, and she
would have maintained a hopeful and determined outlook for the
future—one in which her son would have every opportunity to grow
mentally and physically strong and achieve a full sense of manhood
by acquiring his freedom.

Records reveal that Tanner owned no other slave children in
1862, which means that Isaac likely spent much of his time alone
under the care of an elderly slave woman who watched over him
while America performed her duties. The tradition of communal
child care ensured the availability of maternal figures to feed small
children, keep an eye on them, and correct any behaviors deemed
dangerous to their present and future safety. Clearly, someone needed to supervise Isaac while America was attending to her responsibilities in the Tanner home or performing other errands required of
her. On occasion, she may have been able to steal some time away
from the Tanner residence after completing her chores of cook-
ing, cleaning, and washing. On small farms, domestic servants like
America were allowed some flexibility in their comings and goings,
as long as they met their masters' needs. America may have been allowed to attend to Isaac after she fulfilled all her daily duties in the
"big house," working under the strict supervision of the Tanners.

Like most children born in slavery, young Isaac was unaware of
his status as human chattel. If it had been up to his mother, he would
never have learned that he was the property of another human being. She did her best to satisfy her child's needs, comforting him at

night when he cried for affection and preparing their meals from the meager rations provided for their subsistence. Perhaps America risked taking some crumbs from the Tanner kitchen—a transgression that could have resulted in flogging.

It is unclear whether Isaac was America's first child, the first to survive beyond birth, or the first she was allowed to keep. If she bore children before Isaac, they may have been taken from her and sold at the Clark County court day or at Cheapside in Lexington to raise funds or pay debts. Or they may have been sold to "soul drivers" from St. Louis, Missouri, or Louisville, Kentucky, as they passed through the Bluegrass on their way to the slave markets of New Orleans.[33] In any case, Isaac was too young to be aware of the world outside the farm or to understand the dramatic changes taking place during this heroic time in American history. For people of African descent, their dreams of deliverance were coming true.

By the summer of 1862, the war had taken hold of the nation, and enslaved blacks in the Bluegrass listened to their white masters talk openly about the battle at Fort Sumter in South Carolina, the "black Republican" conspiracy to end slavery and take the property of good white people, and their constant fear of slave uprisings. For most African Americans, both enslaved and free, the notion of liberation from the peculiar institution and overt racism became a real possibility as long as the Union soldiers kept coming. Furthermore, freedom fighters like Charles Lenox Remond, Harriet Tubman, Frederick Douglass, and Sojourner Truth were constantly agitating white people to see blacks as human beings and challenging black folks to fight for the freedom they longed for. In Kentucky, abolitionism was as old as the state and its constitution. However, its meaning in the Civil War era was much different from that understood by the early settlers. Previous generations had argued against extending the institution of slavery beyond the "Old Dominion" of Virginia because it promoted idleness among white men and diminished the value of work.

The philosophical position of abolitionists had evolved since then. For men like William Lloyd Garrison, the abolition of slavery was essential to the moral life of the country: the "degrading

vassalage of the entire North to the accursed Slave Power" resulted not in a Union of honor, he claimed, but in disunion and dis-
honor.[34] Garrison believed, as did many New England abolitionists,
that black men and white men were equal in the eyes of God. Kentuckian Cassius Marcellus Clay had been an early advocate for the
gradual emancipation of slaves, but by the 1860s, he had become
a stringent proponent of the abolition of slavery. He gave speeches
throughout the state under threat of violence from both slaveholders
and nonslaveholders who adamantly opposed the potential increase
in the population of free blacks. Given the climate of the country
and Clay's support of President Lincoln, his position in favor of full
emancipation for African Americans became an immovable force in
Kentucky politics.

As America Murphy struggled to care for her son and satisfy
the daily needs of the Tanners, she would have been well aware of
the drama taking place around her. She would have paid attention to
the movements of the Union and Confederate armies, both of which
would have a significant influence on her future as a slave and her
son's future as a freeman. By the spring of 1863, Federal troops and
Confederate rebels challenged each other for control of the border
state of Kentucky. As a pivotal geographic, political, and strategic
location, the Bluegrass region became the focus of John Hunt Morgan, who traveled north through Kentucky to Ohio in an attempt
to distract Union commanders. Unlike South Carolina and the ten
other states that seceded, Kentucky remained a Union state and was
therefore under the protection and control of the Federal government. Kentucky slaveholders loyal to the Union were allowed to keep
their human property unless their slaves were impressed by Federal
troops to work at the various encampments throughout the state.
All white persons who were arrested as rebels, who were known to
be Confederate sympathizers, or who actively supported the rebel army, financially or otherwise, could take an oath of allegiance
if they wanted to remain free. The penalty for violating the oath
was death.[35] Those who refused were arrested and had their property confiscated by Federal troops, including their human chattel,
which were deemed "contrabands of war."[36] It is not clear whether

enslaved African Americans in the Bluegrass completely understood the particulars of the Emancipation Proclamation, believed that it was real, or understood the conflict the nation was embroiled in. More than likely, a great number recognized that their freedom was linked to President Lincoln's efforts to keep the nation together.

There can be no doubt that America Murphy believed her prayers were being answered each time she saw or heard of a Union soldier near the Tanner farm. Like most enslaved black men and women, she reflected on the gravity of her situation and was cautious not to express her joy and anticipation too loudly, so as not to arouse the ire of her master. However, in private, in the darkness of her cabin, she would have dropped to her knees and tearfully thanked God for smiling on her and her people and for blessing her with the opportunity to see her child attain his freedom.

With war at the doorsteps of their masters, enslaved African Americans, including the placid yet courageous America Murphy, understood that drastic changes were taking place. This heroic age would draw the masses of oppressed black people together to fight for the right to live free—or die in the process. And through a series of opportunities, circumstances, and luck, they would find the strength to develop the skills, abilities, and confidence to succeed socially, politically, and economically.

For children born at this moment in American history, their future was being shaped by circumstances and forces beyond their control. For Isaac, the America of his ancestors was dissolving, and the laws that proclaimed him the property of another were crumbling under the weight of revolution and rebellion. Men and women he did not know, but who would come to know him as an adult, were changing the world, inspired by thoughts of freedom. Isaac was a child of the great movement to lift the black masses from the "depths of slavery to the height of liberty and manhood." The boy born in slavery in Clark County, Kentucky, would become one of the millions to benefit from the sacrifices of those who came before him and from the bravery of the black soldiers, including his father, who fought and died under the banner of freedom during the Civil War.[37]

# PART 2

# *Rise*

# 3

# Seizing Freedom

Almost immediately after Abraham Lincoln was elected president in November 1860, the country split down the middle. Tensions had been building for nearly forty years, since the Missouri Compromise, and the Republican Party's platform of limiting the expansion of slavery into the Federal territories sent a shock wave through the United States. Historians may argue that the causes of the Civil War were multiple, yet all would agree that the linchpin was the issue of slavery.

Other than the radical abolitionists who believed the institution was morally and religiously wrong, white Americans in the North, South, and West became agitated over the possibility of a change in the status quo if the position of the lowly Negro was elevated. In the North, nativists and Irish immigrants railed against the thought of blacks gaining access to the rights and privileges of citizenship, which would mean increased competition for jobs. In the South, advocates of the "Slave Power" chafed at the thought of their way of life being attacked. They believed in the much-debated notion that blacks were natural slaves and whites their natural masters, and each depended on the other for survival. In the West, advocates of popular sovereignty, which threatened the balance of power in the United States, sought to exclude any elevation of the

Negro beyond his status as subordinate to the "white race."[1] What is more, immigrant and nativist whites did not want their future success and sense of entitlement to the land and its resources to be jeopardized by the Negro question: what to do with 4 million black people. Overall, a majority of whites wanted to maintain the racial hierarchy supported by the Constitution and reinforced by custom.

Not surprisingly, African Americans saw things differently, especially black leaders who had committed their lives to fighting slavery. Prior to the beginning of the Civil War, black writers expressed the opinion that it was time for the "black man to learn to stand firmly upon his feet—his own feet" and pursue a greater degree of freedom beyond the control of white men and their traditions.[2] In addition, radical abolitionists, antislavery organizations, and colonization societies challenged the validity of owning human beings, becoming more vocal in their efforts to destroy the "Southern way of life" while advancing a more just and respectable national character. Conversely, the Slave Power, with its Northern supporters and government constituents, decided that the institution was too important to lose, forcing the country into a transition that would intensify sectional tensions and ultimately lead to civil war.

With the Compromise of 1850, which included a more stringent fugitive slave law, African Americans faced an avalanche of fierce refusals, all choreographed to "suppress and crush out" any "agitation for Liberty and human equality."[3] What seemed to be an attempt to defend the rights of slaveholders became a siren call for those who were paying close attention to the unfolding political contest. The Fugitive Slave Act of 1850 eroded what little stability African Americans had gained over time. From this defensive position, black leaders launched an assault on the institution of slavery, challenging their community to be brave and to speak the truth.

Under the protection of the Fugitive Slave Act, slave catchers, bounty hunters, and "nigger stealers" roamed the streets of Northern cities in search of runaways to return to their masters. Freeborn or manumitted African Americans living in Philadelphia, New York, Boston, or Cincinnati had no defense against accusations that they were runaway slaves, and agents sometimes stole them from their homes in pursuit of the rewards for recovering human chattel. On occasion, free black men would be kidnapped and sold into the cotton fields of the Deep South, never to be heard from again. Cavalier attempts to remove former slaves from the comfort of their homes in the urban North sometimes resulted in violent confrontations between former masters or bounty hunters and members of the black community seeking to protect their own. Moreover, under the law, whites as well as African Americans were required to assist in the capture of blacks accused of being a runaways. In effect, the law entitled the Slave Power to reach beyond its borders and into the lives of those who wanted no part of slavery. To avoid being caught and returned to the South, runaways used the Underground Railroad to get as far north as they could travel.[4] From 1850 to 1860, thousands of former slaves made their way to Canada, where they came under the protection of the British government, and set up communities in cities such as Windsor, Montreal, and Toronto.

The Fugitive Slave Act forced African Americans to defend their natural right to be recognized as human beings and to resist at all costs the doctrine that guaranteed their perpetual servitude. When former slave William Parker of Christiana, Pennsylvania, gave shelter to a fugitive slave owned by Edward Gorsuch of Maryland, bloodshed ensued. Gorsuch and his men asked Parker to submit to a search of his premises, and when Parker refused, the slave hunters began firing on the residence. Parker and his men defended themselves, and the exchange left Gorsuch dead and his son wounded. Parker was hurried out of the county to Canada, where he found refuge and protection under the British flag. The other men involved were indicted for treason against the United States.[5]

The September 18, 1851, issue of the *National Anti-Slavery Standard* carried a commentary on the bloody confrontation: "Love of liberty is no less powerful in men whose skins are black than in those of light complexions, it need surprise nobody that in the game of slave-hunting . . . it should sometimes happen that the hunted become the mark for bullets, and the law of self-preservation, and not the Fugitive Slave Law, be obeyed and triumph." Parker, who had defended his right to freedom, was lionized by Frederick Douglass, who wrote: "Parker and his noble band of fifteen at Christiana, who defended themselves from the kidnappers with prayers and pistols, are entitled to the honor of making the first successful resistance to the Fugitive Slave Bill."[6]

Parker's resistance was just one of many examples of how blacks, abolitionists, and antislavery advocates responded when the evils of slavery threatened to expand beyond the geographic boundaries of the South. Northern whites generally did not care for the Negro, but they regarded the "slave hunters searching for human prey in northern neighborhoods" as opportunistic man stealers and kidnappers.[7] Being forced, under the law, to assist slave hunters and law enforcement officials in their pursuit of so-called runaways may have been responsible for engendering antislavery sentiments among many private citizens in the Northeast.

Perhaps the most significant development during this tumultuous period was the action taken by Dred Scott, an enslaved servant of U.S. Army physician John Emerson. Since 1833, Scott had accompanied Emerson in his travels across the country into the free states and throughout the free territories. After Emerson's death in 1843, his widow hired out Scott and his wife to work for different families in the St. Louis area. In 1847 Scott sued Mrs. Emerson for his and his wife's freedom, stating that Dr. Emerson's frequent moves between posts in the free North and the slave South had, in fact, emancipated Scott and his family. Scott won an early decision in 1850 in the St. Louis Circuit Court but then suffered a defeat in the Missouri Supreme Court. At that point, Emerson's widow turned over her legal affairs to her brother, John Sandford, who continued to fight to restore her property. The 1854 reversal of the Missouri Supreme Court's ruling gave Scott grounds to petition to have his case heard before the U.S. Supreme Court. The mere fact that Scott was able to challenge his assumed status as a slave and a noncitizen in court was a moral victory for African Americans who were watching the drama unfold.

In 1856 the Supreme Court heard the arguments of Dred Scott and John Sandford. The decision handed down by Chief Justice Roger B. Taney confirmed to whites that the inferior status of black men in America would be perpetuated forever. Taney advanced the argument that slavery was secure "wherever the Constitution of the United States extends" and that Congress lacked the power to prohibit the institution's natural growth and expansion.[8] Furthermore, with regard to Scott specifically, Taney's interpretation of the Constitution was clear: "colored persons of African descent have no rights that white men are bound to respect," and "colored [men] of African descent are not and cannot be citizens of the United States."[9] In other words, black men—whether enslaved or free—would never achieve equality with whites. African Americans could not—or, rather, they should not—expect any help from U.S. law, which was intended to protect citizens, not the property of citizens. Blacks in America were at the mercy of the white majority.

By 1858, with Abraham Lincoln as its primary spokesman, the newly formed Republican Party gained momentum for its direct challenge to the Southern Democrats' stronghold on national politics. In a series of debates with incumbent senator Stephen A. Douglas of Illinois, Lincoln was successful in restructuring the issue of slavery. Douglas, the principal framer of the 1854 Kansas-Nebraska Act, which repealed the Missouri Compromise and initiated the bloody fight over Kansas by pro- and antislavery factions, was popular with Southerners. In his final debate with Douglas on October 15, 1858, in the town of Alton, Illinois, Lincoln professed that the "real issue in this controversy" was that "one class . . . looks upon the institution of slavery as a wrong, and . . . another class . . . does not look upon it as a wrong." In a sympathetic plea to men of common means and simple ambitions, Lincoln argued, "What has ever threatened our liberty and prosperity, save and except the institution of slavery?"[10] In the end, Lincoln lost the Senate race to Douglas, but two years later, Lincoln and the Republican Party's antislavery position won the presidency of the United States.

By 1860, African Americans understood that the Republican Party's "opposition" to slavery was not a declaration of freedom for blacks based on moral grounds; rather, it was a confirmation of the continued abuse of the so-called Negro under the guise of the Constitution.[11] In other words, with regard to black empowerment, the Republican Party was no better than the Southern Democratic Party: both wanted to maintain dominance over the black race and continue the abuse initiated by the founding fathers. Black intellectuals such as Martin Delany, Frederick Douglass, Charles Lenox Remond, and Alfred M. Green understood the limitations of supporting the Republican Party, but they knew which side of the equation African Americans would have to be on if they hoped to change the fortunes and futures of 4 million people.

On December 20, 1860, after deliberations on the future of the United States and the possibility of forming a separate nation, South Carolina became the first state to secede from the Union. It was followed by Mississippi, Florida, Alabama, Georgia, and Louisiana in January 1861; Texas in February; and Virginia in April.[12] A month earlier, Ohio representative Thomas Corwin's proposed constitutional amendment allowing the slave states to continue to regulate and control the institution of slavery within their borders passed the House and was endorsed by Congress. However, because of tensions and political posturing on both sides of the conflict, the Southern states refused to acknowledge the efforts being made to prevent war. On April 12, 1861, the South Carolina militia attacked the Federal position at Fort Sumter, marking the beginning of an inevitable war that would shape the nation's future. Most important, the war would determine the fate of people of African descent born in the United States and denied the rights, privileges, and protections of the U.S. Constitution.[13]

The war's beginning was marked by excited commentary among black leaders who recognized its significance to the liberation of African Americans. On April 20, 1861, an editorial in the *Weekly Anglo African* conveyed African Americans' hopes regarding the outcome of the war:

> This is but another step in American Progress. We say Progress, for we know that no matter what may be the desires of the men of Expediency who rule, or seem to, the affairs of the North,—the tendencies are for Liberty.
>
> God speed to conflict. May the cup be drained to its dregs,

for only thus can this nation of sluggards know the disease and its remedy.

The strife will be deadly, but the end is certain. It matter not whether the Government is successful, whether the Union is preserved, the ideals underlying the struggle will triumph. Forms are but the dead cerements,—the rattling husks and dry shells which buried shall rot away, while the vital principle within, germinates into newer and more glorious manifestations of Life and Beauty.[14]

The same day the editorial was published, Alfred Green, a Philadelphia schoolteacher, spoke to black Philadelphians recalling the unfairness with which previous generations had been treated after their military service, but he resisted the notion of giving up the perpetual quest to be recognized as human beings and citizens based on what he called "past grievances." Instead, Green made a passionate plea to Philadelphia's affluent black community: "Let us, then, take up the sword, trusting in God, who will defend the right, remembering that these are other days than those of yore; that the world today is on the side of freedom and universal political equity."[15] Furthermore, Green argued that free men marching and fighting as soldiers against the Confederate army would inspire a sense of confidence in those held as human chattel, elevating their sense of purpose and prompting them to fight for their own freedom.

More than anything, men such as Green understood that black men had to be willing to seize their freedom and claim both their manhood and their citizenship. African American leaders believed that once black men proved their worth on the battlefield, there would be no denying them full citizenship rights and privileges in the country of their birth. Black leadership stood firm and refused to be dissuaded by the cool rebuke of native white Americans and Irish immigrants, who knew what was at stake if free blacks were allowed to assert their will and challenge the validity of slavery and their status as second-class citizens. Affirming the legacies of their grandfathers and fathers who had fought in the Revolutionary War and the War of 1812, respectively, African Americans knew that military

service provided access to a breadth of possibilities for self-improve-
ment and a greater sense of belonging, along with the opportunity
to expunge the negative claims against them.

Through a series of tracts, public speeches, and newspaper articles, black leaders instructed the black community how to use the
war's mission of keeping the Union together as a vehicle to abolish
slavery and remove the social, political, and legal barriers to their
full citizenship status. One of the foremost abolitionists was black
orator Charles Lenox Remond, who prior to the Civil War had argued most eloquently, "In spite of slavery and negrophobia, in spite
of the American Constitution,—I believe we have rights against the
world in argument, and in believing this, I hold it to be our right
and duty to defy the men and bodies who shall, in this late hour,
undertake still to crush us in the dust."[16] Remond's words resonated
loud and clear with free urban blacks, whose lives were in constant
turmoil due to their precarious position in a country that did not
value blackness or fully recognize their freedom. Enslaved blacks in
the South, who suffered under a brutal system that made a mockery
of the Declaration of Independence and confirmed the U.S. Constitution's support of white supremacy, were no better off than their
Northern urban cousins.

By the fall of 1862, much of America was embroiled in the
Civil War in one way or another. From the coast of Maine to the
goldfields of California, Americans took sides on the issues at the
center of the fighting: the expansion of slavery, states' rights, and
the Federal government's ability to wage war against its own people.[17] Initially, President Lincoln was not in favor of freeing the 3.9
million slaves inhabiting the American South. Like a majority of
"black Republicans," he believed the institution of slavery was best
suited to its current location and would eventually die out if it were
prevented from expanding into the Federal territories. Lincoln believed that slavery was "an evil not to be extended, but to be tolerated and protected only because of and so far as its actual presence
among us makes that toleration and protection a necessity."[18] Essentially, the Republican Party's only guarantee to the wretched
souls of the South was that they would continue to toil under the

same system their forebears had endured for generations, with no respite but death. Free blacks would have few protections under the law primarily because the party's position was to safeguard the interests of nonslaveholding white men: antislavery in this context meant anti–black labor and competition in support of pro-white labor and prosperity.

Understandably, African American participation in the Civil War was neither embraced nor recognized as necessary by politicians and nativists. As one politician put it, the conflict between North and South was "a white man's war" to be settled by white men alone.[19] Meanwhile, Irish immigrants, who sought to keep blacks at the bottom of society as leverage for their own rise, desperately clung to the possibility of being recognized as white so they could demonstrate their patriotism.[20] Black men steadfastly believed that they too would be liberated from the grips of tyranny and oppression when their patriotic contributions were tallied.

Earlier in the century, black physician and intellectual Martin Delany discussed the nature of "True Patriotism" in an essay published in the abolitionist paper the *North Star*:

> Patriotism consists not in a mere professed love of country, the place of one's birth—an endearment to the scenery, however delightful and interesting, of such country; not simply the laws and political policy by which such country is governed; but a pure and unsophisticated interest felt and manifested for man—an impartial love and desire for the promotion and elevation of every member of the body politic, their eligibility to all the rights and privileges of society. This, and other than this, fails to establish the claims of true patriotism.[21]

Clearly, Delany's observations challenge the idea that patriotism is blind and entails bending one's will to the desires of the nation. A true patriot, in Delany's words, is one who works for the "promotion and elevation of every member of the body politic" and who protects and respects each individual's right to live free from tyranny and oppression. The American Civil War gave black men the oppor-

tunity to display their courage and loyalty to the nation, recognizing
that their lives and futures hung in the balance.

In the spring of 1862 President Lincoln issued his preliminary
Emancipation Proclamation in an attempt to stop the war and begin
the healing process. Knowing that the time was right, thousands of
African American men began liberating themselves, running away
to join the Union effort. In the state of Kentucky, officials of the U.S.
military and a large portion of the general public rejected African
American men—both freeborn and enslaved—who volunteered to
help crush the Southern rebellion. Many of those opposed to African American participation claimed the conflict had nothing to do
with slavery but was a Federal effort to keep the nation unified.[22]
Regardless, President Lincoln made it clear that the course of American history was set, and citizens of the nation could not escape the
fact that "in giving freedom to the slave we assure freedom to the
free, honorable alike in what we give and what we preserve. We shall
nobly save or meanly lose, the last best hope of [the] earth."[23]

On January 1, 1863, Lincoln formally issued the Emancipation Proclamation, declaring that "all persons held as slaves" in the
states seceded from the Union were free and that "such persons of
suitable condition, will be received into the armed service of the
United States." In support of Lincoln, Frederick Douglass and other
black leaders challenged all black men to seize their freedom with
both hands. By the spring, tremendous battles had been fought and
thousands of American lives lost in the process, but as a result of
Lincoln's mandate, the U.S. military had been authorized to enroll
black men for armed military service. Thus began the push to allow
black men to serve the Federal government as soldiers in an effort to
demonstrate and claim their manhood and citizenship, while seizing
freedom and liberty for all African Americans.

## Kentucky

Before the 1860 election, Kentuckians did not support Lincoln.
Many were agitated by his position against the expansion of slavery, which they thought would shape the Federal government's at-

titude toward the South in general. Fresh in the minds of most Southerners was Lincoln's 1858 address at the State Republican Convention in Springfield, Illinois, where he had delivered his "House Divided" speech. In that address, Lincoln clearly stated that the future of the United States pivoted on the slavery question, and the country could not survive as half slave and half free. After Lincoln won the presidency, states across the South held conventions to discuss withdrawing from the Union. Southern politicians believed that states had a constitutional right to leave the Union because the Federal government, an agent of the states, threatened their sovereignty.

Between April 1861 and July 1862, Lincoln's policy toward states that had seceded created a breach in trust for those that had once been loyal to the United States. Kentucky's most prominent citizens, many of whom were slaveholders themselves or benefited directly from the institution, signed up to fight the Federal government, based on the belief that President Lincoln and the Republican Party had gone too far by violating their right to hold slaves. As a result of this clear rupture between sectional powers, many Kentuckians, who were heavily dependent on slave labor for their wealth, rebelled against the Federal government and its power to dictate the lives of free men.

One of these men was John Hunt Morgan. Born in Huntsville, Alabama, in 1825, Morgan moved with his family to Lexington when he was a small boy. His mother, Henrietta Hunt Morgan, was the daughter of the distinguished Kentucky merchant, horse breeder, and slaveholder John Wesley Hunt, who is widely recognized as one of the first millionaires to settle west of the Allegheny Mountains. Hunt was a powerful force in business, politics, and agriculture. In the early part of the nineteenth century he was responsible for importing racehorses to Lexington, with the goal of improving the quality of the region's horseflesh.[24] Hunt's cord and rope manufacturing business in Lexington turned the hemp grown on his farm (using slave labor) into the packaging and shipping materials required to support the South's cotton industry (another crop cultivated and harvested by slaves).[25] John Hunt Morgan and his brother

C. C. Morgan followed in their grandfather's footsteps as manufacturers, slaveholders, and businessmen in Kentucky.

In 1862 Kentucky voted to side with the Federal government in the conflict. Morgan, however, believed Kentucky should maintain its neutrality and was unwilling to accept the Union's position on slavery and the dissolution of states' rights. He thus began a campaign to disrupt the Federal government's presence in Kentucky, using his familiarity with the land and his proven ability as a military leader to cut across the state with his cavalry company, destroying lines of communication and wreaking havoc wherever he could. With the generous support of Kentuckians sympathetic to the rebel cause, Morgan challenged the Union troops at every turn. From April to December 1862 Captain Morgan was responsible for raids that relieved farmers and Union supporters of their horses, cattle, and weapons; burned railroad tunnels to disrupt the flow of supplies to Federal troops throughout Kentucky; and captured more than 2,000 Federal soldiers.[26]

The violence surrounding David Tanner's Clark County farm, where America and Isaac Murphy lived, must have been both exciting and daunting. Five days prior to Isaac's second birthday, on January 1, 1863, President Abraham Lincoln issued his Emancipation Proclamation, abolishing slavery in the states that had seceded from the Union. Those sweet words of freedom no doubt lifted the hearts and souls of those who hoped one day to see the promised land their forebears had assured them was just beyond the horizon. Lincoln's words rang clear, affirming that the day of deliverance had arrived for those held in bondage: "That on the First Day of January, in the year of our Lord one thousand, eighteen hundred and sixty three, all persons held as slaves within any State or any designated part of a state, the people whereof shall then be in rebellion against the United States, shall be then, henceforward, and forever free." Lincoln's strategy was simple: create instability within the Confederacy by freeing those at the center of the conflict, thereby delivering the death blow to the heart of the institution.

As the effects of the radical document unfolded across the country, black abolitionists' vision for "colored people" varied. Individuals such as Sarah Parker Remond, the sister of Charles Lenox Remond, spoke loudly and widely in defense of the freedom of enslaved and free African Americans and their right to develop as whole human beings. In her address to the International Congress of Charities, Correction, and Philanthropy in London, Remond argued that the "real capacities of the Negro race have never been thoroughly tested; and until they are placed in a position to be influenced by the civilizing influences which surround freemen, it is really unjust to apply to them the same test, or to expect them to attain the same standard of excellence, as if a fair opportunity had been given to develop their faculties."[27] In other words, Remond was anticipating a transition period from slavery to freedom, and she was asking for patience and compassion on the part of society. Newly freed blacks would need time to shed the influences of their previous condition (one that was not of their choosing) and develop the necessary skills to succeed as full citizens of the United States and the world. Remond's observations were important to the full-fledged emancipation of blacks, and this understanding was central to the forward movement advocated by black abolitionists, who recognized the window of opportunity provided by the war and the need to take full advantage of it to achieve their freedom.

After the Emancipation Proclamation, the area around the Tanner farm became active with the sights and sounds of war, as individuals sought to claim the state for their own side of the conflict. Also active were the area's black slaves, many of whom stole away as soon as they got the chance, even though, by law, they were not considered free because Kentucky had not seceded. In defiance of their masters, African Americans fled to claim what was theirs under the banner of the Federal government: freedom. Federal campsites throughout the state became swollen with masses of old and young blacks seeking refuge and sanctuary. With so few blacks left on the farms, there was no one to harvest the corn, barley, hemp, and wheat; no one to tend the animals; and no one to wait hand and foot on their masters.

Up to this time, enslaved blacks' existence had consisted of satisfying a multitude of demands and desires that were not their own, providing living proof of the fiction of white supremacy, and living in fear of displeasing their masters and mistresses. How would they respond to their new status as free in this time of war and uncertainty? What did liberty mean to men and women shaped by a brutal system designed to extract as much from them as possible while giving little, if anything, in return? How would they deal with the burden of being liberated from the fetters of servitude? Where would they turn for advice? President Lincoln may have signed the Emancipation Proclamation, but in the hearts and minds of African Americans, God was the great architect who had willed their freedom, and in God they found strength.

Before 1864 African American men were not mustered into the military as soldiers but were "impressed" as laborers to build walls, draw water, cook, and tend to cattle.[28] Wherever Union military personnel were busy securing defensive positions in the state, African Americans identified these Federal posts as portals to freedom and sought work there driving teams of horses, working in barns, and constructing roads.[29] It is instructive to know that between 1861 and 1864, more than 100,000 African American men and their families ran away to federal encampments in the state of Kentucky, seeking freedom and opportunity under the Union flag. With no formal policy in place, it was up to camp commanders to decide whether to allow them entrance. Because Kentucky remained loyal to the Union, the property of its self-proclaimed Unionist slaveholders was not covered by the Emancipation Proclamation. Thus, most self-emancipated slaves seeking the security of Federal encampments were either turned away or returned to their masters. The relatively few black men and women permitted into the Federal camps served as personal servants to commissioned officers, helped build fortifications, worked as teamsters, washed clothes, and cooked.

Some high-ranking officers refused to protect the property rights of Kentucky's slaveholders. One example was Colonel Smith D. Atkins of the Ninety-Second Illinois, stationed near Mt. Sterling, Kentucky. Atkins would not send "runaways" back to their masters, even though they petitioned for the return of their human chattel. "I will not make myself & my regiment, a machine to enforce the slave laws of Kentucky & return slaves to rebel masters," he wrote.[30] Atkins was unwilling to abandon the wretched souls he believed he had sworn to protect. In November 1862 Colonel Atkins and his regiment came face-to-face with an angry mob of white Kentuckians in Winchester, not far from the Tanner farm. They threatened to remove the black men, acting as servants, from the regiment's lines as it marched toward Lexington. After repelling the challenge to his authority to harbor contraband of war,[31] Atkins ordered the men of the Ninety-Second to load their weapons and fix their bayonets, in anticipation of what they might encounter in Lexington. Scenes such as this no doubt gave hope to the bondsmen and -women awaiting a change in their status as slaves. To the enslaved, hope was the great equalizer in the war that refused their participation.

Frederick Douglass, who, prior to the Emancipation Proclamation, had publicly admonished President Lincoln for not recognizing the humanity of those designated human chattel, now heaped praise on the commander in chief for inspiring a more tangible sense of hope for the indigent and degraded black masses. Douglass recognized that it was far too easy to depend on the law to try to change the direction of the war, and he had an intimate understanding of the situation blacks found themselves in. He was quick to put into perspective the challenges that lay ahead, writing in January 1863: "The price of Liberty is eternal vigilance. Even after slavery has been legally abolished, and the rebellion substantially suppressed . . . , there will still remain an urgent necessity for the benevolent activity of the men and the women who have from the first opposed slavery from high moral conviction."[32] Douglass knew that, by issuing the Emancipation Proclamation, Lincoln had destabilized the institution of slavery in the Confederate states while protecting it in the states that remained loyal to the Union. But if slavery was, in fact, an evil that the nation could do without, it would have to be eliminated everywhere. In other words, even the loyalist states would have to emancipate their slaves if Lincoln's antislavery document were to have the desired effect on the nation.

To be clear, the acceptance of African American men into the military challenged the traditional white supremacist agenda, which found no value in blacks and failed to recognize their contributions. Black abolitionists challenged the war's aims, seeking black participation as a public rebuke for the injustice of slavery. It is within this context that the image of the "colored soldier" rose once again as a symbol of racial destiny and possibility. For African American men who served as Union soldiers, "Federal blue" came to embody manhood, bravery, and freedom.[33] If African Americans found solace in Lincoln's gesture, they took Douglass's words to heart, imploring black men to fight for their freedom and that of their families. Camp Nelson was an important development in achieving that freedom.

## Camp Nelson

In June 1863 the Army of the Ohio, under the direction of Major General Ambrose Burnside, began to construct a strategically important supply depot and encampment on 4,000 acres southwest of Lexington in southern Jessamine County. During the previous year, the Union army had sustained great losses in men and strategic positioning due to a lack of access to food stores and ammunition. With the loyalty of Kentucky hanging in the balance and Confederate troops advancing throughout the state, Burnside and his newly formed Army of the Ohio had to prepare to ward off a full-scale invasion. Indeed, the disruption of supply and communication lines by General John Hunt Morgan and Major General Kirby Smith forced Union army officials to remedy the situation and create a substantial defensive position from which to repel the rebel invaders. Confederate guerrillas, whose forays behind Union lines destroyed rail transportation, supply chains, and communications, had to be dealt with if the Federal government wanted to maintain control of Kentucky, a critical border state. The new depot would also support the hard-fought positions of the Union army stretching north to the Ohio River and south to the Tennessee border. The site chosen was situated on the "high plateau above the Kentucky River" to the north and Hickman's Creek to the south. To the west was an area fortified by 400-foot-high cliffs, which made the location defensible against enemy attacks. On June 12 the depot was officially named

Camp Nelson, in honor of the recently murdered Major General William "Bull" Nelson, who had been the commander of the Army of Kentucky.[34] The location of this supply depot in the Bluegrass region became an important factor in the Union army's success in the southern theater of war and was a critical element in the liberation of African Americans throughout the United States.

To construct the necessary facilities, including the waterworks, barracks, hospitals, and stables, General Burnside authorized the use of slaves from nearby farms. Other black men, both free and enslaved, were impressed from surrounding cities and farms or confiscated as contraband from rebel sympathizers (as authorized by the Confiscation Act of 1862) and put to work building the camp, as were those individuals who escaped from slavery and found refuge at the encampment. These men were responsible for digging "entrenchments and forts" and functioned as the "chief laborers on the road and railroad projects" surrounding Camp Nelson.[35] Additionally, on August 10, 1863, Brigadier General Jeremiah Tilford (J. T.) Boyle, commander of the District of Kentucky, authorized the impressment of 6,000 African American males between the ages of sixteen and forty-five (including free blacks) living in the counties surrounding Camp Nelson to construct lines of transportation from Lebanon to Danville, Kentucky. Boyle's order made it clear that slave owners would be compensated for the use of their property on a monthly basis through the voucher system. However, any slave owner refusing to meet the demands of the army could have his property confiscated.[36]

While military personnel negotiated with the loyalists of central Kentucky over the use of their slave labor, African American men, through their interactions with white Union soldiers, free blacks, and other men of a similar condition, were beginning a process of transformation that was unprecedented in American history. In Kentucky, enslaved blacks who came into contact with those who had been liberated from their rebel masters discovered that they could imagine a future without the daily oppression that had been their reality. Many northern Union soldiers considered the institution of slavery alien and un-Christian, and their very presence among and interaction with those considered inferior undermined the system of abuse and initiated a series of changes among white and black men alike. As a result, both were changed forever.

What began as a strategic decision to build a supply depot for the Army of the Ohio in central Kentucky quickly became one of the most important events for the deliverance of African Americans since the war began. For those blacks who were expected to contribute only labor to support the efforts of those fighting the war, Camp Nelson presented a world of new, exciting, and previously unimaginable possibilities.[37] Indeed, as they gained access to food, clothing, shelter, and training in a variety of useful occupations, black men began to grasp the significance of the moment. They were on the verge of a new epoch in American history.

Contributing to blacks' personal growth were sympathetic military officials, who were willing to use their power and influence to challenge the laws and traditions of the South and expand the role of black men in securing the Union. In August 1863 Adjutant General Lorenzo Thomas, an advocate of allowing black men to serve as soldiers, approved General Burnside's recruitment of blacks into the Union army, even though the War Department believed it was unnecessary to enlist "Negroes" as troops.[38] More than anything, Congress and the War Department wanted to prevent the loyalist slave owners in Kentucky from getting upset and crying foul at the Federal government's change in policy. But in reality, the damage had already been done. Scores of African American men left the fields, factories, and stables of their owners to join the movement to save the Union and themselves. Thousands walked or marched down the dirt roads leading to Camp Nelson; others cautiously snaked their way through the fields in search of the freedom they believed they would find within the walls of the camp.[39] Whether they would get the chance to take up weapons and fight and die like their brothers in arms at Fort Wagner or later at Fort Pillow remained to be seen.[40] Nonetheless, it was only a matter of time until they discovered a new sense of purpose for their lives.

By the beginning of 1864, the completed depot was attracting white loyalist refugees from Tennessee, on the run from the rebels' fury. At the same time, changes in U.S. policy related to the military recruitment of enslaved and free blacks in Kentucky became more focused. In December 1863 the Army of the Department of the Tennessee began signing up black men from nearby southwestern Kentucky, disregarding the rights of loyal Kentucky slaveholders.[41] In a letter to General Boyle, Colonel Cicero Maxwell, stationed at Bowling Green, Kentucky, accounted for the "consequences of having recruiting stations for negroes in Tennessee close to the border." He continued: "I am told no distinction is made between the loyal and disloyal owner, but I do not know what to suggest, though it does seem to me an outrage that the Slaveholder who has been true and loyal through all the troubles of Southern Kentucky, should receive no more consideration than the traitorous sympathizer with the causeless, wicked Rebellion, and who has actively given it aid and encouragement."[42] Clearly, Kentucky slaveholders had reason to be alarmed. But momentum was on the side of the "Negro," especially after the Emancipation Proclamation, the draft riots in New York, and the growing need for able-bodied men to crush the rebellion at its core.

On February 24 Congress added a supplement to the national enrollment act, providing for the conscription of slave men in the border states and promising "compensation to loyal owners of up to $300 for each slave who volunteered."[43] The result of the policy was threefold: it provided the Federal government with the military personnel required to continue to fight the war; it compensated slave owners for their human property; and it opened a doorway to freedom for African American men who served, and eventually for their families. Unfortunately, it did not pertain to families resulting from abroad marriages; the act applied only to family members owned by the same master.[44]

Some slaveholders took advantage of the opportunity to be compensated by the Federal government for their legal property; others refused to allow their slaves, whom they considered inferior and subhuman, to wear a uniform and claim any measure of equality with white men. Resisting the congressional mandate to enlist slaves to meet the army's quota, slave owners protested the audacity of black men who would claim their freedom at the cost of white slaveholders' property, profits, and pride. Many threatened to destroy the families left behind by these black soldiers, vowing to sell off their wives and children to places in the Confederacy if they did not return to their owners. Others took out their anger and satisfied their bloodlust by showing extreme cruelty to the family members of these newly liberated black men. In sworn depositions, the wives of black Union soldiers gave accounts of their suffering at the hands of their masters for the actions of their husbands. Patsy Leach, owned by Warren Viley of Woodford County, a prominent Bluegrass horseman,[45] testified to the cruelty unleashed on her:

> When my husband was Killed my master whipped me severely saying my husband had gone into the army to fight against white folks and he my master would let me know that I was foolish to let my husband go he would "take it out on my back," he would "Kill me by piecemeal" and he hoped "that the last one of the nigger soldiers would be Killed." He whipped me twice after that using similar expressions. The last whipping he gave me he took me into the Kitchen tied my hands tore all my clothes off until I was entirely naked, bent me down, placed my head between his Knees, then whipped me most unmercifully until my back was lacerated all over, the blood oozing out in several places so that I could not wear my underclothes without their becoming saturated with blood.[46]

In an effort to save her own life, as well as the lives of her five children, Mrs. Leach ran away to Camp Nelson, seeking shelter and protection from Federal troops.

Other women described similar treatment as retaliation for their husbands' answering the call to serve the Union cause. Clarissa Burdett, the wife of Private Elijah Burdett of the Twelfth U.S. Colored Artillery, recalled in her March 27, 1865, deposition that her master had hit her in the head with an ax handle when he learned her husband had enlisted. Fearing that her master might kill her in a blind rage, Clarissa decided to join her husband at Camp Nelson, leaving her four children behind and not knowing when she would see them again. Hurt by the treatment of their wives and children, and emboldened by their new sense of pride and purpose, some black soldiers confronted their indignant former owners, many of whom had lost faith in the Federal government once it allowed "men of color" to rise to the patriotic challenge and fight for their own freedom.

There can be no doubt that America Murphy knew that enslaved black men were being recruited for military service and that slave masters were protesting—sometimes violently—the loss of their property. After Jerry Skillman enlisted, what were America and Isaac's experiences on the Tanner farm? Would she be punished for Jerry's enlisting? Would she ever see him again? Would his children (America had recently given birth to her second child, a daughter) get the chance to know their father? These questions and more had to run through her head as she imagined Skillman wearing his blue uniform, marching in line to the sound of a fife and drum, and perhaps dying while defending his and his family's freedom. Her life and the lives of her children were connected to Skillman's fate as a soldier.

Sometime before June 24, 1864, Jerry Skillman and another man, who may have been his brother Charles, left the Skillman farm in Bourbon County and headed west to Lexington to enlist in the Union army. Whether J. W. Skillman brought them to Lexington and collected the $600 due him or whether they left on their own is not known. What we *do* know is that on June 24, 1864, the two brothers, along with 512 other African American men, swore to fight to preserve the Union and to follow the laws of the U.S. government. At some point, Private Jerry Skillman would change his name to Burns, probably in an effort to make it more difficult for his owner to find him. It is also possible that his father's last name was Burns, and this was a gesture to honor the memory of a man he had barely known but who remained important to him.

From Lexington, the brothers marched to Camp Nelson under the command of the white officers responsible for the recruitment of Negroes.[47] To the great pleasure of Adjutant General Thomas, more than 1,500 black recruits volunteered in Kentucky that June. The newly appointed superintendent of Camp Nelson, Colonel Thomas D. Sedgwick, "was charged with the work of organizing colored troops" into effective fighting units.[48] Under Sedgwick's command, more than 5,000 black recruits were trained in soldiering and fighting in preparation for the coming tests of their fortitude and bravery. But even at Camp Nelson, blacks were subjected to abuses by whites who lacked the basic morality and self-control that were supposedly at the core of civilized society. In a letter to Dr. John Strong Newberry, founder of the U.S. Sanitary Commission, field operative Thomas Butler observed that the black recruits "were employed to strengthen the defenses" of Camp Nelson, which enhanced its "almost perfect impregnability." However, they were housed in substandard accommodations, forced to wear the old uniforms of white soldiers, and "poorly fed, receiving nothing but what could be taken with their bare hands, and not more than half rations at that."[49] These conditions, whereby black soldiers were overworked and undernourished, contributed to high rates of disease and death and affected their morale. For some, slavery had been more humane than soldiering.

Prior to the 1864 Conscription Act, black soldiers who had left without their masters' consent were often reclaimed by their disgruntled owners, who came to camp to collect them and used various means of persuasion to get them to leave. Those who were unwilling to go voluntarily could stay in camp if their owners were not loyal to the Union. Those whose masters were Unionist were returned to them and often suffered great cruelty as punishment for running away. Some had their ears cut off or were tied to trees and horsewhipped. There were even cases of black men being killed by their former masters. Some were shot in the head in clear view of observers; others were taken some distance away, where they were tied down and "flayed alive."[50] Despite the danger, black men increasingly risked their lives to travel to Camp Nelson. For those who made it through the gates, it represented a journey from slavery to freedom. For those given the opportunity to wear the "Federal blue" uniform, it represented the achievement of something that had long been denied them: public recognition of their manhood.[51]

In spite of the obstacles, African American men and boys left their masters' farms by the hundreds to join up and claim freedom as enlisted men in the U.S. Army. On the way to recruitment centers in Lexington and Louisville, many black volunteers were viciously assaulted and brutalized by whites, who opposed their recruitment as soldiers and the elevated status it gave them.[52] Fortunately, the will and determination of these black men could not be crushed by the negative responses of white Kentuckians, most of whom had been conditioned to believe that blacks were inferior. The time had come for Kentucky's black sons, brothers, and fathers to join the ranks of the brave, standing shoulder to shoulder on the verge of history.

What began in May as a trickle of volunteers became a tidal wave by September, as African American men clamored to fight for a cause greater than the preservation of the Union: their freedom. Indeed, by the end of the war, 23,703 black men from Kentucky had enlisted in the Union army; this was second only to Louisiana, with 24,052. However, Louisiana's Native Guard consisted mostly of free men of color who were well-educated businessmen from New Orleans. In contrast, a majority of Kentucky's black soldiers were former slaves fighting for their freedom on the battlefields of the South.

Elijah Marrs, who would become a sergeant in the Twelfth U.S. Colored Heavy Artillery, was one of the thousands of men in Kentucky's great black regiments. He wrote a compelling narrative of his life, including his experiences as a slave on the Robinson farm in Shelby County, Kentucky, and his time as a soldier. Marrs describes the day he decided to leave slavery behind and join the ranks of *les fils courageux de l'Afrique noire*—the brave black sons of Africa: "I remember the morning I made up my mind to join the United States Army. I started to Simpsonville and walking along I met many of my old comrades on the Shelbyville Pike. I told them my determination, and asked all who desired to join my company to roll his coat sleeves above his elbows, and to let them to remain so during the day. I marshaled my forces day and night. I had twenty-seven men, all told, and I was elected their captain to lead them to Louisville."[53] Marrs's decision to free himself from slavery and encourage others to pursue the same goal is inspiring. Such individual initiatives would have a great impact on the mass exodus of African Americans who passed through Camp Nelson and other portals of freedom. For African American men like Marrs and Jerry Skillman, their manhood became inseparable from their service as soldiers in the Civil War, where "freedom and equality" rested on the willingness to sacrifice one's life in defense of one's claim to humanity, manhood, and citizenship.[54]

Like the families of most black soldiers, Jerry Skillman's followed him to camp. When America and her children arrived at Camp Nelson, where they slept, and where they ate are unknown. However, records show that shortly after black men were mustered into their regiments and marched off to drill and train, their wives and children usually followed. In many cases, once slave owners learned the husbands had enlisted in the Union army, they turned out the wives, sending them away and forcing them to fend for themselves and their children. Although they were discouraged by military personnel, most wives felt they had no choice but to follow the roads leading to Camp Nelson, already swollen with those seeking redemption.[55] There is no evidence that America Murphy and her children were expelled from the Tanner farm, but it is likely that she, three-year-old Isaac, and her infant daughter were among the multitude seeking deliverance from slavery at Camp Nelson.

Within a few weeks of establishing residence at the camp and perhaps finding work as a washwoman or a cook, America would have heard about the decision to bar civilians from entering Camp Nelson. In a memo dated July 3, 1864, Brigadier General Speed Fry ordered that "only able bodied Negroes of lawful age who express a desire to enter the U.S. service shall hereafter be permitted to enter" the camp. Furthermore, "any old men, women or children shall under no pretense whatever be allowed to pass the line of Pickets at this Post."[56] For whatever reason, the soldiers standing guard ignored this order and continued to let people pass through and take up residence on the already congested grounds. Between the end of July and late November, the population of African American women and children in the camp doubled from 200 to 400. Food and clothing were limited, and to provide shelter for the increasing population, brothers, husbands, and fathers constructed shanties and tents from materials found both inside and outside the camp. The military post began to look like a refugee camp rather than the staging ground for assaults on the enemy.

It did not help that the experiment in emancipation was under attack by both government officials and the general public. Many remained skeptical of black men's ability on the battlefield, even though their bravery had been proved "beyond further doubt" at Milliken's Bend.[57] Assistant Secretary of War Charles A. Dana noted, "The bravery of the blacks at Milliken's Bend completely revolutionized the sentiment of the army with regard to the employment of Negro troops. I heard prominent officers who formerly in private had sneered at the idea of the negroes fighting express themselves after that as heartily in favor of it."[58] Dana's sentiment was supported by Adjutant General Thomas, who pushed hard to recruit able-bodied black men from Kentucky to serve the Union cause. By July 20, three "colored" regiments under the command of Colonel Thomas Sedgwick had been fully "organized, clothed and armed" out of the thousands of recruits available. Indeed, the 114th and 116th Colored Infantries and the Twelfth U.S. Colored Heavy Artillery were held in "readiness to repel any attack" by rebels and to respond to the need for troops in the theater of war.[59]

By October, Jerry and Charles Skillman were privates in Company C of the 114th Colored Infantry under the command of Major Andrew J. Hogan. They were embracing their new lives as soldiers and were prepared to fight for their freedom and that of their families. This was especially true of Jerry, whose wife and children were daily reminders of his purpose in life: to gain their freedom through his service. Isaac may have been too young to understand everything happening around him, but there can be no doubt that it left an indelible impression on him. Children know when to fear and when to rejoice, based on the reactions of the adults around them. They are accustomed to reading the faces of adults to discern how they should respond.

Abolitionist John G. Fee, a member of the American Missionary Association and the founder of Berea College, was a strong supporter of the recruitment of black men, and he believed Camp Nelson could meet many of the needs of its black population. With the support of Captain Theron E. Hall, Fee began a program to educate the black soldiers, providing religious training, compulsory education, and practical skills that would allow them to function as contributing members of society.[60] More than anything, black soldiers gained an advocate in Fee, who saw them as "noble men . . . made in the image of God, just emerging from the restraints of slavery in the liberties and responsibilities of free men, and of soldiers."[61] Fee convinced military officials to support his plan to change the fortunes of blacks through education and obtained the use of a large schoolroom as well as copybooks, slates, and other valuable supplies.

In early August the Reverend John A. R. Rogers visited Camp Nelson and made the following observations about Fee's work:

> I have just returned from a visit to Camp Nelson and Berea, greatly cheered by what I saw. At Camp Nelson I found brothers Fee and Vetter, and their thirteen volunteer assistants, teaching the colored troops. The teachableness of the colored soldiers, their eagerness to learn, and their rapid progress, were alike surprising and gratifying. I have never seen more rapid progress made by anyone then by them. . . . I can but think that the black men to whom brother Fee preaches there—and he preaches to not a few of either the black or white race—are destined to exert a great influence. Colored soldiers will be leaders among colored men.[62]

Like Fee, Rogers was a proponent of African American equality, and he recognized that the war was an opportunity to change whites' attitudes toward their darker brothers.

However, what Fee and Rogers overlooked were the problems at the camp. The large number of runaway slaves created discord when their owners came looking for them. And although the military leadership was quick to take new recruits, there was little support for their families. With very few opportunities for black women to find employment as personal cooks and washerwomen, some traded sex for food; a number of families starved and were forced to return to slavery. All this would change after November 22, 1864, when the decision was made to forcibly evict all nonessential personnel.[63]

As the winter approached, General Fry issued the order to displace the most vulnerable occupants of Camp Nelson. Although the white workers had been provided for and were not in danger of being expelled from camp, the colored people were subjected to the cruelty of military efficiency. In what was described by several eyewitnesses as the "coldest [weather] of the season," with the wind "blowing sharply," black women and children were loaded onto wagons with whatever they could carry and taken north of the camp. At gunpoint and under "threat of [violence and] death" if they returned, the elderly, the sick, and mothers with their children began the sojourn north toward Lexington in search of shelter.[64] Soldiers then dismantled the makeshift community of rough tents and huts, stacked everything into piles, and set them ablaze. From outside the camp lines, the displaced African Americans could only watch as the smoke rose in great curls of blue, gray, and black. Amid the crying of children and the wailing of women forced out into the night, their husbands, fathers, and brothers watched helplessly from their barracks, unable to attend them, afraid of being shot dead for disobeying a direct order. Although some of the displaced women and children made their way to Nicholasville and Lexington, 102 perished, including several small children.

The "deliberate cruelty" on the part of the Union command became news throughout the nation. Abolitionists such as Horace Greeley, publisher of the *New York Tribune*, blasted the Federal government and officials of Camp Nelson, publishing an account of the expulsion: "At this moment, over *four hundred* helpless human beings—frail women and delicate children—having been driven from their homes by *United States soldiers* are now lying in barns and mule sheds, wandering through the woods, languishing on the highway, and literally starving, for no other crime than their husbands and fathers having thrown aside the manacles of slavery to shoulder Union muskets."[65] In a sworn deposition, Private Joseph Miller of Company I, 124th U.S. Colored Infantry, described in detail the expulsion of his family from Camp Nelson and the death of his son:

When I came to Camp for the purpose of enlisting about the middle of October 1864, my wife and children came with me because my master said that if I enlisted he would not maintain them and I knew that they would be abused by him when I left. I had then four children, ages respectively ten, nine, seven and four years. On presenting myself as a recruit, I was told by the Lieut. in command to take my family into a tent within the limits of the Camp. My wife and family occupied this tent by the express permission of the aforementioned Officer and never received any notice to leave until Tuesday November 22nd when a mounted guard gave my wife notice that she and her children must leave Camp before early morning. This was about six o'clock at night. My little boy about seven years of age had been very sick and was slowly recovering. My wife had no place to go and so remained until morning. About eight o'clock Wednesday morning November 23rd a mounted guard came to my tent and ordered my wife and children out of Camp. The morning was bitter cold. It was freezing hard. I was certain that it would kill my sick child to take him out in the cold. I told the man in charge of the guard that it would be the death of my boy. I told him that my wife and children had no place to go and I told him that I was a soldier of the United States. He told me that it did not make any difference he had orders to take all out of Camp. He told my wife and family that if they did not get up into the wagon which he had, he would shoot the last one of them. On being thus threatened my wife and children went into the wagon. My wife carried her sick child in her arms. When they left the tent the wind was blowing hard and cold and having had to leave much of our clothing when we left our master, my wife with her little ones was poorly clad. I followed them as far as the lines. I had no Knowledge where they were taking them. At night I went in search of my family. I found them at Nicholasville about six miles from

Camp. . . . I found my wife and children shivering with cold and famished with hunger. They had not received a morsel of food during the whole day. My boy was dead. He died directly after getting down from the wagon. I know he was killed by exposure to the inclement weather. I had to return to Camp that night, so I left my family in the meeting house and walked back. I had walked there. I travelled in all twelve miles. Next morning I walked to Nicholasville. I dug a grave myself and buried my child. I left my family in the Meeting house—where they still remain.[66]

Clearly, such cruelty could not be forgotten by those who experienced it. The insensitive treatment of the sick and the frail, those unable to fight off starvation and cold, was a deliberate act intended to rid the army of unwanted responsibilities. It is possible that America Murphy and her children were forced to leave Camp Nelson that November, and, similar to Joseph Miller, Jerry Skillman may have attempted to save his family. But he likely found little support from the soldiers charged with dispatching the women and children into the cold Kentucky night. The failure to protect the smallest and weakest African Americans reflects the embedded social and political reality captured in the historical moment: black lives meant something only when they served white aims and goals. Even though Miller and Skillman and others like them were empowered to assert their manhood in the context of protecting the Union and pursuing their individual freedom and liberty, they were not free to protect their families.

After learning of the plight of the 400 colored women and children ejected from Camp Nelson and General Fry's role in executing the order, Captain Theron Hall began to protest their abuse up the chain of command. Hall, an advocate for African Americans' transition from slavery to freedom, wrote to Captain J. Bates Dickson in Lexington: "More than four hundred poor women and children families of Colored soldiers have been sent from Camp the past week. Some have died and all are in a starving condition. They are sitting by the roadside and wandering about the fields. Can you not induce the General to interfere on their behalf? No more potent weapon could be placed in the hands of the rebels to prevent enlistment than this. The whole community are loud in denouncing the outrage."[67] As a result of Hall's efforts, Dickson ordered Fry to provide the families with the necessary food and shelter and even instructed him to "erect new buildings" and welcome the refugees back into camp.[68] Fry, who believed he was in the right, was unwilling to budge on his decision to expel those who were nonessential to the functioning of a military installation. Even after receiving a direct command from Brigadier Major General Stephen Burbridge, Fry still refused to allow the wives and children back into camp and went so far as to have Hall arrested for agitating the situation.

At all levels, it was understood that events at Camp Nelson made the Federal government look bad and might discourage black volunteers from enlisting. Fortunately, by the middle of December, General Fry was removed as commander of Camp Nelson, either at his own request or under pressure from his superiors. His successor, Adjutant General Lorenzo Thomas, began a program to accommodate the wives and children of the black soldiers. He appointed Captain Hall as the new superintendent of refugees and Reverend Fee as supervisor of spiritual and educational development. With these changes, Camp Nelson became the most important place in Kentucky and in the nation for black people making the transition from slavery to freedom.

By January 1865, Camp Nelson was once again functioning as a portal to freedom for self-emancipated blacks in Kentucky. Under the guidance of Hall and Fee, soldiers' wives and children, including America, Isaac, and her daughter, had access to shelter, food (albeit military rations), and education. Private Jerry Skillman, meanwhile, had witnessed firsthand the consequences of military efficiency and callous decision making. His wife and children had been ejected into a harsh and hostile environment, without care or concern for their lives. The helplessness felt by Skillman and his fellow soldiers, and their guilt and anger over the loss of their loved ones, only confirmed their great purpose. The future had to be different. It was up to them to ensure that the world—or at least the United States—was fit for black people to live in.

## "Freedom Will Be Theirs by the Sword"

While Camp Nelson was adjusting to changes in leadership and revising its policies toward housing, feeding, and educating the wives and children of black soldiers, dramatic changes were also taking place in the Union army, particularly in the theater of war around Richmond, Virginia, the capital of the Confederacy. In early November 1864 Lieutenant General Ulysses S. Grant directed that black regiments from the armies north and south of the James River be combined to create the all-black Twenty-Fifth Corps. Grant's decision to mount an aggressive campaign to end the war required a concerted effort and the consolidation of all available troops into fighting units capable of maintaining pressure on the enemy. The decision to amass an all-black corps was radical, but it was endorsed by President Lincoln, Secretary of War Edwin M. Stanton, and Assistant Secretary of War Charles Dana as an effective use of manpower. Still, the military brass was not convinced of black soldiers' ability to fight, even though the examples of Fort Wagner and Milliken's Bend should have been proof enough.[69] Furthermore, a number of Northern military officials were concerned about white soldiers' morale if they were forced to accept the reality of black men in uniform. But President Lincoln wanted to end the bloody war, and General Grant wanted to make it happen.

To lead the all-black Twenty-Fifth Corps, Grant selected the highly capable twenty-nine-year-old Major General Godfrey Weitzel. Grant was well aware of Weitzel's extraordinary ability to lead men into battle and direct them under fire. A few months earlier, on September 29, 1864, Weitzel had been assigned to command the Eighteenth Corps while General Ord recovered from injuries sustained during the capture of Fort Harrison.[70] In the fighting, Weitzel and his men not only sustained their position but also captured more than 300 Confederate soldiers and officers, allowing them to gather intelligence about the conditions at Richmond and the strength of its forces.[71] This information would be important for Grant's spring 1865 campaign to capture the city, and the Twenty-Fifth would provide the additional muscle needed to deprive the enemy of rest and thus win the war.[72]

On January 3, 1865, Colonel Thomas D. Sedgwick, commander of the 114th U.S. Colored Troops stationed at Camp Nelson, received Special Order No. 3, instructing his regiment to depart immediately and head to Virginia. The 114th, 115th, and 116th Infantry Regiments, all from Camp Nelson, were three of the thirty-two black regiments absorbed into the newly formed Twenty-Fifth Corps. Privates Jerry and Charles Skillman were members of the 114th. There can be no doubt that the Skillmans and their fellow soldiers were filled with pride when they learned they would be joining the fighting at Richmond. Yet they could not help but recall the fate of their fallen comrades from the Fort Pillow Massacre and, most recently, the Battle of Saltville, where black soldiers had been killed after being captured and held as prisoners of war. For men like Jerry Skillman, whose goal was freedom from the stigma of race and its limitations, this was an opportunity not only to claim their manhood but also to become an example of what a man should be: resolved, determined, and unshakable in his commitments.

Within days of celebrating his son Isaac's fourth birthday, Jerry Skillman left in pursuit of his destiny. After saying his good-byes and holding his smallish four-year-old in his arms one more time, Skillman loaded up his field pack, shouldered his government-issued Sharps carbine, and fell in with his regiment. As the eleven companies formed a column numbering more than 1,000 men and began their eighteen-mile trek toward Lexington, behind them marched their fears of inadequacy and inferiority. However, the closer they got to Lexington, the more confident they became in their abilities as soldiers, growing taller with the knowledge that they were being counted as men. They were greeted in Lexington by an enthusiastic crowd of Union supporters, well-wishers, and black folks overtaken with joy at the sight of their fellow blacks marching off to glory. After boarding their train, the men of the 114th, including Jerry Skillman, envisioned what lay ahead. Since the previous June, he had waited patiently to serve. Now, as a free man, as a soldier racing toward the fight in Richmond, he imagined both the beginning of one world and the end of another, converging.

When the 114th arrived at Chaffin's farm sometime between January 6 and 10, they were assigned to the First Division of the Twenty-Fifth Corps in the Third Brigade. Skillman and his fellow soldiers quickly fell into the daily routine of drilling and preparing to march into battle when called on. The men were well aware of the fighting taking place around the farm; there had been reports of enemy skirmishes and snipers shooting at black soldiers. Still, the black Yankees remained enthusiastic about the opportunity to serve and adjusted to their new environment. By the second week in February, more than 13,000 "colored soldiers" had been absorbed into the Twenty-Fifth Corps, and all of them were waiting for the chance to prove themselves in battle.

On February 20, 1865, a memorandum from Major General Weitzel was read to all the men under his command, expressing both his expectations for victory and his recognition of their great purpose in the war against rebellion:

In view of the circumstances under which this corps was raised and filled, the peculiar claims of its individual members upon the justice and fair dealing of the prejudiced, and the regularity of the conduct of the troops, which deserve those equal rights that have been hitherto denied the majority, the commanding general has been induced to adopt the Square as the distinctive badge of the Twenty-fifth Army Corps. Wherever danger has been found and glory to be won, the heroes who have fought for immortality have been distinguished by some emblem, to which every victory added a new luster. They looked upon their badge with pride, for to it they had given its fame. In the homes of smiling peace it recalled the days of courageous endurance and the hours of deadly strife and it solaced the moment of death, for it was a symbol of a life of heroism and self-denial. The poets still sing of the Templar's Cross, the Crescent of the Turk, the Chalice of the hunted Christian, and the White

Plume of Murat, that crested the wave of valor, sweeping resist-
lessly to victory. Soldiers, to you is given a chance in this spring
campaign of making this badge immortal. Let history record
that on the banks of the James 30,000 freemen not only gained
their own liberty, but shattered the prejudice of the world and
gave to the land of their birth peace, union, and glory.[73]

How Jerry Skillman responded to this glowing compliment or what
the black soldiers said among themselves as they fastened their badg-
es to their uniforms we will never know. However, we can imagine
that Weitzel's challenge to rise up and be counted as men who were
lovers of "peace, union and glory" must have moved them to tears.
The badge of the Twenty-Fifth Corps, a simple blue square, became
symbolic of the overall purpose of the war for these black men.
Many had joined the army to flee the cruelty and degradation of
slavery; others saw it as an opportunity to kill white men responsible for their pain and suffering. Nevertheless, thousands understood
that their greater purpose was to shatter the institution of slavery
and the prejudice found in the world, while claiming their manhood
in the process. All these black men, once deemed unimportant to the
Federal effort to secure the Union, unfit to serve as soldiers, and un-
worthy to wear Union blue, were on the verge of capturing the city
that maintained the fiction that white supremacy and black inferiority were inherent and ordained by God.

      As March came to a close and winter slowly turned to spring,
the First and Second Divisions of Twenty-Fifth Corps were readied
to complete the final surge against General Lee's forces. The division commanders, Brevet Major General August Kautz of the First
and Brigadier General William Birney of the Second, prepared their
seasoned soldiers to advance beyond the Confederate lines with the
intent of ending the war. On March 27 the Army of the James, of
which the Twenty-Fifth Corps was a part, was coordinated to move
against Richmond, and the Second Division came under the immediate command of Major General Ord. From Weitzel's notes, we
know that on the morning of March 28 he had under his command
Kautz's division, a division of the Twenty-Fourth, the Fifth Massa-

chusetts Colored Cavalry, and an additional 500 mounted cavalry-men from Mackenzie's command.[74] Attached to the First Division, Private Jerry Skillman's 114th Regiment was poised to take part in the fall of Richmond.

While Weitzel maintained his position on the outskirts of Richmond, General Grant led the assault against Petersburg. After six days of fighting, it became evident that the rebel forces had been demoralized and were pulling back. On the morning of April 2 Petersburg was taken, and with it the strength of the Confederacy. The defeat at Petersburg alerted the rebel troops in Richmond that the end was near. On the morning of April 3 Weitzel ordered his men to prepare to enter the city, which was now ablaze from fires set by the Confederates in an effort to destroy tobacco stores, buildings, and other materials believed to be valuable to the Yankee soldiers.[75] The Union soldiers, including Skillman's regiment, entered the city to secure it, put out the fires, and restore order.

Chaplain Garland H. White, a former slave and member of the Twenty-Eighth U.S. Colored Infantry, entered the besieged capital city amid thousands of freedmen and -women. "I became so overcome with tears," White wrote, "that I could not stand up under the pressure of such fullness of joy in my own heart."[76] Blacks cheered as the soldiers marched up Main Street playing the drums and carrying the colors of their corps and country. The spectacle of black men in blue uniforms with shoulders erect and heads held high, maintaining complete discipline, was burned into the minds of the spectators, who recognized that the day of jubilee had finally arrived. After ten days of occupation, the First Division, along with remnants of other brigades and regiments, was relocated to a camp outside of Petersburg near Swift Creek.[77] In a letter dated April 11 that was printed in the *Philadelphia Inquirer*, the writer recounts the behavior and efficiency of the all-black Twenty-Fifth Corps:

> The First Division of the Twenty-[Fifth] Army Corps . . . has been performing garrison duty at Richmond, and took a very prominent part in the capture of that city. It is composed en-

tirely of colored regiments, with the exception of the artillery and a squadron of white cavalry.

On nearing Petersburg the division took a short rest and then marched through the city, presenting company and platoon fronts. The streets were filled with citizens, curious to witness the appearance and evolutions of so large a body of "Black Yankees." No matter how deep seated the prejudice of the people here may have been against colored soldiers, their excellent behavior, exact marching, skillful evolution, and true military bearing were eminently calculated to dissipate any existing antagonism. They moved through the city with the exactness and regularity of machinery, and not a word escaped the lips of any one of them.[78]

It is unclear whether the Twenty-Fifth Corps' relocation was precipitated by the military's desire to calm the black masses or to save white southerners from the embarrassment and humiliation of having black men rule over them. The black soldiers were also having a significant influence on former slaves, which created an unstable and volatile environment for whites who were trying to hold on to their land, their property, and their dignity.[79]

On April 15 the nation learned of the assassination of President Abraham Lincoln, shot by actor and Southern sympathizer John Wilkes Booth while attending a production of *Our American Cousin* at Ford's Theater in Washington, D.C. The president's death shocked the nation, leaving it without the great architect of the war to maintain the Union and without a great advocate for the freedom of blacks in America. Southern sympathizers rejoiced, while former slaves mourned the loss of their champion, the "Second Father of his Country."[80]

Meanwhile, the Twenty-Fifth Corps, still stationed near Petersburg, became the focus of a government conspiracy to remove black soldiers from Virginia. In a memo to Grant, Major General Henry W. Halleck wrote:

General Ord represents that want of discipline and good officers in the Twenty-fifth Corps renders it a very improper force for the preservation of order in this department. A number of cases of atrocious rape by these men have already occurred. Their influence on the colored population is also reported to be bad. I therefore hope you will remove it to garrison forts or for service on the Southern coast and substitute a corps from the Army of the Potomac, say Wright's, temporarily.

It seems very necessary to prevent the rush of the negro population into Richmond and to organize some labor system in the interior immediately as the planting season will be over in two or three weeks. Unless this is provided there will be a famine in this State. For this purpose I shall occupy Fredericksburg, Orange or Charlottesville, Lynchburg, and a few other points. To perform this duty properly requires officers and men of more intelligence and character than we have in the Twenty-fifth Corps.

Grant responded quickly, instructing Halleck to place the "Twenty-fifth in a camp of instruction either at Bermuda Hundred or at City Point until some disposition is made of them for defense on the sea coast." Grant also entrusted Halleck to implement a labor system to "employ the idle and prevent their becoming a burden upon the Government."[81]

On May 1, 1865, General Halleck assigned all colored troops in the Department of Virginia to the Twenty-Fifth Corps, which would immediately be sent to a camp of instruction, and "no more colored troops would be enlisted."[82] Once he learned of these actions, Major General Weitzel wrote to the assistant adjutant general of armies in the field, Lieutenant Colonel T. S. Bowers:

Colonel: I have heard through several unofficial sources that the troops of my corps are charged with having committed an unusual amount of irregularities while in and about Richmond, and that these reports have reached the ears of some of the highest commanding officers in the service. As I have a telegram from my immediate commander, Maj. Gen. E. O. C. Ord, commanding Department of Virginia, that nearly all of the irregularities complained of were committed by black and white cavalry, which either did not belong to my corps, or had been with it but for a few days; as I know positively that others were committed by the convicts in soldiers' clothing, liberated by the rebels from the penitentiary at the evacuation of Richmond, and as I with my two division commanders, Bvt. Maj. Gen. A. V. Kautz and Bvt. Brig. Gen. R. H. Jackson, both officers of experience in the regular army, believe the troops of this corps to be not only as well behaved and as orderly as the average of other troops, but even more so. I respectfully request to know whether any such charge as above referred to has been either officially or unofficially made by any responsible person. The behavior of my entire corps during the last month has been most excellent. Only one complaint has been made by the people of the vicinity, and this I traced to troops that did not belong to it.[83]

Weitzel's letter of inquiry was not answered directly. Instead, he received a telegram from Halleck on May 18, 1865, telling him of Grant's order to remove the Twenty-Fifth Corps to the Rio Grande by ocean transportation, which was scheduled to arrive at City Point, Virginia, in two days. A good soldier, Weitzel complied, and there is no record of him protesting the injustice levied on the Twenty-Fifth Corps. But antiblack sentiment was present throughout the war, especially among the military brass, which were willing to sacrifice black men as fodder but unwilling to compromise the fiction they had come to depend on.

It is not clear whether Jerry Skillman was on the ship headed for Texas. Records show that by July, he was back at Camp Nelson in Kentucky, listed as part of the invalid corps. Whether he was injured during the siege on Richmond or had taken a bullet earlier, while in camp at Chaffin's farm, is not known. Skillman died at Camp Nelson on July 27, 1865, if not from combat wounds then most likely from tuberculosis or one of several other diseases easily spread in close quarters.

With the death of her husband, it was up to America to protect her son from the harsh and often cold world. Her experiences as a slave and her time at Camp Nelson would influence the choices she made for him. Young Isaac Murphy, who would have been four years old at the time of Skillman's death, was too young to understand what was happening. It would be years before he could take pride in knowing that his father had been recognized as both a brave man and a free man. And like a majority of African American boys of his generation, Murphy would come to admire his father's resolve and the courage it took to wear the uniform that represented freedom, manhood, and citizenship. He too would have to stand up for what he believed in.

## 4

# From the Silence
# and the Darkness

## *1865–1869*

In the summer of 1869 the highly anticipated total eclipse of the
sun enshrouded the earth in darkness for what seemed to some like
an eternity. Scientists had foretold of the "startling and impressive"
sight that would appear in the sky on August 7.[1] Still, this natural
occurrence turned frightful and disconcerting to those who had a
limited knowledge of the universe and therefore gravitated toward
their religious roots to explain the darkening horizon. But on the
day in question, few could turn away from the tremendous spectacle that resembled the colliding of heavenly bodies and, to the naked
eye, appeared to be a prelude to the end of the world.

In American newspapers and magazines, astronomers and as-
trophysicists quantified the precise minutes and seconds when the
moon would cover the sun, leaving only the corona, the outer edge,
visible. Newspaper editors advised readers to use colored or smoked
glasses or pieces of glass with a "thin, even coat of dark varnish"
to view the eclipse.[2] In the *Atlantic Almanac*, Charles S. Peirce pro-

vided an explanation of the event and opined that the "total eclipse, whose path lies through a large and thickly settled portion of our country, is an event whose interest cannot be exaggerated."[3] The reading public, especially those of financial means, took note of Peirce's observations and made plans to travel to the best locations to view the eclipse. Thousands migrated into the projected path to witness the display of awe and wonder.

In the weeks prior to the heavenly phenomenon, hundreds of scientists also migrated across the country to the 140-mile-wide belt stretching from the Atlantic Seaboard to the agricultural Midwest, where they set up their bulky telescopes and cameras to observe and capture the sequence of events leading up to the total solar eclipse. Indeed, train cars delivered parties of bespectacled men weighted down with equipment, accompanied by their assistants, to the most favorable spots among the dozens listed as "excellent for observation." From Leesburg, North Carolina, to Burlington, Iowa, distinguished astronomers and wealthy star gazers settled in to observe the celestial event of epic proportions.[4] Chemistry professor Henry Morton of the Franklin Institute was well positioned at Burlington, near the west bank of the Mississippi River, on August 7. The highly acclaimed scientist and intellectual hoped to obtain images of the drama unfolding in the heavens above. Using a Merz and Mahler telescope with a Frauenhofer friction-governor clock and specially fitted lenses to accurately record the changing position of the moon, Morton photographed the eclipse with pinpoint accuracy.[5] His images clearly captured the volatile nature of the sun's outer surface, with Venus and Mercury visible in the distance.

While scientists like Morton used the eclipse to prove theories related to activity on the surface of the sun and to record the planets' movement through the solar system, others viewed the natural occurrence with feelings ranging from dread and gloom to curiosity and approbation. To the faithful, the "sickly green hue" that blanketed the earth and made a frightful sight of the land, causing domestic animals to wander the fields and birds to fly distracted in the dimly lit sky, was but one revelation of the power of the "Omnipotent Creator."[6] To the uneducated masses, the mysterious event unfolding in the heavens signified an uncertain future. Some saw the eclipse as an antecedent to death and destruction, which were sure to follow such a foreboding display of otherworldliness.

Yet for others, the natural phenomenon was a clear sign of the end of one era and the beginning of a new epoch in human history. To the forward-looking and learned, the eclipse metaphorically marked the end of a world that had grown old and tired. Out of the terrible silence and darkness consuming the land there emerged a beauty reflecting the process of renewal and rebirth. For African Americans, whose lives had been changed by the Civil War, the rights and privileges attained through Federal legislation, and the burgeoning possibilities for social, economic, and political growth, their eyes were fixed on a future in which they emerged from the darkness of slavery into the light of full citizenship. More than anything, the solar eclipse was a sign from the heavens that the future was written in the stars, and no white man on earth had the ability to change it. For America Murphy (who might have been using her married name, Burns) and her son Isaac, this sign in the sky could have meant a number of things or nothing at all. But one thing was certain: if change was inevitable and ordained by God, Isaac's future was tied to the racial destiny of a people grounded in their faith in things unseen.

Sometime after the death of Jerry Skillman (Burns), America and her two children left Camp Nelson and traveled to Lexington, which was teeming with former slaves in search of opportunities to express their newfound freedom. Depending on the time of year, the health of her children, and the available means of transportation, the eighteen-mile journey could have taken several hours or a few days. There are many reasons why America would have chosen to leave Camp Nelson, most of which were closely tied to the numerous changes taking place both in the Bluegrass region of Kentucky and throughout the United States after 1865.

First, passage of the Thirteenth Amendment to the U.S. Constitution on December 26, 1865, officially marked the beginning of Reconstruction throughout the South, giving former slaves both their freedom and the momentum to gain access to citizenship rights, including the right to vote. Federally sponsored organizations such as the Freedmen's Bureau, headed by General Oliver O. Howard, supported blacks who were struggling to adjust to freedom and their new place in society.[7] Unfortunately, this political gesture, which was intended to elevate the status of former bondsmen, in no way guaranteed that whites would accept blacks as part of American society proper. In fact, throughout Kentucky, violence against freedmen increased in the rural areas around Lexington. African Americans were subjected to public displays of humiliation, sexual abuse, and mass murder by whites, most of whom refused to acknowledge that the Civil War had changed anything.

Angry that free blacks were being supported by the Federal government and competing for and acquiring economic opportunities that had once been reserved for whites, vigilante groups formed, led in part by Confederate veterans. They armed themselves and patrolled the country roads, terrorizing blacks and driving them back to the farms of their former masters.[8] On numerous occasions, African American men and women were beaten, raped, and had their ears cut off or their "skulls broken" by night riders, brutal patrollers, and a rising homegrown terrorist group known as the Ku Klux Klan.[9] After the Civil Rights Act of 1866 was signed into law, white resentment burst forth as a torrent of hatred and violence against the Federal government and blacks. This resentment was punctuated by the lynching of black men who tried to assert their freedom.

Between 1866 and 1868 white Kentuckians committed hundreds of crimes against the freedmen, in an effort to reinstate "home rule."[10] Still, some whites were willing to accept former slaves into society and give them the opportunity to become contributing members of the community. But beyond the religious motivations of the American Missionary Association, white interests in the freedmen generally had more to do with the workforce and economic needs of manufacturers and less to do with social justice and gaining the franchise. Quite plainly, white businessmen still needed the muscle of black men and women. But these whites who employed blacks also became the focus of night riders and midnight assassins, suffering property destruction, death threats, or worse by white men determined to curb the progress of the colored people.

America Murphy may have decided to leave Camp Nelson because of overcrowding, dwindling supplies, and a lack of employment opportunities at the Federal encampment for a widow with two small children. Despite the recent policy changes, many of which resulted from the November 1864 expulsion of women and children from the camp, there were still too many people drawing on the limited services and supplies available. In 1865 the camp's population increased significantly, owing to a surge of new enlistees who brought their families with them. By the fall of 1865, there were more than 2,400 women and children at the Federal encampment. Poverty and disease quickly turned the portal of freedom into a tomb of death. Within a year, 90 percent of the inhabitants would be gone; those who survived would leave in search of better accommodations and opportunities.

By September 1866, when Camp Nelson came under the control of the Freedmen's Bureau, there were 250 inhabitants remaining, most of them the wives and children of soldiers assigned to the Twenty-Fifth Corps, which was still stationed at the Rio Grande in Texas. Although they resided within the walls of the camp, the soldiers' families were not safe. White ruffians known as regulators began to terrorize the residents of Camp Nelson. Bent on vengeance against blacks, especially black soldiers, these former Confederate soldiers and men of similar temperament recognized the vulnerability of the women and children there and began an all-out assault on the encampment. With the absence of military force (most Federal troops had been sent to urban locations), "armed raiders descended upon the camp," abusing and killing unarmed black men and former soldiers in front of their wives and children.[11]

The Reverend Abisha Scofield, the white administrator of a refugee facility and school, was confronted by regulators, who strongly advised him to stop supporting and teaching former Kentucky slaves.[12] When he refused, the regulators threatened to shoot Scofield and his family if they did not leave Kentucky immediately. Taking the threat seriously, Scofield left the state, never to return.[13] This type of violent intimidation was common throughout the South, especially where former bondsmen came under the guidance and care of well-intentioned whites, as well as black teachers and missionaries. These individuals understood the power of education as a gateway to greater rights and privileges, and they prepared the former slaves to participate as full citizens of the United States through literacy. However, their success threatened illiterate and poor whites, who recognized that education gave former slaves a sense of citizenship and autonomy from white power.

In response to this threat, white men (especially the poor) volunteered to enforce the rigid customs of slavery to undermine the efforts of missionaries throughout the South.[14] Many of the white and black missionaries and teachers serving the needs of the freedmen did so under the banner of Christian service and what they believed to be the will of God. However, they soon realized the ungodly nature of human beings—specifically, whites adamantly opposed to African Americans' elevation to citizenship. The lack of protection by the Federal and local governments severely hindered their goal of educating blacks and preparing them for life beyond slavery. As a result, many missionaries and teachers were run off from the encampments, rural towns, and freedmen's schools where they were needed.

If not motivated to leave Camp Nelson because of conditions there, America may have decided to go because of the death of Jerry Skillman. Having lost her husband but not her will to survive, America was no doubt determined to find a place in the world where her children could take advantage of their newly gained freedom. Still, she would need some assistance negotiating the dynamics of the quickly changing world, and the lack of family members at the encampment made her vulnerable to abuse by the racial paternalism of the Freedmen's Bureau and by others who might take advantage of her situation. America may have decided to go to Lexington to seek the security of family members there. She was familiar with the city and its African American community. Former slaves and free blacks had established viable institutions during the first half of the nineteenth century, and by the beginning of Reconstruction, their organizational skills were turning blacks into a community of workers, consumers, and politically active citizens. These institutions would be an integral part of the development of African American social, political, and economic movements and the expansion of individual notions of manhood and womanhood.

The Emancipation Proclamation, the Civil War, and the Thirteenth Amendment were dramatic developments responsible for transforming former slaves into an effective network of religious leaders, educators, and businessmen. The racial destiny of African Americans was tied directly to their ability to develop and utilize communal networks, their will to survive, their religious faith, and their ultimate goal of being recognized as human beings. African Americans maintained a degree of control over their situation that was largely undetected by white society. Nevertheless, upon reaching Lexington, America Murphy would experience "discrimination in employment and access to public accommodations" and fall victim to legalized brutality.[15]

Ultimately, it was likely a combination of factors that led to America's decision to leave the deteriorating situation at Camp Nelson. Slavery had officially ended, and Reconstruction had begun as an earnest attempt to protect the newly freed from abuse and to elevate their status. America, like most former slaves, understood the importance of educating her children and the need to find work to support their full transition from slavery to freedom. Still, slavery's abolishment was not yet a reality to all Americans. Whites still ruled with impunity in most parts of the Bluegrass, and African Americans worked hard to establish a foothold in a society that many found foreign and intimidating. How were former slaves supposed to reconcile the fact that they had been treated like animals? What was freedom supposed to look like? What was it supposed to feel like? Who was going to protect their children? Whatever the psychological, social, and political effects of slavery, America's task was simple: ensure the future of her children. America's love would protect them, and her vision of Isaac's future would ultimately lead to his success.

Although the evidence is somewhat fragmented, it is likely that by the spring of 1867, America Murphy and her two small children arrived in Lexington, seeking shelter and protection with family and friends in the ramshackle housing available. The bustling city must have been a frightening sight to six-year-old Isaac, who was accustomed to the rural surroundings of Camp Nelson and the daily routine provided by his mother. Isaac would have to learn very quickly how to navigate the urban sea of hard- and gentle-faced people pressed together in the narrow confines of the city's black community.

A mecca for African Americans seeking to reinvent themselves as free men and women, Lexington became a stronghold for Kentucky blacks during Reconstruction. Prior to the Civil War the African American population of Lexington was 3,080, or about 30 percent of the city's almost 10,000 inhabitants. Of that number, 2,480 (80 percent) were enslaved African Americans, and 600 were free Negroes.[16] Although the "malady of slavery had been with Lexington from the beginning," prior to Reconstruction, blacks and whites in the city lived somewhat uncomfortably as neighbors.[17] The households of free and enslaved African Americans were interspersed among those of whites, for whom they worked as domestic servants and as laborers in a variety of manufacturing tasks. Antebellum Lexington was a lively scene, where African Americans represented the bulk of the workforce that made modern living possible. In fact, enslaved African Americans cleared the land to make way for "Athens of the West."[18] The muscle of black men and women was responsible for the wealth enjoyed by white Kentuckians prior to Reconstruction. As historian John D. Wright explains:

There were blacks everywhere, engaged in a great variety of tasks. In the morning, many could be seen going to the Market House where, at the various stalls, other blacks were butchering meat or selling vegetables, fruit, and flowers. Early in the morning, many of the male blacks headed for the factories, or to other tasks as bricklayers and masons, blacksmiths and carpenters, or perhaps to work on the building of the Lexington & Ohio Railroad. Others would be driving wagons or carriages, repairing streets, digging sewers, tending horses and equipment at the livery stables. Others performed the thousand and one menial tasks at the Phoenix Hotel and many other inns and taverns. Domestic servants in hundreds of residences performed innumerable tasks to keep the daily routine operating successfully.[19]

Clearly, the institution of slavery, especially in the city of Lexington, had produced a dependency on blacks. During Reconstruction, most of the South would continue to rely on blacks' service and labor in an array of occupations. This would prove important for both America and Isaac.

By 1867, African Americans were clustered in former slave housing in the back alleys of Lexington and crammed into the limited accommodations available along railroads, under bridges, near dank cemeteries, and in the makeshift hamlets on the edge of town.[20] The influx of freedmen and their families created a tremendous demand for low-cost housing. Housing projects sponsored and built by Lexington's political elite were virtually thrown up on the edge of the city. Attorney John A. Prall created Pralltown southwest of the city center between Colfax and Prall Streets and South Limestone Street and the railroad tracks; George B. Kinkead created Kinkeadtown out of low-lying land located between Maple and Ohio Streets and Fourth and Fifth Streets; Bruce's Addition was created by wealthy hemp manufacturer William W. Bruce on land near his rope factory between Seventh Street and the city limits; and Goodloetown was established by the editor of the *Kentucky Statesman*, William Cassius Goodloe,[21] on a plot of land located north of East Main Street and Midland down to Third Street.[22] On these poor-quality, low-lying lands surrounding the city, opportunists and philanthropists catered to and took advantage of the swelling population of blacks migrating into the city.[23] These locations became the physical spaces where new African American communities developed, dependent on the charity of white men, black benevolent societies, and "kinship relations" for survival.[24] The "bottoms," as they became known as, represented both a physical location in the city and an imagined psychological state where there was no place to go but up.

By the spring of 1870, the number of black inhabitants had jumped 133 percent to 7,171, accounting for almost half the population. With this increase came a range of social, economic, and political changes for those in search of something resembling freedom and opportunity.[25] The racially charged climate was both daunting and liberating to former slaves. Yet in the changing landscape of the nation, especially in the South, cities were the only places blacks could turn to for security. For African American residents of Lexington, this new sense of community was directly influenced by a "rigid system of segregated housing patterns" adopted by the city fathers in response to the influx of freedmen.[26]

When Isaac, his little sister, and his mother arrived in Lexington, they sought out family and friends, not unlike many newly transplanted rural African Americans from the Bluegrass. The ability to locate relatives and friends in the city speaks to the active kinship network that existed during slavery and the desire of those who had been displaced by the institution to reconnect with family members. Among the masses of migrants, vagrants, and homeless jamming the streets, America and her children found their way to the home of a friend, Cora Jordan, whom she likely met on the Tanner farm before the war.

In Maydwell's 1867 directory of Lexington, Eli Jordan is listed as residing at Third Street and Corporate Line, near what would eventually become Goodloetown. Eli, his wife Cora, and their two daughters, twelve-year-old Lizzie and eleven-year-old Cora, welcomed America and her children into their already cramped space.[27] The Jordan family depended on the patriarch to earn an income and generate a degree of security. Eli Jordan did so as a horse trainer and hostler, whether because that was the only job he could find or because he had done similar work as a slave. In the Bluegrass, horses and slaves had been the alpha and the omega of the region's economic, social, political, and cultural life before the Civil War. During Reconstruction and into the late 1890s, former slaves' influence on the horse industry would make the difference between success and failure. Most important, Eli Jordan would become one of the most influential men in the life of six-year-old Isaac.

Born in slavery in 1822, probably somewhere near Louisville, Kentucky, Jordan was recognized as one of the premier trainers in the Bluegrass during the 1870s. He worked for James Williams and Richard Owings of Williams and Owings Farms of Lexington and for J. W. Hunt Reynolds of Fleetwood Farms in Frankfort. His success in identifying and training talented horses, as well as jockeys, was on a par with that of Ansel Williamson, the celebrated trainer at Robert Atchison Alexander's Woodburn Farm. In terms of training the black community's children to be successful, Jordan instilled in his daughters a sense of purpose that extended beyond the narrow definition of success based on material gain. In a sense, Jordan became a surrogate father to America's children, sharing his understanding of horses, the ways of white folks, and the joy of a job well done. Isaac may have been the son Eli never had, and he impressed on the boy his definition of manhood, the importance of prudence and honesty, and the benefits of being consistent in all things. A smallish child, Isaac had already suffered the loss of his father and felt his mother's absence as she tended to the day-to-day necessities of survival. He would one day reflect on his bleak beginnings and the efforts of Lexington's black community to protect him from the temptations of city life. In adopting a morally sound, if not wholly Victorian, approach to life as an adult, Isaac would become an exemplar for black boys and men who admired his manliness, success, and prudence.

There can be no doubt that the worldly Jordan, among others in Lexington's black community, took on the responsibility of shaping the youngest members to be productive citizens who would not only cherish freedom and equality but also honor the memory of those long passed and their dreams of freedom. Given the limited opportunities in Lexington and the obstacles set up by whites, African American leaders invested their energies in uplifting the race through spiritual guidance and fellowship, in addition to strongly promoting their children's education and teaching them the virtuous qualities of hard work, morality, and temperance. Indeed, the freedmen recognized that their hopes and dreams for a fairer, more just, and more prosperous future could be achieved only by investing in themselves and their children. The individual and collective destiny of all black people was inextricably linked to inspiring a sense of purpose in the children of the newly emancipated masses. This was achieved through the two most important black institutions in Lexington during Reconstruction: the black church and the freedmen's schools.

Regardless of the community's overarching plan for the future of black Kentuckians, America Murphy had to be the primary wage earner, caregiver, and protector of her family. Needing to find gainful employment, she would have ventured out into the city in search of a job, likely leaving her children under the watchful eye of Cora Jordan. America may have knocked at the back doors of the homes of wealthy and middle-class whites; stood on the steps of the county courthouse at Cheapside, waiting to be asked to clean; or walked the streets and alleys of Lexington in search of some way to provide for her children and herself. Frequently, black women without the protection of husbands or other men were forced into prostitution. Whether America succumbed to that pressure is unknown, but the possibility exists.

By 1868, America Murphy was listed on the roster of potential taxpaying adults living in Lexington. However, with no firm address established, she probably remained with the Jordan family until the spring of 1869 while she adjusted to urban life and sought suitable housing. Sadly, America's daughter, whose name has been lost to history, died sometime between the spring of 1868 and the spring of 1869. The youngster likely succumbed to influenza, pneumonia, or diphtheria, the most prevalent causes of childhood death in postbellum Lexington.[28]

## The Way and the Light

An estimated 4 million former slaves were set adrift in American society with the dissolution of the institution of slavery. These individuals, most without skills, education, or economic power, depended on the government and numerous benevolent societies to help them find their way in a world that was frightening yet filled with possibility. In less than five years, blacks had gone from being human chattel to citizens, and they were on the verge of getting the right to vote. Although a majority of former slaves had a basic understanding of what freedom meant in terms of being able to move about the countryside, most needed help in making the mental, physical, and spiritual transformation required to become self-sufficient. They needed direction and leadership, which had to come from within the black community if freedom were to be established and experienced as a natural phenomenon.

By 1866, conditions were ripe for African Americans throughout the South to satisfy their desire to be acknowledged as full-fledged human beings. For generations, the institution of slavery and the brutal conditions of servitude had combined to produce a mythic notion of freedom tied to the biblical promised land—an imagined place looming somewhere north, just over the horizon. Although an estimated 100,000 blacks were liberated by the Underground Railroad between 1850 and 1860, and thousands more escaped through other means, those enslaved blacks left behind understood that the dream of physical freedom was not easily realized. To run away was, in essence, to steal another man's property. The consequences of being caught were too great for most to attempt to escape. For a majority of blacks who lived in the South, this kind of freedom did not arrive until Federal soldiers in Union blue marched past their farms and into Southern towns and cities, leaving scores of liberated blacks in their wake. Others claimed their physical freedom after the Emancipation Proclamation was read to them from the porches of their masters' homes by Federal officers seeking to secure the former slaves' loyalty in an effort to unravel the Confederacy from within. Still others recognized they were free only when word spread that General Robert E. Lee had surrendered at Appomattox after his "rebs" were defeated by colored soldiers outside Richmond. In this way, freedom was connected to a corporeal reality that required the individual's physical removal from the institution of slavery by force or by legal means.

To say that this was the only sort of freedom for the enslaved is to ignore their most influential form of resistance. Grounded in traditions brought from Africa, and expanded with the adoption of Christianity in North America, religion encouraged a spiritual freedom that was easily hidden from whites.[29] Slave preachers often held secret meetings on the farms and plantations of the South to discuss African Americans' purpose in the world and what the future might hold. Christianity was regarded as a form of redemption whose "great moral and religious principles . . . lie at the base of an elevated and sound moral" society.[30] Indeed, it was their sense of spiritual freedom that prepared African Americans for emancipation, which they attributed to their prayers, their patience, and, of course, the will of God. This ability to elevate themselves above their physical limitations and therefore resist their masters' authority had long been an integral part of black life in the South. Nevertheless, at the core of this spiritual freedom was African Americans' ability to organize themselves into an effective body politic capable of undermining their masters' control over how or what they thought. This underground or invisible network of people actively involved in "building and fortifying community life" empowered black men and women to take leadership roles.[31]

By the beginning of Reconstruction, organizing their communities into cohesive units that could respond to external challenges and the needs of their members became a priority for black leaders. Like the government officials directly connected to the Freedmen's Bureau, African Americans recognized that economic, social, and political chaos was sure to accompany the migration of former slaves from rural areas of the South and border states like Kentucky and Missouri to urban and semiurban locales near their former homes. African American religious leaders also recognized the need for a structured transition to guarantee that freedom was not temporary. Black leaders fully understood what was at stake for former slaves and the future of the race, and they strategically planned how to become contributing members of society based on religious values, republican concepts of life and liberty, and hard work.

Against this backdrop, the black church emerged as a force in the state of Kentucky. Its ministers and its members were critical participants in the overall program to educate former slaves and their children, while advancing new ideas about the value and place of blacks in American society. In Lexington the black church was the primary gateway to freedom, education, equality, and opportunity for African Americans, especially the children, most of whom had been born into slavery. Through the church's guidance and leadership, these children developed into exceptional examples of manhood and womanhood. During the latter part of the nineteenth century, the roster of successful black Lexingtonians included doctors, lawyers, businessmen and -women, politicians, ministers, horse farm owners, horse trainers, and, of course, jockeys.

Kentucky's first all-black church was founded in 1785 by Peter Duerett, a slave from Virginia who was known as "Old Captain." Duerett's First African Baptist Church was established in Lexington on land owned by pioneer John Maxwell, who apparently believed that slaves should be allowed to worship as they pleased, especially if it provided order and discipline to an inferior caste of people.[32] The population of enslaved African Americans increased in the Bluegrass between 1800 and 1820, and by the time Old Captain died in 1823, the African Baptist Church had more than 300 members. Most of these were slaves, but church members also included the handful of free blacks living in Lexington, such as Samuel Oldham, Rolley Blue, William Gist, Solomon Walker, and Jason Bullock.[33] These men were church trustees and the leaders blacks turned to in times of need. As odd as it sounds, Lexington's free and enslaved black population created a world where they could function with some sense of normalcy. The black church nurtured this sense of community and became the center of this stability.

After the passing of Duerett and some controversy over the church's direction and its future leadership, the membership asked London Ferrill, a well-known and respected free black preacher, to take over the pastorate of First African Baptist Church. Ferrill, hoping to elevate the church's current status as an unrecognized assemblage of slaves and free blacks, petitioned the Elkhorn Baptist Association for membership. The white association refused to acknowledge the all-black church until it had been firmly established that Ferrill was ordained and endorsed by the community's most

prominent white citizens. After a series of closed meetings and pe-
titions supporting the new preacher, Ferrill assumed leadership of
the congregation in 1824 and proceeded to increase its membership
through mass baptisms of urban-dwelling slaves and free blacks.[34]
Although Ferrill was readily accepted by most of the Lexington
community, jealousy seems to have played a role in Harry Quills's
attack on the preacher. Quills tried to have Ferrill, a Virginia native,
removed from his pastoral duties and from Kentucky, arguing that
no free colored man born outside the state could stay for more than
thirty days. Lexington's white community, including livery stable
owner Jeremiah Murphy, signed a petition that granted Ferrill the
right to come and go as he pleased.[35]

Over the course of his thirty-two years as head of First African Baptist Church, Ferrill baptized more than 5,000 black folks
seeking deliverance from their worldly pains. There can be no doubt
that Ferrill's guidance provided his congregation with the hope they
needed to withstand the machinations of slavery on a daily basis.
Trusted by the white patriarchs of Lexington not to inflame animosities between blacks and whites, Ferrill was allowed some flexibility
in his teaching and preaching. In keeping with the Christian tradition and public ritual of marriage to validate a couple's commitment
to each other in full view of their community and in the eyes of God,
Ferrill performed marriages between enslaved men and women, pro-
nouncing them joined "until death or *distance* did them apart."[36]

At the height of his popularity, Ferrill became an exemplar of
selflessness, resolve, and leadership when Lexington was hit by an
outbreak of cholera in 1833. Along with white Lexingtonians General Leslie Combs, William Solomon, Benjamin Gratz, John Keizer,
and others, Ferrill acted heroically, caring for the sick and dying and
burying the dead at the risk of his own life.[37] Unfortunately, Ferrill's
wife was one of the 500 Lexingtonians to die in the epidemic, out
of a population of little more than 6,000.[38] Ferrill's commitment to
the community during this time of great turmoil won the hearts and
loyalties of many of Lexington's elite.

While Ferrill was building the First African Baptist Church into
a revered religious organization, its membership ebbed and flowed

according to the internal politics of the church, the in-migration of new slaves and their denominational beliefs, and the desire of some individuals to establish and lead their own separate churches. By the beginning of Reconstruction, Lexington had six black churches, many of which had spun off from Old Captain's original congregation. These churches were Pleasant Green Baptist, Independent Baptist, First African Baptist, a Methodist Episcopalian church, a Christian church, and an African Methodist Episcopalian (AME) church. Because Baptists made up a majority of the population, they had the greatest influence on the institutions connected with freedom, especially education.

In August 1865, four months before slavery was officially abolished in Kentucky, the State Convention of Colored Baptists was created under the guidance of Henry Adams, pastor of Louisville's Fifth Street Baptist Church. Adams had been responsible for growing the black membership in the white First Baptist Church in Louisville, and he had led a movement to create a separate place of worship for blacks, helping to establish the Colored Baptist Church in Louisville, with 475 members, in 1842.[39] The 1865 convention brought together prominent black church leaders from central Kentucky to plan a strategy for collective growth and stability for the freedmen pouring into cities such as Lexington and Louisville. Some of these former slaves were running from terrorist activities in the rural parts of the state, where they received no protection from the law.[40]

After several days of meetings and deliberations, the convention attendees formalized a constitution and formed committees dedicated to developing a program of free education throughout Kentucky, increasing membership, and expanding the faith. These organizational efforts of the black church in Kentucky were furthered by members of the various congregations and benevolent societies, who were committed to educating former slaves and free blacks. For the Reverend James Monroe, who had taken over leadership of the First African Baptist Church in 1862, the education of black children was essential to the success of the great experiment of emancipation. What is more, Reverend Monroe demanded that black children in Lexington receive the education they deserved in order to fulfill their destinies as learned, informed, and God-fearing citizens who could lead their community in the future.

In 1867 Reverend Monroe and his Lexington congregation hosted the annual General Association of Colored Baptists convention, where the delegates' primary concerns were the continued and future education of ministers and the development of schools for children. Monroe had already begun his work against the challenging climate of Reconstruction, especially the fact that whites viewed the education of blacks as detrimental to their power over former slaves and an affront to traditional ideas of American citizenship. Increasingly, the church's role as the center of spiritual and rudimentary education evolved to include strong political activism, whereby religious leaders used their collective voices and connections to the powerful white elite to challenge legislative rulings against African Americans. Nevertheless, during Reconstruction, the education and welfare of black children remained the priority for black ministers throughout Kentucky.

## "With Labor and Education for Your Motto"

The resilience of black Kentuckians had been forged in the fires of slavery, poverty, and degradation. They emerged from their subjugation hungry for the opportunity to prove their worthiness of all the rights and privileges of full citizenship. Although denied access to the franchise, African American leaders such as Frederick Douglass, Martin Delany, and John Mercer Langston continued to argue for the civil and political rights of black people. Not only had "colored" soldiers served, fought, and died in the Civil War to preserve the Union; black people had been at the very core of the nation's success and deserved their freedom based on merit. In other words, freedom was their birthright; it had been paid for by the labors of their forebears and their own efforts on behalf of their unyielding masters. What is more, black leaders understood that education was central to a true sense of freedom and the key to a full understanding of democracy. Education prepared the individual to participate in society as an enlightened and informed citizen capable of making erudite decisions, thereby gaining access to the social mobility and political power indicative of a successful community.[41]

At the beginning of Reconstruction, schools across the state of Kentucky were established in and by African American communities long before the Freedmen's Bureau, the American Missionary Association, and other benevolent societies stepped in to help former slaves learn to read and write. Through collaborative efforts, freedmen and -women raised the necessary funds to purchase land for schools, pay teachers, and buy books. Clearly, African Americans understood that education and literacy were tied to black destiny and black power. To fulfill the deafening demand for education, many church-based schools allowed both children and adults to attend. Indeed, a number of the facilities offered day schools for children and night schools for adults, as well as Sabbath schools for moral and religious education.

During slavery, African Americans recognized that knowledge was power, but by Reconstruction through the political process, they came to realize that book knowledge was empowering. While day schools groomed and prepared African American children to enter a world where their intellect and work ethic would take them far, night schools taught adults to be knowledgeable and politically active participants in the American system of democracy capitalism. Education was deemed such a necessity that when work became difficult to find in Lexington, African Americans went back into the fields of their former masters to earn enough money to pay for their children's tuition and books and for teachers' salaries. Black Kentuckians certainly took seriously the possibilities offered by Reconstruction, especially in terms of advancing their children and gaining the franchise.[42] In Lexington, the African American community was a strong supporter of education and used its limited resources to open schools in the most important centers of black social activity: the church.

In April 1865, before the Freedmen's Bureau was organized, dozens of religious organizations, benevolent societies, and independent philanthropists provided funding and materials to organize day schools in homes and churches. These initial piecemeal efforts were supported by community fund-raising and directed by ministers and church trustees. In the same month the Freedmen's Bureau began operation, one of Lexington's first schools for black children was opened at the First African Baptist Church under the supervision of the Reverend James Monroe. There were sixty pupils, and each one had a spelling book and a story book for lessons.[43] In May the Reverend Edward P. Smith, a representative of the American Missionary Association (AMA), visited Lexington to survey the needs of the freedmen and their children. Smith observed that the First African Baptist Church had one of five schools operating in the city and charging tuition of $1.25 per month for each child.[44] Thus, for a majority of families, including those of black Civil War veterans, school was not an affordable endeavor. To pay for their children's education, parents had to raise money from outside the community due to overpopulation in the city, which led to a shortage of jobs.

Leaders of the disparate but solidifying African American communities recognized that all children needed access to proper schooling if the promise of enlightenment and full citizenship was to be achieved. In most cases, children "manifested the same dogged commitment to their education" as adults did to the recognition of their birthright and their humanity.[45] Black children were the main reason African American leaders continued to fight for the franchise, no matter how dangerous the consequences or the means whites used to deter their progress.

By October 1865, less than two months after the State Convention of Colored Baptists first met in Louisville, Reverend Monroe, a charter member of the convention, had begun soliciting money from his 1,500 members to pay the salaries of teachers to staff community schools.[46] Reverend Smith's fortuitous visit to Lexington (he had been delayed in the city while on his way to Nicholasville) led to AMA support not only for Monroe but also for other schools in the area.[47] Smith's primary observation had been the lack of literate and capable teachers for the eager students. It was common knowledge that before the AMA and the Freedmen's Bureau became involved in the education of African Americans, local church schools such as those at Pleasant Green Baptist Church and Main Street Baptist Church were staffed by semi-illiterate teachers who did their best but inevitably failed to impart the fundamental elements of a proper education.[48] Until more qualified teachers could be hired, the schools would not fully satisfy the children's educational needs.

Thanks to the proximity of Camp Nelson and the commitment of the Reverend John G. Fee to educating its inhabitants, children like Isaac Murphy had the opportunity to learn from some of the better teachers in the Bluegrass.[49] Reverend Edward P. Smith knew of Miss E. Belle Mitchell, a mulatto woman who had briefly taught at Camp Nelson, and he sent word, through Miss Mary Colton at the camp, of a teaching position available in Lexington. A gifted teacher, Mitchell was asked to "take charge of a free school for the children of colored soldiers," most of whom were poor.[50] She relocated from her parents' home in Danville to Lexington, where Mr. and Mrs. Henry H. Britton willingly opened their home to her "for the good of the race." Mitchell was thus introduced into the aspiring class of Lexington—the elite African American men and women who valued education, social mobility, and the power that comes from being well connected to those in power.[51]

The Brittons, whose home was located on the northwest corner of Mill and New Streets in the Second Ward, were considered "honest, industrious and frugal people, [who] were among the first and highly respected families and citizens of Lexington."[52] A freeborn mulatto and self-educated businessman, Henry Harrison Britton ran a barbershop serving white men only, located next to the Broadway Hotel. He employed several barbers, including Thomas Jackson and James H. Scott. Britton would become very wealthy from his business ventures and would use his capital to purchase luxury items such as a piano and a carriage for his family's transportation. He belonged to a variety of benevolent societies dedicated to the uplift of African Americans in Lexington and was a member of the inaugural board of directors for the Colored Fair Association in 1869.[53] Like her husband, Laura Marshall Britton was mulatto, the daughter of a slave woman and her master, Colonel Thomas F. Marshall of Woodford County. The wealthy Colonel Marshall provided Laura with an above-standard education for any young girl—white or black—at his expense and most likely under his direct guidance and supervision.[54]

Like other women of her class and position, Laura Britton probably served as a community matriarch, ensuring the moral uprightness of the children, especially her own. Strict members of the Episcopalian Church, the Brittons undoubtedly exemplified proper middle-class sensibilities and served as a model for other black families.

The seven Britton children were well known throughout Kentucky for their intellectual capacity and musical ability. Julia Ann was recognized as a musical prodigy and a "remarkable performer on the piano," holding parlor concerts before the Civil War in the homes of William Preston and John Hunt Morgan.[55] Sometime between 1869 and 1870, the Brittons moved to Madison County, where the children were enrolled in Berea College to continue their educational and intellectual development. In particular, Julia and her sister Mary would blossom as intellectuals. After graduating from Berea in 1874, Julia moved to Memphis, Tennessee, where she married and started a music school. In Memphis she also became heavily involved in civil rights, becoming a charter member of the National Association for the Advancement of Colored People (NAACP) in 1909. Mary Britton became a teacher and was the first African American woman to practice medicine in Kentucky.

Clearly, Reverend Monroe's request for assistance from the AMA was answered and supplemented by members of the black community with considerable status and power, including the Brittons. The church school at First African Baptist Church, under the direction of the AMA, Miss Mitchell, and Reverend Monroe, satisfied the desires of both parents, who wanted their children to learn to read, write, and do arithmetic, and community leaders, who sought to transform the future of black Lexington through education, self-mastery, and successful assimilation into society. The school also provided the community's youngest members with the best examples of manhood and womanhood and demonstrated the benefits of upward mobility, political activeness, and an understanding of progressive ideas. More important, regardless of the freedmen's motivations for relocating to Lexington and despite the city's obvious limitations, African Americans created a proactive cultural, social, and political environment that attempted to redefine family, marriage, and community and advance communal cohesiveness. Among Lexington's progressive community, religion, temperance, education, and hard work were the foundations for the future. To succeed in Lexington, one needed to have a vested interest in the community, its children, and its overall welfare. Communities were composed of individuals, but individuals need communities for support, protection, and a grounded sense of identity.

In keeping with the mission of the black Baptists' convention—which was to preach the Gospel and train the black community through Christian education—in addition to their rudimentary education, children were instructed in proper etiquette and hygiene to prepare them to serve their community, participate as upright citizens, and lead the race to new horizons.[56] This approach to education would allow future generations of African Americans to function in society as disciplined, self-directed, and purpose-driven individuals. The future of both Lexington and Kentucky was dependent on this particular generation's access to education and acceptance of religious values, which would prepare them for all the rights and privileges of citizenship.

Although there were a number of problems with school supplies, and a majority of the students lacked proper nutrition, Belle Mitchell's average class size grew to sixty-nine by November 1865.[57] The number of children attending school in Lexington increased primarily due to the in-migration of refugees from Federal encampments and rural black families fleeing the violence of the countryside. White resistance to educating former slaves varied, based on their class and their understanding of race as a concept. In the rural towns and hamlets surrounding Lexington, the economic difficulties of white farmers, many of them former slaveholders, "caused . . . them to oppose any prospect of extending education or welfare agencies which would involve an increase in taxes" to pay for Negro education and thus ruin the South's traditional labor pool.[58] Others considered schools for former slaves a waste of time and resources and refused to have anything to do with uplifting a so-called inferior race of people. The most extreme cases involved the burning of school buildings and the violent intimidation of black preachers and white teachers who sought to enlighten former slaves through religious and moral education. Many were run out of town, afraid they would be shot for teaching Negroes.[59] To a majority of working-class and poor whites, elevating the Negro to the level of a socially conscious citizen threatened all that was common and familiar.[60] The idea of being equal to or less than the Negro drove whites to unimaginable acts of violence, including lynching, to reclaim what they had lost in the Civil War and Reconstruction: ignorance of their common humanity with other human beings.[61] Whites had been exposed as the victims of a cruel joke: they were no better than the next man, unless, of course, they imagined themselves to be so. Some would rather drape an American flag around a dog and call it a citizen than concede that the Negro was a human being deserving of citizenship.

By the time of Reconstruction, the image of the black man as inherently inferior, ignorant, and hopelessly corrupt was no longer universally applicable. Education was quickly becoming the most accessible way to shed the weight of history and the myth of white supremacy; it empowered former slaves to imagine a future of freedom and prosperity. This proposition was difficult for white men—both the wealthy elite and the illiterate poor—to accept. The race-based social, economic, and political hierarchy at the foundation of American society in general and Southern society in particular was changing before their eyes and shifting under their feet. If blacks could read, write, and discuss the finer elements of government and politics, how could they be ignorant and backward and at the bottom of society? Black education was a direct threat to white identity, citizenship, and power, and those whites who were unable to accept this break from tradition threatened to plunge Kentucky into a race war.

On December 18, 1865, the Thirteenth Amendment was ratified, and Secretary of State William Henry Seward made it official: slaves in the state of Kentucky were free. Immediately, Kentucky lawmakers began devising ways to derail federally funded and supported reforms advanced by the Freedmen's Bureau. By February 1866, the Kentucky General Assembly adopted the following measure, creating a special fund to pay for the education of black children:

> All taxes hereafter collected from negroes and mulattoes in this Commonwealth shall be set apart as a separate fund for their use, one-half, if necessary, to go to the support of their paupers, and the remainder to the education of their children.
>
> In addition to the tax already levied a tax of two dollars shall be levied on every male negro and mulatto over the age of eighteen years, and, when paid into the treasury, shall go into the fund aforesaid.
>
> The trustees of each school district may cause a separate school to be taught in their district for the education of the Negro and mulatto children, to be conducted and reported as other schools are; and when this is done, they shall receive their proportion of the fund set apart in this act for that purpose.
>
> No part of said fund shall ever be appropriated otherwise than pursuant to this act, in aid of common schools for negroes and mulattoes.[62]

In theory, this measure would have established a formal education system for black children in Kentucky, as well as a fund to care for "paupers"—aged and debilitated former slaves who were unable to find work and support themselves. In practice, however, the monies collected were not used for black education; they were spent on white schools and disbursed to former slave owners to compensate them for their losses and help them support older blacks still living on their property. Monies left over were absorbed into the general state fund, never to be recovered.[63]

As a direct consequence of the abuse of the so-called Negro Fund, the black community rallied to address this miscarriage of justice. For some, the Civil War was still alive and kicking, and black folks were prepared to defend their position alone, if need be; however, they understood that without the help of the Federal government, their chances for success were limited. Those opposed to the Thirteenth Amendment sought to unravel blacks' transition from slaves o free citizens by any means possible. Allies of the freedmen understood the power behind the ability to read a book, understand the law, and exercise the right to vote. Those invested in the process of black citizenship and suffrage recognized a moral obligation to see justice served.

General Oliver O. Howard, commissioner of the Freedmen's Bureau, promoted Negro suffrage and education to ensure that former slaves became functional citizens of the United States.[64] Howard was certainly aware of the conspiracy against him in the White House. Early on, President Andrew Johnson used the Freedmen's Bureau as a political whipping boy to denounce the radical Republicans as a "new set of slave-masters . . . [who,] under this new system" of Reconstruction, would work blacks as if they were slaves, at the expense of the Federal government, and keep any financial benefit to themselves, at the cost of the taxpayers.[65] Johnson attempted to appeal to white Southerners by undermining and threatening to scuttle the push for black enfranchisement, arguing that "already the colored man had gained his freedom during the war, and if he and the poor white came into competition at the ballot-box, a 'war of races' would result."[66] In reality, that war had already begun. The battlefronts were set: the schoolroom and the ballot box.

Johnson vetoed the freedman's bill, which would have extended Federal protections to African Americans in the South, in an effort to ensure the enforcement of blacks' rights. This led to a debate in Washington that was settled by Congress on April 9, 1866, with passage of the Civil Rights Act.[67] Lincoln Republicans recognized President Johnson's ploy to undermine one of the main goals of Reconstruction: citizenship and suffrage for former slaves. Johnson's sympathetic policy toward the South and negrophobes, as well as his own racism, presented a challenge to General Howard and his Freedmen's Bureau. Still, the "Christian general's" strong conviction about doing what was right and moral guided his steps. Howard's purpose was to create a vehicle by which citizenship rights could be obtained by black men who had remained steadfast in their pursuit of education and temperance and understood the true meaning of citizenship. Only this, Howard believed, would right the injustices of slavery and the exclusion of blacks as an inferior class of people. As Reconstruction moved into high gear, members of the African American community looked to the Freedmen's Bureau as the gateway to first-class citizenship.

General Howard's persistence, along with that of his assistant commissioner of Tennessee and Kentucky, General Clinton Fisk, assured blacks that slavery was, in fact, "a dead letter."[68] Yet, even with the support of the Freedmen's Bureau and the American Missionary Association, black education in the South proceeded slowly and sporadically. However, in cities such as Louisville and Lexington, where the black church was strong and the black community resilient, education was directly connected to the destiny of African Americans—especially the aspiring class of professionals who assumed leadership.

One of the most impressive schools in Kentucky was the Howard School, which opened in Lexington in the fall of 1866. Through the fund-raising efforts of black women such as Laura Britton, Arrena Turner, and Theodorcia Scroggins, the tuition-free school was opened in the Ladies Hall on Church Street, the building having been purchased by some of the city's prominent black leaders.[69] Supplied with teachers, materials, and funding from the Freedmen's Bureau and the AMA and money from the Negro Fund, the Howard School was the premier institution of black learning in Lexington.[70] In its first year of operation, the 500 students enrolled were instructed by three teachers: Sarah B. Todd, Dora Brooks, and J. H. Phillips. The AMA later hired Belle Mitchell to teach and to be an example of an intellectually challenging, morally sound, and community-oriented "colored" citizen.[71]

Samuel C. Hale, an instructor from South Carolina, was hired to enhance the teaching corps at the Howard School. Appointed assistant superintendent of education for Kentucky by General Howard, Hale would be responsible for implementing a number of advances in the education of Lexington's black children. Certainly, Hale's appeal was closely connected to the documented success of the all-black Saxton School under the supervision of Francis L. Car-

dozo, a mulatto educator who constructed a curriculum to support
the ongoing development of black children in the South with well-
qualified black teachers.[72] In the September issue of the *American
Missionary*, Hale writes of his arrival in Lexington, his interaction
with the teaching staff, and the community's reaction to the education of black children. Most important, he accounts for the changing political environment of Lexington, which had swung in favor
of funding for the freedmen's schools:

> Our colored school board applied to the trustees and county
> school commissioner, and they agreed to so far recognize us as
> teaching one of the public schools in the city, as to draw for us
> the share of public funds coming from taxes upon colored peo-
> ple, and over five hundred dollars came into the hands of the
> treasurer of our school board, who, after paying bills for coal
> and repairs, turned over near $300 to the A.M.A. Though this
> is but a small part of the cost of supporting so large a school,
> yet, it is a step in the right direction—the beginning of a sup-
> port of common schools by tax, and as such we rejoice in it.
>
> Our school building, located on what is known in Lexing-
> ton as Church St., is a brick structure, and answers our pur-
> pose well, so far as it goes. The chief alterations needed are to
> make the larger rooms smaller by folding doors and to have
> them better supplied with more convenient seats. Our seats are
> without desks, and writing has been taught by classes—a few
> desks being provided for the purpose at one end of the large
> upper room.
>
> A school house bell is very much needed to secure prompt-
> ness in our scholars. Will some friend send us one?
>
> We feel that successful schools are reconstructing the pow-
> er of Kentucky and such we must have at Lexington.[73]

Hale's tenure at the Howard School lasted only two years (he moved
to Cleveland, Ohio, and opened a country store), but he contributed
tremendously to the development of Lexington's African American
community, and many of the children he taught would achieve great

things in the latter part of the nineteenth century. Unfortunately, Hale's efforts to move the race forward would be forgotten by the end of the century, a casualty of the times.

The official records of the Freedmen's Bureau show that between 1866 and the end of 1867, the thirteen schools in Kentucky funded by the bureau had close to 10,000 students enrolled. The Howard School could boast of having at least 1,121 black students during that same period. In December 1868 Oberlin graduate John G. Hamilton joined the staff of the Howard School as its principal, after serving in the same capacity at the Ely Normal School in Louisville for six months. We do not know the reason for his short tenure at the Ely School, but reports from T. K. Noble, assistant to the chief superintendent of schools, document Hamilton's early success in Lexington.[74] Unfortunately, Hamilton's long-term impact on the Lexington community would be connected to his position as cashier for the Freedmen's Bank and the drama that followed the financial crash of 1873 and the bank's collapse in 1874.

Besides the Howard School, there were five other schools in Lexington that served the educational needs of African American children and adults. Under Hale's guidance, the number of schools in Kentucky grew exponentially between 1867 and 1869, especially in the larger cities and more populated areas, where teachers could be recruited and whites tolerated the presence of an educated black populace. Still, the black leadership constantly lobbied for state support; they organized themselves into a powerful body politic capable of arguing for the needs of the black masses. One of the most impressive demonstrations of this emerging power occurred in the summer of 1869.

On July 14 in Louisville, Kentucky, more than 2,000 people jammed the streets between Fourth and Jefferson, near the Benson Theater, to attend the Colored Educational Convention. The stifling 100-degree temperature did not deter those concerned about the future of their children and the race from attending one of the most important public meetings held in postbellum Kentucky.[75] The standing-room-only crowd was anxiously anticipating the speechifying of prominent guests from around the country, including the

Reverend John G. Fee, black Civil War veteran and civil rights activist Martin Delany, and distinguished black representative of the Federal government John Mercer Langston. At 2:00 that afternoon, one of the main organizers, Colonel Benjamin Runkle of the Freedmen's Bureau, addressed the impressive crowd: "You have come up through oppression, darkness and slavery to civil liberty," he began. "And you are yet to be respected by all the good people of this country. Gathered together as you are, with labor and education for your motto, and justice and equal rights as your aim, you must succeed, and I know you will yet become equal to any people within the domain of the land—the home of all the oppressed of the earth." The sweltering mass of black folks received Runckle's words with the enthusiasm of a revival; applause and shouts of "Amen" followed his remarks as he sat and listened attentively to the rest of the program.[76]

There were 230 delegates present at the convention, representing almost every county in the state. Lexington's contingency included Henry King, James Turner, John Tandy, and E. R. Wells. The delegates endured the oppressive conditions in the hope of ensuring the education and full citizenship of all black Kentuckians and ending the violence against them. After the formal nomination and election of officials, including the selection of King and Tandy as vice presidents and Wells as the sergeant at arms, the president-elect, Elder H. J. Young of the Quinn Chapel of Louisville, addressed the assemblage. He reminded those present why they had come together under the banner of Christian brotherhood, justice, and the future of the race. Young suggested that the "two most important duties of the Convention was to petition the United States Congress to make further appropriations for the education of the colored people in Kentucky; and second, to petition the State Legislature to give them assistance."[77]

On day two of the convention, while the delegates and wordsmiths agonized over language, intent, and a united vision for the future, spectators in the Benson Theater were treated to a magnificent display of oration by several speakers, including John Mercer Langston (the great-uncle of Langston Hughes). A man possessing tremendous knowledge of politics, culture, and human nature, Langston wove a tapestry composed of notions of their collective destiny, using their emancipation from slavery as a point of departure for his discussion of the direction in which "the race" was heading. Recalling the 20,000 slaves gathered outside Louisville on the Fourth of July, 1865, to hear General John Palmer read the Emancipation Proclamation and declare them free men and women, and the sound of those men and women thanking God for deliverance, Langston reminded his audience that the journey was far from over. The current denials of their citizenship, their right to a quality progressive education, and their right to testify in court were battles yet to be fought. More important, they were battles that needed to be won. Indeed, the future of the race hinged on what he identified as the true "test of equality," which he believed, quite plainly, was achievement. Langston argued that there "has been no change made by God since our emancipation. No man is called of the brotherhood that is not equal in the measure of arms, of muscles, in the measure of bodily strength, in demonstration of vigorous intellect." For Langston, equality was not a status conferred by men based on socially constructed definitions; it was a common humanity shaped by the "hands of his Maker."[78]

On the final day of the convention, the executive board read the seven resolutions that, among other things, demanded equal representation, support for education, and protection under the law. The resolutions also recognized the benevolent societies that supported the freedmen and their transition from slavery to freedom. Finally, the delegates implored the young men and youth of the state of Kentucky to "learn trades and engage in agricultural pursuits as a proper mode of supporting themselves and giving encouragement to mechanics and agriculture," which would provide for their families.[79] Besides the unified position taken in the resolutions, what stood out was the unity demonstrated by the 230 delegates from across the state who had come together to serve the social and political needs of African Americans. At the end of the three-day conference, spectators in attendance, especially those from urban parts of the state, had been whipped into a jubilant frenzy of anticipation: they would gain access to education for their children and themselves, win the franchise, and be recognized as fully vested Americans. Unlike the spectators, however, the reform-minded delegates knew their job was not over. The hard part would be convincing the Kentucky legislature of the merits of providing access to equal education, establishing viable businesses to support the development of an independent class of freedmen, and giving them a political voice. For the freedmen, achievement might be the true "test of equality," but resilience and vigilance would be the true test of courage and manhood.

## Eternal Striving as the Price of Liberty and Success

If the success of the 1869 Colored Educational Convention was an indicator of the will of black Kentuckians, the same could be said of the Colored Fair Association, founded in the fall of the same year. Within a month of the Louisville convention and four days after the solar eclipse of August 7, 1869, two of Lexington's convention delegates, Henry King and James Turner (one of the men responsible for acquiring the building for the Howard School), assembled African American leaders from their community to create a business in support of the resolutions proposed during the Colored Educational Convention. W. D. Johnson describes the founding of the Colored Fair Association:

> On August 11, 1869, a mass meeting was held at Ladies' Hall in the city of Lexington. Henry King, from his active and earnest work and enthusiasm in the enterprise, was made Chairman, and Henry Britton, Secretary. The object of the meeting being stated by the chairman a permanent organization was formed. Henry King was elected President; H. H. Harvey, Vice President; James Turner, Treasurer; Henry Scroggins, Secretary; and a Board of Directors, consisting of five members, James Harvey, Thomas Slaughter, George Perry, E. G. Smoot and Theodore Clay. These were the first to be thus honored by this enterprise.[80]

At the initial meeting, the board developed a mission and vision for the organization, which was no doubt directly in line with the Louisville convention's mandate to change the circumstances of colored people throughout the state of Kentucky. The members decided to offer a limited number of shares, at $10 per share, to outside investors; this not only expanded the funds available to the organization but also allowed individuals to invest their hard-earned money in the development of their community. Indeed, in addition to using their capital to expand opportunities for freedmen in the region, the board created a tool for racial uplift and local pride.[81]

Under the leadership of Henry King, George Perry, James Turner, and Henry Scroggins, the organization generated the necessary momentum to demonstrate racial progress in agricultural and mechanical enterprises, animal husbandry, and entrepreneurship, giving Lexington the prestige of being the most successful black community in the state. The association's first fair was held October 6 to 9 on rented land outside Lexington, near Newtown Pike Road. From all accounts, the event was a success, showcasing local produce and livestock raised by black farmers; women's proficiency in preserving, baking, sewing, and knitting; and an array of entertainments, ranging from horse and trotting races, band performances, and speakers—most of whom pontificated on the importance of republican values, temperance, and gaining the vote. Although exact numbers are unavailable, evidence suggests that between 2,000 and 6,000 visitors attended the fair over the four-day period, with an estimated net profit of $1,368.[82]

Over the course of twenty-five years, the breadth and depth of Lexington's Colored Fair Association grew, attracting tens of thousands of visitors to the Bluegrass to witness one of the finest displays of achievement "among the Afro-American race."[83] In ways both intended and unintended, the entire African American community benefited from the annual fairs. Exhibitors displayed their wares, crops, and skills, competing for hundreds of dollars in premiums; the city's hack drivers, porters, food and drink hawkers, and artisans plied their trades and generated income. Certainly, black business leaders took advantage of the annual fairs to generate income, demonstrate their usefulness in industry and agriculture, and distinguish themselves from the less reliable and less vigilant. The lead-

ership of Lexington's Colored Fair Association promoted eternal
striving as the price of liberty and success.[84] By the end of the 1860s,
black Lexington was coming alive, and individuals were working together to increase their communal wealth.

By 1869, America Murphy had made the transition from a rural
to an urban existence. Records show that between 1866 and 1869,
America moved her family from one end of the city to the other,
no doubt in search of stability. After leaving the Jordans' home on
Third Street and Corporate Line, she moved to 17 Jordan's Row;[85]
apparently, America moved her family as often as needed to maintain a roof over their heads. Over that four-year period, Isaac might
have attended one or more of the schools in Lexington: the Howard School, on Church Street between Upper and Mulberry; the
school at Pleasant Baptist Church, on the southeast corner of Lower
and Maxwell; the Talbott School, on Upper Street between Third
and Fourth Streets; the First African Baptist Church school, in the
building on the southwest corner of Short and Dewees; the Methodist Episcopal church school, on the south side of Water Street near
Ayres Alley; or the Christian church school on Fourth, between Upper and Mulberry.

In the fall of 1867 the Howard School had more than 500
students attending classes, and six-year-old Isaac might have been
among them. Through the guidance of Howard's qualified teaching
staff, children like Isaac had every opportunity to develop a deep
sense of morality and discipline, while acquiring the virtuous character traits needed to succeed. Most important, teachers such as
Samuel Hale and Belle Mitchell would have reinforced the lessons
Isaac's mother had instilled in him during the waning years of slavery and after their move to Lexington.

There is documentation that on April 19, 1869, America applied for her late husband's pension through the Pension Bureau
Office in Lexington.[86] Unfortunately, we do not know whether she
could support her claim to the bureau's satisfaction. Indeed, because
slave marriages were not recognized as legal and binding, and because of the complex nature of slavery, former slaves might have

several spouses and numerous children from different relationships. Therefore, a pension claim for a black Civil War soldier likely required a rigorous examination of the facts. If she managed to prove her claim through an array of self-generated and corresponding documentation—applications, letters from character witnesses, and affidavits—America would have received payments of $10 a month—a significant amount of money for a woman trying to survive in a postslavery society where friends could be hard to come by.

As noted earlier, sometime between the winter of 1868 and the spring of 1869, America's daughter died. Tax records indicate that America, one child, and a male over the age twenty-one lived together at an undisclosed residence in Lexington. There are two plausible explanations for this living arrangement. The first is that America found a new male companion, and she and her son took up residence with him. This could have been Simon Williams, who is listed on the 1870 census as the head of household at the First Ward residence where America, three of her siblings (Anne, James, and another sister named Anne), and her son Isaac all lived. Williams, a Civil War veteran who had served in the Twelfth U.S. Colored Heavy Artillery at the Battle of Richmond, returned to Camp Nelson at the end of the war to await his discharge from the army. There is a good chance that America knew Williams from Camp Nelson. After mustering out on April 4, 1866, Williams likely arrived in Lexington and became acquainted (or reacquainted) with America. With both of them seeking shelter and companionship, they may have decided to move in together.

The second explanation is that America, who had been born in Lexington, reunited with her father, Green Murphy. Evidence suggests that Green was none other than Jeremiah Murphy, the white livery stable owner who, years earlier, had defended preacher London Ferrill from Harry Quills. One of the first innkeepers in Lexington, Jeremiah Murphy established his business on Mulberry Street in 1806. Within ten years, he purchased several pieces of property throughout the Bluegrass, including a stable "next to the county jail," where he maintained horses for leisure and business activities.[87] Although not on record as a turfman of any significance, he was involved in the early development of the industry west of the Allegheny Mountains.[88] In 1834 he sold a portion of his landholdings to the Kentucky Association, established to "improve the breed of horses by encouraging the sports of the turf."[89] Records from 1840 indicate that a Jeremiah Murphy owned three female slaves on his Scott County farm, right outside Lexington, near Georgetown Pike. One of these women might have been a slave named Anne, America's mother.

In the 1859 *Lexington Directory*, Jeremiah Murphy is listed as the proprietor of a livery stable on the east side of Mulberry between Main and High Streets.[90] Based on the location of his stable, his involvement with horses, and his long history in the Lexington community, he likely had access to the living accommodations at 17 Jordan's Row (where America moved with her family), the building that once housed Henry Clay's law office and would later house the offices of Benjamin Gratz (B. G.) Bruce's *Kentucky Livestock Record*, an early authority on Thoroughbreds and horse racing. What is more, Murphy owned the lot near Cedar and Broadway that America would eventually purchase. Thus, it seems likely that Jeremiah and Green Murphy were one and the same—and America's father— and he was probably the adult male living with her in 1869. Besides shelter and protection, this arrangement would have allowed eight-year-old Isaac to get to know his grandfather, listen to his stories from the past, and ask questions about his family: Who were his relatives? What was his grandmother like? And perhaps other, more uncomfortable questions about race, slavery, and the selling of human beings. We will never know, but this void in the historical narrative is ripe for inquiry.

Based on different accounts, we have an image of Green Murphy as a central figure in the everyday life of early antebellum Lexington. An acquaintance of Robert Todd, Henry Clay, and John Wesley Hunt, Murphy was a businessman who loved horses. He was probably responsible for introducing Isaac to horses and discussing the beautiful beasts with the boy. One might assume that having a grandfather who wanted him to become a jockey—a story corroborated by Eli Jordan—shaped Isaac's destiny. But it is reasonable to believe that because of his small size, he eventually would have been recruited by turfmen to ride their horses as an exercise boy. Clearly, living in Lexington—one of the centers of Thoroughbred horses and racing prior to the Civil War—provided the perfect opportunity for Isaac to pursue a career as a jockey. It is possible that in addition to encouraging Isaac's career, Green Murphy influenced his work ethic and character, helping to make Isaac the exemplar of virtue and eloquence he would be known for.

In addition to his grandfather, young Isaac was watched over by his mother, his other kinfolk, and community members who knew that the temptations and distractions of urban life could easily lead even the most well-mannered child astray, into a world of frivolity and mischief. In Lexington, the burgeoning black community worked hard to establish the infrastructure necessary to support the concept of respectability as an invaluable currency gained through education, temperance, and achievement. This infrastructure functioned to communicate a sense of success that all could admire and aspire to. In other words, Murphy's future success as a jockey, how he carried himself, and how he was perceived by his peers were connected to the sense of racial destiny being infused in the first generation of black children able to attend school and grow to maturity with confidence in the Bluegrass region.

In promoting achievement as the credo for gaining full citizenship, African American leaders sought to inculcate a feeling of racial destiny that inspired a healthy enthusiasm for self-reliance, education, and political activism. Most important, this sense of racial destiny was supported by the independence that developed when black individuals created businesses and participated in fraternal organizations and churches, all of which allowed black Lexingtonians to establish and maintain a strong, progressive sense of community at the beginning of Reconstruction.[91] Within the context of racial destiny and the ideology of respectability, black churches and their leaders promoted education for children and work as a noble endeavor for adult males, policing their members to deter any unsavory activities that might damage the race or diminish the progress made. In extolling the benefits of temperance, frugality, and hard work, the black leaders of Lexington kept an eye toward the future, even though a majority of former slaves lived in the present and had little understanding of what racial destiny entailed. Who could blame them for their lack of enthusiasm for self-reliance, education, and political awareness when they still had nothing to show for their newly acquired freedom? What is more, this sense of racial destiny was supported by members of the aspiring class, those who emerged from the embers of slavery with at least some power, based on their proximity to the elite.[92]

As a subscriber to the ideology of respectability, America Murphy found work as a laundress for several white families in Lexington. Recognizing that the fast-paced urban environment was not conducive to her son's full acceptance of the values that she and the more progressive members of her community considered necessary for his future development as a man, America made choices to protect her son's future. In the shadows of the 1869 solar eclipse, America was no doubt awed by the spectacle of the moment, and perhaps she found a renewed sense of purpose. Indeed, from the silence and the darkness, a new day was dawning for America and Isaac. He was her reason for living, and eventually, he would become her greatest achievement.

# 5

# The New Order of Things

## *1870–1874*

On the day after New Year's 1870, three to four feet of snow blanketed central Kentucky—the heaviest snowfall in the state's history. Whiteness enveloped the countryside, and in the clear, predawn sky following the storm, an aurora borealis was visible as far south as Lexington.[1] This was an unusual occurrence in the Bluegrass, and only those rising before the sun crested the Allegheny Mountains in the east would have witnessed the natural phenomenon.[2] On the morning in question, between the hours of 3:00 and 5:00, farmers in central Kentucky would have been starting their days, tending to livestock, milking cows, and gathering eggs from chicken coops. They would have mused over the dancing streaks of bluish-green light in the northern sky. Most did not understand that charged particles ejected from the sun and carried by the solar winds caused these magnificent displays, which were usually visible only in the Far North, in places like Alaska, Canada, and Iceland. What did it mean to see such a sight so far south? Had the earth's magnetic poles shifted? Had there been some "extreme event," whereby the amount of material ejected from the sun was so massive and powerful that the greenish glow could be seen for more than 3,000 miles? Whatever the farmers might have thought or wondered, few if any wrote about it, and complete accounts are difficult to find.

Like the farmers, horse trainers, grooms, and stable boys would have been tending to their early-morning chores, ensuring the comfort of the Thoroughbred horses in their care. Primarily black men who were former slaves, these individuals would have been up early enough to see the awe-inspiring bluish-green light in the sky and wonder what was happening to the world. The boys and young men working the stables would have relied on the knowledge and wisdom of the older trainers to explain the meaning of such natural phenomena. To these older men, the sky was a mystery, and its secrets were divine in nature—not meant to be known by men. On the morning in question, an older trainer might have shared stories with his young apprentices about the early days of slavery in Kentucky, when it was believed that if a child entered the world under a sky aglow with fire and light, that child was special and gifted and had the ability to change the fortunes of his people.

Thus, these black men and boys might have seen the northern lights as a sign of the future success of the colts and mares they were preparing for the spring races. In Kentucky, if a horse were born during such a celestial phenomenon and had markings on its coat similar to those in the sky, it would be named to memorialize the event, and each time it won a race, the past event would be recalled with enthusiasm and excitement. The names Comet, Asteroid, and Nebula were not common, but neither were the horses that possessed them. A Thoroughbred horse born under an aurora borealis and marked with a jagged white stripe or blaze on its face might inspire a dramatic name like Aether, the elemental god of the sky. Its particular value and purpose would be tested in April and May on the training tracks and proved in the heat of July and August at the numerous courses throughout Kentucky, the South, the West, and the Northeast. These exhibitions were not limited to demonstrating the strength, resilience, and beauty of the horse and increasing the financial gain and prestige of their owners. These performances were inextricably linked to the reputations of the black trainers who brought them to the line, the black grooms who took care of their needs, and the black jockeys who rode them to their full potential.

In 1826 the Kentucky Association, dedicated to the development of agriculture and livestock, was founded by a group of prominent farmers, politicians, and businessmen, all of whom were breeders or patrons of central Kentucky's Thoroughbred horses and owners of slaves. The combination of land, capital, and slave labor had ensured that horse breeding played an important part in the development of the state, and the association's primary objective was clear: "To improve the breed of horses by encouraging the sport of the turf."[3] While serving as an outlet for members' leisure activities, the association also promoted the various interests of the farms and factories located on the outskirts of Lexington's bustling urban environment. Central Kentucky produced Thoroughbred horses, livestock, hemp, tobacco, and, prior to the Civil War, slaves, and Lexington's politically powerful sought to expand the market for these goods and services beyond the state line. Elisha Warfield, John Wesley Hunt, General Leslie Combs, Dr. Benjamin W. Dudley, John Brand, and John Boswell—the same men responsible for establishing the Kentucky Association—would charter the Lexington and Ohio Railroad in 1830, with the dual purpose of creating a more reliable means of transportation and promoting trade with northern markets and beyond.[4]

After four years of political, sectional, and environmental challenges, the initial rail line was completed as far as Frankfort, Kentucky, linking the capital to one of the state's most productive centers for economic development and providing a more efficient means of transporting central Kentucky politicians to and from their seats of power.[5] Unfortunately, the rail line would take another forty years to complete, as the politics involved in constructing a railroad to Louisville proved more of a hindrance than first imagined. In addition, the outbreak of the Civil War in 1861 killed such projects until peace was established during Reconstruction.

In spite of these events, the Kentucky Association and its mission to improve the horses of the Bluegrass continued to flourish, thanks to the innovations of men such as Robert A. Alexander of

Woodburn Farms in Woodford County. Alexander's operation became the model for horse farms throughout the United States. With
the assistance of head trainer Ansel Williamson and a dozen or so
other black men serving as grooms and jockeys, Woodburn Farms
brought more than a few champions to the line each spring, including the famed Asteroid, son of Lexington. Indeed, from 1857 until
well after Alexander's death in 1867, Woodburn Farms reigned as
the pride of the Bluegrass, a jewel in the crown of central Kentucky.

By January 1870, a significant number of dramatic events had
occurred in and around Lexington, making the appearance of the
aurora borealis seem appropriate. Like the solar eclipse of August
1869, the northern lights may have led some residents of the Bluegrass to theorize that change was again on the horizon. Others may
have seen the aurora borealis as a sign of the philosophical shift taking place in Kentucky, with black men gaining access to citizenship
and securing the right to vote with ratification of the Fourteenth
and Fifteenth Amendments. Obviously, Kentucky was not physically
shifting to the geographic North, but the state was becoming more
Northern in its philosophy. It had reestablished itself as a stronghold for the party of Lincoln, as black men found their political
voices and were encouraged by their white Republican friends to exercise their rights as citizens as frequently as possible. In contrast,
many other white Kentuckians, both rich and poor, were vehement-
ly and violently opposed to "Negro suffrage" and wrapped themselves in the garb of "lost cause" identity politics, refusing to accept
the changes occurring in Kentucky and throughout the South.[6]

The fact that Kentucky blacks were free, had gained the rights
and privileges of citizenship, and were on the verge of attaining suffrage challenged the core beliefs of whites who saw themselves as
superior to people of African origin, regardless of their proven ability to rise above their previous status as human chattel. These white
men worked hard to deny black rights by systematically punishing
those African Americans with social, political, and economic aspirations. Blacks, along with white politicians, business owners, and
average citizens who favored changes to the status quo, became the
targets for these disillusioned and disoriented white men, most of

whom still suffered from the trauma of losing the Civil War and held on to the notion that white male power required black subjugation at the institutional and communal levels. Unable or, in some cases, outright unwilling to accept the inevitability of change, these men continued to fight the war of rebellion on the local front; they fought to maintain the American principles ordained by the founding fathers, who had claimed the divine right of white men over the land and promoted white dominance over the Negro as necessary to the development of the country and a truly authentic American identity.[7]

To be sure, by 1870, the city of Lexington was in the midst of a revolution. Led by ministers, newly empowered black men, and hardworking black women, Lexington's black community was alive with the pulse of progress and hungry for the promises made to those who were willing to trust the often maligned political process of self-government in this "new order of things." Although a small sample of articles from various Kentucky newspapers might lead one to believe that few blacks understood the power being bestowed on them through the Fifteenth Amendment, one article in particular illustrates that some leaders of the black community were well aware of its significance. In the *Kentucky Statesman*, black leaders from Frankfort called for a "Colored Men's Convention":

We, the colored citizens of the city of Frankfort, have duly considered the condition of our people throughout the State of Kentucky, and knowing as we do that there are many of our people not aroused to what is being done, and that there is a great work before us and a great responsibility resting upon us—knowing the intentions of our good Democratic friends who have for years been battling against the colored men, depriving us of the rights of citizens, depriving us of that which we gained at the point of a bayonet, denouncing us ignorant and incapable of self government. In view of these things, we, as a committee, with the right invested in us by the popular will of all the colored citizens of the city, at a public meeting held on the 24th, call a State Convention to meet in the city of

Frankfort on the 23rd day of February, 1870, to discuss and prosecute means appertaining to the political issues of the day, and to the vital interest of our race throughout the State. Each county is authorized to send three delegates to each thousand population. Each delegate is advised to come prepared to defray his personal expenses of the Convention. There will be due notice given by sending circulars all over the State. We hope all loyal editors will publish this article throughout the State.[8]

Clearly, blacks throughout the state of Kentucky were ready to act to secure their right to vote and claim their share of the American franchise.

For young Isaac Burns Murphy, Lexington was the perfect place to grow up. It was a place where radical black thought and action originated; it was a place where a young black boy could develop an identity grounded in the communally supported philosophy of self-reliance, achievement, and prosperity. By choosing to remain in Lexington, America Murphy exposed her son to a community participating in the great movement to reconstruct the body politic of the United States to include blacks as valuable citizens and contributors. The question, however, was how to accomplish this in a state that had been both pro-Union and Southern during the Civil War,[9] and where a majority of white men still claimed to be superior to blacks. This would be the challenge for aspiring blacks and their hopeful yet naïve offspring.

By mid-August 1870, nine-year-old Isaac and his mother were living in the First Ward, in the Lower Street cluster of homes set aside for African American inhabitants.[10] According to the 1870 U.S. census, America and Isaac had taken the last name of Simon Williams, a day laborer who was listed as the head of the household. Whether this was a loving marriage or one of convenience, a physical relationship between two consenting adults in need of companionship, or a mistake on the part of the census taker in assuming that Simon and America were husband and wife will never be known. Also living at the same residence were three other adults—Anne, James, and another woman named Anne, all with the last name Murphy—perhaps America's siblings. According to the census data, all the adults worked, with the exception of the older Anne, who was twenty-five and was listed as keeping house, and America, who was recorded as being twenty-nine years old (according to other records, her actual age was closer to thirty-nine) and was listed as being "at home."

Of those living at the residence, only Isaac and America were literate, which meant they were able to read and write. Simon Williams could read, probably a result of being stationed at Camp Nelson and taking advantage of the education provided by the American Missionary Association. The census also reveals that Isaac attended school in 1870. Based on the location of their residence, he probably attended the school at Pleasant Green Baptist Church, where the pastor, the Reverend Morrison M. Bell, taught the day school to supplement his income.[11] Along with the other children, many of whom also lived in the Lower Street cluster of homes, Isaac would have been drilled with Bible lessons and challenged to memorize the Ten Commandments and other passages.

Whether America Murphy was religious is not known. However, it is safe to say that she, like a majority of blacks during this period in American history, understood the power and purpose of religion to ease the physical and psychological pain of the past, the unpredictable present, and unknown future. It is unclear whether she attended Sunday services regularly or evening prayer meetings on Wednesdays or Fridays. Nor do we know whether she participated in the various church activities that helped maintain the stability of the black community. Chances are good that she did. Because she did not work outside the home, America had the opportunity to be an active member of the church, to volunteer at the Sabbath school held on Saturday mornings, or to take part in Reverend Bell's program for the moral education of black children, giving her a sense of purpose within her community.

As part of Lexington's radically progressive and politically active black community, America may have attended the Republican Club meetings held on Saturday nights at Pleasant Green Baptist Church. There, she would have learned about the importance of maintaining a politically active community and utilizing the power gained through the Civil War amendments, as well as the usefulness of white Republican friends such as William Cassius Goodloe, a former politician and editor of the *Kentucky Statesman*. Goodloe's efforts to represent the issues of the African American community in the pages of his biweekly newspaper advanced awareness of the political process, which would be essential to constructing and broadening ideas about freedom, equality, and citizenship. Another critical supporter of the black community was John G. Hamilton, the superintendent of colored schools and principal of the Howard School. In addition to advocating the education of black children, Hamilton helped the freedmen save their money and acquire home mortgages. On November 8, 1870, Hamilton opened a branch of the National Savings Bank and Trust Company, also known as the Freedmen's Bank, on the corner of Upper and Church Streets. General D. S. Goodloe, William's brother, served as chairman of the bank's advisory board, consisting of A. M. Barnes, Colonel John A. Prall, W. S. Taylor, the Reverend James Monroe, and Henry King (secretary).[12] As both cashier of the bank and superintendent of the colored schools, Hamilton was responsible and held accountable for the black community's financial and educational development.

Another valuable ally was Llewellyn P. Tarleton Jr., a well-known lawyer and politician who would become editor of the *Kentucky Statesman* in 1871 and secretary for the committee exploring the development of the railroad through Lexington. By all accounts, he was capable of great leadership and stamina, but as a defender of African American rights and privileges, he was exceptional; the pages of the *Statesman* resonated with his viewpoints and opinions on the rights of African Americans. In 1883 Tarleton would argue before the U.S. Supreme Court on behalf of John Bush, a black man accused of murdering Annie Van Meter, the daughter of a farmer. According to Tarleton, Bush had not received a fair trial in Kentucky in 1879, and his case was one of the first heard by the Court regarding the denial of black rights under the Fourteenth Amendment.[13]

Prior to ratification of the Fifteenth Amendment, black women focused their activities on the issues that concerned them most:

the villainous activities of the Ku Klux Klan and the lynching of black men, the need for safe working environments, the acceptance of blacks' testimony against whites, and the education of black children. After the amendment's ratification, even though black women were still excluded from voting, they influenced the eligible male voters in their community and damned those black men who cast their lot with the Democratic Party for self-serving reasons.[14] Throughout the South, black men who had accepted money or clothes in exchange for voting the Democratic ticket sometimes suffered isolation, humiliation, and, in the most extreme cases, death at the hands of those blacks who believed black Democrats were race traitors who intentionally worked against the progress of the race.[15] In Lexington, Democrats attempted to appeal to black voters' memories of their slave past, when life was "simpler" for the Negro, or they threatened to take away jobs if blacks did not vote for the white man's party.[16] It is unclear to what extent Democrat-supporting blacks were abused by their community, but they likely saw the folly of their decision to endorse those who would reenslave a freedom-loving people.

Meetings to address the political questions of the day were well attended by the black men and women who represented Lexington's colored community. At these gatherings, the city's politically active and politically powerful assembled to express their "gratitude" as well as their "grievances."[17] Reverend Bell, like his fellow pastors serving black congregations, worked hard to keep the faithful focused on the Christian teachings of temperance, humility, and brotherhood. Churches were places where noble examples of muscular Christianity were rewarded with praise and identified as paragons of exceptional virtue. Bell's church provided not only a spiritual home for America and her family but also role models of acceptable male behavior for Isaac.

## A Community of Strivers

A year before relocating to the Lower Street enclave, America and Isaac lived at 17 Jordan's Row, near the corner of Short and Upper Streets and across from the county courthouse, also known as

Cheapside. Black people had once been sold at Cheapside, but now, in the middle of Reconstruction, the monthly livestock sales were coming under the scrutiny of the more cosmopolitan Lexingtonians, who were interested in creating a less odiferous business district, void of its agrarian and slave past. Within a six-block radius of the residence on Jordan's Row were more than a dozen black business-es, and some of the most prominent members of Lexington's black community lived within walking distance of the Cheapside market.

Blacks were scattered throughout the central part of the city but were becoming exceedingly concentrated in the suburbs of the First, Second, and Third Wards. Sensing the anxious if not alto-gether paternalistic gaze of whites, whose philanthropy and power-ful political connections had lifted some of the barriers to progress, members of the black community who lived near the courthouse were compelled to move from their former rental homes into hous-ing projects built on the periphery of downtown Lexington, beyond the view of the white elite. Still, even as the black community be-gan spreading out east and north of the courthouse, as well as south across the railroad tracks past Vine Street, white men maintained control through surveillance, real estate development, and political manipulation.

Despite a depressed if not outright anemic economy, a few of the 7,215 African American inhabitants were able to establish so-cial, political, and economic footholds in the postbellum city of more than 14,000. Black businesses, many of which had been established before emancipation, gained a new clientele during Reconstruction and were able to take advantage of the growing population, espe-cially on Hunt's Row, or Vine Street—the "black main street."[18] African American businessmen such as Ferdinand Robinson, Isaac Lee, George Tandy, and Henry Scroggins were cornerstones of the black community. Robinson, a mattress manufacturer, provided products and services to all of Lexington. Isaac Lee and George Tandy had a confectioner's shop that sold sweets and bakery items. Henry Scroggins's barbershop on Hunt's Row serviced black men and, quite possibly, white men who were not prejudiced toward the barber's primary clientele. These men were highly regarded for their integrity and sense of purpose—strivers in every sense of the word. Based on their financial success and standing in the community, these four were among the dozen or so black men who formed the community's core leadership, providing advice and direction. Scroggins would be an especially significant contributor to the economic, social, and political development of the community.

In addition to being secretary of the board of directors of Lexington's Colored Fair Association and the future founder and editor of the *American Citizen*, Scroggins was an outspoken member of the Republican Party and an advocate for self-reliance and black empowerment. As chairman of the Colored School Committee, he constantly argued for fair and equal funding for Lexington's black schools and pushed his fellow community leaders to defend black children's right to a quality education. In January 1870 the *Kentucky Statesman* published a letter signed by Scroggins and other black leaders who were dissatisfied with the Lexington School Committee's decision to consider the availability of school aid from other sources before distributing monies from the Negro Fund.[19] They wrote:

There is something wrong somewhere. The officers in Louisville certainly ought to know that there [are] 1500 children in this city. If they don't know, they are certainly well paid to know. The Bureau has not given us any information of any change in regard to the sums of money paid last year. If any change has been made, we have had no official report; and if it remains the same, where does it go? If it still remains the same are only 300 children to be benefitted by it, when three times that amount are thrown in the streets, for that one building will not accommodate more than 300 children. We claim a part of that government money for the poor children, for it is theirs. We are determined to stand up for these children. We now ask are you willing to divide your $200 equally of government money with us for our $1.10 tax money—you having 30 children and we having 400, and perhaps in a short time will have double that number. We hope the School Committee will take good care of our money and employ teachers of good moral character and who have stood an examination before the Commissioner; put them under reasonable pay and dismiss them when they deem it necessary; and visit and pay the same attention to our schools as they do to the city schools. Now let our disputing come to an end, and let us try to better understand each other. We must educate, and when educated, we will have different views and different feelings, and knowledge of a higher sphere of things. Let us work for the masses. As for our white teachers, we have the highest regard. We have been with them four years. They come from good families in the North, are highly cultivated both in manners and religion, and are worthy of the best society—some are graduates of the best colleges of the North. They are noble and high-minded, and such friends of mercy we can never forget. We cannot do without them, nor do we want to be without them while we are so poor and dependent upon their noble charities. We are very thankful to the Christian Society that sent them to us, and who pay them, as we are too poor to do more at the present for ourselves.[20]

Scroggins argued that the five black schools in Lexington served more than 1,500 children, and funding should not be withheld or divided based on a set of rules designed to reward schools favored by the American Missionary Association or the Federal government. Monies intended for all five schools had consistently gone to the one school that was already heavily supported by outside funding. Without their fair share of government funds and county tax funds (from taxes paid by blacks), which altogether would amount to $650, unsupported teachers had to turn away one-third of the community's black children due to a lack of resources. This lack of financial support was unacceptable, given that black men, some of whom did not even have school-aged children, worked hard to make a living and pay their taxes to ensure the education of black children.

Out of necessity, Henry Scroggins and other local African American leaders became politically active, demanding adequate funding for black schools. They rallied to challenge the cavalier policies of the Lexington School Committee, whose members' chil-

dren were not directly affected by the irresponsible decision to withhold funding from needy and deserving schools. The father of two
school-aged children himself, Scroggins understood that education
was the key to their future.

Although we cannot be sure, Isaac Murphy probably attended
the Howard School on Church Street, which was only two blocks
from his residence on Jordan's Row. The pride of Lexington's black
elite, the tuition-free Howard School was sponsored by the American Missionary Association and supported by local benevolent societies. It was considered a model for colored schools throughout the
state; only the Ely School in Louisville was thought to be more advanced. Under the direction of new principal John G. Hamilton, the
teachers of the Howard School worked to ensure that the children
of washerwomen, stable hands, barbers, and farmers were ready to
take their place in a world much different from that of their parents.
In fact, most of the students' parents were illiterate, but they knew
that education and religion were the greatest gifts they could give
their children.

Because the community was dependent on the efforts of all its
members, Isaac would have known of men such as Henry Scroggins,
James Turner, and Henry King—three of the leaders in the fight
for education, access to public accommodations, and all the privileges of citizenship. Other important businessmen in Lexington's
black community were Lawson Hawkins, who ran a grocery store
on Broadway near Main Street, and Nathan Bibbs, whose home-
based storefront was located on Upper and Winslow. These businesses provided necessary goods and services, and their proprietors
served as examples of success and independence. Isaac and America
probably visited all these places of business at one time or another.
Like most children, Isaac would have been especially attracted to the
sugary sweets made by Lee and Tandy, and he may have convinced
his mother he deserved a small piece of candy on their trips down
Vine Street to buy the necessities of daily life.

Feeding the spiritual and educational needs of the black community, and still within a six-block radius of the Murphy home,
were four of the six active black churches in Lexington: First Afri-

can Baptist Church on Short and Dewees, led by the the Reverend
James Monroe; the First Methodist Episcopal Church on West Upper between Second and Mechanic, led by the Reverend G. H. Graham; Independent Baptist Church on Merino and Main, led by the
Reverend Frederick Braxton; and the Christian Church on Fourth
Street between Upper and Mulberry, led by the Reverend Alexander Campbell. In addition to the Howard School on Church Street,
the Talbott School on Upper between Third and Fourth Streets was
within walking distance for Isaac.[21] America and Isaac thus had access to everything they needed, except maybe steady employment.

Before moving to Madison County sometime around the spring
of 1870, Henry and Laura Britton assisted in expanding the possibilities for blacks in Lexington. A barber who served only white men
at his shop near the Broadway Hotel, Britton was able to maintain
his family's finances and lifestyle while developing important relationships with some of the most powerful white men in Lexington.
He participated in organizing the Howard School, and his involvement in the Colored Fair Association helped garner the support of
black community leaders as well as white Republican lawmakers
and landowners, who saw the enterprise as a positive initiative. Over
time, the Colored Fair Association would become one of the most
important endeavors for blacks in and around Lexington, providing
numerous opportunities to expand agricultural businesses, services,
and leisure activities for the tens of thousands of visitors to the Bluegrass each year.[22]

The Colored Fair Association was the brainchild of Henry
King, a house painter who lived on Mill Street between High and
Maxwell Streets. Outspoken, resilient, and an advocate for black
self-reliance, King participated in the initial Colored Educational Convention and provided critical leadership in Lexington's development as a stronghold for Republican activism, cementing the
community's future as an important place for black progress. His
leadership in expanding opportunities for blacks in agricultural and
mechanical industries through education, business, and politics was
both practical and necessary to stimulate his contemporaries' steadfast pursuit of a full life through good works.

Men like Britton, King, Robinson, and Scroggins were examples to black boys like Isaac Murphy. They illustrated what black men were capable of achieving in business and in the community, and they demonstrated the importance of giving back to the community by providing opportunities for others. Indeed, for those men and women poised to claim "freedom, literacy, and political and economic independence," their faith and hope could carry them only so far.[23] To be successful during this period in African American history, one had to be tough, determined, and resilient.

Isaac and the many other young men and boys who witnessed the measured success of their community's elders were not the exclusive beneficiaries of black men's striving for independence. Black women also wanted a better future and strove to improve life's possibilities. America Murphy's work as a washerwoman and domestic servant kept food on the table and Isaac in suitable clothing. We will never know the actual details of how America dealt with the daily realities of nineteenth-century Lexington, but it is safe to assume that some of her experiences were universal among black women in her situation. However, unlike Laura Britton and the wives of Henry Scroggins and James Turner, who were protected from the abuses experienced by black domestic servants and washerwomen, America had to negotiate life in the former slave state where, to a majority of whites, blacks were still considered insignificant yet necessary.

By December 1870, America seems to have parted ways with Simon Williams. Tax records indicate that America Burns (her married name) purchased a lot, valued at $570.50, in the city's First Ward in the Lower Street cluster of homes near Cedar and Broadway, not far from her previous address.[24] The deed book reads:

And at the Special terms of December 1870, an order was entered directing the undersigned to make and execute a Deed of conveyance for said property to America Burns by consent of the said Ferdinand Robinson. Now therefore, this indenture, made and entered into this 3rd day of December 1870 between John Toll (et al.) and the Master Commissioner by Barack G. Thomas Master Commissioner of the Fayette Circuit Court of

the first part and America Burns of the City of Lexington and
State of Kentucky of the Second part. [Illegible] that for and in
consideration of the promises and full payment of the purchase
price aforesaid, the receipt whereof is hereby acknowledged
this [part] of the first part has granted, bargained, and sold to
the part of the second part and her heirs and [illegible] as alone
described the following described property to wit; commenc-
ing at the corner of an alley on Cedar Street moving North said
street in a North westerly direction forty-seven feet to Matilda
Wheeler's line, hence at right angles with said Wheeler's line
one hundred feet. Hence in the Southeasterly direction forty-
seven feet to said alley hence with said alley to the beginning,
being the same property that was consigned to Mary Masterson by Jeremiah Murphy by deed dated May 6th 1865.[25]

How America knew Ferdinand Robinson, the Lexington mattress
maker, and how he was involved in the property acquisition are intriguing questions.[26] There is a good chance that Robinson was part
of her kinship network—those relationships African Americans
maintained throughout slavery and beyond.

Property ownership was an accomplishment for any nineteenth-
century woman; for a black woman, it was a progressive milestone.
America was one of only a few African American women in Fayette
County to hold a deed to a city lot. Looking ahead, America recognized that property ownership could create additional opportunities
for her son and herself, so she invested her hard-earned money, as
well as the money she received from her husband's pension,[27] in their
future. Her purpose seems to have been greater than just a desire to
live comfortably. America may have been hoping to accrue the kind
of family wealth that would allow her son to own his own labor and
be his own man.

Historian Patricia Hill Collins describes black women like
America as "outsiders within," or "people who no longer belong
to any one group."[28] This position allows them to occupy a void in
the continuity of societal interactions. According to Collins, black
women during Reconstruction occupied this particular space: they

lacked both the patriarchal power of males and the empowered femininity of white females. African American women were both seen and unseen, used and abused by their own men and by the white men who preyed on them outside of the protection of their community. Yet these women retained important roles in terms of gaining access to information, given their close proximity to whites in the course of their work as domestic servants. In other words, they used their "invisibility" to their advantage.

Like most black women who worked for the white elite, America was well aware that she needed to work hard, save her money, and invest in the future. In the antebellum period, during interactions at church, picnics, and other social gatherings, freeborn blacks would counsel former slaves about the importance of saving for the future, and there is no doubt that they listened to their freeborn contemporaries and benefited from their experience. Although savings accounts and real estate investments were reserved for a limited few with the necessary resources, land became more affordable during Reconstruction, and some black families were able to pool their money and acquire city lots or small farms with the help of white employers or trusted members of the community.

Lexington's black community was more advanced socially, economically, and politically than African Americans elsewhere in the South, due to the number of free blacks who were educated, owned businesses, and were well connected to powerful white men who shared information with those they deemed exceptional or extraordinary. However, the right to vote became the most celebrated possession of black Lexingtonians in the early 1870s, as many white men became the embodiment of the devil himself, tormenting blacks without fear of repercussion or remorse.

## "A Regular Reign of Terror"

The idea of Lexington as the site of a new revolution, with blacks as the protagonist, harks back to the beginning of the American Republic and the fight to be free from British rule. Not dissimilar to those colonists battling for life, liberty, and the pursuit of happiness,

African Americans in Lexington and throughout the South fought to claim their rights as human beings and to end injustice. More than anything else, blacks understood that freedom meant control of one's destiny. As a small boy growing up during these revolutionary times, Isaac Burns Murphy encountered and experienced these liberating forces both directly and indirectly. Lexington was the perfect place to prepare a young man to claim his share of the American franchise. Even so, Isaac would have been scarred by the dark forces attempting to crush his people's progress toward full citizenship and, in the process, inflict as much pain and wreckage as possible.

Throughout Lexington, African Americans were constantly reminded of the oppressive forces scheming against them. The Fifteenth Amendment to the Constitution, ratified in early 1870, stated that the "right of citizens of the United States to vote shall not be denied or abridged by the United States, or by any State, on account of race, color, or previous condition of servitude." Unfortunately, this only accelerated the abuses inflicted on former slaves and their families. At the beginning of Reconstruction, former Confederate soldiers roamed the countryside in search of blacks to take out their "wrath at the Federal Government."[29] Most poor whites opposed efforts to elevate the Negro through legislative enforcement, educational advancement, and the political advocacy of white radical Republicans. In reality, they were intimidated by black competition for jobs, landownership, and political power. Furthermore, these whites recognized that once former slaves obtained positions of power, "poor white trash" might be seen as more "niggerly" than blacks. Major landowners, most of whom had farmed hemp and corn and bred horses prior to the Civil War, had lost tens of thousands of dollars in human chattel and had thousands of acres of farmland going unused, and now they feared being reduced to the social equal of the "inferior" race. All these feelings created opportunities for collusion among these various classes of angry white men.[30] This unified front by the white majority created a response that would shape race relations in Kentucky in particular, and the South in general, for more than 150 years.

Rejecting every aspect of black freedom, "counter-Reconstruction organizations" formed parties of renegades, vigilantes, and regulators to instill fear in blacks and in those whites who tried to change the culture of Kentucky.[31] Groups of white men wearing sheets or costumes with elaborate designs intended to intimidate and to arouse black superstitions roamed the countryside under the cloak of night. Before the Fifteenth Amendment provided for Negro testimony, they could do so with no fear that any blacks, male and female, would be able to identify them as the perpetrators of such crimes. Blacks in the rural parts of Fayette County were most vulnerable to attacks by the Ku Klux Klan and its "regular reign of terror."[32] Black farmers and their families, living in isolation in the countryside or in the small hamlets surrounding Lexington, were preyed on by bands of the Ku Klux Klan. Klan members served up whippings and then dragged their victims until the flesh was torn from their bodies. Outrages such as castration, rape, murder, and lynching were common in the 1870s, and the bodies of victims were often displayed as warnings to other independent-minded former slaves. Many of these acts of violence seemed to be spontaneous, directed at unsuspecting black farmhands, old women, ministers, disabled black men (including former soldiers), and hardworking individuals just trying to make a life for themselves and their families. Yet some of these outrages were clearly meant to make a statement about the political concerns of the day.

On the night of November 1, 1872, three members of the Hawkins family—Samuel Hawkins, a black man who had helped organize black voters for the Republican Party, his wife Mahalia, and his seventeen-year-old daughter Fanny—were taken from their home outside of Lexington, near the Jessamine County line, by members of the Ku Klux Klan.[33] The next day, all three were found dead: they had been shot, drowned, and hanged from the limb of a tree suspended over a cliff near the Kentucky River.[34] This horrendous execution of an entire family was but one example of the barbarism unleashed by whites on blacks who merely wanted to live as free men and women. Many of these outrages were, in fact, assassinations of black leaders, intended to remind black Kentuckians what might happen to them if they continued to press for their rights.

Clearly, these murders were the work of disgruntled white men who feared black power and were threatened by black manhood. Black men who educated themselves and their families, who were dedicated to achieving social and economic success, and who were committed to voting to defend the Republican agenda of granting all citizens equal rights and protection under the law, were a threat to white men suffering from the trauma of an exposed racial reality: The myth of white supremacy was breaking down, and that white men were no better than black men.[35]

Men like Henry King, Henry Scroggins, James Turner, Henry Britton, Ferdinand Robinson, and George Perry worked to establish order in the black community and negotiated with Lexington's most prominent white leaders for the advancement of blacks. These men also ensured the survival of their children by teaching them how to deflect the hatred of whites and turn it into the energy required to take advantage of opportunities, achieve their goals and dreams, and even flourish as professionals. Indeed, for Lexington's black community to succeed, it would have to find fertile ground in the hostile environment promoted by anti-Republican Democrats and antiblack white supremacists, of which there were plenty in both the city and the nearby countryside. The most fertile ground, in fact, was the soul.

The vision of the future created by these African American leaders motivated the swelling black population to get behind them. In the midst of dramatic social, political, and economic changes taking place in Lexington, the black community also suffered violence—lynching, murder, rape, and property damage—perpetrated by white men who loathed the reality of black suffrage and the development of an independent, self-reliant, confident black man. The political voice provided to blacks by the Republican Party, the in-migration of blacks from farms on the outskirts of the city, and black Lexingtonians' burgeoning awareness of their racial destiny led to an increased self-awareness and a sense of purpose for black youth. They believed that nothing was impossible for those who were hopeful and persistent, even as white hatred and violence toward blacks became more predictable and remained woefully unimpeded. All these changes and challenges would influence the character of black Lexingtonians and their future in the city for generations.

## The Cruelty of Trust

On April 21, 1873, America Burns opened a savings account at the National Savings Bank and Trust Company (Freedmen's Bank) branch in Lexington. She became one of more than 1,000 local women, men, and children to deposit their hard-earned income in what they believed was a secure institution created to protect their money and thus their futures. Like so many others, America and her fellow depositors saved what little they had, hoping to keep their dreams of success and achievement alive. Each time these hardworking individuals made their way to the corner of Upper and Church Streets to place whatever sum they had accumulated into the hands of John G. Hamilton, the bank's cashier, they dreamed a little more. On the same day America opened her account, Spencer Talbott, a forty-nine-year-old laborer and widower, deposited $6.25, and William Coleman, a thirteen-year-old schoolboy, deposited $0.35.[36] Hamilton recorded each of these transactions in the branch's ledger book, as well as in the depositor's personal passbook. It is instructional to know that printed in each bankbook was a chart showing the amount of interest that could be generated for a "man [or woman] who saves ten cents a day every day for ten years."[37] In nineteenth-century dollars, the amount accumulated after ten years could have been used as a down payment on a farm or on a city lot with a new home or for a child's college tuition. To the farmers, wage laborers, washerwomen, cooks, draymen, brick masons, schoolchildren, and barbers patronizing the Freedmen's Bank, their bankbooks were symbols of their prosperity and aspirations.

The Freedmen's Bank ledger listed deposits ranging from a few cents to thousands of dollars. In total, the estimated holdings of the Lexington branch amounted to a little more than $25,000.[38] Although the amount in America's account is not known, the fact that she put any money in the bank indicates that she was able to find and keep work, perhaps washing and cleaning for white families; her late husband's pension ($8 to $10 per month) would have supplemented those wages. Like others, America assumed that the bank was safe; its Washington, D.C., branch boasted assets of more than

$6 million. The Freedmen's Bank also promised a return of 6 per-
cent interest on all deposits. For America, this must have been a god-
send. With her savings plus interest, and her ownership of a city lot
worth $400 in 1873, she was beginning to reap the rewards of her
hard work and determination.[39] As far as America was concerned,
she had established the foundation for a new life filled with possibilities for herself and her son.

Initially chartered by an act of Congress and authorized by
President Abraham Lincoln, the National Savings Bank and Trust
Company was established in the District of Columbia on March
3, 1865, its primary objective being to "receive on deposit for safe
keeping and investment for *their* benefit, all sums that might be offered by 'persons lately held in slavery' from one dollar up."[40] To
guarantee the success of the "simple mutual savings bank established for the benefit of black people," the charter required that at
least "two-thirds" of the bank's deposits be invested in U.S. Secu-
rities, including stocks, bonds, and Treasury notes.[41] However, the
National Savings Bank and Trust Company was not legally connected to the Federal government. Owned solely by the depositors, who
were the investors, the bank was a philanthropic endeavor intended to support black people's transition from slaves to wage earners
and to provide their descendants with examples of self-reliance and
self-help by instilling the economic concepts of industry and thrift.
A bankbook was like a badge of honor, a symbol that an individual
had risen above his or her previous condition and become a respectable citizen.[42] With the support of stalwarts such as Frederick Douglass and John Mercer Langston, trustees of the Washington, D.C.,
branch, and Congressman Robert Smalls and Major Martin Delany,
trustees of the South Carolina branch, blacks were easily convinced
of the prudence of saving their money in local branches, and they
believed (mistakenly) that the Federal government was responsible
for their investments. By 1872, the number of branches throughout
the South had increased to thirty-four; there was also a branch in
Philadelphia and one in New York.

On November 8, 1870, John G. Hamilton opened the Lexington branch of the Freedmen's Bank with the support of black

and white community leaders.[43] Hamilton was thus responsible for the black community's savings and, as superintendent of colored schools, the education of its children. Promoting industry and thrift as necessary to achieving the promises of freedom and citizenship in America, Hamilton, the bank's advisory board, and community leaders enthusiastically promoted the savings bank as the proper place for striving people to put their hard-earned money. Within this context, the Freedman's Bank provided both a catalyst for the development of black economic power and a progressive political discourse on participation in the American franchise.[44]

To attract depositors, Hamilton and advisory board members held public meetings at black churches, the Ladies Hall, and other venues where they could talk to the black community about saving, thrift, and sobriety as the pathway to citizenship in a capitalist society. To educate potential depositors about the moral benefits of investing their money in the Freedmen's Bank, Hamilton likely distributed pamphlets to his curious but cautious audiences related to the "sins against thrift."[45] At these meetings, Hamilton argued that it was each man's responsibility to "earn all he can honestly; to use it for the support of his family and for sending his children to school. All after that he should put by in some safe place where he will get interest on it."[46] Advertisements for the bank in the *Kentucky Statesman* claimed that it had deposits of "over sixteen million dollars" and that "any amount received" was eligible to have interest paid.[47] Responding to Hamilton's benevolence and black leaders' call to support what they believed was a government-sponsored institution, black Lexingtonians deposited their money in the local branch, trusting that their nest eggs would grow into healthy birds they could live off of.[48]

By June 1873, the people's faith in the Freedmen's Bank was reflected in the total amounts deposited and withdrawn at the thirty-four branches over the seven years since its founding: deposits of $49,629,354.25 and withdrawals of $45,600,684.82, leaving a balance of $4,028,669.43.[49] However, what seemed to be a well-organized, government-sponsored gesture in support of equal opportunity and self-reliance quickly became a profit-making enterprise for the less scrupulous American businessmen controlling the bank's financial decisions. To officials, it was obvious that this noble effort to elevate the black masses had become the victim of a lack of oversight and regulation. What is more, the country's economic downturn exposed the untrustworthiness of some of the bank's cashiers, charged with protecting the interests of their loyal investors. Poor accounting practices and substantiated rumors of unsecured loans to speculators that had been lost without explanation incited a run on the bank, depleting a majority of its capital.

Frederick Douglass, who took over as bank president in March 1874, tried to save it from sinking further into the abyss. Unfortunately, losses were too great, and once the Washington, D.C., branch failed, branches across the South, including the one in Lexington, were unable to pay back their investors. By June 28, the Lexington branch had closed its doors, leaving more than 61,000 depositors, including America, penniless and holding "worthless notes."[50] Sadly, most of these investors never recovered their losses; nor did they recover their faith in the promises of a government run by white men. For America Burns, however, there was no time to mourn the loss of her life savings. She had to come up with a plan to protect her son from the poverty that was sure to follow her financial misfortune. More problematic, she developed tuberculosis (consumption), and her life seemed to be slipping back into the shadows of obscurity.

## An Excellent Student and a Promising Jockey

By the time of the bank's failure in 1874, thirteen-year-old Isaac had been attending school for some time. But sometime that year, America decided to apprentice her son to horse breeder James T. Williams, the business partner of Richard Owings, for whom she washed and cleaned. This decision may have been a response to the loss of her savings, and it is possible that otherwise, Isaac would have been able to stay in school. In the days and weeks leading up to her decision to let Isaac go, America no doubt consulted with her father, Green Murphy, and with family friend Eli Jordan. She must have turned the decision over in her mind a thousand times or more, seeking a better solution. What is more, she had become very sick and was in desperate need of financial assistance and medical care. Of all the reasons why Isaac became a jockey, the final factor may have been his mother's poor health and her desire to give him some security before she died. America wanted to save her son from an unknown and destitute existence. These circumstances led to Isaac's discovery of his ability to pilot 1,200 pounds of horseflesh capable of running thirty-five miles per hour.

During an 1885 interview, James T. Williams recalled the day America brought Isaac to him: "One day a colored woman called upon me with the request that I employ her boy to exercise my horses," Williams explained. "The woman was a consumptive, and stated she believed her life might be prolonged if her son was employed."[51] Still, America must have had reservations about exposing her son to the seamy side of horse racing: gambling, drinking, and carousing in the red-light districts. At the root of her decision was the understanding that Isaac would soon have to face the world on his own, and he would need some sort of skill if he was going to survive and be successful.

America's resourcefulness led her to use her connections to her employer Richard Owings and her friend Eli Jordan, who worked as a trainer for the Williams and Owings stable. On the advice of Jordan, America likely approached Owings directly about any apprenticeship opportunities for her child.[52] Even at thirteen, Isaac was a small and sensitive boy who was very close to his mother. In securing her son's position as an apprentice, America clearly had three goals: to protect Isaac from being orphaned and left to negotiate the temptations of the city alone; to provide him with useful skills that could secure him a modest income in the future, while maintaining his virtuous upbringing; and to obtain a small income to offset her living expenses and perhaps delay her death.

James T. Williams and Richard Owings maintained a space at the old Kentucky Association Race Course in Lexington, the oldest racing club in the state. Like most turfmen of the mid- to late 1870s, Williams and Owings were always looking to improve their stock of Thoroughbreds, as well as employ quality riders.[53] In fact, by the 1880s, the region surrounding Lexington was called a "breeder's paradise" for its green pastures, its high-quality horseflesh available for sale, and its talented jockeys.[54] Like a majority of turfmen in the South, Williams and Owings used African American boys and men as their main source of labor—grooms, trainers, exercise boys, and jockeys. African Americans were integral to the development of the horse-racing industry, and they knew how to succeed. Although there were white jockeys and white stable boys, African Americans predominated on the dozen or more major horse farms in the six counties surrounding Lexington. In the beginning, they had ridden side by side with a small number of great white riders, but as African Americans became more successful at competing among themselves and with their white counterparts, the sport changed to fit the converging social, political, and economic circumstances.[55]

As horse racing "became . . . a profitable business venture, with the book-maker as a recognized factor, the great jockeys jumped into national popularity."[56] By winning big-money races such as the Suburban, the American Derby, the Kentucky Derby, the Saratoga, and the Latonia Derby, African American jockeys became widely known. By the 1890s, with their achievement in the sport of horse racing and their financial success, African American men gained the attention of those white men who saw black success as a threat to white supremacy.

In the mid-nineteenth century, the labor performed by blacks constituted "nigger work" to most whites, and they wanted no part of it. However, by the end of the nineteenth century, with the economy in a downward spiral, increased competition for jobs, and thousands of dollars available to successful jockeys, white men no longer saw working in stables and around smelly animals as synonymous with drudgery, and they began to compete with blacks for positions as jockeys. However, the ability to ride on the American turf was a skill that had to be taught by a master trainer, and fortunately for Isaac, Eli Jordan agreed to take him on as a student of "horsemanship" and groom him for life as a jockey.[57]

After securing Isaac's position as a stable boy under Jordan,

America likely insisted that "Uncle Eli" make her boy adhere to a certain set of Christian mores and values: no drinking, no tobacco, no foul language.[58] Thanks to Isaac's small stature—standing less than five feet tall and weighing no more than seventy pounds—he soon earned a new position as an exercise boy at the stable.[59] His daily routine consisted of waking up before dawn to feed, water, and groom the horses; clean the stalls; and report to Jordan on the animals for which he was responsible. As an apprentice, Isaac "would have slept in the barn, up in the straw with the other boys. . . . He wasn't training to be a jockey. He was training to ride races," which would make a jockey out of him.[60] On the racetrack, Isaac and the other apprentices took their lessons just like children in school, and they always obeyed Jordan.

After being thrown from his first mount, appropriately named Volcano, an embarrassed and intimidated Isaac settled in to learn the art of riding from Jordan, the best horse trainer in Fayette County. Coaxing his young pupil to get back up on the fiery horse, Jordan taught him how to take control of the animal through the confidence of his seat. Isaac trusted Jordan's judgment and, risking injury and further humiliation, remounted the temperamental yearling, eventually breaking the horse and securing both their futures in horse racing. Jordan would later comment that Isaac listened to him and followed directions, demonstrating that he was an excellent student and a promising jockey. Known to be dependable and responsible, Isaac was by all accounts a "nice, quiet, lovely boy" who did not swear or gamble.[61] Under the expert guidance of Uncle Eli, Isaac excelled, learning the intricacies of riding races and working toward mastering the art of pace.

To train and prepare the young boy's mind and body for the rigors of competition, Jordan had his student ride fast quarter-, half-, and one-mile lengths, timing him at each interval and telling him exactly how fast he had traveled. Through this process, Isaac would get a feel for the horse's ability and learn every detail about the particular horse he was riding: its morning disposition, its temperament and character under stress, how fast it could run on a full stomach, and the pace it was capable of. Jordan also taught him how to negotiate a wet or muddy track; how to use the horse's body to defend himself against unscrupulous jockeys; and, most important, the value of being honest in a sport where one's reputation could determine how many mounts one received. In short, to become a successful jockey, Isaac not only had to develop horse sense; he also had to master every detail of each race, and most important, he had to master himself.[62]

Indeed, as an apprentice, Isaac spent time among the horses in the stables, allowing him to get a feel for the animals and an understanding of his own capabilities. In learning the many critical aspects of horse racing, Isaac established a foundation of knowledge that turned him into an expert in the art of pace, a skill he would later use to defeat the competition in more than 600 races.[63] For spectators, Isaac's excellent seat and his command of a race defined him as a master rider whose performance as a jockey mirrored the quality of his manhood.

After less than two years, the thoughtful, quiet boy had become a jockey of considerable talent. His rise to fame would be the result of a virtuous disposition learned as a small boy and a sense of achievement as a jockey of exceptional physical ability and moral courage. In learning how to ride races, control the pace of his mount, and disregard the constant beckoning of temptation, Isaac was able to take full advantage of the opportunity his mother provided. By the spring of 1875, it was time to see how well he could perform.

# PART 3

*Revelations*

# 6

# Learning to Ride
# and Taking Flight

## 1875–1880

By his fourteenth birthday, Isaac's apprenticeship in the stables of James T. Williams and Richard Owings began to pay off. In the beginning, no one could have imagined that the little boy from Lexington would become the greatest representative of horse racing the state—maybe even the country—would ever produce. What is even more amazing is that despite his greatness, Isaac remained humble and focused in a sport where dishonesty and treachery prevailed. Like most boys filled with potential, Isaac would have had little hope of achieving success without sponsorship and guidance, so the opportunity to demonstrate his talent with horses was inestimable. For the next eight years, Isaac's rise would be shaped by a series of events far from his day-to-day activities on the racetrack or in the quiet time he spent by himself. In some ways, his path was created by circumstances outside his comprehension and beyond the narrow world of Lexington and the Bluegrass. Isaac was fortunate that he began his journey headed in the right direction.

Before becoming an apprentice jockey, Isaac first had to prove his salt as a stable hand.[1] Eli Jordan, who had known Isaac since he was a small boy, would recall years later that he was quiet and "always in his place," and Jordan could always put his "hands on him any time, day or night." Isaac "was one of the first up in the morning, ready to do anything he was told to do or help others. He was ever in good humor and liked to play, but he never neglected his work, but worked hard summer and winter."[2] This seriousness suggests that Isaac's mother had instilled in him the value of hard work and the savvy to take advantage of his opportunities. America was a smart and determined woman who clearly recognized the character traits her son would need to find a place in the world for himself. In addition, Jordan's tutelage gave him both a sense of purpose and the skills he needed to succeed. It seems that Isaac, like his mother, was both smart and determined; this was reflected in his work ethic, which would lead to his later success and consistency, which became his signature quality.

Isaac learned that horses depended on people for everything. Stable boys were in charge of feeding and grooming the horses they were assigned to care for. Isaac slept in the stall of his charge and was responsible for keeping it clean. This involved removing the droppings and used bedding, separating the soiled straw from what was still usable; sweeping the hard dirt floor and allowing it to dry out; and then replacing the bedding with a thick layer of clean wheat straw or wood shavings, depending on the cost and availability of materials, as well as the temperament of the horse. Isaac was also responsible for transporting the solid waste material to the drying area away from the stables, where it would eventually be hauled away and used as fertilizer by local farmers and gardeners.

These tasks and others were vital to the welfare of the horses and had to be performed daily, without fail. Neglecting this routine could jeopardize the horses' health, especially a newly foaled colt or filly, and it could mean a severe beating or worse for the stable boy who forgot his responsibilities. Whether Isaac and his fellow apprentices were abused by head trainer Jordan or stable owner Williams for neglecting their chores is not known. However, physical punishment was considered an acceptable consequence for apprentices who failed to properly feed, groom, and exercise their animals.[3] This was part of the conditioning process for those who wanted a chance to wear the black and red colors of Williams and Owings.[4]

Fortunately, Isaac was conscientious about always being in his place when called on, so he probably avoided beatings, and given their personal relationship, Jordan may have had more patience with him than with the other boys. Early on, Isaac demonstrated a commitment to his calling. After performing his early-morning tasks of feeding and watering the horses and preparing them for their morning workout, he watched the exercise riders putting the horses through their paces. Isaac's first assignment as an exercise boy was to ride George Rice's horse Volcano, which promptly reared up and threw him to the dirt track. At that moment he had two choices: get back on and try again to control the horse, or run away and hide. In reality, there was nowhere for him to go. His mother was dying of tuberculosis and needed the money he earned working at the stable; his father was dead; and his few remaining blood relatives had moved away to Covington, Kentucky, just across the Ohio River from Cincinnati.[5] So he made the only decision possible for a boy whose prospects were as narrow as they were shallow: he got back on the horse.

After their workouts, the exercise boys helped the grooms rub down and massage the horses to ease their muscles and to feel for tight ligaments and firm flesh. Still learning about the habits of horses, Isaac watched the grooms' technique for brushing and combing the horses to put them at ease.[6] Isaac understood that he had a lot to learn if he wanted to become a successful jockey. There were plenty of other boys and men who aspired to the fame and life of ease enjoyed by the Napoleons of the turf, who rode fast and lived even faster. But not everyone had the know-how and the talent to control a horse and get it to perform well enough to win. Indeed, although they were separate, the horse and its jockey were, ideally, one entity as they charged around the oval track in pursuit of victory. And for a select few, immortality would be their reward. As exciting as it seemed, the life of a nineteenth-century jockey was filled with danger, but the potential rewards compelled a few brave souls to choose the saddle and reins, the post and paddock, as a way of life. In his poem "Aintree Calls," British poet Will Ogilvie expresses the essence of what it means to be a jockey: "Danger beckons yet to daring / And the colours wait for wearing / While Fame proffers gifts for sharing."[7] Through trial and error, young Isaac learned to be fearless. Through the teaching of Jordan and the advice of fellow jockeys, he learned how to ride races and win stakes. Isaac was a quick study, and everyone saw that he was born to ride. He had the head and the heart for *les belles bêtes:* the beautiful beasts.

In early February 1875 Benjamin Bruce's Lexington-based *Kentucky Live Stock Record* reported that the "prospect for fine sport at this place is more flattering than it has been for many years, judging from the number of horses in training in this section."[8] Along with the Williams and Owings stable, others preparing for the spring races included H. P. McGrath, B. G. Thomas, J. A. Grinstead, A. Keene Richard, General Abe Buford, F. B. Harper, Daniel Swigert, and T. J. Megibben. The number of quality horses had increased over the last few years, and the new stakes race in Louisville had been on all their minds during the winter months. Horses nominated for the inaugural meeting of the Louisville Jockey Club were being prepared for the race that was destined to be a showcase for quality Kentucky-bred Thoroughbreds such as Aristides, Ten Broeck, Bob Woolley, Clemmie G, and Kilburn. Quality black jockeys would also participate in the event, although, at the time, they were still a somewhat invisible presence. These jockeys included Oliver Lewis, William Walker, William Lakeland, Howard Williams, Dick Chambers, and Raleigh Colston Jr., all from Kentucky and all proven champion pilots of horseflesh. These men's names would be lost to history because, whether black or white, the jockey was not as important as the horse, which was being showcased for sale to the highest bidder. This would change significantly as the popularity of horse racing increased and the public began to demand exciting races based on rivalries between horses and, eventually, between individual jockeys and their ability to bring home a winner with style. By the later years of the nineteenth century, black jockeys were increasingly excluded, owing to a number of factors, including jealousy among white jockeys, who saw the huge salaries earned by successful blacks as an affront to white men; collusion between owners and white jockeys to bar blacks from the richest stakes races; and hostility toward blacks in general during the 1890s, when lynching reached its peak in America.

On February 25, 1875, Williams and Owings shipped their string of horses to Louisville, under the care of Eli Jordan, to begin training for the Jockey Club race.[9] The decision to train in Louisville was probably based on several factors, such as the desire to introduce the horses to the new track, get a feel for the track's speed and where the low points were, and take advantage of the new facilities built by the Louisville Jockey Club. The owners and trainer may have gone early to observe the competition and create a plan of action for each horse based on the jockey's ability and the field of competitors. The Association Course at Lexington, where the Williams and Owings stables were located, was connected to Louisville and Nashville via railroad, so transportation was not a problem. From Lexington, they could travel south and test their horses at smaller tracks along the way, such as Crab Orchard, some forty-six miles south of Lexington.

The records are unclear regarding how many races Isaac had prior to the first one in Louisville, but he claimed his first official race was in May 1875 at the Crab Orchard track.[10] The oldest circular track in the state, Crab Orchard was a great testing ground for potential stakes-winning horses and reliable, talented jockeys.[11] Here, among his peers, Isaac "rode several races" and secured his first win on B. F. Pettit's chestnut filly Glentina (future winner of the Louisville Jockey Club's Colt and Filly Stakes).[12] According to Murphy, he rode Lady Greenfield in a losing effort in 1875 prior to his victory on Pettit's filly, but it "marked the real beginning" of his life as a professional jockey.[13] We cannot know how the impish yet resilient boy handled his first victory or how Uncle Eli responded to his pupil's success. Isaac may have been modest and humble, smiling slightly but not wanting to draw too much attention to himself, or he may have laughed out loud at the joy and elation of putting it all together. We can only imagine how a fourteen-year-old boy coming into his own would have acted.

It is not known whether Isaac traveled to Louisville with Jordan, to set up the accommodations there, or journeyed south to Nashville with the rest of the boys, where Williams had entered his colts in stakes races beginning on May 4.[14] If he went south, Isaac may have had one or two mounts at the Nashville Blood Association Meeting on the Williams and Owings horses Creedmore, Fair Play, or Playmate, all of which either won their respective races or placed in the top three. At Nashville, even if he did not ride, Isaac would have helped with stable duties, grooming, and preparing the horses for their races. This experience would have been invaluable to young Isaac, who still had much to learn about how races were run, different ways of riding at race meets, and the rules of the match race format, whereby additional weight was added to a horse as a handicap to determine the champion among horses of different breeds, ages, or sexes. In some cases, the outcome of a match race was determined by the best two out of three or three out of five heats.

Isaac also would have been schooled on the dangers of gambling on horses. Essentially, Jordan would have told Isaac that good jockeys don't gamble; they don't have to. If Isaac was a good boy, he would get what he deserved. In later years, he would draw from this wisdom provided by Jordan and others, and Isaac would become a role model for other young jockeys who hoped for financial security and the opportunity to ride in stakes races.

In an 1889 interview, Isaac said he had to "laugh as he thought of himself in those old days," yet he seemed to value coming up, albeit briefly, through the Association Course, also known as the "Chittlin Switch" racetrack, at Lexington to become a jockey of some ability.[15] Although in the spring of 1875 he had been training as a jockey for less than a year, he had learned the value of a good seat and the details of riding a horse at maximum speeds, and he was gaining an understanding of the art of pace. Still, Isaac was untested in big-time stakes races, where lives could change for better or worse on any given day. By mid-May, Isaac was in Louisville to test how well he had learned from his mentors, Jordan and Williams, and from his mother. Everything was working in his favor, and he was preparing to take flight in a world filled with possibility.

## Louisville and New Beginnings

In May 1875 the Kentucky spring was chilly. However, the winter-like temperatures did not prevent curious crowds of patrons, horse-racing enthusiasts, and men of the turf from descending on Louisville for the inaugural races at the new horse park. Indeed, under the banner of Kentucky pride and advancement of the state's long-standing tradition of horse breeding and racing, the streets of the river city were filled to the brim with eager black and white faces anticipating something new and thrilling on the horizon.[16] For the thousands who traveled to Louisville to participate in the spectacle, the atmosphere was more than electric: it was contagious. Many of the attendees were interested in seeing the best Kentucky-bred horses run fast; others came to bet on their favorites and, if they were lucky, go home with some easily won cash. Bachelors arrived in town looking not only for trackside entertainment but also for that which could be found in the red-light district and the many saloons throughout the city, where unattached women could be persuaded to engage in sin at an affordable price. Families also came to the inaugural event. Fathers brought their sons to participate in the fair-like atmosphere as a rite of passage and to mark the day the races came back to Louisville.

For the gentlemen of the turf, especially those with a genteel philosophy of breeding and running horses and a desire to export their stock to enthusiastic customers in the East and across the Atlantic in England and France, Louisville became a mecca for well-bred horses and a new commercial center. Breeders such as Woodford County's Daniel Swigert, Franklin County's J. W. Hunt-Reynolds, and Fayette County's H. P. McGrath would use the new venue to showcase the quality of the horseflesh available on their farms, as well as the quality of the trainers, grooms, and jockeys they employed. As boosters and beneficiaries of Kentucky's most important industry, these men joined with others of considerable influence, power, and wealth to pool their resources and develop a new model for horse racing that would benefit Kentucky's identity as the Thoroughbred capital of the United States, if not the world.

That May, however, the focus was on the new course located in the Louisville suburbs, still surrounded by farms and the rural landscape from which it had been carved. The design of the Louisville Jockey Club and Driving Park was based on the tracks and courses in Europe. Its principal founder and chief organizer, Meriwether Lewis Clark, was no doubt taken aback by the throngs of people who came to usher in a new era in Kentucky horse racing.

In 1872, three years prior to the opening of the Louisville track, a group of gentlemen of the turf, businessmen, and politicians made it known that they wanted to expand Kentucky's horse markets into the East, West, and South. But to do so, and to compete with Lexington, racing would have to return to the city of Louisville on a grand scale. Clark, his influential uncles John and Henry Churchill, and a number of wealthy breeders were convinced that Louisville could become the epicenter of Kentucky's prized Thoroughbred industry. At the request of this distinguished group of Kentuckians, Clark, a former banker and tobacco merchant, traveled to Europe for the sole purpose of studying horse racing there and developing a new approach to American racing based on the grand spectacles organized by the English Jockey Club. In Europe, the "Sport of Kings and of the aristocracy" was steeped in tradition and ritual unlike that found in America.[17] While in England, Clark met fellow Kentuckian and former vice president John Cabell Breckinridge, who introduced him to members of the Jockey Club.[18] These interactions would prove significant not only to the development of the racetrack in Louisville but also to the sense of pride in Kentucky horse racing.

While in England, twenty-seven-year-old Clark visited the Newmarket Heath course, where the Two Thousand Guineas Stakes was held; Epsom Downs, where the Epsom Derby and Epsom Oaks were held; and the location of the original St. Leger Stakes, held at Town Moor in Doncaster. Clark learned about the history of the Jockey Club, the process of selecting competitors, the origins of certain traditions, and the importance of honor as the basis of success and failure. For two years, Clark immersed himself in the habits of the "most chivalrously honorable" traditions and culture of the turf and, in the process, mastered the many details of managing a race-course. The knowledge he gained would inform the creation of the Louisville Jockey Club and the policies it implemented under Clark's strong leadership.[19] However, unlike the English, American horse breeders were in the racing business to make money. So Clark studied a system of betting used by the French called "pari-mutuel."[20] Although it would take some time for this system to catch on in the United States, Clark saw its possibilities.

Enthusiastic about the future of horse racing in Kentucky, Clark returned to Louisville in 1874 with a plan to change the sport for the better. With the support of a newly formed board of directors that included E. H. Chase, Daniel Swigert, John E. Green, H. Victor Newcomb, J. W. Hunt-Reynolds, W. H. Thomas, and John Churchill, Clark incorporated the Louisville Jockey Club and Driving Park and began to raise funds to build the racetrack itself. One of the unique features Clark proposed to the board was a new racing format that eliminated heat races; each race would be self-contained, and each horse would run only once a day. The emphasis on stakes races also created excitement for the betting public, who could see different races in a single day or over a series of days that showcased Thoroughbreds of different ages. After raising $32,000 through subscriptions, Clark began construction of what would become a monument to Kentucky's genteel past. By the spring of 1875, the track was completed and the gates were opened to the enthusiastic "racegoers" and the voguish petite bourgeoisie engaged in social jockeying at Kentucky's newest attraction.[21]

Matt Winn's memoir recounts his experience on the first day of races at the Louisville track:

The first Derby Day I remember as if it were yesterday. It was May 17, 1875. I was 13—nearing 14—when Col. M. Lewis Clark, the Louisville sportsman, and his associates of the race track which now is Churchill Downs, were making ready for the opening. My father decided to be there. He wasn't a horse player. But this was more than a race day. It was a festival, and my father felt he ought to be at the track to see if the "goings on" would be worth all the fuss the people had been making about the new track, and the new kind of racing.

Clark, in making up his racing programs, had decided to have three races aping the English. One was to be the Clark Handicap, named after himself, because the St. Leger was named after Colonel St. Leger, who had arranged the conditions for the world's first stakes race. Another was to be the Kentucky Oaks, for three year olds, named after the Epsom Oaks. The third and, of course, the most important was to be the Kentucky Derby in which conditions were the same as for the Epsom (or English) Derby. The distance of the Kentucky was fixed at a mile and a half (1 mile, 880 yards) as compared with the Epsom Derby distance of 1 mile, 881 yards.[22]

Clark presided over the inaugural races at the Louisville track. Proof of the track's success was the number of people waiting to enter the Louisville Jockey Club racecourse on opening day.[23]

Beyond the dirt track, the facilities included 150 stalls for horses, a clubhouse for Louisville Jockey Club members, and a grandstand that could accommodate up to 5,000 spectators.[24] Clark and the club's membership understood that the prestige generated by the track, with its European-style racing program and high-quality horseflesh, would add value to Louisville and satisfy horse breeders' aspirations to grow the industry beyond the boundaries of the state. What is more, such a prestigious event would encourage local merchants and horsemen to invest in their businesses and farms to satisfy the anticipated demand in the East. Along with horses and other livestock, Kentucky farmers wanted to export hemp, rope, wool, tobacco, and corn to markets outside the Ohio River Valley. If Clark's European-style races at the new double-cupolaed structure turned out to be a success, Kentuckians would benefit immediately from the local attention and the national publicity. Yet, even as the grandstand and infield filled with people of various occupations, income levels, and racial backgrounds eager for the races to begin, things were far from perfect.

Understandably, the history of slavery and the thousands upon thousands of blacks bought, sold, and bartered in and around the city of Louisville could not be forgotten. Even as times were changing and prosperity seemed attainable, race was an ever-present reality. Following the Civil War, Louisville, like Lexington, had become a popular destination for former slaves from the surrounding rural areas, especially those seeking refuge and protection from the escalating violence unleashed on them and their families in the countryside. By all accounts, the presence of Federal troops in urban areas served as a deterrent against former Confederate soldiers and other dejected whites who terrorized former slaves. Although many wealthy farmers whose livelihoods had depended on slave labor during the antebellum period still depended on the wage labor of blacks during Reconstruction, including those who raised Thoroughbred horses, it is unclear how many of Kentucky's prominent horse breeders were members of the Ku Klux Klan. There is some speculation that the Klan's midnight assassins used horses owned by local farmers who believed blacks were becoming too much of a threat to Kentucky traditions.

Like Lexington, Louisville's black population increased significantly after the Civil War. Between 1860 and 1870, the number of residents grew from close to 7,000 free and enslaved blacks to nearly 15,000.[25] By 1870, numerous religious, educational, and political meetings and conventions were being held in the city by African Americans trying to establish a foothold in society and exercise their rights guaranteed under the Constitution. Leading the black community is such endeavors were the Reverend Henry Adams, pastor of the Fifth Street Baptist Church; his daughter Susie Adams, a teacher at the church's school; musician and teacher William H. Gibson Sr.; and Horace Morris, an accountant and former cashier at the Freedmen's Bank before its collapse in 1874. Their success served as a catalyst for others. Although success was not inevitable, the individual achievements of many blacks encouraged the forward-thinking to take advantage of opportunities as they arose.

Even in the midst of the nationwide scandal involving the Freedmen's Bank, Louisville's African American leadership maintained
its focus on education, religion, work, and savings as integral to
the achievement and social mobility of the community. By demonstrating their value through productivity, order, and faith, African
Americans protected their own psyches and that of the larger black
community from the external abuses perpetrated by that portion of
white society bent on exterminating the Negro in America—or at
least in their particular part of it.

The image of Louisville as a gateway to opportunity and prosperity was countered by the reality of African Americans' ongoing struggles to achieve freedom and citizenship. Overt challenges
to their sovereignty after passage of the Fifteenth Amendment led
numerous individuals to become politically active and agitate for
the right to be recognized as men with the power to change their
own circumstances. A number of the Kentucky horsemen who were
members of the Louisville Jockey Club and Driving Park had been
slave owners, the children of slave owners, or supporters of the former Confederacy. For some of these turfmen, one of the most attractive features of Thoroughbred horse breeding and racing was
the creation of a distinct Southern identity connected to the "lost
cause" narrative. In some ways, the Louisville Jockey Club was a reaction to the Federal government's attempt to pacify and change the
true nature of the so-called traditional Kentuckian through the Civil
War and Reconstruction. This public display of one of antebellum
Kentucky's most influential industries was, in essence, a refutation
of the notion that the North had won the war. In the postbellum
period, Kentucky's most powerful white men used horse breeding
and racing to become the new masters of the Bluegrass, claiming the
honorary titles of colonel and general and, metaphorically, continuing the battle for white supremacy.

On the surface, this newly created sense of identity promised to
boost Kentucky pride as well as the local economy.[26] But not to be
forgotten were those individuals who would make Kentucky's horse
industry a success by shaping the land with their muscle and using
their knowledge of horses to groom and train the spirited foals to

run and win on the racetrack. These black men, many of whom were former slaves, created their own opportunities for social mobility and economic success through the same revived Bluegrass industry. On a tour of Lexington, a farmer from Cincinnati, Ohio, observed:

> Whether it is the normal condition of the outskirts of Lexington or not, it appears as if they were given up to little negroes, in single file, riding horses that were covered as with garments, and looked out upon a sinful world, through round holes cut in their head clothes. One could not but imagine that a circus was always getting ready to start on a parade through the streets. This mixing up of the negro element with the horse is a striking feature of the neighborhood. Wherever you see a horse you see a negro. If the horse is to be ridden, a little "nigger" is perchance on his back; if to be led, it is done by a big negro. It is almost to suggest the idea that while white people *may* have descended from monkeys, the colored race must have been bred from horses, the two affiliate so readily. This theory might be a great comfort to the good white people who are so tenacious of their exclusive descent, and is respectfully referred to the professors of "Darwinianism" for learned consideration.[27]

Although grotesquely ignorant and conditioned by the "Darwinianism" of the time, these observations of the intimacy between black men and horses support the notion that African Americans were invaluable to the development of horse racing in Kentucky.

The value and success of the horses raised on the various Bluegrass farms can be attributed to the black men and boys who devoted themselves to bringing the colts and fillies under their care into their own. And those horses' winnings, breeding fees, and offspring would be responsible for the economic success of the horse industry for generations. Ironically, that industry would try to exclude those who helped create it.

By the spring of 1875, this was Isaac Murphy's world. The wide-eyed boy born during the Civil War and coming of age during Reconstruction had arrived in Louisville, where the Jockey Club's version of the sport of kings had attracted 12,000 spectators to witness the speed of Kentucky-bred horses piloted by skillful jockeys in their colorful silks. Isaac would have seen everything Matt Winn saw from the infield that day, but from behind the scenes—in the stalls, where Eli Jordan and James Williams fussed and fretted over their well-prepared runners, and on the rails near the finish line, where he would watch the end of races and the results. Like the crowd in the stands and Matt in the infield, Isaac was looking forward to an exciting day at the races. He could not help looking at the well-dressed men and women in the grandstand, the assemblage of fashionable ladies in flowery hats and their diamond-pinned gentleman companions, or the array of common folk on the rails along the homestretch. The boy would soon be the focus of their attention, and his performance could either make his career or sabotage his future as a jockey. But luckily, he did not have a mount in the first race or, for that matter, on the first day.

At 2:30, after some jostling among the horses, the official starter tapped the drum to begin the first race. The six four-year-old horses and their jockeys took off around the oval track, each one hoping to claim the first prize. After a beautiful start, General Abe Buford's chestnut gelding Kilburn took the lead and held it for the first mile. At various points in the race, the crowd held its breath when the favorite, William Cottrill's chestnut filly Bonaventure, took the lead, lost it, and then regained it after some prodding by her able jockey, William Lakeland. When Bonaventure managed to hold off the field and claim victory, cheers went up. After two minutes and thirteen and a half seconds, the region's most important horse park had officially been christened. The judges, jockeys, and spectators all recognized that the track was fast, and old records were in jeopardy of falling. Ideally, this would happen during the second event on the program: the Kentucky Derby.

In what was being touted as the premier contest for Thoroughbred horses and breeders, the Kentucky Derby had been designed by Colonel Meriwether Lewis Clark Jr. to equal the Epsom Derby in England. Clark had called on his friend Colonel William H. Johnson, president of the Nashville Blood Horse Association, to officiate at this most important race.[28] Isaac, along with everyone else present, watched as Johnson walked across the dirt track wearing his best suit. They watched him as he drew a line in the dirt to mark the starting point; then he reminded the fifteen jockeys to keep their horses behind that line until the official drum was tapped, signaling the start of the race. It is instructive to note that thirteen of the fifteen jockeys were black, but this was not unusual. As Johnson climbed into the starter's box, Isaac watched the jockeys position themselves and their horses for the best possible start. When Colonel Johnson struck his drum, the field burst forward as if on fire, with the familiar Volcano (Isaac's first mount as an exercise boy) battling General Buford's McCreery for the lead. Both of Henry Price McGrath's horses—Chesapeake, ridden by William Henry, and Aristides, ridden by Oliver Lewis—were in the middle of the pack, with Lewis forcing a heavy pace. Both horses had been trained by Ansel Williamson, who had gone to work for McGrath after the death of Robert A. Alexander, the owner of Woodburn Farm. The thunderous sound of hooves impacting the ground competed with the cheers from the stands as the favorite, Chesapeake, was bested by stablemate Aristides. The chestnut colt opened up a gap between him and the field after the first mile and then dashed unchallenged down the stretch with McGrath's "green and orange colors flying in the wild," to the delight of the crowd.[29] Aristides came within seconds of tying the record for three-year-olds at a mile and a half and netted McGrath the healthy sum of $2,900—not to mention bragging rights to the very first Kentucky Derby victory. Finishing second was Volcano, winning $200 for his owner George Rice and proving his salt in a big race.

Williams and Owings stables also did well that first day. The favorite, Fair Play, won two out of three one-mile heats to take the Association Purse of $400. And in the fourth and final race of the day, Playmate finished out of the money but placed sixth in the field of fifteen. It is safe to say that when Fair Play rounded the final turn, Isaac, the jockey in training, was watching carefully as, coat shining and muscles flexing, the horse bore down the straightaway toward the finish line. Watching from behind the rails, Isaac would be learning how to judge a horse's pace by watching its body movements and looking for signs of fatigue and tightness in its stride. He would be listening to Jordan as he barked instructions to the jockey, telling him when to let the horse run free of the bit and when to punish him with the whip. Or maybe Jordan just let the jockey do his job, leaving the critique until later, when it could be delivered in private and more readily absorbed and understood, and the public would not be privy to knowledge of the horse's or the jockey's weaknesses. It makes perfect sense that Isaac would learn these important lessons by listening and by watching theory and practice merge into performance. He would begin to understand the small margin between winning and losing and the big difference between a job as an exercise boy and a career as the best jockey of the day.

On May 22, the fifth and final day of the Louisville meeting, it was Isaac's turn to ride. His mount was Robert Scott's Lady Greenfield,[30] and the race was the Consolation Purse for horses that had already been beaten.[31] There is no doubt that Isaac was eager to demonstrate what he had learned at Chittlin Switch as an exercise boy and at Crab Orchard as a newly minted jockey. After a few words of encouragement from the other jockeys, Isaac mounted his horse and was led to the track. All of a sudden, Isaac's big moment was at hand. With everyone watching, it was time for him to show exactly what he knew and achieve the primary objective for any new jockey: finish the race alive. Jordan's instructions to Isaac were probably quite simple: get the six-year-old mare off the line at the tap of the drum and run her to the finish line. But whatever they were, it didn't matter in the end. Isaac was the last off the line. In no time, Lady Greenfield was distanced by the field and finally cantered past the judges' box to the applause of the exhausted crowd, ending the first Louisville Jockey Club meeting.

Isaac might not have appreciated this recognition from the crowd; it would have been embarrassing and humiliating to perform so poorly. But he would have many other opportunities to ride past the judges' stand to the cheers of spectators. On those occasions, he would understand that their applause was an expression of appreciation for his skill in the saddle. He would use this first race as a reminder to always compete, regardless of the horse he had under him. This was one of many lessons he would learn from his first ride in Louisville.

What did Eli Jordan think of Isaac's initial performance at Louisville? Did he laugh to himself when the mare failed to get off the line, or did he look for signs of a great jockey being born? We can only speculate, but it seems likely that he used the experience as a teaching tool for his young, eager jockey. Jordan himself may have been a jockey at one point, as were most black trainers of his generation. Weight, age, and fading ability forced many out of the saddle and into the role of trainer, molding both horses and boys into winners. Jordan would have understood if Isaac froze when the drum was tapped. He knew that the jostling and slashing from other jockeys could intimidate a young boy trying to become a man in a do-or-die occupation. Master trainer that he was, Jordan understood the desire to be successful, and he knew how to get what he wanted out of a horse and a young jockey, especially one who trusted his every word and command. Whatever the exchange between trainer and jockey was after the race ended and Isaac weighed out, it likely included a constructive critique that helped Isaac understand what he had done right and where he had failed.

Given Isaac's future success, it is obvious that he took Jordan's criticism to heart. Yet he was still just a boy, and he may have taken his failure hard, even crying once he was out of the public eye, where his peers could not see him and question his toughness. Or he may have demonstrated the same stoically cool demeanor that would characterize his later victories, seemingly achieved without much effort. Or perhaps this loss gave him the incentive to work even harder to become the most successful jockey of his generation—maybe of all time.

In any case, we can assume that Jordan began a regimen to condition Isaac to anticipate when to get off the line, having him practice hundreds of times. In other words, Jordan drilled Isaac in the proper techniques to stay in control of the race before it became a race. He also would have taught him to know the strengths and weaknesses of the horse he was riding, as well as the strengths and weaknesses of the other horses in the field. Isaac needed to develop an awareness of everything going on around him at all times, anticipating the unexpected and trusting his instincts at every turn. The lessons would be ongoing. But Isaac was bright and willing, and his commitment was obvious to all who saw the little yellow boy with long arms, some ability, and a good seat. Despite the loss at Louisville, the fourteen-year-old had passed the first test for a professional jockey: he came back for more.

## Winning It All

Looking back on the career of Isaac Murphy, Philip St. Laurent wrote glowingly about the "cool and assured" way he guided his horses, sometimes with a simple "whisper" to coax his steed across the finish line to win by a nose. In his match races on Salvator, against Ed Garrison riding Tenny, Isaac became famous for two things: "winning and handling his mounts gently." Over the years, Isaac had proved himself head and shoulders above the competition. According to St. Laurent, "That's the way Murphy proved things. He won races."[32] What exactly he had to prove is not mentioned, but by the 1890s, there were several issues affecting black Americans that Isaac could not avoid, even on the racetrack.

The most prevalent was the so-called Negro question, whereby whites wondered what to do with the nation's more than 7 million blacks, who were considered alien in the country of their birth. Whites wanted nothing more than to rid themselves of "the stain" of slavery, on the one hand, and the competition by blacks, on the other.[33] Solutions to the supposed problem were posed by historians such as Philip Bruce, who demonized African Americans as naturally savage and incapable of achieving a sense of civility after emancipation:

> The return of the race to the original physical type, involves its intellectual reversion also. The alteration of its mental character will be disclosed in the development of simpler and more distinct intellectual traits; with the elimination of mulattoes,

the points of mental difference between the blacks and the white will grow more apparent. So far, the only persons of unusual capacity whom the former race has produced have been men who were sprung, either directly or remotely, from white ancestry. . . .

The reversion to the original type is apt to make the Negro a more dangerous political factor, because it will increase his inability to grasp enlightened ideas about public policy.[34]

Bruce promoted the concept of reversion, suggesting that, because of their nature, blacks were destined to become extinct socially, politically, and culturally. His theory also claimed that because mulattoes had "white" blood, the elimination of mixed unions between blacks and whites represented a break in the civilizing of the darker race. In other words, blacks were recognized as a threat to a civilization in which whites once again dominated as masters of their own destiny.[35]

By 1890, black intellectuals had recognized and articulated why white men were so adamantly opposed to the progress of the black race: fear of economic competition was a cloaked reference to fear of black masculinity. If a black man who had once been at the bottom of society proved himself capable of achieving and sustaining success, what could be said about a white man who had never been a slave yet has achieved nothing? Black men's successful competition with whites for jobs, security, and power came to define white masculinity as less potent and therefore less manly. This new reality framed numerous contests between white and black men in the latter part of the nineteenth century.

For Isaac Murphy, his contests against white rivals like Ed Garrison and Jimmy McLaughlin became more significant to racing fans. They still watched to see which horse won the race, but some became more concerned with which race (black or white) won the competition. Horse racing had been good to Isaac, and he had been good for horse racing. What he thought about the Negro question, how it influenced his riding, or whether he became more determined to win because of the growing tensions between the races is not clear. What we do know is that in the spring of 1876, Isaac was a year older and wiser. The most important issues on his mind were the quality of his seat and his understanding of the art of pace. The future was still undefined, and so was his place in it.

By the spring 1876 meeting of the Louisville Jockey Club, Isaac had gained additional experience with the horses owned and managed by the Williams and Owings stable. He had also gained ten pounds. Although Isaac's weight gain—he now tipped the scales at eighty-seven pounds—seemed to bolster his ability to control his mounts, other jockeys were not so lucky. Isaac was probably aware of some of the harsh methods they used to keep the pounds from adding up, including being buried in manure, running and riding while wearing heavy wool sweaters, limiting their food intake, and practicing a regular regimen of vomiting (which, as we now know, can damage the esophagus and rot the teeth, due to stomach acids).

During the winter, Isaac and Eli Jordan no doubt discussed some the finer points of riding to win, especially how to judge the pace of a race and the speed of a horse. When the weather was right and the horses were ready, Jordan began training his eager apprentice in the field, where Isaac excelled. To get as close to his horse as possible, Isaac would have spent hours in the saddle, learning how the horse's shoulders moved in anticipation of the inevitable impact of its feet on the ground. He would have learned how to balance himself in the stirrups, using his knees and hips and head as he and his charge attacked the course with raw determination and intent. He would have felt the rush of accelerating from a dead standstill to speeds that felt like he would leave the earth forever if he just leaped off the horse with his arms open. Finally, he may have visualized himself riding the perfect Kentucky Derby, as Oliver Lewis had in 1875.

For those involved in the horse-racing business, the work was never ending, especially as it related to developing the next champion Thoroughbred. In the Bluegrass, most trainers and turfmen knew which horses were primed to win the stake races at Nashville, Lexington, and Louisville and which ones could succeed back east at Saratoga, Long Branch, and Monmouth Park. Horses that showed well in the early spring and were in peak condition by June had their legs under them and could begin training for the fall races. Controlled tests to measure a horse's submission to the will of the trainers and jockeys provided a glimpse of the animal's temperament and character both under stress and under ideal circumstances. The profits to be made from investing in a good horse and a proven winner could be phenomenal—earnings from the sale of horses, stud fees, and the auctioning off of foals of a winning breed. However, to win races and make money, one had to do two things: get the horse to run fast, and get the jockey to run smart.

Like the horses, the jockeys underwent conditioning and tests of endurance, especially those who were talented but still unproven, like Isaac. The more real competitions they could ride in, the better they would become. Each time they climbed onto the back of a well-conditioned, well-prepared animal, they had an opportunity to show the maturity and instincts needed to be successful. But there was a catch. The jockey had to want to win more than the trainer, more than the owner or breeder, and more than the other jockeys in the field. And he had to convince the horse he was riding to run fast enough to win the race. Isaac was that kind of jockey. Later in his career, Isaac's good friend and attorney Llewellyn P. Tarleton asked him about the potential of a particular young rider. Isaac sternly replied, "He can't expect to get up and ride right without work and exercising. It was practice that made me know when I was going a 45 or 50 gait."[36] Putting in the necessary work made Isaac great.

It is intriguing to think of Isaac as a track rat, always willing to exercise any horse available to be ridden. Maybe he even imagined what it was like to be a horse, running fast with the wind blowing past him. He likely befriended *les belles bêtes* with apples and carrots and kept some feed stuffed in his pocket to reward a spirited colt, resisting the saddle or bit, for his good work and cooperation. Isaac and the horses he rode most frequently became kindred spirits. He watched as they ate, slept, and ran freely, getting to know them and understand their habits. Not all jockeys shared Isaac's patience with the horses; some preferred to use the riding whip to intimidate and punish a horse for not running fast enough, demonstrating who was in control. Isaac, however, connected with horses in a way that seemed to create an agreement between equal parties. Isaac may have wondered to himself what the horses were thinking when they saw him. Did they like him? Could they understand him? Isaac saw and understood each horse as an individual with a distinct personality and particular likes and dislikes. Knowing each of his partners so well gave Isaac the edge, allowing him to win on any horse at any time.

In addition to spending time with the horses and training with Jordan, Isaac no doubt benefited from listening to the wisdom being doled out in huge doses by the old philosophers who hung out at the stable and the racetrack, all eager to impart the tiniest bit of information to guarantee an advantage over an unsuspecting rival. Although there is evidence that a number of these men were former colored troops and veterans of the Civil War, there is no indication that any of them knew Isaac's father. If they had, that would have been an important part of Isaac's growth as a man—sharing memories of his father with men who knew him and might have fought beside him during the war. These are just some of the gaps in African American history that we long to know but never will.

Although he was still a year away from participating in his first Kentucky Derby, Isaac had the opportunity to prove his abilities in other races over the five-day period in 1876. In fact, in the Louisville Ladies Stakes for two-year-olds, he showed the skills that would make his name synonymous with dramatic finishes. On May 17, the third day of the meet, Isaac was the jockey of choice to ride Williams and Owings' Springbranch in a field of ten that included another horse from the same stable, Classmate. At the tap of the drum, the field got away, with the bay filly Princess out in front. After only "a few yards," Classmate took the lead, followed by Lizzie Whipps and Isaac on Springbranch.[37] After the three-quarters pole, Isaac managed to maintain his third position, holding off Eva Shirley and Glentina. Down the stretch, Springbranch answered Isaac's call and sprinted past Lizzie Whipps and gained ground on Classmate, only to lose the race by two lengths. Isaac finished second and in the money, which was good for his employer and therefore good for him. He was still learning how to wait for the right time to let his horse open up and get to the finish line first. His second ride atop Springbranch, in the Tennessee Stakes, was not as successful; he finished out of the money in fifth place.

From Louisville, the Williams and Owings stable traveled north to Cincinnati, Ohio, to participate in the Cincinnati Jockey Club meeting at Chester Park, one of the new racecourses in the Midwest. Inaugurated in 1875, the same year as the Louisville Jockey Club, Chester Park fixed its spring racing schedule to come after the Louisville races and before the meetings at St. Louis.[38] Officials in Cincinnati understood the value of their city as a major hub between those two other destinations for wealthy owners and breeders, as well as the masses that followed the turf.[39] To accommodate patrons of the turf, the Marietta and Cincinnati Railroad created a special train from downtown Cincinnati, near the corner of Pearl and Plum Streets, to Chester Park. Judge Edgar M. Johnson, president of Cincinnati's Queen City Jockey Club and a lawyer by trade, helped build the racecourse to boost the Cincinnati economy as horse-racing insiders and fans traveled to the city.[40]

Similar to Louisville, Chester Park was energized by a new enthusiasm for racing, and local citizens flocked to the track to enjoy the spectacle of daring jockeys defying death as they piloted their 1,200-pound torpedoes around the dirt tracks designed for that purpose. At the four-day event in Cincinnati, Isaac did not fare so well, finishing fourth in two races on two different days.[41] But again, at this stage of his career, what he needed was experience. To continue to develop as a jockey who was capable of winning races consistently, he had to ride as often as he could, testing out Jordan's instructions and critiques, as well as his own self-evaluations. Still, nothing could have prepared Isaac for the politics of the turf and the unintended consequences—both positive and negative—of trying to win at all costs.

In September, at the annual Lexington meeting at the Kentucky Association racetrack, Isaac took a giant leap forward. In the second race of the fifth day, the Colt and Filly Stakes, he won aboard P. Bennett's Glentina, the chestnut filly previously owned by B. F.

Pettit, and the same horse Isaac had ridden for his first win at Crab Orchard the previous spring. On this particularly cool and cloudy day, Isaac put everything together, beating a field of horses that included Baden-Baden, a future Kentucky Derby winner, as well as McWhirter and King Faro, both winners of major stakes races. The editor of the *Kentucky Live Stock Record* provided a detailed account of the race:

> After several false starts Major [B. G.] Thomas sent the eleven away to a most capital start. The field was so large and the horses crowded together so close on the turn that it was impossible to say who had the lead until half way round the turn, when Glentina's colors showed in front, King Faro who was cut off by the crowding on the turn was second, the remainder of the lot pretty well bunched. Just after passing the quarter, 25 seconds, King Faro showed half a length in front of Glentina with Harry Peyton, Baden Baden and Headlight lapped a length from them. No change occurred down the back stretch or past the half mile, 50¾ seconds. *Coming around the lower turn Glentina again showed her nose in front*, with Baden Baden lapped on King Faro. They passed the three quarter pole, 1:18, in this order, and on entering the homestretch Glentina increased her lead and finally won by a length, King Faro in second, half a length in front of Harry Peyton, third, who in turn was lapped by McWhirter, fourth, Baden Baden fifth, Allen Pinkerton sixth, Endorser seventh, Bradamante eighth, Headlight ninth, Blarneystone tenth, Victory eleventh. Time, 1:45½.[42]

In this race, Isaac demonstrated the style that would make him not only a consistent winner but also a popular jockey among owners. He was growing into his full potential, and everyone saw it, including his mother, America.

Sometime during the fall meeting in Lexington, after his win on Glentina, Isaac decided to change his surname from Burns to Murphy. Why would Isaac choose to distance himself from the memory of his father, a Civil War veteran who had fought against slavery? What was the benefit of taking the last name of his grandfather Green (Jeremiah) Murphy? Evidence suggests that Isaac took his grandfather's name as a gesture of respect and to honor the man who had taken in a desperate America and her children in their time of need. The other alternative is that he did it because his mother asked him to. And being an obedient child who loved and respected his mother, and perhaps because of her poor health, Isaac chose to honor his mother's wishes. But why would America ask her son to change his name? The answer is unclear and open to speculation. However, it is possible that Jerry (Skillman) Burns was not Isaac's father. Jerry may have adopted Isaac as his son, and Isaac may have already known and accepted this, taking Burns as his last name because that was the name of the man who had cared for him as a father. But at this point, Isaac may have decided to change his name to set the story straight for himself and to stay connected to his real past.

We cannot be sure how Isaac spent his leisure time, but he probably had few free days to lose himself in the streets of Lexington or spend time with his mother. It is likely that during the winter months of November through January—or, in modern terms, the off-season—Isaac sought out his mother's company, but his time with her was probably limited because of her tuberculosis. Still, it seems safe to assume that America maintained an ongoing relationship with her son, despite her illness. They may have attended church together at one of the six black churches listed in the 1876 directory. While we will never know for sure the inner workings of the relationship between Isaac and America, one thing is clear: she placed her son on the path he seemed born to follow. America was important to Isaac, and he would be committed to fulfilling her vision for him long after her death in 1879.

Isaac's first official ride under his grandfather's name was a dramatic success, even though he was four and a half pounds overweight. On September 21, 1876, the second day of the fall meeting of the Louisville Jockey Club, the ninety-one-pound jockey again rode Springbranch, entered in the Bluegrass Stakes for two-year-

olds. The field of stellar Thoroughbreds included Belle of the Meade,
Glentina, Felicia, and Miss Ella. After a series of false starts, each
jockey trying to get the jump on the others, the race began with
Isaac in the awkward position of being in the lead. By the half-mile
pole, the gap had been closed, with Belle of the Meade and her jockey Scott challenging Isaac and Springbranch for the lead. Keeping
his cool, the rookie jockey maintained his pace and piloted Springbranch beautifully around the lower turn. With the two horses now
running side by side and entering the homestretch, Isaac asked his
light-flanked filly to give a little more, and she responded by opening
up her stride and separating from the challenger to win by a length.[43]
With this victory, Isaac Murphy the jockey was born. But at that
moment, no one could have known that the small fifteen-year-old
with thin lips and a straight nose would create such a demand for
great horses and even greater jockeys.

Overall, Isaac had a good showing at Louisville. He finished
second to Alexander Keene Richards's Redding atop T. J. Megibben's Eaglet, and he had a fourth-place finish on Bennett's Glentina
in the Sanford Stakes. The records for the rest of the 1876 season are
fragmented. It is not clear whether Isaac rode in the Nashville Association meeting in October. However, records indicate that the Williams and Owings stable was there and that several of their horses
competed and won major stakes races, so Isaac may have participated in some of these wins. Official records indicate that Isaac had
mounts in fifteen races and recorded victories in two: at Lexington
and at Louisville. However, if he rode in additional races in Nashville, he easily could have increased his mounts to twenty and his
wins to four or five.

It is instructive to know that during this period, top jockeys
rode 150 to 300 races per season, primarily because there were fewer horses and fewer races compared with later in the century. A jockey's salary could vary from $15 to $100 per month if he rode for a
single stable, plus whatever bonuses he received for winning. Some
jockeys, such as William Walker, frequently bet on the horses they
rode, hoping to make extra money.

Now that he was a professional jockey, Isaac's life was about to change—his understanding of his new career, the world in which it functioned, and his place in it. How he would adjust and what choices he would make would be just as unique as his talents on the racetrack.

## The End of an Era of Progress

With the election of Republican Rutherford B. Hayes to the presidency in 1876, the "bargain between Big Business and the South" was about to change the trajectory of progress in American society, especially as it related to blacks' ability to retain the rights gained through the Thirteenth, Fourteenth, and Fifteenth Amendments.[44] In Kentucky, Republican politicians argued over the future of the South, which was still unwilling to admit its "own acts of 'madness, folly, and wickedness' [toward blacks]; instead of taking the Negro by the hand and leading him in a friendly way in to the paths of virtue, intelligence and material prosperity, they [Southerners] have appealed to the passions and prejudices of race against race, until they have excited the ignorant and vicious deeds of violence and outrages . . . which cast a dark shadow over the entire South."[45] Unfortunately, the hotly contested election, the arguments in favor of the nation's growth and the development, and the hatred of the Negro by whites in both the North and the South resulted in compromises that not only threatened to start a new civil war but also put African Americans at the mercy of white Southerners who were still seething over losing the war, losing their property, and seeing their former slaves gain power and use it to refute and deny the idea of white dominance.

Almost immediately after the Federal government removed troops from the South, Southern planters and Southern Democrats set out to disenfranchise blacks by denying them access to the ballot box "by force, by economic intimidation, by propaganda designed to lead him [the Negro] to believe that there was no salvation for him in political lines but he must depend entirely upon the thrift and the good will of his white employers."[46] With the election of Hayes, segregation found a friend in Washington who was willing to promote the destruction of African American life as mere sport to enable growth and prosperity: the new basis for American capitalism.

In *Slavery by Another Name*, Douglas A. Blackmon writes lucidly about the consequences of the return of "white political control" in the South. In states like Mississippi, black life was already criminalized through legislation outlawing vagrancy. In a majority of Southern states, blacks faced the possibility of being jailed and forced to work under conditions that were, in some cases, worse that slavery. Blackmon writes: "By the end of Reconstruction in 1877, every formerly Confederate state except Virginia had adopted the practice of leasing black prisoners into commercial hands. There were variations among the states, but all shared the same basic formula. Nearly all the penal functions of government were turned over to the companies purchasing convicts. In return for what they paid each state, the companies received absolute control of the prisoners."[47] In other words, to feed the South's need for cheap labor and to reassert white privilege and power, the law and big business conspired to subjugate and reenslave African Americans through convict leasing programs.

In some Southern states, black boys under the age of fourteen were arrested for misdemeanors and petty crimes, or just for being orphaned and homeless. These mostly innocent victims were sent to convict camps with adults for terms ranging from a few months to life. In Kentucky, the first prison leasing contract was signed in 1825; by 1877, it was on the verge of expansion as white leaders debated the best way to answer the Negro question.[48] The extent to which African Americans in Lexington experienced the consequences of American racism and the new Southern capitalism is not known. However, if Isaac had not been apprenticed to Williams and Owings by his mother, or if she had died before he was established in some occupation, he might have ended up in one of those convict camps, leased to a company looking to fill its labor quota with able-bodied blacks.[49] Fortunately for Isaac, his career as a jockey was taking off like a rocket. There seemed to be no end in sight to his success.

In April 1877 James Williams bought out his partner, Richard Owings, for an undisclosed amount of money and shipped his stable of horses to Nashville in preparation for the annual meeting there.[50] In addition to Williams, Isaac rode for several other owners, including the firm of Rice and Bethune and J. W. Hunt-Reynolds, the proprietor of Fleetwood Stock Farm. In Nashville, Isaac finished third in his first four races; his lone victory came on day three on Williams's Vera Cruz in the Cumberland Stakes for three-year-olds. In both one-mile heats, he successfully piloted the bay colt to impressive wins over the field of competitors.[51] Similar to his performance the previous fall, Isaac did extremely well for a novice jockey. His victory on Vera Cruz demonstrated that he was learning to judge the ability of the horse under him, as well as the abilities of the other horses in the field. In the final heat, King William jumped into the lead from the start, but by the half-mile pole, Isaac had brought Vera Cruz up and was challenging for the lead. There was something special about how he handled his horses down the stretch. With a little encouragement from Isaac, they responded and won by whatever it took—a length, a head, or a nose. In this race, Vera Cruz answered his request. The season was only beginning, and there would be plenty of close finishes to come.

Isaac had to be hoping that this season would solidify his career as a full-fledged jockey who was free to negotiate contracts and earn a set salary plus bonuses for victories. His apprentice's salary, which was paid to his mother, was obscenely low, considering the progress he had made over the past two seasons. An increase in salary would allow Isaac's mother to live more comfortably and perhaps try one of the numerous cures for consumption publicized in the *Lexington Observer* and *Lexington Daily Press*. Although these remedies were experimental at best and opportunistic quackery at worse, none would benefit America. Unfortunately, the real cure was decades away, and America had less than three years to live. But Isaac may have thought about the possibility of saving his mother's life from time to time.

Isaac arrived back in Lexington in time for the May 12 start of the Kentucky Association meeting. Riding Classmate in the Phoenix Stakes, Isaac was able to negotiate the turns on his home track but failed to close the distance on Bradamante and lost by a length. The next day, on J. R. McKee's Waterwitch, he won the Filly Stakes in dazzling fashion. Coming down the stretch, Isaac piloted the chestnut filly past Queechy like a missile, winning by a head. These dramatic finishes gained the public's attention.

By 1877, Isaac was no doubt maturing as he was increasingly exposed to the world beyond Lexington. What he thought about the election of Rutherford B. Hayes, the loss of Federal protection for blacks in the South, or the possibility of a war with Spain over Cuba, we will never know. But at the very least, he had to realize that one did not have to be white, educated, or middle class to be concerned about race, politics, and business. For most urban-dwelling blacks, their race represented a political position and therefore presented limited economic opportunities. Luckily for Isaac and other black jockeys, they were still somewhat insulated in horse racing. For the most part, at least in the South, whites still saw working with animals as "nigger work," and they gladly let the "darkies" occupy most of those positions. Very soon, that would change. And Isaac would have a major role in transforming jockeying into a highly lucrative profession, and therefore one that was highly sought after by whites, who viewed black jockeys' high salaries as an affront to white boys, who could ride horses too.

In the meantime, James Williams, Eli Jordan, and Isaac Murphy made their way to Louisville on the special excursion trains from Lexington to prepare for the third meeting of the Louisville Jockey Club. Isaac was scheduled to ride in his first Kentucky Derby, piloting Vera Cruz. Benjamin Bruce, editor of the *Kentucky Live Stock Record*, wrote glowingly of the first day: "Never in the history of the Kentucky turf with all its splendid antecedents, has the promise been so bright or the prospects flattering for a brilliant meeting as the forthcoming one of the Louisville Jockey Club."[52] The weather on May 22, the first day of the races, was beautiful and "tempered by a gentle breeze," and those sitting in the infield were anxious for the races to begin.[53] After the first race, the spectators took up their positions all around the track and in the stands to witness the third installment of the spectacle that represented Kentucky pride, as well as its future: the Kentucky Derby.

In the field of eleven capable three-year-olds, Isaac's only advantage was his understanding of Vera Cruz and how to ride him. He had ridden the horse on numerous occasions and was well acquainted with his temperament, but different competitions and different fields can bring out the best and worse in athletes, even horses. After several false starts and a pause in the action, the field was off, but Vera Cruz had a poor start; the horse "reared and plunged" and was left behind.[54] Isaac regained control over the temperamental animal to finish strong—in fourth place—but out of the money. Most believed that Vera Cruz would have won the Derby "if he had not unfortunately been left at the post."[55] Many years after the race, Isaac expressed the same sentiment: "I have always thought I should have won the Kentucky Derby that year . . . had not Vera Cruz, my mount been left at the post. Vera Cruz was a superior race horse, but was never sound and when this is considered his career was all the more remarkable."[56]

During the final days of the Louisville Jockey Club meeting, Isaac had two other mounts; he finished first on Fair Play in a heat race on the sixth day, and he came in fourth on Classmate in a final-day "purse race" sponsored by a consortium of Louisville hotels. Early on the morning of the last day, the clouds had dispersed and the threat of rain had subsided, and the track was filled with racing fans and others interested in watching history unfold. They crowded the infield, the grandstand, and the areas surrounding the track to see Frank Harper's five-year-old bay stallion Ten Broeck, ridden by Isaac's friend and mentor William Walker, race against the clock.

Horses born in the Bluegrass were bred for speed, and Ten Broeck was capable of running very fast. In the time trials, he broke the American record for the mile at 1:39¾ and ran the best two miles, at 3:27½; the best three miles, at 5:26¼; and the best four miles, at 7:15¾.[57] Newspaper headlines read: "Ten Broeck's Great Race," "Ten Broeck Cuts Down the Fastest Two Mile Record Three Seconds," and "A Glorious Event in Old Kentucky: Ten Broeck the Fastest Horse in the World."[58] The glory of "Old Kentucky" had been realized, and horse racing had emerged as a national spectacle worthy of coast-to-coast press coverage. The widespread attention garnered by this particular feat was the beginning of a number of changes in horse racing, the Bluegrass, and those who participated in the sport, especially Isaac Murphy.

That season, Isaac would ride for the first time at Saratoga, giving eastern horse-racing aficionados a glimpse of his abilities with *les belles bêtes*. The boy from Lexington was about to enter a world where fast horses, politics, and gambling were an integral part of the decadent realm of the eastern kings of the turf and their style of horse racing, which would directly and indirectly affect the entire nation.

Horse racing in the East had been in existence longer than the United States of America. When and where it was perfected mostly depended on who had money to spend on horses, where venues for racing were available, and whether people were interested in watching Thoroughbreds run around dirt tracks in the suburbs. In post–Civil War New York, wealthy investors such as Leonard Jerome, August Belmont, Cornelius Vanderbilt, William R. Travers, and John Hunter supported the sport's revival, and a new culture of horse racing was developed for the large crowds of spectators who could afford to spend time and money doing whatever they pleased.[59] Tracks were built at Saratoga Springs, Jerome Park, and Monmouth Park at Long Branch to satisfy the need for class affiliation and elevation. Writing about horse racing in New York, historian Steven Reiss observes, "Wealthy New Yorkers were creating racing stables because of personal satisfaction with their horses' accomplishments and a desire to enhance and certify their elite status."[60] By the 1870s, the resort town of Saratoga Springs, New York, became synonymous with the changing nature of the turf: it was obstinate, crooked, and unclean. Still, the lucrative purses in the East and the chance to showcase the pride of the Bluegrass drew Kentuckians to the Adirondacks version of Sodom and Gomorrah, where gambling, drinking, and other vices were rampant among the well-connected, well-heeled, and, most likely, well-armed.[61]

In 1862 gambler, former prizefighter, and future congressman John Morrissey led the push to make Saratoga Springs a destination for wealthy patrons who were interested in casino-style gambling and entertainment. Within a year, he added four days of horse racing to the growing list of activities, which included carriage rides, horseback riding, and boating. Seeking to expand the sporting aspect of the upstate New York resort, Morrissey formed the Saratoga Racing Association for the Improvement of the Breed, with the backing of Leonard Jerome, John Purdy, Cornelius Vanderbilt, William R. Travers, and John Hunter, who also became founding members of the organization. When the opportunity presented itself, the association secured an additional 125 acres to construct a new track and a grandstand capable of seating 5,000 spectators, with enough space left over to entertain as many as 10,000 on the grounds surrounding the track.[62] The races were not always the most popular entertainment in Saratoga, and the racetrack's clientele found numerous other ways to spend their time and money—at the shops lining Broadway, in the local restaurants, and in the private hotel parlors where "Cubans" provided "musical entertainment" to the fashionable and the restless.[63]

The resort town was also a haven for an array of working-, middle-, and upper-class blacks. During the antebellum period, free blacks migrated to Saratoga Springs to work for wages as bellhops, waiters, or washerwomen in the hotels and boardinghouses and as trainers, stable boys, grooms, and exercise boys at the track and stables. Blacks were the main source of labor at the United States and Grand Union Hotels and in the town's restaurants; others worked as carriage drivers, transporting resort patrons to the train station or the racecourse or just taking them for a leisurely drive along the expansive avenues. Saratoga provided a significant amount of income for many seasonal workers who lived in New York, Philadelphia, or other nearby locations in the off-season.

Historian Myra Armstead writes that the postbellum "growth of the black population in Saratoga Springs" was tied to the service industry, but the gambling economy expanded blacks' financial opportunities, allowing them to generate "peripheral income, as proprietors of permissive" black businesses.[64] And although African Americans were permitted to ride as jockeys, historians Ed Hotaling and Steven Reiss note that black owners were barred from entering their horses in races, and black spectators were barred from the seating area, probably in the grandstand.[65] Armstead suggests that although Saratoga's African American community was transient and relatively small compared with the visiting white clientele, it found a way to partake in the festivities. An article in the July 19, 1865, edition of the *New York Times* notes that one of the many attractions in Saratoga was a lecture "by an intelligent colored gentleman from Africa in the Baptist Church."[66] The identity of this "intelligent colored gentleman" is unknown, but the account of this particular event in the history of Saratoga's black community is intriguing.

It is important to note that during this period, tensions between blacks and Irish immigrants and Irish Americans were once again on the rise, particularly with regard to employment opportunities. Not that long ago, New York had been the site of the 1863 draft riots—a response to the Conscription Act.[67] Given the country's prevailing racism and economic instability, impoverished Irish and native white men responded violently to the law, which allowed draftees to avoid military service if they hired substitutes or paid $300 to buy their way out. Unwilling to participate in a war to free blacks, who would ultimately compete for and possibly take their jobs, whites lashed out. First they attacked draft offices, but then blacks became the targets of their hatred. Black men, women, and children were tortured, hanged, and burned by mobs of whites of all ethnicities who joined in collective opposition to black suffrage and opportunity. By 1877, the seasonal jobs once reserved for blacks had become appealing to "vast numbers of Catholic Irish immigrants," who used their whiteness and the specter of violence to oust blacks from these previously undesirable jobs.[68] This would happen in other occupations as well, including that of jockey.

By 1876, under the guise of the Saratoga Racing Association, John Morrissey sought to control horse racing in the East and the gambling activity related to it. Morrissey's strong-arm attempt to restructure racing in New York in favor of Saratoga Springs—that is, to ensure that races at the resort took precedence over all other scheduled meetings—was part business and part vendetta. In 1867 Morrissey had a falling-out with his partners in the luxurious casino at Saratoga, professional gamblers H. P. McGrath of Lexington and John Chamberlain of St. Louis. Shortly afterward, McGrath left New York for Kentucky, and Chamberlain began planning for Monmouth Park at Long Branch, New Jersey.[69] It is not clear why the partnership dissolved, but it is possible that McGrath and Chamberlain were willing to fix races by having jockeys pull horses and having betting operators lower the odds to encourage unsuspecting patrons to wager more money. Trusted by the wealthy and well positioned, Morrissey probably asked his partners to leave to protect his distinguished board of directors, and himself, from scandal.

To guarantee first-rate racing at Saratoga Springs, Morrissey believed they had to ensure the quality of the horses participating. To do so, racing officials decided to penalize stables whose horses had run in races within five days before the Saratoga Springs meeting. For Kentuckians traveling to the East to compete at Monmouth Park, the penalties represented an escalation of political maneuvering by racing officials to seize commercial control of the sport. On June 16 the *Kentucky Live Stock Record* observed:

The Monmouth Park races begin on June 30th and to prevent horses from running at Long Branch, the Saratoga Association programme penalizes winners over any other course after June 25th. The penalties range from 5 to 12 pounds. We thought turf interests had received a sufficient backset in New York this year by the suppression of pool selling, without any additional handicapping; but in this it seems we were mistaken. These penalties imposed on winning horses at Long Branch may work injury to that meeting, and while it does, it is certain to injure Saratoga in a like degree. It is a declaration of war against owner and other associations which they may accept to the great injury of both meetings. Penalties like handicaps are not popular with the American racing public, and the best thing Saratoga can do is at once abolish these penalties.[70]

The commercialization of racing as an entertainment for the masses, the prevalence of high-stakes gambling, and the New York legislature's banning of pool selling forced many unique aspects of the sport to change.[71] Whereas Kentucky turfmen had once been welcomed and had introduced some of the best-bred animals in the country, along with some of the best jockeys, this new era of horse racing was shaped by a politics of the turf that was exceedingly influenced by the wealthy, the politically powerful, and the plungers who wagered fortunes on the outcome of races, many of which they influenced. The eastern racing circuit, with its connections to the nation's wealthiest families, became a haven for horse-racing aficionados from around the country who wanted nothing more than to establish themselves as members of the moneyed elite. Less influential were those interested in the improvement of the breed.

For Isaac Murphy, the chance to race in the East was both a blessing and a curse. When he arrived in Saratoga Springs, where he stayed and ate, and which individuals he interacted with are not known. What we do know is that his monthlong stay in Saratoga exposed Isaac to African Americans from different backgrounds, professions, and occupations; Spanish-speaking Cuban musicians who moved between the elite white society they played for and the black community they lived in; and the anti-Semitic movement initiated by Henry Hilton, whose "interdiction" of Jews from the Grand Union Hotel was supported by hotel patrons. We also know that Isaac put on one hell of a show in his debut at Saratoga Springs.[72]

On July 31, the fifth day of racing, the weather was clear and the track was sound from the steady "drying wind, and a warm sun."[73] Riding the energetic Fair Play, one of the favorites, Isaac was poised to compete against the field of eastern horses and jockeys that included George Lorillard's Lucifer, ridden by Harris; the Dwyer brothers' Vermont, ridden by Sayers; and T. W. Doswell's Rappahannock, ridden by Hughes. After a poor start, Isaac was unable to get a feel for the field and finished an unimpressive fifth. But this was just the first race, and Isaac would have a month to gauge the riding styles of the eastern jockeys and study the temperaments of the different horses.

The following day the weather was clear and attendance was high. It was a good day for the jockey from Lexington to show what he was capable of. In the third race, a heat race of three-quarters of a mile for a $300 purse, Isaac was once again piloting Fair Play. At the start, D. J. Crouse's Auburn jumped out in front with Isaac right behind, pressing the lead. Miscalculating, Isaac waited too late to make his move and lost the first heat by a length. However, he adjusted his strategy in the final two heats. He allowed Auburn to get away quickly, but at the lower turn and into the straightaway, Isaac leaned forward, signaling to Fair Play to open up, and the horse responded. There was one difference in the final heat: Isaac used the whip just enough to motivate his mount to win convincingly—a rare display of coercion by the usually cool horse whisperer.[74] But Isaac was not yet proven. During the second meeting at Saratoga, from August 5 to 22, he would get closer to perfection.

Of the six races Isaac started, he won three: twice on Vera Cruz and once on Fair Play. Consistently improving and demonstrating his ability to judge the pace of the field and maintain control of the race, Isaac got his horses to the finish line by the slightest of margins, winning by a head or a nose. On the third day of the second meeting, in a dash race of a mile and three-quarters for a $600 purse, Isaac apparently intimidated the other jockeys from attacking the track and running aggressively. In fact, based on the account in the *Kentucky Live Stock Record*, the other jockeys seemed to be waiting for Murphy, who provided an excellent start as the pace was slow, steady, and "quite uninteresting." However, after the first mile the race became a sprint to the finish between Isaac on Vera Cruz and George Barbee on Tom Ochiltree. Not until the end of the race did Isaac let his horse go to the lead, and with the very last jump, Vera Cruz "headed Big Tom" at the finish line.[75] The sixteen-year-old master in the saddle had captured the attention of everyone at the Saratoga Springs horse park. He was making a name for himself by beating the best in the East.

Returning home to Lexington, the conquering hero likely began to prepare for the fall meeting of the Kentucky Association, scheduled to start on September 17 on what could be considered Isaac's home track. In his free time, he likely interacted with various members of the community at church, at the barbershop, or on Vine

Street (Lexington's black Main Street), where his accomplishments on the track may have been praised by his admirers. Upon his return home, Isaac probably learned of the movement to leave Lexington for Nicodemus, Kansas, and the role played by the Reverend Morrison M. Bell of Pleasant Green Baptist Church.[76] Although the end of Reconstruction marked the end of the era of progress for black-white relations in America, especially in the South, a place like Nicodemus provided hope for a people in search of "racial uplift."[77]

As president of the Nicodemus Colony, Reverend Bell and his officers, which included Isaac Talbott, W. J. Niles, Daniel Clarke, Jerry Lee, William Jones, and Abner Webster, promoted a new beginning for the "colored people" of Lexington. An outgrowth of the movement started by Benjamin "Pap" Singleton, the Nicodemus Colony offered three specific enticements to African Americans who were willing to move to Kansas: access to land and the opportunity to become self-sufficient; escape from the violence of the South and the white men who perpetuated the degradation of blacks; and security for their families, especially their children, whose future looked bleak if they stayed in Kentucky, where their perceived value was based on their usefulness to whites.

Printed in bold letters across the top of a broadside announcing the migration to Nicodemus was this statement: "All Colored People That Want to Go to Kansas, on September 5th, 1877, Can Do So for $5.00."[78] The officers of the Nicodemus Colony understood the need to convey the seriousness of the venture to the masses, and they printed the following resolutions on the same broadside to clarify the mission and goals of the expedition:

> WHEREAS, We, the colored people of Lexington, Ky., knowing that there is an abundance of choice lands now belonging to the Government, have assembled ourselves together for the purpose of locating on said lands. Therefore,
>
> BE IT RESOLVED, That we do now organize ourselves into a Colony, as follows:—Any person wishing to become a member of this Colony can do so by paying the sum of one dollar ($1.00), and this money is to be paid by the first of September,

1877, in installments of twenty-five cents at a time, or otherwise as may be desired.

RESOLVED, That this Colony has agreed to consolidate itself with the Nicodemus Towns, Solomon Valley, Graham County, Kansas, and can only do so by entering the vacant lands now in their midst, which costs $5.00.

RESOLVED, That this Colony shall consist of seven officers—President, Vice-President, Secretary, Treasurer, and three Trustees. President—M. M. Bell; Vice-President—Isaac Talbott; Secretary—W. J. Niles; Treasurer—Daniel Clarke; Trustees—Jerry Lee, William Jones, and Abner Webster.

RESOLVED, That this Colony shall have from one to two hundred militia, more or less, as the case may require, to keep peace and order, and any member failing to pay in his dues, as aforesaid, or failing to comply with the above rules in any particular, will not be recognized or protected by the Colony.

Based on the available evidence, 900 families caught "Kansas fever" and signed up to leave with the expedition.

On September 6, the *Lexington Press* reported the mood of the previous day's departure of no more than "two hundred and fifty, men, women, and children" as they boarded train cars heading for Ellis, Kansas, to begin life anew.[79] According to historian Nell Irvin Painter, in "September 1877 the second and largest addition, 350 settlers, came to Nicodemus with Reverend M. M. Bell of the Nicodemus Colony, under the aegis of W. R. Hill.[80] In March 1878 Hill would bring another group of 150 people from Scott County, Kentucky, to Kansas. Nicodemus represented a new start for blacks in search of land, opportunity, and a sense of freedom not found in the previous places they had called home.

There is no question that the state of Kentucky in general and the counties surrounding Lexington in particular were not the friendliest of places for African Americans. Between the end of the Civil War and the end of Reconstruction, brutal crimes against blacks, especially lynching, became part of the daily lives of African Americans throughout the state. As historian George Wright asserts, "Although poor, young, uneducated blacks were the primary victims of white violence, no black person within Kentucky was immune from attacks by whites. Furthermore, the entire legal system upheld white violence by refusing to apprehend, charge, and convict white offenders of blacks, thus ensuring that all Afro-Americans were at the mercy of whites."[81] In other words, whites were complicit in denying blacks their humanity through the criminalization and destruction of black life in the Bluegrass. Those who chose to leave Lexington saw no other way to save what mattered most: their lives and the lives of their children.

Isaac could not have missed the commotion at the train station on the day so many people (called Exodusters) left Lexington, and he probably understood why they left. But if Isaac intended to pursue a career as a professional jockey, he would have to construct his own identity in a way that supported his economic pursuits and protected his psychological need to be recognized as hardworking and productive. He would eventually have to cultivate a persona of masculinity tied to the Victorian ideal espoused by aspiring middle-class professional men of the period. In addition, Isaac would have to demonstrate a nonthreatening attitude that was honest and trustworthy in relation to the white patriarchy and its unyielding need to be appeased.

In Lexington, amid the sadness and excitement of the departed Exodusters, Isaac still had a job to do, and he showed well at the Kentucky Association's fall meeting. Out of nine starts, he won three: twice on Vera Cruz and once on Alexander Keene Richards's L'Argenteen. Most important, Isaac began riding for the impresario of Fleetwood Stock Farm, J. W. Hunt-Reynolds, piloting Blue Eyes to a third-place finish in the Colt and Filly Stakes. Less than a month later, at the Louisville Jockey Club's track, Isaac demonstrated his ability to be a consistent winner. On October 1, the first day of the fall meeting at Louisville, ninety-eight-pound Isaac rode Vera Cruz to victory in his first major stakes race—the St. Leger. Later, he would say of this particular victory, "I have often thought of that day. Success made me very happy."[82] In the very next race he won on L'Argenteen, finishing cleanly and coming away with a "big cantor by a length."[83] Over the seven-day period, Isaac won five of the seven races he started, including the Galt House Stakes for three-year-olds on Abe Buford's Lizzie Whipps. In his final race of the season, at the Maryland Association meeting in Baltimore, he won again on Vera Cruz in the Breckinridge Stakes for three-year-olds; the competition from the East including August Belmont's Susquehanna and David McDaniel's two entries, St. James and Major Barker. A description of the race in the *Kentucky Live Stock Record* paints a picture of how Isaac awed spectators with his breathtaking finishes:

> When the flag fell Major Barker took the lead, Susquehanna second, Vera Cruz third, St. James fourth, Wash Booth fifth and Oriole sixth. Before reaching the quarter St. James was in the lead some six lengths, Wash Booth second, Oriole third, Vera Cruz fourth, Major Barker fifth and Susquehanna sixth. St. James opened a gap of twenty lengths in front of Oriole, who was lapped by Vera Cruz. No change at the three-quarter pole, and as they came back to the stand St. James was ten lengths in front of Vera Cruz second, Wash Booth third, Oriole fourth, Susquehanna fifth and Major Barker sixth. Vera Cruz gradually closed the gap on St. James, and by the time they had reached the lower turn he was within a length, and as they entered the homestretch he showed a length in front, and galloping along won the race in a canter by two lengths in front of Wash Booth third, Oriole a bad fourth, Susquehanna fifth, Major Barker sixth.[84]

That the little jockey from Lexington had become a master of the turf was obvious to anyone paying attention. Rather than a struggle to make his horse work beyond its natural capabilities, Isaac's performance as a jockey was artistry, as he coaxed his mount to move at the pace required. For Isaac, riding had become as natural as breathing.

## Seasons of Death and Renewal

After his success in 1877, Isaac was in for some changes. Sometime between the beginning of the off-season and January 1878, Isaac's mentor and father figure, Eli Jordan, left the Williams stable and became head trainer at the Hunt-Reynolds stable. One possible clue to the reason for the parting of ways was the death of Williams's "valuable and richly bred young stallion Creedmoor" on November 6, 1877. Foaled in 1873, the chestnut colt, a son of Asteroid, stood sixteen hands high, "had excellent legs, broad, flat knees with immense bone and great substance. His racing career had been extremely good," so his premature death due to colic must have been a blow to Williams.[85] Whether Jordan was directly responsible for Creedmoor's death through his own negligence, or whether it was the fault of an assistant trainer, groom, or stable boy assigned to care for the four-year-old, Jordan was the trainer on record, so ultimately he was responsible and may have been fired. For the first time since he began working as a stable boy, Isaac was without Jordan. In the long run, this separation would prove invaluable to his development as both a jockey and an individual.

By the end of May 1878, Isaac had ridden in several meetings: the Nashville Blood Horse Association meeting, where he won two of three races on Williams's Fair Play and Shortline; the Kentucky Association meeting, where he finished second in the Blue Ribbon Stakes on R. H. Owens' Leveler and third on Vera Cruz in the sweepstakes race on the second day; and the Louisville Jockey Club meeting, where he finished in second place in three of the five races he started.[86] Clearly, Isaac was not in top form. Perhaps the absence of Jordan was affecting his performance; Williams's instructions to Isaac may not have been what he was accustomed to, negatively influencing the results. There is a possibility that Isaac was hoping to be released from his contract so that he could join Jordan at Fleetwood. One could speculate that he purposely lost races to diminish his status with Williams. However, this is unlikely; Isaac would not have damaged a relationship that was so important to his career as a jockey, which was just beginning to flourish. In addition, a black boy refusing to follow the directions of a white man would have been too risky. Common sense and ambition would have kept the humble, quiet Isaac out of trouble.

The Williams stable traveled to Cincinnati for the Queen City Association meeting at Chester Park, scheduled to start on May 30.

Arriving a few days early allowed both the horses and the jockeys to get accustomed to the track, its surface, and other particulars, such as knowing where the headwind was and where to make the winning jump on the field. On June 1, a generous crowd of 2,500 spectators came out to enjoy the races under clear skies. As Isaac trotted Classmate onto the track and positioned himself and his horse behind the starting line, he could not have anticipated the events that followed and the repercussions they would have on the rest of his life. In an 1889 interview, he recalled the incident that cost him four months of salary and bonuses:

> I have been exceedingly fortunate in keeping the respect of starters and racing officials, and thus avoiding the ban of suspension with but one single exception. . . . I was riding Classmate in a race and a boy started to cross me, not only cutting me off, but running the risk of injuring both the mare and myself. As it was, it knocked the mare to her knees, but I soon pulled her together and was quickly in the race again. Another boy, Link Gross, who was in the race was also jostled by the same daring rider, and, Link's temper getting the best of him, he struck the offending lad in the face. The blood spurted on my shirt, and when the latter claimed foul against me and brought charges of my having hit him, the officials looked at the shirt and blood, and putting more faith in the circumstantial evidence than in my denial, disqualified Classmate for the head, fined me $25 and suspended me for a year.[87]

During his suspension, Isaac might have exercised horses for Williams or for other owners, who would have jumped at the opportunity to have their horses trained by a talented jockey. Or it is possible that his suspension forced Isaac to find work elsewhere, in some other occupation. Prevented from earning a living as a jockey, Isaac temporarily returned to a state of poverty. In hindsight, however, the suspension may have been the best thing for his career and perhaps his life.

Four months passed between Isaac's suspension from racing

and his exoneration and eventual reinstatement on September 11, 1878, by the president of the Queen City Association, Edgar Johnson, who "later on apologized for his hasty action."[88] By this time, Isaac may have been released from his contract with Williams, because a jockey who could not race was of no use. In the same 1889 interview, Isaac recalled that the suspension cost him "considerable at the time, since I was a poor lad and the money I earned by my riding was all I had to live on."[89] This statement implies that Williams did not continue to pay Isaac during the suspension, but we do not know Williams's version of events. It may not have been the best of circumstances for Isaac, but it seems to have worked out to his advantage once he made his way to Frankfort, where Jordan was now working for Hunt-Reynolds.

Hunt-Reynolds was from one of the oldest families in Kentucky, a grandson of Lexington merchant John Wesley Hunt, a breeder of fine racehorses. Hunt-Reynolds was continuing his grandfather's legacy while indulging his lifelong passion for horses. A brief glimpse into his life is important to understand the type of man he was and the influence he would have on Isaac's future.

Born to Anna Taney Hunt and William Bell Reynolds in 1846, J. W. and his sister Catherine were raised by their mother's sister, Mary Hunt, and her husband, Judge John Hanna, after their mother died and their father was unable to care for them. The Hannas, who had no children of their own, adopted their niece and nephew. As part of the Hunt family, J. W. grew up with his first cousins, John Hunt Morgan (the future Confederate general) and his brother C. C. Morgan, who loved horses and rode them "like demons over the countryside."[90] John Hunt Morgan's skills as a horseman would be documented in the reports of Union officers, who noted his use of guerrilla tactics in raids on Union depots and supply lines and his ability to evade capture. The fact is that Morgan knew the land better than the Union soldiers chasing him. As boys, he, his brother C. C., and their cousin J. W. had stayed in the saddle from dawn to dusk, pursuing adventures on horseback.

As soon as Catherine was old enough, Mrs. Hanna sent her to New York to attend Madame Chageri's Seminary for ladies, where she would learn to be a proper lady. However, after the outbreak of the Civil War and the death of Judge Hanna in 1861, Mrs. Hanna moved with the children to Frankfurt, Germany, to escape the violence and uncertainty in Kentucky. J. W. attended the University of Heidelberg, where he studied history, politics, languages, literature, and the arts. By all accounts, he was an "ebullient spirit" who quickly developed into a mature and effusive gentleman.[91] He met his future wife, Meta Fleetwood Westfeldt, in Germany; she was also attending the University of Heidelberg and was an intellectual force equal to her future husband. It is not clear whether they married in Germany, in Kentucky, or in New York City, where Meta's father, Gustav Westfeldt, was a coffee merchant.

We do know that after the Civil War, Hunt-Reynolds returned to Frankfort with his sister and his aunt. After settling in and adjusting to the changes that had taken place in Kentucky, he began the process of establishing his livestock farm, concentrating on Thoroughbred horses. Within a few years of his return to the United States, and using the substantial wealth inherited from his father, grandfather, and uncle, Hunt-Reynolds purchased "637 acres of high, rolling land, mostly set in grass" and surrounded by trees, near the Kentucky River on the Frankfort and Louisville Turnpike. Named after an ancestor of Meta's, Fleetwood Stock Farm was completed sometime between 1867 and 1868.[92] J. W. and Meta's only child, Meta Christina Hunt-Reynolds, was born January 20, 1869.

In the Frankfort community, J. W. served in a number of capacities: as a member of the Knights Templar and Commandery, on the board of the directors of the Frankfort Agricultural and Mechanical Association, and as a delegate for Ascension Episcopal Church at the annual convention in Louisville.[93] A generous person who "gave a hand in every public enterprise, and took the lead in many social interests," Hunt-Reynolds was considered a man of unimpeachable character.[94] It is unknown where he stood on the race question and whether he was a member of the Ku Klux Klan or participated in the lynching of blacks.

Over the course of ten years, Hunt-Reynolds built an estate worth an estimated $82,000, with additional assets in Louisville

real estate.[95] Although genial and scholarly, Hunt-Reynolds was also
competitive: he wanted his horses to win. J. H. Walden, Hunt-Reynolds's trainer and the superintendent of his Fleetwood Stock Farm,
was responsible for maintaining the property but was inconsistent
in bringing home winners. Hunt-Reynolds was a founding member
of the Louisville Jockey Club, and despite all his work to ensure the
quality of Jockey Club meetings, his horses fell short. Hunt-Reynolds's decision to hire Eli Jordan as his new head trainer was a sign
that he was anxious to put it all together: his investment of time, energy, and resources to improve the breed and his patience in working
to develop the perfect Thoroughbred. When Isaac decided to join
Jordan and ride for Fleetwood, he started down a path that would
establish his reputation as a consistent winner, an individual of radi-
ant character, and an exemplar of manly virtues.

On Wednesday, September 11, the third day of the Kentucky
Association's fall meeting, Isaac made his debut wearing the red and
white colors of Hunt-Reynolds's Fleetwood stable. In his first race
after his suspension, Isaac took the reins of the bay colt Caligula in
a mile-and-a-half "Selling Sweepstakes Race" worth $525. After a
"fairish start," the field of six set out on a feverish pace to gain momentum in an effort to capture the lead and eventually the victory.
Isaac waited for the right moment to guide his spirited horse to the
front. As the "platoon" rounded the lower curve and entered the
stretch, Isaac and Caligula made their move. Without hesitation,
they surged into the lead and held on to win by two lengths.[96] On
day four, riding Ed Turner for Taylor and Company in a match race
against Dan Swigert's Mexico, Isaac kept the pace where he needed
it and broke away to win easily by two lengths. Two days later, the
editor of the *Kentucky Live Stock Record* remarked on the result:
"Ed Turner bowled over Mexico in the mile and half race. Isaac
Murphy, who has been reinstated, rode him with artistic skill and
judgment."[97] Clearly, the horse world was taking notice.

At Louisville that fall, Isaac struggled to find his rhythm and
gain a sense of familiarity with the horses. He finished in the money in six of his twelve races but had no victories. His rival from the
East, James McLaughlin, won a majority of the races he started, and

Isaac finished behind him in every race except the last one. What is most significant about that final race was an incident that validated Isaac's character and honesty. On the seventh and final day of the races at Louisville, Isaac was asked to replace Spillman, the jockey riding J. C. Murphy's bay colt Edinburgh, in the third race of an all-ages contest of one-mile heats for a purse of $300. It is not clear why Jockey Club president Meriwether Lewis Clark removed the assigned jockey and selected Isaac to fill in.[98] Did he suspect that the jockey had pulled Edinburgh in the first heat? Had Spillman said or done something that led Clark to believe he was plotting to bring shame to the club and the track?

Earlier in the year, on the Fourth of July, the Louisville Jockey Club had hosted a big $10,000, four-mile match race between Kentucky's Ten Broeck, owned by Frank Harper, and California's champion mare Mollie McCarthy, owned by Theodore Winters. Clark heard rumors that the great black jockey William Walker was going to throw the race. In an interview, Harper recalled the confrontation between Walker and Clark:

> The jockeys were called up to receive their instruction from the Judge. Col. Clark said . . . "I hear there are suspicions that you are going to throw this race. You will be watched the whole way, and if you do not ride to win, a rope will be put about your neck and you will be hung to that tree yonder (pointing the tree just opposite the Judges' stand), *and I will help to do it.*" Walker tried to answer him, and say that he did not want to ride in the race, but Colonel Clark would not let him speak.[99]

It is likely that Isaac was at that race to support Walker, his friend and mentor, and heard the threat against his life if anything in the race looked suspicious.

Given the history of lynching in Kentucky and the seriousness of the accusation, the threat was a real one. Clark demanded unwavering honesty in the saddle, especially among the black jockeys. However, there were too many variables in a race—unforeseeable circumstances or obstacles—that might result in a loss and be construed as intentional, leading to the death of an innocent jockey. Did the white boys receive the same threats if they lost? Probably not. Why were black jockeys subjected to this kind of abuse? Quite plainly, it was part of the history of the sport in Kentucky and the traditions associated with black labor and white power. Historian Maryjean Wall identifies the connection between wealthy "landowners who bred horses" and the violence inflicted on blacks in Kentucky.[100] The fact is that numerous members of the Klan were local farmers and gentlemen of the turf who refused to accept the changes brought about by the Civil War. Reconstruction had come to an abrupt end, and Southern white men were no longer under surveillance by the Federal government, allowing them to perpetrate violence against blacks undisguised and in broad daylight. Blacks were slipping back into a state of nonpersonhood: the "socially dead."[101]

Whatever Clark's motivation was for choosing Isaac as the replacement jockey for Edinburgh, no one contested it. He finished second, but in front of his rival McLaughlin.[102] It is quite possible that this particular episode in his early career informed or confirmed Isaac's decision to always be honest and avoid the temptations of gambling that led jockeys to pull horses and throw races. He would tell his fellow jockey John "Kid" Stoval that if he were honest, he could get all the mounts he desired. That was true for the time being, but there would soon be other unsavory influences to deal with.

Through the end of the 1878 season, Isaac's superb riding elevated Fleetwood to the premier stud farm for Thoroughbreds in the Bluegrass. It was also home of the best jockey in the state of Kentucky, if not the entire South. But he still had to prove himself back East.

Prior to the start of the 1879 season, eighteen-year-old Isaac had ballooned up to more than 130 pounds. This marked the beginning of his battle with weight and the debilitating disease that afflicted a majority of jockeys of the late nineteenth century and cost some of them their lives. Isaac's weight gain was not the result of overindulgence; the winter months spent away from horses and the track gave his body a chance to recover from the stress of maintaining a low riding weight. (Later, like most professional athletes, Isaac would spend the off-season savoring his well-deserved rest, dining, traveling, and otherwise enjoying his wealth. As he eventually learned, there was a price to pay for success.) No longer the lithe and light-weight exercise boy, Isaac was overweight in the spring of 1879 and needed to drop thirty pounds as soon as possible.[103] Most jockeys did not have nutritional programs or structured exercise routines to help them keep fit and active during the off-season. Scientifically sound techniques of weight control for athletes were decades away.[104]

There were several methods for "training down." Fred Taral used to run with several sweaters on to increase perspiration, and Ed "Snapper" Garrison ran behind a moving wagon holding onto the "tail board." Other jockeys took Turkish baths or sparred with boxing gloves to lose weight. Although it was supposedly effective, most jockeys avoided the old-fashioned method of sitting in a pile of manure to induce perspiration. In extreme cases, jockeys used starvation diets to lose weight quickly or "purged" after eating.[105] Some jockeys used enemas or natural laxatives, like "black draught," to clear their bowels. Learning from other jockeys, Isaac eventually developed his own method, which in time would prove both beneficial and costly. For now, he simply went without food and took extended walks, covering several miles, in the weeks and days before a race.[106] As he got older and heavier, the results of his rigorous and dangerous weight-loss routine left Isaac weak and ineffective at the beginning of each season, but once he was at his optimal weight, he managed to maintain it by eating eat fruit and small pieces of "very rare steak."[107] Between races, he spent a considerable amount of time resting, attempting to recover from the tremendous fatigue and strain on his body that came from trying to control his spirited mounts while in a perpetual state of hunger.

When Isaac mounted Falsetto for the Phoenix Stakes at the Kentucky Association meeting on May 10, 1879, he had dropped more than thirty pounds and was probably feeling weak. After numerous false starts, the race began with Trinidad, ridden by Allen, in the lead. Isaac kept Falsetto back and waited until the furlong pole to rush "between Scully and Ada Glenn, throwing the latter off her stride, and winning the race on the post by a neck."[108] Though exhausted, he won two other races over a three-day period.

After winning the stakes race in Lexington, and no doubt feeling pleased with his performance, Isaac and the Hunt-Reynolds stable made their way to the Louisville meeting. May 20 was clear and warm, the track was fast, and "attendance was very large." In the first race, atop Hunt-Reynolds's Fortuna, Isaac took control of the race, only to have it end in a dead heat with William Jennings's Glenmore. In the second race, the Kentucky Derby, Isaac rode Falsetto again, but he waited too long to reel in the colt named Lord Murphy, ridden by white jockey Charlie Shauer. In what was described as "a most exciting race," Falsetto came on like a dynamo "within forty yards of the stand where Lord Murphy drew clear and won the race by a length and a half."[109] Although he probably thought he should have won the Kentucky Derby, the race was still in its infancy (not the premier contest it is today), so Isaac considered it just another race. It was just one of the 100 or more starts he would have that season. Still, he may have felt the need to redeem himself in his remaining races, and by the end of the meeting he had nine wins, including the Louisville Cup on Fortuna, the Tennessee Stakes on G. W. Bowen and Company's Wallenstein, and the Merchants' Stake on Hunt-Reynolds's Blue Eyes.

From Louisville, Isaac traveled to Missouri for the St. Louis Jockey Club meeting from June 10 to 14, where he won two out of four races riding for James Williams, including the first race of the engagement on Checkmate. He left St. Louis and headed for the Chicago Jockey Club meeting, scheduled for June 21 to 27, where he won with S. and R. Weisiger's Incommode and finished in the money on L. P. Tarleton's Solicitor, D. McIntyre's King Faro, and Brien and Spencer's Captain Fred Rice. He then traveled to Michigan for the first meeting of the Detroit Jockey Club, held from July 1 to 4. That event promised to attract prominent "horses from Ohio, Kentucky and Tennessee stables, as well as Martin & Baldwin's Pacific Stables."[110] Winning twice on the second day on Williams's Checkmate and Enquiress, Isaac swept the entire card the next day, riding to victory on Checkmate, Bonnie Oaks, and Glenmore twice. Two days later in Milwaukee, Wisconsin, he came close to duplicating that success; he brought home three winners and might have swept the entire program if he had had a mount in the last race.[111] Thus far, the 1879 campaign was Isaac's most successful to date.

Because the spring and fall racing seasons overlapped, and because jockeys who were under contract went wherever their stables sent them, they had little time to explore the communities they visited. Local entertainments and cultural events may have been plentiful and attractive to a young bachelor, but after competing on the track, he was likely ready for bed. Opportunities for companionship may have been limited for Isaac: another train ride, another city, another boardinghouse, another paddock, another paycheck—and another woman? It is possible that Isaac had sexual relationships before he married, but abstinence would also make sense, considering the racial uplift programs promoting temperance, abstinence, and community building through achievement.

During Reconstruction, African American community leaders advocated abstinence as a demonstration of civility, Christian morals and values, and a progressive orientation toward the future. As historian Michelle Wallace explains, African Americans worked hard to "construct themselves as members of [a] collectivity not just because they and their forebears shared a past, but also because they believed their futures to be interdependent."[112] This somewhat magical disposition allowed individuals to claim their humanity not only through their personal achievements but also, in the case of black men, through their public exhibitions of Christian uprightness, temperance, and gentlemanly decorum that represented the progress of blacks as a whole. What better crusader for morality than Isaac—a man-child who entered the lion's den every day of the racing season and emerged not only unscathed but seemingly strengthened by confronting his temptations? This, of course, is problematic: we cannot know what Isaac did in private. The prevalence of public teetotalers who drink in private and ministers who sin is a clear indication that some performances are for public consumption, while others are private, reserved for personal scrutiny, self-critique, and self-judgment.

As monotonous as the life of a jockey might sound, it was a

great opportunity for a talented young man to see the country and, if good fortune was on his side, make enough money to marry, settle down, and perhaps have a string of horses to run. This may have crossed the eighteen-year-old's mind now and again, as he imagined what his future would look like when he got too big to ride.

By the fall of 1879, Isaac was a rising star and no newcomer to Saratoga Springs. His 1877 race on Vera Cruz had created quite a stir among patrons of the turf, who caught a glimpse of a new type of jockey who was intelligent, calm, patient, and disciplined. He gained the attention of some of the most powerful breeders in the East, whose jockeys failed to match Isaac's single-minded focus on his work. When he arrived at Saratoga in 1879, what were the spectators anticipating from Murphy? Surely, they had read the newspapers and were aware of his dominance at Louisville, Detroit, and Milwaukee races. They may have had a pretty good idea of the outcome, but like any race, nothing was certain.

On June 16, a full month before the races opened at Saratoga, Eli Jordan and the Hunt-Reynolds stable arrived to begin training for the meeting. Sometime after his last race in Wisconsin, Isaac boarded an eastbound train headed for New York.[113] What were traveling conditions like for Isaac? In those cities and towns that drew the color line, they could have been almost anything—from riding in unsafe and unsavory conditions to being ejected from his seat by a white man unwilling to sit in the same car with a black man—even (or perhaps especially) one who seemed to be a social equal or a middle-class professional. Anything other than the stereotypical "coon" or "Sambo" could be an affront to a white man's sense of privilege. In the 1870s and 1880s numerous legal actions were brought against railroads for not protecting the rights of black passengers or for actively enforcing separate car policies by denying blacks access to available seating.

By the time Isaac arrived in Saratoga, the resort town was a crush of humanity—white women dressed in the latest fashions from Europe, wealthy men holding court on the piazzas of the various hotels, and sporting men looking to fill their pockets with winnings based on hot tips and inside information.[114] On Saturday, July 19, the

weather was lovely, the track was in good condition, and the crowd
was anxious for the first race to begin. Along with the white visitors,
"African American tourists and conventioneers" participated in the
festivities where they could, enjoying the benefits of their wealth and
mixing with other middle-class strivers, rubbing elbows—both literally and figuratively—with the obscenely rich. It is safe to assume
that all were looking forward to the day's main event—the prestigious Travers Stakes—and the performance of Spendthrift, the new
prize of New York financier and turfman James R. Keene. White
society may have considered blacks second-class citizens, and some
excluded their darker brothers from the human race altogether, but
everyone at Saratoga agreed that the little jockey from Kentucky was
exciting to watch, especially when he won such big races with such
uncommon style. After the Travers, however, horse-racing fans talked about Isaac Murphy with new enthusiasm:

> In 1879, the last year in which the owners of the great racing
> stables of the seaboard met at Saratoga in force, at the time
> when George Lorillard's Sensation, Grenada, and Rosalie came
> in first, second, and third in the Flash Stakes, a chunky colored
> boy appeared with quiet old Eli Jordan, the able trainer for
> J. W. Hunt-Reynolds of Kentucky. A large delegation of New
> Yorkers had come to back Spendthrift for the Travers, the three
> year old event of the year. While the applause which greeted
> Spendthrift was making the great colt prick his ears, the col-
> ored boy appeared on Falsetto. The way the boy handled Fal-
> setto and won the race attracted the attention of turfmen from
> all sections. The Kentuckians were wild with joy; they threw
> their hats in the air and carried off the coveted trophy from its
> pedestal in front of the grandstand. The lad repeated his vic-
> tory by winning the Kenner Stakes, at two miles, on Falsetto.
> The boy's name is Isaac Murphy. He has had remarkable suc-
> cess on the turf.[115]

Spendthrift, the favorite, was a quality Thoroughbred born on
Daniel Swigert's farm outside Lexington and purchased by Keene

for $15,000 after the colt went undefeated as a two-year-old. But in the end, it was the quality of the jockey that mattered most. New York had become the showplace for two of Kentucky's most prized exports: fast horses and brilliant jockeys. Eighteen-year-old Isaac guided Falsetto to a two-length victory over Spendthrift, ridden by Feakes. In a postrace interview that appeared in *Spirit of the Times*, we get a glimpse of Murphy's thoughtfulness and intellect:

I met Murphy, who rode . . . [Falsetto]. He is a bright youth, and although his winter weight was over 130 lbs., he can under the reducing process, ride at 105 lbs. I inquired of him what were his instructions in the race, and he said:

"I had no instructions, except that I was to win the race."

"With such instructions, do you not think you laid away rather far for the first mile?"

"Well, I don't know sir. I wanted a waiting race. I thought Spendthrift was the horse [I] had to beat. I did not know about Harold, but I believed that my horse could win from either of them if I could get the race put upon a brush down the homestretch, and I kept away from them to keep them from becoming alarmed. I was always within striking distance, and you know when Spendthrift went away down the backstretch I was ready for the move."

"Yes, that is true, but why did you go up to Harold and Jericho, at the half mile, and then fall away again?"

"I did not care for Jericho, but while I thought Spendthrift was the dangerous horse, I wanted to go up to Harold to see how he felt, so I tapped Falsetto with the spur one time, went up to them, felt of Harold, found him all abroad, sprawling over the course, and saw he was out of the race, and I fell back to keep Feakes from thinking I was at all dangerous."

"How did you get between Harold and the pole on the turn?"

"I didn't intend to go upon the turn, but when we started toward the stretch Harold was tired and unsteady, and he leaned away from the pole and gave me room to go in. I thought it better to run for the position than to have to run around him, so I jumped at the chance and went up between him and the rail. I steadied my horse here a moment to compel Harold to cover more ground on the turn, and beat him good, for he was very tired, and just before we got to the stretch I left him and went off after Spendthrift."

"Where did you catch him?"

"Just after we got straight into the stretch."

"Did you have to punish Falsetto?"

"As I tell, when I went up to Harold at the half mile, I hit him one with the spur. Then when I ran between Harold and the pole I gave it to him again. When I got to Harold, I laid there a little while, and kept touching my colt with the right spur, to keep him from bearing out to Harold, and also to make him hug the pole. He is a long strider, and is inclined to lean out on the turns. I kept the spurs pretty busy in him until I got to Spendthrift. Here Feakes drew his whip, and Spendthrift refused to respond to it. So I stopped and let Falsetto come along, but I kept urging him with the reins. He moved so strong that I did not have to punish him any more."

"Is Falsetto a free mover?"

"No, sir, not generally. He does not run on the bit, but ran better on it today than I ever knew him. He held it till I hit him with the spur the first time—the end of a mile and a quarter. He turned it loose as soon as he felt it and never took hold of it again."[116]

This exchange between Isaac and the reporter reveals three important aspects of the race: he knew his horse, he knew the other horses in the field, and he knew himself. His skill and his knowledge of how to ride races, not just run horses, gave him a distinct advantage over the other jockeys. Most impressive was the way he directed and orchestrated the outcome of the race, calmly calculating his options with a "steady hand, a quick eye, a cool head, and a bold heart."[117] Also impressive was his command of the English language, his confidence, and his intellect, which could not have been cultivated in the stables among the horses and the waifs attending them. For that, Isaac had his mother and Lexington's black community to thank.

Through his performances on the track and in the media, Isaac attracted a following among the throngs of Victorian groupies in the stands, who idolized the wealthy owners and patrons, and among horse-racing fans, who read the newspapers to keep up with his results. His success also attracted the attention of sporting men who were willing to pay jockeys to manipulate races and change the outcome. According to his obituary, Isaac was offered "enough [money] to buy a Bluegrass farm if he would have agreed to lose on Falsetto in the Kenner Stakes," three weeks after his win on Falsetto in the Travers.[118] As far as we know, Isaac did not take the money; instead, he guided Falsetto to another win over Spendthrift.

Although jockeys were not considered professionals in the same sense as doctors, lawyers, politicians, and businessmen, it took considerable skill to ride races. With his performances and his interviews, Isaac was elevating the profession through his representation of muscular Christianity, honesty, and consistency. Murphy's standards, his artistic approach, and his professionalism may have challenged the definition of both jockeys and their work.

During the Saratoga races, Isaac wore the colors of his two most consistent benefactors, James T. Williams and J. W. Hunt-Reynolds, and he attracted the attention of Californian E. J. Baldwin, whose horses finished poorly at the meeting. Winning races consistently with style and grace in front of the wealthiest men in America would be to his advantage as the new decade began. But sadly, while Isaac was at Saratoga his mother, America, died.

The Fayette County commissioner's supplemental schedule of recorded deaths from June 1879 to May 1880 lists the death of America Burns in August 1879 of complications related to consumption and cancer of the rectum.[119] It is hard to imagine how she must have suffered, but nineteenth-century cases studies of women being treated for rectal cancer are revealing. Walter Harrision Cripps describes a woman who could have been America: "She was very thin and emaciated, and for some time had been unable to work as a laundress. For more than a year she suffered discomfort in the rectum, and had lost blood from time to time, a muco-purulent discharge being persistent. During the last few months the pain had greatly increased, her nights were sleepless, she was tormented with the constant desire to go stool."[120]

The form that reports America's death contains invaluable information: her age, her race, where she and her parents were born, the cause of death, and the attending physician. What it does not tell us is where she died. Did she die in a hospital or in an alleyway? Who discovered her body? And finally, who contacted her son? Did he receive a telegram informing him of his loss? Did he share his grief with Eli Jordan, a minister in Lexington or Frankfort, J. W. Hunt-Reynolds, or one of his fellow jockeys, like William Walker?

Surely America was proud of her sole surviving child. We can only imagine that as she took her last breath, she was confident that her boy would be all right. He was educated, independent, and successful; his character, honesty, self-effacing nature, congenial demeanor, and altogether cheerful outlook on life were imprints of America Murphy Burns, her family's history, and her wishes for her son's future. Where she is buried and who attended the service are not known. Even Isaac and his magical disposition could not save his mother or himself from falling through the cracks of American history, with its tendency to make invisible the stories at the root of African American success and achievement.

Despite the loss of his mother, Isaac ended the year on a positive note, winning the St. Leger on G. W. Darden's Lord Murphy and finishing in the money in six of seven races at Louisville. After returning to Frankfort, to the home he shared with Eli Jordan and several others, Isaac likely reflected on all that had happened, perhaps turning to his mentor and surrogate father for support. Being a thoughtful person, he may have kept a journal where he recorded his meditations on life, along with information about his number of wins, the character of the horses he rode, the different cities and horse tracks he visited, and new acquaintances he made. At Fleetwood Stock Farm, J. W. and Meta Hunt-Reynolds may have consoled their young employee, whom they had grown close to. Having lost his own mother at an early age, J. W. may have helped Isaac deal with his grief. Acknowledging that children honor their parents by fulfilling their dreams for their offspring, the men may have discussed the finer points of what it meant to be a man in nineteenth-century America. Although their friendship would have been problematic for a number of reasons linked to the history of slavery, white supremacy, and the persistence of violence against blacks, J. W. and Isaac may have found common ground that allowed them to go beyond a formal employer-employee relationship or one based on the social construction of race and the definitions of black and white. An indirect result of this fostered kinship tie would be Isaac's formulation of a new black masculinity. Black jockeys of his generation could enjoy the elevated status of professional men who joined social clubs, served as community leaders, and represented the best class of citizen. Professionalization supported class stratification and development, which legitimized citizenship for some but barred others from participating.

Professionalization of what had been deemed "slave work" during the antebellum period and "nigger work" during Reconstruction dramatically changed the notion of how a jockey should act both in and out of the saddle. Isaac won the respect of owners and spectators, who had grown to expect and appreciate his measured riding and exciting finishes. They respected how he went about his work, and they enjoyed watching him perform. Still, Isaac was no doubt aware of the widespread perception of African American men as holdovers from slavery and a problem to be dealt with by the rope or the lash. But Isaac, who was better educated than the average black or white man, used his facility with language to explode the caricatures that represented black men as half-witted, effete, and inconsequential to the outcome of important events. Even in the midst of the success enjoyed by Isaac and other black jockeys such as William Walker, Oliver Lewis, James "Soup" Perkins, and Anthony Hamilton, images of stereotypical "colored boys" riding hoses began to appear more frequently as advertisements and reminders of the preferred social, political, and economic status of black men in America. Fortunately, Isaac was just getting started.

Drawing on the example of successful blacks in Lexington,

Louisville, and Frankfort, Isaac understood that achievement and will alone could not refute and deny the imposition and audacity of white supremacy. One had to refine, reform, and represent oneself in society. However, very few black jockeys were able to win over the public with the charm and gentlemanly sensibilities Isaac conveyed by the way he dressed, his body language, and his reserved air of confidence and humility. Clearly, Isaac believed that being successful required discipline. This understanding helped him shape his ideas about himself and make plans for a future beyond the saddle that would include marriage, children, the purchase of real estate, and ownership of a string of horses. But in addition to mastering the necessary riding skills, Isaac would have to master himself and the ever-present temptations in the burgeoning spectacle of horse racing.

By the spring of 1880, Isaac would be a year older and wiser in the ways of the turf and life's disappointments. During the winter months, he may have joined Frankfort Baptist Church, attended public lectures about black suffrage, and even taken advantage of educational opportunities at the local school for blacks. Isaac would go into town to get his hair cut at the barbershop, purchase clothes and shoes,[121] and satisfy his other indulgences, whatever they were, with like-minded individuals. And he would meet his future wife, Lucy Carr.

Still, the status of blacks in Frankfort was no different from that of blacks throughout Kentucky. Those who were seen as threats to white power were singled out and persecuted for their advocacy of black citizenship rights. A Republican stronghold, Frankfort had one of the most active black communities in the state in terms of pushing back against the aggressive agenda to jettison the gains won in the Civil War and the radical policies of Reconstruction. Unfortunately, the collusion among state and local governments and wealthy, middle-class, and poor whites undermined the democratic process and hindered blacks' progress. White men worked with impunity to regulate, criminalize, and eliminate black lives. The amount and degree of violence and lawlessness visited on African Americans—in a state where Christianity was professed to be the

foundation of civilization—were shameful. It would be another decade before Kentucky passed an antilynching law to protect its black
citizens from white mob violence. If Isaac learned anything from
the black community of Frankfort, it was that his relationship with
J. W. Hunt-Reynolds, the city's favorite son, was vital to protect him
from jealous white boys who thought that his success limited theirs.

There is good reason to believe that white Kentuckians considered blacks a detriment to the progress of the state, as well as the
country. In March 1880 a writer in the *Kentucky Live Stock Record*
suggested the following:

> If the negro would leave the State, it would be greatly benefit-
> ted thereby, both in wealth, population and increased develop-
> ment. The negro in large numbers, be he slave or freeman is
> detrimental to the development of the country, as history of ev-
> ery slave State in the Union has demonstrated.
>
> As a class, with few exceptions, they are ignorant, indo-
> lent, dull, improvident, and any thing but enterprising citizens.
> Nothing has done so much to retard Kentucky's progress as
> negro labor, which has hung like an incubus upon her devel-
> opment, and the sooner our people are convinced of the fact
> the more rapid will be our increase in wealth, prosperity and
> power.[122]

Of course, the writer ignores the history of slavery and the human
equity poured into the state's development by people of African descent. Nor does the author recognize that the wealthy had no desire
to provide other white men with opportunities to climb economically, socially, or politically; their sole objective was profitability and
the power wealth provided.

Arguments like these would be responsible for a gradual de-
cline in the employment of black boys and men as jockeys at major
tracks across the country. On the major horse farms in the South
and at tracks in the East, African American trainers and jockeys
were already losing ground as whites began to consolidate power
around Negro hating. But in Isaac Murphy's case, his phenomenal

success on the turf still drew the attention of owners who wanted him to guide their horses in the major stakes races, which of course increased his earning capacity significantly. In the 1880 season Isaac rode at weights from 100 to 113 pounds for ten different owners, including J. W. Hunt-Reynolds and H. P. McGrath. Over the course of four months, however, the popular jockey rode in only thirty-two races, posting ten victories and a dozen second-place, seven third-place, one fifth-place, and one eighth-place finishes. In the month of August, Isaac was absent from the track at Saratoga Springs—or any other track, for that matter. This could be explained by any number of things—an injury or illness, or perhaps some violent act against him by those hoping to sabotage his success. One other possibility is that America Murphy's death, recorded as occurring in 1879, actually took place in 1880; this would justify Isaac's absence in August, placing him in Lexington making preparations for his mother's burial. Wherever Isaac was in August, the next month would bring another tragedy.

In September, in between the Lexington and the Louisville Jockey Club meetings, the Hunt-Reynolds family departed Fleetwood to attend the Westfeldt family reunion in Shufordville, North Carolina, right outside of Asheville. J. W., Meta, and their daughter Christina left Frankfort the week of September 15. J. W. probably planned to spend some time with the Westfeldt family before joining Eli and Isaac in Louisville for the races. Prior to their departure, J. W. had been suffering from an undiagnosed sickness, but based on published reports, he was in relatively good health. However, on the evening of September 22, 1880, thirty-four-year-old J. W. Hunt-Reynolds died from a ruptured blood vessel in the brain.[123] Two days prior, he had complained of a headache but did not seek the advice of the local doctor. Hunt-Reynolds's contributions to the turf would not be forgotten. With J. W.'s death, Isaac lost not only a generous mentor and employer but also his security in the horse-racing world. He would have to find other owners to ride for to fulfill his destiny. In this time of great disappointment, loss, and uncertainty, Isaac had to take hold of his future.

# 7

# An Elegant Specimen of Manhood

## *1881–1889*

In the early spring of 1881, Isaac found himself largely alone, having lost his mother in 1879, followed by the passing of J. W. Hunt-Reynolds, his mentor and employer, in the fall of 1880. Other than Eli Jordan, who had been a father figure to Isaac since childhood, he had no family connections. There is no evidence that his mother's siblings kept in contact with their nephew after leaving Lexington sometime before 1873. Now twenty years old, Isaac would have sought female companionship among the young black women in the Frankfort community, near his home on the Fleetwood Stock Farm.

Although it was not uncommon for jockeys to marry, the reality of a jockey's life made marriage difficult. There would be long periods of separation as he traveled around the country for six to nine months of the year, and there were no guarantees of a steady income that a family could depend on.[1] As a result, most jockeys remained single, seeking companionship whenever and wherever they could find it. Bawdy houses, saloons, and cabarets were patronized by heroes of the turf, some of whom lived hard by day and harder by night.[2] How many jockeys contracted venereal diseases, participated in sexual trysts with male prostitutes, or came to ruin as a result of their sexual desires is not known, but we do know that there was no shortage of venues near racetracks where men could satisfy their carnal desires. Despite the well-publicized images of high culture associated with horse racing—its wealthy white patrons, elegant gambling facilities, and extravagant parties—sex work was a prevalent feature of jockey clubs.[3] Essentially, jockey clubs were homosocial environments catering to the maintenance and elevation of white male privilege for their elite membership. These all-male clubs served to reinforce white male power over minorities, women, less powerful white men, and immigrants. Indeed, through minstrel shows, performances by Irish actors and musicians, and burlesque shows by women from an array of backgrounds (but most of whom lacked the protection of honest labor and domesticity), the jockey club embodied traditional ideas related to racism, sexism, and classism. These clubs also may have served as a liminal space for elite experimentation with the homoerotic, with cross-dressing white men in blackface providing racial and sexual ambiguity. Historian Eric Lott suggests that blackface minstrelsy functioned to mediate "white men's desires for other white men" or to fulfill a "fantasy of racial conversion" representative of sexual envy of or desire for black men.[4] Clearly, these jockey clubs were off-limits to black jockeys and trainers.

Through horse racing, Isaac was exposed to a variety of venues that promoted illicit sex, drinking, and gambling as cultural and social norms. In cities across the country, these types of establishments in African American communities gave black heroes of the turf the occasion to interact with locals, while contributing to the local economy by spending their money on the numerous pleasures available.[5] Nightlife became an integral part of the racing experience. We do not know whether Isaac participated in any of these social activities, whether he indulged in transient sexual encounters in the various cities he visited or abstained from sex until marriage, or whether he pursued a relationship with a young lady in Kentucky of a character similar to his own. We can only imagine that the quiet, religious young man was exactly what he seemed.

Isaac began to focus on what he wanted to achieve through his career as a professional jockey. He likely saw his life as a series of decisions that, if he chose wisely, would ultimately lead to success and accomplishments beyond the track. He had achieved his manhood in the saddle and could not afford any distractions or setbacks that might jeopardize his favored position among the owners. Barring any unforeseen acts of God, Isaac planned to use his talent to construct a viable representation of nineteenth-century manhood that would be taken seriously by the powerful whites he had to impress, while laying the foundation for a life beyond jockeying. Both on the track and in public, he presented himself as a professional man whose skill and talent were invaluable. This self-awareness of his value and earning potential had been cultivated in Frankfort, under the guidance of Eli Jordan and J. W. Hunt-Reynolds. Historian Ed Hotaling, among others, has suggested that Isaac also benefited from the "refined and sympathetic" talents of Meta Hunt-Reynolds, who "took an interest in him."[6]

Isaac had been with the Hunt-Reynolds family for just under two years and may have grown close to Meta and eleven-year-old Christina during that time. Isaac's likable nature, sharp intellect, and boyish appeal made him attractive to those who recognized his potential. But whether Meta became "another important role model, a molder of character and manners," as Hotaling suggests, is not known.[7] However, there is reason to believe that she was taken by the boy's ability to read and write, his affinity for honesty, and his religious declarations. Her interest seems less connected to narratives of white matriarchal subjectivity of black children and adults and more like that of an employer generally concerned about the welfare of a valued employee, or perhaps a teacher wanting the best for a prized pupil. As we shall see, Isaac's contributions to the success of Fleetwood Farm and the support of J. W.'s widow added to his achievements and his popularity.

The widowed Meta Hunt-Reynolds refused to fall in line with traditional notions of femininity and decided to keep her husband's legacy alive and continue to run their horse farm in the Bluegrass. Less than a month after she buried her husband, the *Cincinnati Daily Gazette* reported that "Mrs. J. W. Hunt-Reynolds will not sell the race horses, but will train them next season."[8] As the wife of one of the founders of the Louisville Jockey Club, she remained committed to the purpose of Fleetwood Farm: improvement of the Thoroughbred for the development of Kentucky's commercial and agricultural industry. The question was whether club president Meriwether Lewis Clark, secretary D. W. Johnson, and the other board members would accept her. Presumably out of respect for J. W. Hunt-Reynolds, the club did not publicly resist the membership of a woman in the Louisville Jockey Club—which, up to now, had been a private reserve for Kentucky's most prominent white men. Only time would tell how club members really felt about recent developments and how willing they were to change their well-entrenched positions on race, class, and gender. For the time being, they allowed Meta to make this public gesture in her husband's memory.

Securing the assistance of Eli Jordan, Meta prepared for the challenges of running a horse farm. At the time, it was unheard of for a woman to undertake such a task, but it was not impossible. Businesses like Fleetwood Farm were generally all-male domains; women merely added some softness and civility to the rough and manly atmosphere, acting as aesthetic accoutrements at race meets or in the members-only clubhouse. But Meta was up to the task of operating the business she had likely helped her husband develop over the dozen or more years of their marriage. Her determination to step in may have been an indicator that Fleetwood Farm was as much her creation as J. W.'s. Meta may have contacted her father and brothers, who were coffee merchants, to ask their advice, but horses were outside their area of expertise. She would have to depend on the help of those in the know: Eli Jordan and Isaac Murphy.

One sign that Meta was knowledgeable about the procedures related to Thoroughbred management was that on April 18 she registered three foals recently born at Fleetwood Farm: a chestnut filly named Whisperina, a brown filly with a blazed face and four white feet named Facsimile, and a bay filly named Fleta.[9] How Eli Jordan felt about working for a woman is not known. Perhaps the seasoned trainer of champion horses saw it as a chance to test his own ideas about grooming and training, which he might have been reluctant to express under a male owner. Perhaps the fifty-eight-year-old Jordan just saw it as a sign of the times.

Although there was increased competition between blacks and German and Irish immigrants for better-paying jobs, black trainers and jockeys were still favored over whites. It is also important to note that between 1880 and 1883, the immigration of Europeans accelerated, while the Chinese immigrants who had settled in the West were being excluded from American life as an indigestible element in the "body politic."[10] Historian Anna Pegler-Gordon argues that this separate and unequal immigration policy—or "twin tracks" for inclusion and exclusion—began as early as 1875 with the Page Act, which prohibited the immigration of Chinese women who were prostitutes or the second wives in polygamous marriages.[11] This act of Congress not only revealed a deep-seated belief in the institution of marriage as a contract between one man and one woman of consensual age but also shed light on the assumption that Chinese culture threatened American notions of democracy. This rejection of polygamy also manifested as a growing contempt for Mormonism during the 1880s; polygamy was seen as a social and cultural evil that made a "mockery of marriage" and led to the "self-degradation" of women. Endorsement of the practice threatened American life in general and mainstream Christianity in particular. In other words, polygamy was a battleground not only for a cultural war against the Chinese but also for a religious war against the Mormons, who "had long been derided for their bizarre religious beliefs, their secretiveness, their hierarchical organization, [and] their unquestioning obedience to self-proclaimed prophets."[12]

The Chinese Exclusion Act of 1882 made it clear that the Chinese were not welcome in America. It castigated the hardworking people who had helped connect the nation through the building of the Transcontinental Railroad. Similar to African Americans, the Chinese sought economic security and social mobility wherever they could be found, and most were willing to do work that white men would not. In the words of nineteenth-century African American scholar Alexander Crummell, this form of "temporal prosperity" was the first step for people in need of "self-dependence" who sought to "raise themselves above want, and to meet the daily needs of home and family."[13] Unfortunately, because the Chinese were willing to work for low wages and in dangerous conditions, they aroused the hatred of white men, who argued that the Chinamen were taking white men's jobs and were "likely to overwhelm" the country with their numbers.[14]

These events reflected the growing tension over labor practices throughout the United States, especially in urban industrial areas, where blacks and immigrants competed for opportunities to work. Within the "bounds of whiteness," Irish and German immigrants constructed an identity based on their position as the newly disadvantaged and the need to forge relationships with other identifiable whites to deny blacks and Chinese access to social, political, or economic power. Thus, as historian Abby Ferber argues, "white identity developed . . . as a consolidation of privilege" and as an act of denying nonwhites the opportunity to become equal contributors to the labor market.[15] This neo-white movement, fueled by economic tension, fear of competition, and public contradiction of the inherent inferiority of blacks and Chinese, was the basis for black- and yellow-faced minstrelsy. Masking such anxieties behind playful yet violent portrayals of "intractable social conflicts" fueled the production of racial caricatures—African Americans as animalistic and subhuman, and Chinese as vile and shiftless. This, in turn, fed the growing practice of mob action as a corrective public exercise against violations of the social order.[16]

For Isaac Murphy and other black jockeys, the racetrack represented democracy at its best. Indeed, the opportunity to succeed was available to anyone brave enough to ride a horse, but those whose skill exceeded that of the average jockey could attain much more. Isaac's success would eventually generate jealousy among the white boys who conspired to exclude "coloreds" from the tracks. In the Northeast in particular, tens of thousands of Irish immigrants aggressively challenged African Americans' economic opportunities, and the racetrack would be the scene of both real and metaphorical confrontations between blacks and whites in the coming decades. The fight was believed to be for dominance of America, achieved by reaffirming one's place in society through one's productivity. Beyond the simple equation that work provided income, which in turn provided social mobility, economic stability, and political influence, European immigrants equated work with power, and power with whiteness. This notion of whiteness as an unchallenged position and possession fueled violence against black men for minor infractions and imagined transgressions against white male privilege. Of course, these acts were instigated by rabid racists, social Darwinists, and angry Southerners who could not bring themselves to honor the Federal government's claim that people of African descent were, in fact, American.

To be sure, the African American leadership did not allow these accusations, degradations, and outright attacks on the character of blacks to go unchallenged. In June 1881 Frederick Douglass eloquently argued:

Of all the races and varieties of men which have suffered from this feeling [of prejudice], the colored people of this country have endured the most. They can resort to no disguises which will enable them to escape its deadly aim. They carry in front the evidence which marks them for persecution. They stand at the extreme point of difference from the Caucasian race, and their African origin can be instantly recognized, though they may be several generations removed from the typical African race. They may remonstrate like Shylock—"Hath not a Jew eyes? Hath not a Jew hands, organs, dimensions, senses, affections, passions? Fed the same food, hurt with the same weapons, subject to the same diseases, healed by the same means, warmed and cooled by the same summer and winter, as a Christian is?"—but such eloquence is unavailing. They are Negroes—and that is enough, in the eye of this unreasoning prejudice, to justify indignity and violence.[17]

To Douglass, "slavery created and sustained" the prejudice experienced by African Americans in every corner of the nation.[18]

Although there was ample evidence that the race had grown from its previous condition of ignorance, stupidity, servility, poverty, and dependence by gaining access to education and economic stability, the threat of the Negro becoming a social equal inspired an epidemic of lynchings throughout the South, including Kentucky. How Isaac handled being part of an identifiable pariah class, whether he worried about the possibility of violence against him because of his success, and how he adjusted his travels to avoid potential confrontations with white men are not known. Yet we know that he had to interact with white men of various classes and occupations, all of whom were capable of meting out brutal punishment. We can be fairly sure that within the racially charged environment of horse racing, Isaac experienced painful reminders of his sanctioned place in society. How he handled these transgressions would be answered in the saddle during the 1881 season.

## Making a Name for Himself

By May 1881, Fleetwood Farm, now under the control and direction of Meta Hunt-Reynolds, was prepared for the spring season. With master trainer Eli Jordan in charge, the Hunt-Reynolds horses were primed to begin their campaign at the annual Kentucky Association meeting in Lexington. When Benjamin Bruce, editor of the *Kentucky Live Stock Record*, visited Fleetwood Farm as part of his annual reporting on the progress of Thoroughbreds in training in the Bluegrass, he noted that Fleetwood's string of racers was under the control of Eli Jordan, "who had trained and brought to the post such capital horses as Whisper, Felicia, Fortuna, Blue Eyes and Falsetto."[19] In prior years, Bruce's reports had focused on what owner J. W. Hunt-Reynolds was anticipating for the coming season, with little concern for the trainer. In 1881, however, there was no mention of Meta as the new owner of Fleetwood Farm or her intention to run one of the most successful stables in the Bluegrass. Instead, the article concluded with a somewhat lukewarm commentary on the future of the farm: "Barring accidents, the Fleetwood Farm stable will fully sustain the reputation it acquired during the life of its lamented owner, Col. J. W. Hunt Reynolds, and before the snow flies we expect to see the Fleetwood colors, red, white sleeve, red cap, leading the van for some of the most important events of the season of 1881."[20] Whether Meta considered this an insult to her leadership of Fleetwood Farm is unknown. However, she trusted that her wise trainer would perform as well for her as he had for her husband. It is safe to assume that she expected the same from her most prized employee, Isaac Murphy.[21]

On May 7, the opening day of the Kentucky Association meeting, the sky was clear and bright, and a "gentle breeze from the East" played over the large crowd of spectators.[22] In the first race of the day, Isaac, riding at 112 pounds atop Clarissima in a $150 purse race, finished second behind his friend John "Kid" Stoval on J. S. Boyd's Harry Gow. On the second day he won riding J. R. McKee's Pope Leo in a heat race valued at $1,350. Fleetwood Farms had only three entries in the entire meeting, and Isaac rode only one of the three. Why he competed in only two races during the six-day engagement, and why Fleetwood Farms had only Clarissima on the track, when there were reportedly fifteen horses in training for the spring races, is unknown. Isaac's limited mounts may have been an indicator of future weight issues or a larger issue related to Meta's new role as the owner of Fleetwood Farm. Although there is no tangible evidence that the membership of the Kentucky Association objected to the blurring of gender boundaries and the presence of a female owner, one cannot help but wonder if the all-male board of directors barred Fleetwood horses from full participation. Again, nothing of this nature was reported in the newspapers, but it is possible that the association did not want to publicize the decision to exclude Mrs. Hunt-Reynolds from the Jockey Club, preferring not to disclose the goings-on in the inner sanctum of the clubhouse.

By the beginning of the Louisville Jockey Club meeting on May 17, the entire Bluegrass racing community had had a chance to process the idea of a woman as an owner. In response to Meta's new position as the only "queen" of the turf, the board of directors barred her participation. Although her gender had no effect on how Fleetwood Farm's horses or jockeys performed, her mere presence in the all-male preserve challenged long-standing rituals and traditions. The main authority on all turf-related issues in the Bluegrass, the *Kentucky Live Stock Record*, remained silent on the whole affair. While some men probably admired her decision to run Fleetwood Farm, Meta Hunt-Reynolds challenged Kentucky turfmen's cherished self-image as traditional Southern gentleman: chivalrous, chauvinistic, and inherently self-doubting.

The Louisville Jockey Club's decision was no doubt a disappointment to Meta. Although it did not affect her ability to run Fleetwood Farm, it damaged her ability to make it a viable and valuable business. In essence, if she was not allowed to enter her horses in events, she would be unable to find buyers to purchase her stock at a premium. What is more, the Jockey Club's decision had a negative effect on Isaac. Most owners had already engaged their primary jockeys for the season: no mounts meant no money for the talented jockey.

For the first four days of the Louisville meeting, Fleetwood Farm did not have a single horse in a race. And not until the fourth day did Isaac have a mount, finishing fourth and out of the money on J. T. Williams's Checkmate.[23] On the fifth day, however, there seems to have been a compromise: Eli Jordan was allowed to register and race Fleetwood's horses under his name. Jockey Henderson, riding the bay colt Maretzek, finished last in the Tobacco Stakes for three-year-olds. This outcome was repeated on the seventh day in the Merchants' Stakes, with the valuable bay colt Uberto ridden by Bratton. Isaac rode Checkmate in the same race, finishing fourth and in the money, and two races later he brought Ackerman and Company's Surge across the line for a second-place finish in an association race for a $50 payout. The following day, in the fourth race, Isaac won on Uberto in the Distillers' Stakes for three-year-olds. In a classic Murphy finish, the self-assured jockey waited until the right moment to urge his horse on, winning by two lengths.[24]

Oddly, the Louisville Jockey Club found it less distasteful to allow Eli Jordan, a black man, to register and race horses in the spring meeting than to let a white woman do the same. Somehow, in the very confused and contradictory world of white patriarchy, elevating a black man into the coveted position of "owner" was more acceptable than allowing a white woman to claim economic equality, social standing, and political power. Interestingly, the *Kentucky Live Stock Record* listed Jordan among the successful owners at the Louisville meeting, with Uberto winning $500.[25] Thus, Jordan became the first African American to be listed as a registered owner of a horse in a Louisville Jockey Club meeting.

At the end of the Louisville meeting, the Jockey Club announced upcoming changes that would allow the most talented jockeys to ride more frequently. "We have always been opposed to an extreme heavy scale of weights," said club secretary Johnson. "But it has become absolutely necessary to increase the weights to secure jockeys that are able to ride."[26] These changes would expand Isaac's opportunities to generate income, allowing him to ride for multiple owners over the course of a season.

As for Meta, she found a more hospitable atmosphere at the St. Louis Jockey Club meeting in June. Officials allowed Fleetwood Farm to participate under its own name, not cloaked behind trainer Eli Jordan. Meta's recognition as an owner was important not only to her ability to sell horses but also to her ability to employ the necessary staff to maintain the farm she had vowed to keep.

At St. Louis, Isaac found additional mounts from several owners, including J. B. Sellers, W. C. McGavock, and Louis Riggs. In the four days leading up to his one and only mount for Fleetwood, Isaac won two races and placed second and third in two others. He was proving himself to be a money rider on horses he had confidence in and for owners he respected. On June 10, the fifth day of the St. Louis races, the weather was mild but "attendance was not large" at the afternoon's events.[27] Fleetwood Farm had two horses, Uberto and Maretzek, entered in the mile-and-a-half Merchant Stakes for three-year-olds. Isaac was familiar with both horses but was assigned to ride the bay colt, Uberto. After an even start, Maretzek took the lead and Uberto was in the fourth position, with Murphy trying to stay within striking distance. At the three-quarter pole,

Maretzek was holding on by "two lengths in front of Windrush," with King Nero in third and Uberto trailing.[28] After the first mile, Windrush overtook Maretzek, followed by King Nero in second and Uberto in third. On the turn and down the stretch, the three horses and their jockeys battled head-to-head. Uberto then moved up on Windrush and took the lead, winning the race by a length. Murphy had brought in Fleetwood Farm's first win at St. Louis, with $1,525 going to the victor. By the end of the St. Louis meeting, Isaac was ready for the competition in the East. All he had to do was wait for owners to call him. And call they did.

After his last race at St. Louis, Isaac boarded a train to New York, where the racing was richest in the late summer and fall, especially at Saratoga. What was unusual about meetings in the East was the number of races held in a day—sometimes as many as six or seven. To satisfy spectators' desire for entertainment and provide ample betting opportunities for the gambling set (which, in New York, included just about everyone), the respective jockey clubs set daily programs that included a range of distances—from three-quarters of a mile to a mile and three-quarters—in an effort to fit in as many races as possible. Unlike the West, the East was more concerned with the commercial aspects of racing.

Isaac found mounts with his previous employer, J. T. Williams, and with a number of other owners he knew. On June 16, in front of an excellent crowd on the second day of the Coney Island Jockey Club meeting, Isaac rode Williams's Checkmate to a fourth-place finish, but ahead of his rival Jimmy McLaughlin, who came in seventh. Small victories like this over his eastern rivals added to his growing confidence. Two days later Isaac's moral victory would be dampened by the news that one of the most important trainers in the history of Kentucky horse racing, Ansel Williamson, had died. A column in the *Kentucky Live Stock Record* recorded his significant contributions to the industry:

Many will learn with regret of the death of the veteran colored trainer Ansel Williamson, which took place in this city on Saturday June 18th. Ansel Williamson was some seventy-

**BIRTHS.**

**BIRTHS.**

This document may be the only evidence of Isaac Murphy's birth at the David Tanner farm: the birth of an unnamed black male was recorded on January 6, 1861. (Kentucky, Birth Records, 1852–1910, Ancestry.com; original data from Kentucky Birth, Marriage, and Death Records—1852–1910, microfilm rolls 994027–994058, Kentucky Department for Libraries and Archives, Frankfort)

# MEN OF COLOR, TO ARMS! NOW OR NEVER!

This is our Golden Moment. The Government of the United States calls for every Able-Bodied Colored Man to enter the Army for the THREE YEARS' SERVICE, and join in fighting the Battles of Liberty and the Union. A new era is open to us. For generations we have suffered under the horrors of slavery, outrage and wrong; our manhood has been denied, our citizenship blotted out, our souls seared and burned, our spirits cowed and crushed, and the hopes of the future of our race involved in doubts and darkness. But now the whole aspect of our relations to the white race is changed. Now therefore is our most precious moment. Let us Rush to Arms! **Fail Now and Our Race is Doomed** on this the soil of our birth. We must now awake, arise, or be forever fallen. If we value Liberty, if we wish to be free in this land, if we love our country, if we love our families, our children, our homes, we must strike NOW while the Country calls: must rise up in the dignity of our manhood, and show by our own right arms that we are worthy to be freemen. Our enemies have made the country believe that we are craven cowards, without soul, without manhood, without the spirit of soldiers. Shall we die with this stigma resting on our graves? Shall we leave this inheritance of shame to our children? No! A thousand times No! **We WILL Rise!** The alternative is upon us; let us rather die freemen than live to be slaves. What is life without liberty? We say that we have manhood—now is the time to prove it. A nation or a people that cannot fight may be pitied, but cannot be respected. If we would be regarded *Men*, if we would forever **SILENCE THE TONGUE OF CALUMNY**, of prejudice and hate; let us rise NOW and fly to arms! We have seen what Valor and Heroism our brothers displayed at **PORT HUDSON and at MILLIKEN'S BEND**; though they are just from the galling, poisoning grasp of slavery, they have startled the world by the most exalted heroism. If they have proved themselves heroes, can not we prove ourselves men? **ARE FREEMEN LESS BRAVE THAN SLAVES?** More than a Million White Men have left Comfortable Homes and joined the Armies of the Union to save their Country; cannot we leave ours, and swell the hosts of the Union, to save our liberties, vindicate our manhood, and deserve well of our Country?

MEN OF COLOR! All Races of Men—the Englishman, the Irishman, the Frenchman, the German, the American, have been called to assert their claim to freedom and a manly character, by an appeal to the sword. The day that has seen an enslaved race in arms, has, in all history, seen their last trial. We can now see that OUR LAST OPPORTUNITY HAS COME! If we are not lower in the scale of humanity than Englishmen, Irishmen, white Americans and other races, we can show it now.

MEN OF COLOR! BROTHERS and FATHERS! WE APPEAL TO YOU! By all your concern for yourselves and your liberties, by all your regard for God and Humanity, by all your desire for Citizenship and Equality before the law, by all your love for the Country, to stop at no subterfuges, listen to nothing that shall deter you from rallying for the Army. Come forward, and at once Enroll your Names for the **Three Years' Service.** **STRIKE NOW**, and you are henceforth and forever **FREEMEN!**

| | | | | |
|---|---|---|---|---|
| E. D. Bassett, | John W. Price, | Rev. J. Boulden, | John P. Burr, | Jas. R. Gordon, |
| Wm. D. Forten, | Augustus Dorsey, | Rev. J. Asher, | Robert Jones, | Samuel Stewart, |
| Frederick Douglass, | Rev. Stephen Smith, | Rev. J. C. Gibbs, | O. V. Catto, | David B. Bowser, |
| Wm. Whipper, | N. W. Depee, | Daniel George, | Thos. J. Dorsey, | Henry Minton, |
| D. D. Turner, | Dr. J. H. Wilson, | Robert M. Adger, | I. D. Cliff, | Daniel Colley, |
| Jas. McCrummell, | J. W. Cassey, | Henry M. Cropper, | Jacob C. White, | J. C. White, Jr., |
| A. S. Cassey, | P. J. Armstrong, | Rev. J. B. Reeve, | Morris Hall, | Rev. J. P. Campbell, |
| A. M. Green, | J. W. Simpson, | Rev. J. A. Williams, | James Needham, | Rev. W. J. Alston, |
| J. W. Page, | Rev. J B. Trusty, | Rev. A. L. Stanford, | Rev. Elisha Weaver, | J. P. Johnson, |
| L. R. Seymour, | S. Morgan Smith, | Thomas J. Bowers, | Ebenezer Black, | Franklin Turner, |
| Rev. J. Underdue, | Wm. E. Gipson, | Elijah J. Davis, | Rev. Wm. T. Catto, | Jesse E. Glasgow. |

Because Kentucky had not seceded from the Union, recruitment broadsides like this one would not have appeared in Kentucky until after the Emancipation Proclamation. (Alfred Whital Stern Collection of Lincolniana, Rare Book and Special Collections Division, Library of Congress)

Classes for children and adults were led by teachers hired by the American Missionary Association. (Courtesy of the University of Kentucky Special Collections, Camp Nelson Photographic Collection)

(*Above*) After Captain Theron Hall was appointed superintendent of refugees at Camp Nelson, these houses were built to accommodate the families of soldiers stationed there. (Courtesy of the University of Kentucky Special Collections, Camp Nelson Photographic Collection) (*Below*) At Camp Nelson, black Kentuckians who were former slaves became more empowered. This photograph shows the wives and children of the colored soldiers serving the Union effort. (Courtesy of the University of Kentucky Special Collections, Camp Nelson Photographic Collection)

| NAME OF SOLDIER : | Skillman, Jerry (Alias) Burns, Jerry (alias) | | | |
|---|---|---|---|---|
| SERVICE : | Late rank, _____ Co. C, 114 Reg't U S C Inf | | | |
| TERM OF SERVICE : | Enlisted _____, 1 Discharged _____, | | | |
| DATE OF FILING. | CLASS. | APPLICATION NO. | LAW. | CERTIFICATE NO. |
| | Invalid, | | | |
| 1869 apr 19 | Widow, | 174.318 | 0 | 137.891 |
| | Con Wid | 418.001 | 0 | |
| | Minor | 538.598 | 0 | |
| ADDITIONAL SERVICES : | | | | |
| REMARKS : | | | | |
| | Died _____, 1 , at | | | |

*(Above)* Record of America Murphy (Burns) filing for the pension of Jerry Burns (Skillman). After America's death in 1879, Jerry's first wife, Caroline Skillman, and her son William took up the claim. (Civil War Pension Index: General Index to Pension Files, 1861–1934, Ancestry.com; original data from General Index to Pension Files, 1861–1934, T288, National Archives and Records Administration, Washington, DC) *(Below)* Jerry Skillman's grave site at Camp Nelson Cemetery in Nicholasville, Kentucky. (Courtesy of the author)

The solar eclipse of 1869 was observed at Shelbyville, Kentucky, by professional and amateur scientists from around the country. (Courtesy of the University of Pennsylvania Archives)

The Colored Fair Association's board of directors were some of the most prominent members of Lexington's African American community. Front row (left to right): J. T. Clay, assistant secretary; T. J. Wilson, vice president; Henry Lee, president; A. L. Harden; S. W. Dunn. Back row: H. A. Tandy, Jordan C. Jackson, J. W. Ellis, L. C. Smith. (William D. Johnson, *Negro Business Directory of Prominent Negro Men and Women of Kentucky* [Lexington, 1899], 3)

The Reverend James Monroe (1813–1873) became the leader of the First African Baptist Church in 1862. He presided over several conferences in Lexington related to the spiritual and rudimentary education of black Kentuckians. (Rev. C. H. Parrish, ed., *Golden Jubilee of the General Association of Colored Baptists in Kentucky* [Louisville: Mayes Printing Company, 1915], 190)

On April 21, 1873, America Burns (1831–1879) opened an account at the Lexington branch of the Freedmen's Bank. (Freedmen's Bank Records, 1865–1871, Ancestry.com; original data from Registers of Signatures of Depositors in Branches of the Freedmen's Savings and Trust Company, 1865–1874, micropublication M816, National Archives and Records Administration, Washington, DC)

Broadside advertising "immigration" to the state of Kansas. (Courtesy of the Kansas Historical Society)

## All Colored People

THAT WANT TO

# GO TO KANSAS,

### On September 5th, 1877,

## Can do so for $5.00

### IMMIGRATION.

WHEREAS, We, the colored people of Lexington, Ky., knowing that there is an abundance of choice lands now belonging to the Government, have assembled ourselves together for the purpose of locating on said lands. Therefore,

BE IT RESOLVED, That we do now organize ourselves into a Colony, as follows:— Any person wishing to become a member of this Colony can do so by paying the sum of one dollar ($1.00), and this money is to be paid by the first of September, 1877, in instalments of twenty-five cents at a time, or otherwise as may be desired.

RESOLVED, That this Colony has agreed to consolidate itself with the Nicodemus Towns, Solomon Valley, Graham County, Kansas, and can only do so by entering the vacant lands now in their midst, which costs $5.00.

RESOLVED, That this Colony shall consist of seven officers—President, Vice-President, Secretary, Treasurer, and three Trustees. President—M. M. Bell; Vice-President —Isaac Talbott; Secretary—W. J. Niles; Treasurer—Daniel Clarke; Trustees—Jerry Lee, William Jones, and Abner Webster.

RESOLVED, That this Colony shall have from one to two hundred militia, more or less, as the case may require, to keep peace and order, and any member failing to pay in his dues, as aforesaid, or failing to comply with the above rules in any particular, will not be recognized or protected by the Colony.

The Reverend Morris M. Bell (1844–?), leader of Lexington's Pleasant Green Baptist Church and a community activist, organized the black "Exodusters" migrating from Kentucky to Kansas. (Rev. C. H. Parrish, ed., *Golden Jubilee of the General Association of Colored Baptists in Kentucky* [Louisville: Mayes Printing Company, 1915], 189)

Young Isaac Murphy posing for what may have been his first formal portrait as a professional jockey. (Courtesy of the P. W. L. Jones Collection at Kentucky State University)

John Wesley (J. W.) Hunt-Reynolds (1846–1880) was a gentleman farmer and the proprietor of Fleetwood Farm. The grandson of John Wesley Hunt, Hunt-Reynolds helped make the Kentucky Thoroughbred a national treasure. (Courtesy of the Westfeldt family)

Meta Westfeldt Hunt-Reynolds (1845–1910) was important to Isaac Murphy's development as a man and a jockey. After the death of her husband, J. W. Hunt-Reynolds, she came to depend on the jockey, whose career was just beginning to take off. (Courtesy of the Westfeldt family)

*Carte de viste* of Lucy Carr Murphy (1868–1910). (Courtesy of the Thomas T. Wendell Collection, 1869–1974, Kentucky Historical Society)

The Reverend Daniel S. Bentley (1850–?) was born in Madison County, Kentucky, and attended Berea College, where he was baptized by the Reverend John G. Fee. (R. R. Wright Jr., *Encyclopedia of African Methodism* [Philadelphia: Book Concern of the AME Church, 1916], 38–39)

# First-Class Jockey.

I will make engagements to ride in the
stakes for the coming racing season at Lexington, Louisville, Latonia, Chicago and
Saratoga. I will be able to ride at 110 (possibly 107) pounds. My address until the beginning of Lexington races will be care of
Fleetwood Stables, Frankfort, Ky

4248t          ISAAC B. MURPHY.

Isaac Murphy placed this advertisement in the *Kentucky Live Stock Record*. He
received so many offers to ride that he had to retract the ad after only one week.
(*Kentucky Live Stock Record* 17, no. 11 [March 17, 1883]: 170)

This image of
Murphy appeared
at the end of the
1884 season, after he
won the inaugural
American Derby.
(*Spirit of the Times*,
December 20, 1884)

Ed Corrigan (1842–1924) was one of the principal supporters of Isaac Murphy's career. Corrigan's Pearl Jennings, Modesty, and Freeland were top Thoroughbreds in the 1880s. (Courtesy of the Keeneland Association, John C. Hemment Collection Scrapbooks)

The top American jockeys and horses of 1885 are represented in this promotional poster. Isaac Murphy and Isaac Lewis were projected as two jockeys to watch during the upcoming season. (Root and Tinker, New York; courtesy of the author)

This photograph of Murphy was taken by J. H. Fenton in 1885. (Courtesy of the Library of Congress)

Hoping to prove himself in the East, Elias J. "Lucky" Baldwin (1828–1909) hired Murphy, who was touted as a big stakes winner. Baldwin's willingness to offer Murphy a $10,000 contract would set a standard and eventually change the opportunities for African American jockeys. (Courtesy of the Arcadia Public Library Image Archive)

The Kinney Brothers Tobacco Company produced these cards to advertise its products. Isaac Murphy appeared on three Kinney cards, astride horses owned by E. J. Baldwin: Volante, Los Angeles, and Emperor of Norfolk. (Courtesy of the author)

Advertisements such as this savaged the contributions of jockeys like William Walker, Isaac Murphy, Anthony Hamilton, and Pike Barnes. It reads, in part, "Hi! Dat hoss can jist fly now. I only 'plied jist six bottles of Kendall's Spavin Cure, and it hab taken off all dem four ringbones, two spavins, one curb, two splints, one capped hock and a shoe bile." (Courtesy of the author)

*Isaac Murphy*

Tobacco card from Gold Coin Chewing Tobacco (Julius Bien and Co., Lith, NY, 1887)

ISAAC MURPHY
Champion Colored Jockey

Tobacco card from W. S. Kimball and Company's
Cigarettes. (Courtesy of the author)

This is one of seven tobacco cards produced with Isaac Murphy's likeness between 1887 and 1890. (Courtesy of the author)

Tobacco card from Old Judge and Gypsy Queen
Cigarettes. (Courtesy of the author)

## ISAAC MURPHY.

In the article accompanying this image in the *New York Sportsman*, Murphy comments on riding Salvator: "I'll try hard to win, sir, and my mount is a great young horse, one of the finest I have ever seen. But it's company he'll go against, you know." (*New York Sportsman*, June 21, 1890, 576)

*(Above)* Matt Byrnes (1853–1933), on the left, was a highly sought-after trainer in the 1880s and 1890s. (Courtesy of the Keeneland Association) *(Below)* Murphy's June 25 win on Salvator over Garrison riding Tenny. John C. Hemment's photograph as the horses crossed the finish line is recognized by sports historians as the first of its kind. (Courtesy of the Keeneland Association)

Murphy celebrated his victory on Salvator at the home of trainer Matt Byrnes near Eatontown, New Jersey. (Courtesy of the Keeneland Association)

Jockeys at Morris Park, 1891. Murphy is in the middle row, kneeling behind Anthony Hamilton. Next to Murphy is Willie Simms, who would win the Kentucky Derby in 1896 and 1898. (Courtesy of the Keeneland Association)

In the 1880s and 1890s, at the peak of their success, black jockeys were caricatured as coons in the popular press. Images such as this one humiliated these men and erased any sense of achievement and manhood. (Courtesy of the author)

Image depicting the great 1890 match race between Salvator and Tenny. (Courtesy of the author)

This lithograph of Henry Stull's painting of the match between Salvator and Tenny was a popular depiction of the dramatic race. Note Murphy's posture in the saddle. Stull was probably not at the race but based his painting on the widely circulated accounts of it. (Courtesy of the author)

Isaac Murphy posed for this picture at Morris Park in 1891. (Courtesy of the Keeneland Association)

Ed Garrison (1868–1930) was one of Isaac Murphy's greatest rivals. Their June 25, 1890, match race at the Coney Island Jockey Club is recognized as one of the most exciting in American sports history. (*The American Turf: An Historical Account of Racing in the United States* [New York: Historical Society, 1898], 376)

EDWARD H. GARRISON

Anthony Hamilton (1866–1904) was one of Isaac's closest friends. He left the United States in 1901 to race in Europe. (*The American Turf: An Historical Account of Racing in the United States* [New York: Historical Society, 1898], 395)

In 1895, Willie Simms (1870–1927) became the first American jockey to win a race in England on an American Thoroughbred. (Courtesy of the Keeneland Association)

This image of Murphy was supposedly taken near the fence separating his property from the Lexington racetrack. (Photograph by Harrison Foster)

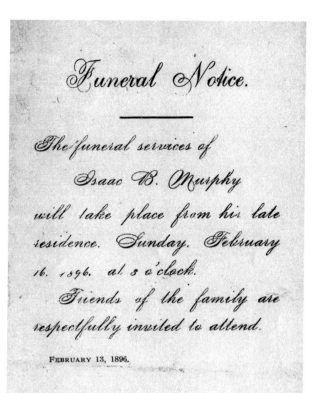

*Funeral Notice.*

The funeral services of Isaac B. Murphy will take place from his late residence. Sunday. February 16. 1896. at 3 o'clock.

Friends of the family are respectfully invited to attend.

FEBRUARY 13, 1896.

The announcement for Isaac Murphy's funeral, held at his home on February 13, 1896. (Courtesy of the Keeneland Association)

Llewellyn P. Tarleton (1846–1916), who wrote Murphy's obituary, remembered the boy who had become an honorable man. "Honor and shame from no condition rise; Act well your part, there all the honor lies." (William E. Bidwell and Ella Hutchinson Ellwanger, *Legislative History and Capitol Souvenir of Kentucky* [Frankfort: Frankfort Printing Company, 1910], 247)

five years of age. He was born in Virginia, and first trained for Mr. T. B. Goldsby, of Alabama, and while under his training [the horse] Brown Dick ran his great three mile race, beating Arrow at New Orleans, La., in 1855, in 5:30¾, 5:28. The late A. Keene Richards purchased Ansel from Mr. Goldsby and he brought out for Mr. Richards Imp. Australian, Sherritt, afterwards changed to Satalite, Glycora and a number of others. About 1861, he took charge of the late R. A. Alexander's stable, and trained Asteroid, Norfolk, Ansel, and a number of other first class horses. . . . When in good health he was a remarkable industrious and attentive man to his business, which was a great secret to his success as a trainer.[29]

Although this account seems incomplete and sterile in terms of Williamson's personal history, the fact is that no one really knew who Ansel Williamson was. Due to nineteenth-century ideas about race and American ideas about destiny, this information was not deemed important.

As American slavery scholar Annette Gordon Reed notes, the "ease and swiftness with which blacks were written out of the social compact indicates that notions of essential differences and inferiority took hold very early on in" the new nation's development.[30] The founding fathers' ideas about commerce and national identity allowed people of African descent to be sacrificed for the good of democracy. The complexities of slavery and the individual experiences of black men and women were rarely shared publicly, for fear of white rebuke and retaliation for contradicting the country's manifest destiny. In the end, only the fortunate few who knew the magnificent trainer and groomer of jockeys would mourn the passing of Williamson the man.[31]

Black children were taught to depend on their elders for advice and guidance, so chances are good that Isaac had looked up to the extraordinary trainer and thus felt a great loss at Williamson's passing. From what we know about Isaac, we can assume that he was respectful and paid tribute to Williamson, someone who was a consummate example of perseverance, industry, and temperance.

From June through October 1881, Isaac lived out of a suitcase, staying at various boardinghouses during the eastern racing season. He may have traveled alone, or he may have traveled with a companion, perhaps a fellow jockey from Kentucky. In between racing at Coney Island, Monmouth Park, and Saratoga Springs, Isaac would have discovered Manhattan, where the cosmopolitan nightlife dazzled the senses of unattached young men with small-town upbringings and big-city dreams. Situated between Twenty-Fourth and Forty-Second Streets, Manhattan's black community was known as the Tenderloin district, and its churches, overpriced tenements, brothels, saloons, and restaurants catered to the distinct tastes and needs of blacks from the South and curious white voyeurs from the North. Historian Marcy Sacks suggests that districts such as the Tenderloin, "among the most congested of any in New York City," increased in population and popularity for a number of reasons. First, these urban spaces were designated for blacks, and the growing number of immigrants from Italy, Ireland, and other European countries drove black Southern migrants away from the more appealing areas of the city. Second, the mainly Irish American police force maintained this color line, so the limited housing and employment opportunities elsewhere in the city led to a "rapid influx of black migrants into" neighborhoods where they felt comfortable among their own.[32]

In *Black Manhattan*, James Weldon Johnson recalls the New York City of his childhood and the neighborhoods where blacks congregated:

In the earliest days the Negro population of New York lived, naturally, in and about the city at the tip of Manhattan Island. In the middle of the last [nineteenth] century they lived mainly in the vicinity of Lispenard, Broome, and Spring Streets. When Washington Square was the centre of fashionable life, large numbers of Negroes engaged in domestic service in the homes of the rich lived in a fringe of nests to the west and south of the square. As late as 1880 the major portion of the Negro population of the city lived in Sullivan, Bleecker, Thompson, Carmine, and Grove Streets, Minetta Lane, and adjacent Streets.[33]

According to Johnson, black Manhattan developed into a black bohemia constituted in part by the Tenderloin district, with its professional clubs and venues where musicians and writers of the era experimented with their art. The red-light district also "nourished a number of ever present vices; chief among them, gambling and prostitution."[34] Black Manhattan was at the forefront in extending the boundaries of the Negro's previous so-called place in the American imagination. In Manhattan, the "Negro jockey constituted the very first ranks of the profession."[35]

While in New York, twenty-year-old Isaac might have wandered the streets of black Manhattan in search of adventure or just to satisfy his curiosity. He might have visited one of the clubs, honkytonks, or other entertainments available. On Sunday, he would have attended services at one of the churches in the Tenderloin district, such as Bethel African Methodist Episcopal Church on Sullivan Street or St. Phillips Episcopal Church on Twenty-Fifth Street.[36] He might have walked down the Great White Way, a portion of Broadway between Fourteenth and Thirty-Fourth Streets, to see the new electric lights being installed under the supervision of black inventor Lewis Howard Latimer. Latimer's patented carbon filament lightbulb and other innovations and patents related to electricity earned him a place alongside Thomas Edison and Alexander Graham Bell, both of whom Latimer worked for as a draftsman and electrician. There is no way to know whether Isaac ever ventured into the Tenderloin district or gazed down the Great White Way, but his time in New York coincided with the changing milieu associated with the burgeoning "diversities of individuality" being cultivated by African Americans in the Northeast, especially in black Manhattan.[37]

While in New York, Isaac would hear of the July 2 shooting of President James A. Garfield at the Washington, D.C., train station by Charles Guiteau, a disgruntled paranoid schizophrenic who had been denied a political appointment at the U.S. consulate in Paris, France. The shot was not immediately fatal, but after suffering for two months from a systemic infection resulting from the wound, Garfield died on September 19 at the age of forty-nine. The following morning Vice President Chester A. Arthur was sworn in at his home in New York by Justice John R. Brady of the New York Supreme Court. Two days later he took the oath of office in Washington before Chief Justice Morrison Waite. Arthur "read a short inaugural address, and issued a proclamation setting apart the funeral day, September 26, as one of national fasting and prayer."[38] As for Guiteau, his three-month trial ended with a guilty verdict, and he was hung on June 30, 1882.

Although President Arthur was a Republican and his policies reflected that affiliation, he was also an advocate for the New South, which meant less governmental oversight of local affairs—specifically, protection of African Americans' citizenship rights under the Civil Rights Act of 1875. Since the Civil War, African Americans had turned to their Republican friends for protection, but the Arthur presidency would prove problematic to those who believed they had a friend in the White House. Ratification of the Thirteenth, Fourteenth, and Fifteenth Amendments had opened the door to freedom, citizenship, and the franchise, but with Arthur's presidency, the government seemed to be taking a step backward. Black leaders and some congressmen looked for help in overturning the concessions being made, while Southern politicians and businessmen were poised to reclaim their former power over African American labor by returning black people to slavery for the good of national pride and productivity.

A sign of the times, the *Kentucky Live Stock Record*, a newspaper usually dedicated to topics related to farming and horse racing, published an article about the "exodus of the negroes from the State," which some Kentuckians lamented as a loss of labor. "Instead of expressing regret," the writer opined, "it is a matter of congratulation, and we should like to see the day when there is not a colored individual in the borders of Kentucky." What is even more striking is the article's advocacy for white labor, "men of brains and muscle" who possess "energy, industry and frugality, backed by intelligence and education."[39] Ironically, these are not the qualities Kentuckians had previously sought in their workers. If they had, black schools would not have been burned down, black men living off their land would not have had their possessions confiscated or destroyed, and black men and women demanding employment contracts and full pay would not have been threatened with death. What Kentucky capitalists really wanted was a new slave—an ignorant shell of a man too fearful to fight for his rights and too hungry to demand what was rightfully his.

White immigrants who saw themselves as equals based on race, if not opportunity, refused to subject themselves to the abuses indicative of slavery. Immigrants wanted to become landowners themselves, not work for other white men looking to squeeze as much cheap labor out of them as possible. Those blacks criticized as "able bodied colored men loafing on the street corners" and indignant Negro women unwilling "to go to the country to work for any kind of wages offered" were actually intelligent and educated about the ways of white folks. These men and women refused to subject themselves to the abuses of sadistic farmers, mistresses, and employers who enjoyed doling out punishments to vulnerable blacks denied the safety of their own communities. Free blacks who knew they had options refused to be reduced to human chattel and chose to migrate to the West.

Within the context of this white derision for blacks, Isaac's success inspired other black people who saw themselves in the jockey. Isaac was a rising star of considerable talent and ability whose achievements posed the question, "If a nigger is not a nigger, then what is a white man?" During his stay in New York, Isaac won fourteen of thirty-four races, placed second in eight others, and came in third in four races. Most of his victories were on Williams's Checkmate and W. C. McGavock's Boulevard. By the end of the 1881 campaign, Isaac had won twenty-two of fifty-two races and enjoyed some popularity among the high-stakes owners and gamblers, including brothers Michael and Philip Dwyer of Brooklyn, "Big" Ed Corrigan of Kansas City and Chicago, New York financier Leonard Jerome (the grandfather of Winston Churchill), and eccentric mining king Elias Jackson "Lucky" Baldwin of Santa Anita Farms of California. These men were capable of accelerating the Kentucky native's career beyond anything he could imagine. Isaac used his reputation as an honest and winning jockey to negotiate terms with these wealthy owners for mounts in stakes races.

These relationships would help Isaac achieve significant milestones during the 1882 season: out of eighty-eight races, he won thirty-three, placed second in twenty, and placed third in ten. Overall, Isaac won an incredible $33,490 for his employers. Isaac's arrival as a professional was reflected not only in the number of mounts he received but also in the quality of the horses he rode. At the Coney Island Jockey Club meeting in September 1882, Isaac, wearing the green jacket and white sash of Ed Corrigan's stable, rode the Kentucky-bred Pearl Jennings in the three-year-old filly stakes race. He won the $600 race by a head in front of Pierre Lorillard's Pinafore and beat two of his rivals in the process—William Donohue and Jimmy McLaughlin, whose home courses were in the Northeast. Most important, this was Isaac's first time riding for Big Ed, who was known as an "arrogant, self-willed despot, a good friend, but a hard hitting enemy."[40] Isaac was well aware of the politics of the turf and the power wielded by people like Corrigan, but Big Ed treated Isaac with respect. It was a mutually beneficial relationship: Corrigan wanted to dominate the racetracks in the Northeast, Midwest, and Far West, and Isaac wanted to ride for an owner willing to pay a premium to the jockey who could help him achieve that goal.

Between the spring and fall seasons in the West and Northeast, Isaac continued to win in the dramatic fashion he was known for. His numerous victories no doubt increased his income for the year and gave a considerable boost to his savings. Although we do not know the specific financial arrangements between Isaac and the owners he rode for, it is estimated that, taking into account fees and bonuses (likely based on a percentage of the winnings), his earnings for 1882 were between $2,000 and $4,000 (or about $50,000 to $97,000 in 2013 dollars).[41] Most important, Isaac was his own man and was able to set his own fees and be paid what he was worth. Eventually, Isaac would even hire his own private valet, a young white boy, to assist him.

At the end of the 1882 season Isaac returned home to Frankfort to recover from the long season of traveling and riding on the national circuit. His success had made him something of a local celebrity, but his achievements would be acknowledged in the national media on the occasion of his twenty-second birthday. On the front page of the January 20, 1883, issue of the *New York Sportsman*, editor C. J. Foster notes Isaac's accomplishments:

Murphy is one of the best jockeys in America, being especially strong in knowledge of pace, coolness, and good generalship. He will soon be too heavy to ride, we fear, in which case Uncle Eli ought to and doubtless will take him in and teach him all he knows about training.

Mrs. M[eta] W. Reynolds  writes as follows concerning him: "Of course I need not tell you of Isaac's honest and trustworthy nature, for the whole of the American turf must be cognizant of that fact; but no one knows it better than I do."[42]

While Foster acknowledges Isaac's superior ability, he also recognizes that his future as a jockey is limited. Still, Foster believes Isaac can have a successful career in horse racing, similar to that of Eli Jordan and the great Ansel Williamson. And Meta Hunt-Reynolds's willingness to express in a national newspaper her personal feelings about the colored jockey indicates Isaac's importance to her and her family.

## On the Path to Happiness and Prosperity

On January 24, 1883, Isaac Burns Murphy married Lucy Carr in a ceremony at St. John's African Methodist Church on the corner of Clinton and Lewis Streets in north Frankfort. The *Frankfort Roundabout* published the following account of the wedding: "Isaac Murphy, the noted colored jockey of Fleetwood Farm, and Miss Lucy Carr of this city, were married Wednesday evening. Quite a number of the young friends of the groom from other places were in attendance, as well as a large company from the city. The ceremony was performed by Rev. D. S. Bentley."[43]

We do not know exactly when and where Isaac and Lucy met.

It is possible (but unlikely) that she worked for the Hunt-Reynolds family as a laundress at Fleetwood Farm. Isaac's introduction to Lucy more likely occurred somewhere in Frankfort's black community of Crawfish Bottom (called the "Craw") sometime between 1878 and 1881. They could have met at a social event hosted by one of three main black churches, at the annual Colored Fair, or at the home of a mutual friend. According to the 1880 census, Lucy lived with her mother and stepfather, Fanny and Granville Lewis, and her sister, Susan Osborne, at a residence on Washington Street in north Frankfort.

Nineteenth-century sensibilities with regard to sex and marriage were not reserved for whites. African Americans also adhered to customs based on the notion of moral reform and social order. In the postslavery, post-Reconstruction environment of Kentucky, African Americans worked extremely hard to demonstrate their civility, Christian morals and values, and a progressive orientation by endorsing abstinence and promoting marriage between the spiritually grounded, emotionally mature, and financially secure. An individual's social, political, and economic responsibilities to his or her community were reflected in decisions regarding sex, temperance, and education.[44] In other words, the magical disposition that Isaac was able to claim through his achievements as a jockey was in fact available to anyone who could publicly demonstrate Christian uprightness, temperance, and gentlemanlike or ladylike decorum. And by becoming an exemplar of these particular characteristics, each individual represented the progress of blacks as a whole.

To understand the young woman Isaac married, some space has to be dedicated to Lucy Carr's background and upbringing. Not surprisingly, the circumstances surrounding Lucy's birth are vague. Born on September 4, 1868, in Frankfort, Lucy was the daughter of Fanny Osborne, a seamstress, and Adam Carr. Between 1850 and 1870 the census lists two men of that name. There was an Adam Carr living in Paducah, Kentucky, in 1850; he was a German immigrant working as a shoemaker, but he disappeared from the historical record thereafter. However, census data reveal that a significant number of Germans and individuals of German descent lived near the Craw, within the footprint of what was clearly recognized as the black community. The other Adam Carr lived in Madison County, where he and his family owned seven slaves, including two female slaves aged twenty-four and forty. There is no way to know whether one of these women was Fanny. Nor is there any evidence that Fanny and Adam were married or even lived together. However, when Lucy died in 1910, her sister named Adam Carr as Lucy's father on her death certificate, leading one to believe that Lucy knew him and perhaps had a loving relationship with him. We cannot be sure which Adam Carr, if either, was Lucy's father. One clue might have been his color, since Lucy was a beautiful light-complexioned woman with red hair.[45] Because Lucy's mother was mulatto and her father was white, Lucy was considered an octoroon. Her red hair and light complexion were not uncommon in Frankfort, especially on Washington Street, where more than 100 mulattoes lived.

Similar to Lexington, the Craw was established after the Civil War when former slaves came to Frankfort in search of housing, employment, and stability. According to census data, between 1860 and 1870 Frankfort's black population almost doubled, growing from 1,282 to 2,335. Historian Douglas A. Boyd describes the Craw as "inexpensive" land containing "humble dwellings for rental to blacks . . . and poor whites."[46] The interracial nature of the neighborhood did not translate to a progressive attitude toward blacks. As noted in chapter 5, in 1870 leaders of Frankfort's black community—including Henry Samuel, Henry Lynn, William Luckett, Edward Smith, H. H. Trumbo, Henry Marrs, Peter Smith, Henry Huggin, and B. J. Crampton—called for a "Colored Men's Convention" to "discuss and prosecute means appertaining to the political issues of the day, and to the vital interest of our race throughout the State." At the February 23 convention, the delegates endorsed resolutions to assert their right to live free after more than 250 years of enslavement and degradation, to continue to support the Republican Party as a show of loyalty, and to claim the "full panoply of American citizenship."[47]

With regard to Lucy's education (and that of other black children), in 1873 the Colored Men's State Educational Union met in

Frankfort to press the state legislature to support the education of black children. The group challenged the state superintendent of schools to release the funding reserved for black schools or prepare to defend his resistance to the request for funds in court. By 1874, the Kentucky legislature had established the uniform school system for Negro children, financed by taxes collected from property-owning blacks.[48] Historian Victor Howard notes that the state superintendent of schools "strongly advocated that the state adequately provide for Negro education."[49] This would be a great advantage for Lucy Carr and the other black children of Frankfort.

By 1880, Crawfish Bottom was a well-established community of former slaves and their children. As productive Republicans, these freedom-seeking, God-fearing, hardworking people managed to maintain their dignity, even in the midst of the degradation and crime afflicting their neighborhood, owing to its location in the bottomlands and its close proximity to the state penitentiary.[50] Adding to the social tension was the economic fissure created by racially motivated hiring practices that aimed to exclude blacks from the labor pool in an effort to keep wages high. As the unemployment rate for African American men increased, so did their frustration; these skilled plasterers, draymen, millworkers, and painters wanted only to assert their manhood and provide for their families. The open competition with German and Irish immigrants for jobs added to the conflicts between the two sets of marginalized Americans. Jobs as coopers, teamsters, bricklayers, and carpenters, which had been available to blacks at the beginning of Reconstruction, were slipping away, along with jobs on the railroad, on the docks, and digging ditches. Occupations such as barber, minister, teacher, porter, and servant remained.

Although black women worked in an array of domestic occupations and were employed as seamstresses, cooks, laundresses, and servants, their importance to the black community went beyond the ability to earn a living. African American women were the glue in their communities, and they acted as a buffer between the white world and the black. They made sure that schools stayed open and church organizations thrived. Lucy Carr learned about her role as a wife and her place in the larger black community by interacting with these older black women. When she married Isaac Murphy, the famous jockey, Lucy must have become somewhat of a celebrity herself: the poor girl who married up. It seems plausible that the newlyweds made their home at Fleetwood Farm while they planned their future together.

Prior to the beginning of the 1883 racing season, Isaac placed an advertisement in the March 17 edition of the *Kentucky Live Stock Record*, under the title "First Class Jockey." In a bold move, he offered his services as a professional jockey who could be contracted to ride at a select number of venues: "I will make engagements to ride in the stakes for the coming racing season at Lexington, Louisville, Latonia, Chicago and Saratoga. I will be able to ride at 110 (possibly 107) pounds. My address until the beginning of the Lexington races will be care of Fleetwood Stables, Frankfort, Ky."[51] Although he published details as to when and where he was available to ride, he omitted any mention of compensation, leaving the terms to be negotiated with each owner. Isaac's ability to read and write and to think critically about what he wanted and how to go about achieving his goals gave him access to the business world that was unavailable to the uneducated. This ability put Isaac on level ground with the owners: he was able to set his own fees and determine the length of his season. In essence, Isaac Murphy was his own boss.

By March 24, he had to announce in the *Kentucky Live Stock Record* that "he has more engagements than he can fill, and that he can make no new engagements" for the 1883 season.[52] If this was an experiment to gauge his worth to the racing public, it worked. The fact that it took only a week to fill his racing calendar was a clear indication that he was a valuable commodity. Isaac was a quality jockey who was not only honest and trustworthy but also a winner. In addition to his own ad, it is possible that some of Isaac's new mounts came as a result of a January 1883 article in the *New York Sportsman*, boosting the Kentuckian as the premier jockey of the day.

Timothy Thomas Fortune, editor of the African American newspaper the *New York Globe*, recognized that Isaac's importance

extended beyond the saddle and the track. A believer in the philosophy of agitation for the sake of the progress of the race, Fortune
challenged his readers to think for themselves and to demand that
their elected officials represent them as citizens of the United States,
not wards of the Republic who were incapable of functioning without the guidance of whites. To refute the notion of the so-called
reversion of the race (used to justify terrorism against blacks), Fortune published "portraits and biographical sketches of prominent
Negroes."[53] He argued that the black press was obligated to "fight
for the rights of our race" and educate black people about themselves and their place in the world.[54] Indeed, from the "pulpit, in the
schools and the colleges, in journalism, in the law, . . . in the prize
ring, in all the life of our civilization, the Afro American is acquitting himself as 'a man and a brother.'"[55] In keeping with this sentiment, Fortune took every opportunity to praise the "modest and
unassuming" Isaac Murphy, elevating the exceptional jockey and
therefore his profession into the realm of respectability.[56]

Clearly, Isaac's reputation and success allowed the Murphys to
enjoy the benefits of celebrity status, including the comforts of an
upper-middle-class lifestyle. Unlike the wives of other jockeys, Lucy
would not have to work outside the home as a maid, laundress, nurse,
or cook. During the nineteenth century (and well into the twentieth),
African American women worked primarily in the homes of white
families, in hotels, and in hospitals. Most were vulnerable to violence,
including rape, and were victimized by the negative image of black
women as licentious and salacious.[57] For a majority of African American women "there would be no room on the pedestal for a southern
black lady," ever.[58] Though Isaac never voiced a plan to protect Lucy
from such indignities, it is clear that their marriage and the wealth
and status generated by his occupation gave Lucy a freedom that was
unavailable to a majority of black women in either the North or the
South. By being educated and part of the aspiring class of African
Americans, and by marrying a highly intelligent, literate, and moral
man, Lucy Murphy would have the opportunity to contribute to a re-
imagining of black womanhood as deserving of respect and consideration. Lucy would have something to say about how she lived her life.

By May 1883, Lexington was abuzz in anticipation of the annual spring races. Lucy may have accompanied Isaac to Lexington, and the couple may have stayed with one of the black families in the city who had known the famous jockey since he was a boy. Henry King, Jordan Jackson, or Henry Scroggins and their families may have hosted the Murphys, ensuring that the newlyweds enjoyed the comforts of home during their visit. Staying at a private residence as opposed to a boardinghouse or a hotel, Lucy would be protected from the roughish elements associated with the races, and she could attend them in the company of friends. This is not to say that Lucy was incapable of negotiating society on her own, but young black women were subject to abuses and outrages by men in general and by white men in particular, who were rarely prosecuted for their crimes.

Isaac was sure to attract a crowd in his hometown; some would be well-wishers, but others would be looking to separate the jockey from his hard-earned cash. Isaac may have donated money to local churches or schools to supplement their stretched resources. Perhaps he even handed out small amounts to orphaned children on the streets. While in Lexington, Isaac probably visited America's grave site, taking Lucy along to introduce his beautiful bride to his mother. After placing flowers on her grave and maybe saying a short prayer to honor her, the couple might have toured the city, traveling by carriage over the dusty streets, with Isaac pointing out the different sights and relating his memories of them.[59] Some of those memories were no doubt sad, cold, and gray; others were happier, of time spent playing, attending school, going to church, or sharing a laugh with his mother. Isaac's success on the oval track had carried him far from his boyhood home, but he would have been reminded of the past at every turn in Lexington, from Cheapside to Vine Street, which was all part of the larger narrative of his people's racial destiny. For Isaac, the bleakness of the past was now overshadowed by the prospect of a bright future with the lovely and supportive Lucy at his side.

On May 9, the first day of the Kentucky Association races, the weather was "warm and delightful," with gusts of wind whirling about and unsettling the loose dust.[60] For the Lexington meeting, Isaac was engaged to ride for McIntyre and Swiney, L. P. Tarleton Jr., and M. E. Clark and Company. In the first race Isaac finished second on Clark and Company's Claude Brannon, three lengths behind F. Water's Vanguard, ridden by Billy Donohue. In his second race of the day he rode Tarleton's Mistral to a fourth-place finish. By day four of the engagement, heavy rains made the track soggy and slow. However, Isaac rode to a first-place finish in a heat race, again on Mistral, securing $300 for Tarleton. In his final race at the Kentucky Association meeting, the Citizens' Stakes for all ages, he finished third on McIntyre and Swiney's Ballard. Although Isaac may have been disappointed in his first races of the season, he knew there were more than enough meetings left to redeem himself.

For Isaac, the 1883 season would be a productive one. His nine victories during the fourteen-day Louisville Jockey Club meeting included some impressive ones: the Louisville Cup on J. W. Loud's Lida Stanhope, the Woodburn Stakes on Chinn and Morgan's Leonatus, and a $2,000 purse victory in the Merchant's Stake on G. W. Darden and Company's Mediator. Especially noteworthy is that Isaac rode for sixteen different owners, whose horses competed for the various purses and stakes available. Increasing his number of mounts fit into Isaac's fee-based system, whereby in addition to a minimum charge, he received a portion of the proceeds when finishing in the money. To guarantee the maximum return for his efforts, Isaac rode only horses that were good enough to contend for the purse money being offered.

His success would continue at the inaugural meeting of the Latonia Jockey Club at Covington, Kentucky, four miles south of Cincinnati. Built on 173 acres of land purchased from the family of Confederate general James Taylor, the track was situated east of the Kenton Hills and consisted of a "massive grandstand and clubhouse on the north side, a [one] mile dirt racing oval, horse barns, and a landscaped infield decorated with flowers and shrubs."[61] For the inaugural meeting, the program offered "twenty-six races, purses and stakes, for the seven days, adding $17,700, a fraction under $3000 each day."[62] By chance or by circumstance, Isaac's first mount at La-

tonia was as a replacement for Billy Donohue, who had been contracted to ride Leonatus for Jack Chinn and G. W. Morgan in the
Hindoo Stakes for three-year-olds. Donohue was pulled from the
race after officials learned that he had bet his life savings on himself to win the Kentucky Derby on Leonatus—which he did.[63] This
was not unusual at the time, but owners were becoming increasingly leery of jockeys who wagered on races in which they participated. How much Donohue won is not known, but it must have been
a significant amount—enough to cause alarm. Clearly, Thoroughbred owners were fearful of jockeys pulling horses in major stakes
races, especially those betting large sums of money with and against
"plungers," who were capable of influencing the outcome of races
through bribery and coercion.

Isaac was already popular among the Kentucky crowd, but Latonia would accelerate his rising fame. Over the seven-day meeting,
Isaac rode in ten races, finishing first in six, second in one, third
in one, and fourth in two. In front of the fashionable crowd, Isaac
won both the Hindoo and Himyar Stakes on Leonatus, for a total
of more than $6,000. In the Hindoo Stakes especially, Isaac demon-
strated his trademark coolness and patience. As reported in the *Cincinnati Commercial Tribune*, "Murphy never moved a finger, not a
word or motion was necessary to encourage the splendid chestnut
who came along in the same easy swinging gait, as if taking a little
afternoon work for exercise, winning 'hands down' literally, so far
as his jockey was concerned. . . . Leonatus was a length in front of
Carter, but he won as he pleased."[64] Five days later, on the final day
of the races, Isaac rode Leonatus to a similar finish in the Himyar
Stakes, winning easily over the field of competitors. Isaac's focus,
patience, and understanding of the horse he was riding convinced
owners that if they wanted to win consistently, the quiet jockey who
did not drink, smoke, or gamble was their best bet.

After Latonia, Isaac moved on to St. Louis and then to Chicago, where he continued his winning ways. He won the Flash, Nursery, and Calumet Stakes on General Harding and the Dearborn and
Green Stakes and the Illinois Derby on Leonatus. Those two horses were the top competitors and the largest winners at the Chicago

Jockey Club meeting. Leonatus, however, was proving to be one of the best of the year, winning all ten stakes races he had entered. Chinn and Morgan's dark bay three-year-old with a white blaze had been bred to run fast; the colt was destined to be a champion. Luckily for them, they had secured a champion jockey, Isaac Murphy, to ride him.

In Chicago, where African Americans made up just a little more than 1 percent of the population, Isaac and Lucy would have had limited choices when it came to lodgings. Still, there were several "refined" and "respectable" families in the "city of neighborhoods" that may have opened their homes to celebrated individuals who were doing good things for the race.[65] It is also possible that the Murphys had friends and kinship ties in Chicago. When Reconstruction ended and the government pulled troops out of the South, a number of Kentuckians moved to the upper Midwest. Historian Christopher Robert Reed suggests that black Chicagoans, whose collective and individual desires for success and achievement were in line with those of black communities across the South and Midwest, would have embraced Isaac Murphy because of his "level of occupational attainment that boded well for future generations of ambitious" African Americans looking to establish themselves as productive citizens.[66]

Isaac Murphy was, without question, becoming one of the most well-known and well-paid professional athletes in America. His popularity among African Americans across the South, West, and Northeast was based on their pride in his accomplishments on the track as well as his public persona as a moral, hardworking, and respectful young man. To numerous blacks, many of whom came from a similar background, Murphy represented their own potential to attain social mobility and economic power. African American newspapers such as the *Indianapolis Freeman, Cleveland Gazette, Washington Bee,* and *New York Globe* would publish stories about and interviews with the well-spoken professional, who was clearly more than just a jockey. Isaac's embodiment of late-nineteenth-century virtues and African American manhood made him into a race hero.

At Saratoga, Isaac finished first in eleven of twenty-eight races and was compared in the media to English jockey Fred Archer, known for his ability on a horse and his gentlemanly decorum off the track. In a *New York Globe* column discussing the goings-on in colored New York society, the affable jockey was mentioned: "Sporting circles in the city were excited over the fact that Isaac Murphy, 'the colored Archer,' landed three winners at the races at Saratoga on Tuesday, . . . the winners being Welcher, Mediator and Force. Mutuals on Welcher paid $101.80, and the colored jockey received a perfect ovation."[67] Of note here is the *Globe*'s accounting of the racing public's response to the jockey's success: "a perfect ovation."

During the thirty-three days of racing at Saratoga, Isaac and Lucy made use of one of the many rental cottages on the grounds of the resort. In fact, Isaac's friend and sometime competitor John "Kid" Stoval had also brought his wife to Saratoga for the grand spectacle of racing. Whether Lucy and Mrs. Stoval were accepted into the circle of the black vacationers and horse-racing fans who were frequent visitors to the resort town is not known. It seems likely that some members of the black petite bourgeoisie would have looked down on the nouveau riche as fraudulent and inauthentic. Regardless, there were plenty of activities for the two women to engage in that did not require membership in a situational elite.

A significant number of black New Yorkers and Washingtonians who made the journey to Saratoga Springs were members of the Grand Union Pleasure Club. The group was apparently formed in response to the exclusivity of white social clubs for the wealthy and those involved in the horse industry. On August 9 the club held its annual reception at the town hall on the corner of Broadway and Lake Avenue, with all the arrangements organized by the officers: J. S. Sears, president; L. A. Walker, secretary; and F. D. Allen, treasurer.[68] The club acknowledged Isaac Murphy and John Stoval as two of the most prominent jockeys in the nation—a status that both men would enjoy, most important, within the context of the black community.

Overall, in the meetings at Lexington, Louisville, Latonia, St. Louis, Chicago, Monmouth Park, and Saratoga Springs, Isaac competed in more than 130 races in 1883, finishing first in 50, second in

30, and third in 15. More important, he continued to cultivate a new circle of friends among the fashionable in the respective locations. His success drew the attention of the well-heeled and well-groomed African American set, which would help guarantee the fulfillment of his plans for his and Lucy's future. For Isaac, it is clear that reputation meant everything, and everything hinged on his reputation: opportunity, success, and his ability to remain relevant in the realm of horse racing.

At the end of the 1883 season, Lucy and Isaac said their goodbyes to the Frankfort community and to Fleetwood Farm. Even though they were only moving to Lexington, in reality, they were entering a whole new world. Both Isaac and Lucy saw themselves as middle class, if not upper middle class. Isaac had proved his ability to generate a significant amount of income, which increased not only their purchasing power but also their opportunities. They left the river town sometime between the end of October and the first week in November and headed southeast to Lexington; there, they would begin a new life together that would take them beyond the narrow confines of the black community. Lucy and Isaac must have realized that along the path to prosperity and happiness there would be those trying to suffocate the dreams of hopeful black strivers like themselves, who were educated and understood the basis of democratic capitalism: free market competition, private property, and opportunities to prosper based on productivity, trust, and honesty.[69] They also had to be aware of the challenges imposed by the U.S. Supreme Court's recent ruling that the Civil Rights Act of 1875 was unconstitutional. In the *New York Globe*, Fortune responded to the Court's decision:

> What sort of Government is that which openly declares it has no power to protect its citizens from ruffianism, intimidation and murder! Is such a Government worthy of respect and loyalty of honest men? It certainly does not enjoy our respect and our loyalty to it is the cheapest possession we have.
>
> Having declared that colored men have no protection from the government in their political rights—declares that railroad

corporations are free to force us into smoking cars or cattle cars; that hotel keepers are free to make us walk the streets at night; that theater managers can refuse us admittance to their exhibitions for the amusement of the public—it has re-affirmed the infamous decision of the infamous Chief Justice Taney that a "black man has no rights that a white man is bound to respect."[70]

As a result of the ruling, private businesses were no longer obligated to serve individuals on an equal basis, as required by the act, which stated that "all persons . . . shall be entitled to the full and equal enjoyment of the accommodations, advantages, facilities, and privileges of inns, public conveyances on land or water, theaters, and other places of public amusement."

Kentuckian John Marshall Harlan, the lone dissenter on the Court, argued that after its ruling the constitutional amendments could not be expected to protect former slaves from persons seeking to deny them their constitutional rights as citizens of the United States. Of the Court's opinion, Harlan had this to say:

My brethren say that when a man has emerged from slavery, and by the aid of beneficent legislation has shaken off the inseparable concomitants of that state, there must be some stage in the progress of his elevation when he takes the rank of a mere citizen, and ceases to be the special favorite of the laws, and when his rights as a citizen, or a man, are to be protected in the ordinary modes by which other men's rights are protected. It is, I submit, scarcely just to say that the colored race has been the special favorite of the laws. What the nation, through congress, has sought to accomplish in reference to that race is, what had already been done in every state in the Union for the white race, to secure and protect rights belonging to them as freemen and citizens; nothing more. The one underlying purpose of congressional legislation has been to enable the black race to take the rank of mere citizens. The difficulty has been to compel a recognition of their legal right to take that rank, and to secure the enjoyment of privileges belonging, under the law, to them as a component part of the people for whose welfare and happiness government is ordained. At every step in this direction the nation has been confronted with class tyranny, which a contemporary English historian says is, of all tyrannies, the most intolerable, "for it is ubiquitous in its operation, and weighs, perhaps, most heavily on those whose obscurity or distance would withdraw them from the notice of a single despot." To-day it is the colored race which is denied, by corporations and individuals wielding public authority, rights fundamental in their freedom and citizenship. At some future time it may be some other race that will fall under the ban. If the constitutional amendments be enforced, according to the intent with which, as I conceive, they were adopted, there cannot be, in this republic, any class of human beings in practical subjection to another class, with power in the latter to dole out to the former just such privileges as they may choose to grant. The supreme law of the land has decreed that no authority shall be exercised in this country upon the basis of discrimination, in respect of civil rights, against freemen and citizens because of their race, color, or previous condition of servitude. To that decree—for the due enforcement of which, by appropriate legislation, congress has been invested with express power—everyone must bow, whatever may have been, or whatever now are, his individual views as to the wisdom or policy, either of the recent changes in the fundamental law, or of the legislation which has been enacted to give them effect.

For the reasons stated I feel constrained to withhold my assent to the opinion of the court.[71]

Harlan knew, of course, that white men would never allow former slaves and their children, whose elevation thwarted white identity and competition, to maintain a firm grip on the franchise of American citizenship. He knew the Court was wrong in abrogating its responsibility to former bondsmen and their children, who had not been allowed to complete their transition from human chattel to fully accredited stakeholders in the nation. The ruling accelerated the ongoing erosion of gains made by blacks through the Civil War and Reconstruction-era legislation, and it validated the sectional and regional abuses of blacks throughout the nation, and particularly in the South. Add to this the developing labor struggle between European immigrants and blacks, and it seemed that a race war was inevitable.

The Murphys might not have grasped the scope of the problem created by the Supreme Court's ruling, but they were not naïve to the fact that white men resented black economic, social, and political power. Clearly, Isaac and Lucy understood that their faith, patience, and resolve would be tested. They would need each other more than ever in the changing landscape of American race relations. Isaac's future success would be firmly grounded in his partnership with Lucy, who would help him build a wall of resistance against the encroachments of white supremacy. Although Isaac's talent as a jockey and his skill with horses, along with the wealth he had accumulated, insulated him somewhat from racism, it was his unimpeachable reputation as a man of principle and honor that mattered most. He used these attributes to refute and deny the lie foisted on African Americans in general and black men in particular that they were inherently inferior and obsolete.

The Murphys moved into their new home at 53 Megowan Street, a formerly upscale white neighborhood that, over the last decade, had become home to more middle- and working-class black families and single individuals. The Murphys purchased their home for $500 from Brigadier General Green Clay Goodloe (U.S. Marine Corps) and his wife Betty, who had relocated to Washington, D.C.[72] The modest Italianate house featured "one large corbelled chimney in the front and one in the rear, Flemish stone courses in the walls, a brick parlor bay window," and other architectural features indicative of middle-class wealth. The home validated the status the newlyweds sought to achieve in their new life together.[73] Rather than the biblical prodigal son returning home, Isaac was more of a conquering hero. The professional jockey exemplified what Lexington's black community deemed important to the progress of the race, along with the success of local businessmen, educators, and political leaders to set good examples for its children. After settling into their new home and beginning the process of weaving themselves into the black community, Isaac was ready for the upcoming racing season.

To transform their new house into a home, Isaac and Lucy likely employed black labor and professionals to decorate and update the interior. They might have purchased furniture from Solomon Blackburn's store on Vine Street, or maybe from stores as far away as Chicago, Louisville, and Cincinnati, to match their class consciousness. The plastered walls of their home may have been papered by a local such as Daniel Carter, using the imported wallpapers of William Morris, the father of the arts and crafts movement, whose tapestries and carpets were popular among the middle and upper classes of England and America.[74] Isaac may have purchased paintings by Edward Troye or Henry Stull or images of famous horses of the time, including those he had ridden in valuable stakes races. These images would be hung in the parlor or in Isaac's personal library, where he would entertain his male visitors, read, or just think.

We know that both Isaac and Lucy could read and write, and Lucy in particular seemed to enjoy intellectual gymnastics. Therefore, it makes sense that their home would be well-stocked with books on various subjects of interest to nineteenth-century intellectuals. Based on late-nineteenth-century tastes, Isaac's library would have been very masculine, with walnut or mahogany bookshelves, a curtain desk, and a reading table. He would have a set of leather-backed chairs for himself and a guest, and gas lamps made of brass, copper, or iron would have been strategically placed. The bookshelves would contain leather-bound volumes by Charles Dickens, Ralph Waldo Emerson, Henry Wadsworth Longfellow, Edgar Allan Poe, Herman Melville, Lord Byron, Washington Irving, and Walt Whitman, along with the works of Frederick Douglass, Edward Blyden, Phillis Wheatley, George Washington Williams, William Still, Alexander Pushkin, and Alexandre Dumas and a well-used copy of the King James Bible. Surely, a library such as this reflected Isaac's education and communication skills, which allowed him to negotiate contracts with horse owners and articulate his thoughts in interviews.

Lucy also would have been settling into her new domestic life. To what extent she was self-conscious about her transition from laundress to middle-class housewife and how long it took her to become comfortable in her new social role are not known. An undated photograph depicts Mrs. Isaac Murphy and her seemingly conservative nature and quiet disposition. Taken sometime between 1883 and 1889, the image captures her style of dress—a white blouse with a lace collar, small hanging diamond earrings, and a diamond pin through the neckline of her blouse—which clearly signifies her class status. Her hair is pulled back in the style of the day, indicative of someone who frequently wore hats as protection from the sun. For some, this was an attempt to keep their complexion from darkening, which could be detrimental to their position in society. Finally, the expression on her face is one of contentment and innocence. Nineteenth-century photography required subjects to remain absolutely still, so a majority of images give the impression that those captured in the frame were serious, stoic, or unhappy. But Lucy's eyes are bright and clear; she looks like a woman who is extremely pleased with her life.

The young couple became members of First Baptist Church and were likely involved in a number of civic activities to advance the community's moral development. Isaac joined the "colored Lincoln lodge of Masons" in January 1890 and was designated the Keeper of Values, a position he earned through his virtuous character.[75] During the nineteenth century, African American fraternal organizations such as the Prince Hall Masons, the United Order of True Reformers, and the Grand United Order of Odd Fellows were involved in a number of civic activities specifically designed to ensure their community's adherence to moral uprightness, educational achievement, and economic opportunity.[76]

Along with the Murphys, Lexington's progressive black community included a number of doctors, lawyers, trainers, barbers, and shoemakers, many of whom had likely known Isaac as a child. Their status in Lexington was important, as they sought not only the benefits of being middle class but also the respectability gained by living among their peers. Unfortunately, by the 1880s, their Megowan

Street neighborhood was undergoing drastic changes, becoming a typical red-light district with gambling, prostitution, and other unseemly activities. In his examination of the life of one of Lexington's most famous madams, Buddy Thompson writes that it is "interesting to note that the Negroes were not consulted in the decision to integrate their neighborhood with prostitutes."[77] Plainly, the Murphys understood that the value of their home was directly connected to its neighbors. Appearances were important to the young couple, who believed that racial uplift was mediated by individual efforts of achievement. Thus, their stay in the house on Megowan Street would be short, although they would retain the property as an investment.

## Skill, Not Luck

In December 1883 Murphy began to be offered large sums of money for his services. The first such offer came from Kansas City horseman Edward Corrigan, whose fiery personality and confrontational style made him difficult to work with. The Canadian-born Irishman had made his money grading roads, constructing railroad beds, and raising cattle on farms in Kansas and Colorado, but he fell in love with the sport of horse racing after losing a few races and a few hundred dollars to a Mormon gambler. As the story goes, Corrigan was supervising the building of "100 miles of the Union Pacific's Oregon short line in the Idaho territory" and "a portion of the Denver and Rio Grande Railroad" through Colorado and Utah when he was challenged to a race in the latter state by a local Mormon.[78] Corrigan may have accepted the challenge as just a friendly competition between men living on the edge of the frontier and for the masculine bragging rights a win would entail, or it might have had a deeper meaning for the man from Missouri, where Mormons were shunned and despised. In any case, given that a horse's performance was considered an extension of its owner's abilities, Corrigan's loss to his Mormon competition could have had a negative effect on his reputation in his home state, especially since their close proximity to the railroad meant that news of his defeat would travel quickly. To recapture his pride, his manhood, and his money, Corrigan sent a representative to Missouri to find a horse capable of running distances of half a mile to a mile. From Moberly, Missouri, he received the bay filly Pearl Jennings, which not only won back Corrigan's money (and then some) but also led the former granite buster to become one of the greatest supporters of the sport of kings. With Pearl Jennings at the core of his success in the West, Corrigan would say that he "made Christians out of all the Mormons in that part of Utah," especially those interested in horse racing and gambling.[79]

By Christmas 1883, Corrigan had secured one of the best jockeys in the business, paying Isaac a retainer of $5,000 (more than $108,000 in 2013 dollars) to guarantee his services at predetermined race meets, while permitting him to ride in other races for other owners (provided they were willing to pay Isaac's fee of $25 per mount).[80] In addition, based on the rules of the American Jockey Club, Murphy would receive the standard $10 for every losing race and $25 for every race won. (Other monetary incentives for jockeys included bonuses of $500 to $1,000 for winning certain stakes races that generated perhaps ten to twenty times that amount.) Based on the media coverage of the contract between Murphy and Corrigan, this was a significant development in horse racing and in relations between jockeys and owners. *Turf, Field and Farm* recognized the team of Murphy and Corrigan as a natural fit that would net the results desired by both parties: "The jockey Isaac Murphy has been engaged by Mr. E. Corrigan for the coming season. Murphy is one of the best on the turf. Mr. Corrigan's stable is made up of [the] finest material, and under the pilotage of Murphy a brilliant career for the Western turfman may be reasonably expected. Mr. Corrigan has spared no money in securing good stock, paying the highest prices, and it will be pleasant to see his liberality rewarded by many victories."[81] Isaac had ridden for Corrigan several times in the past, including piloting Pearl Jennings in a purse race at Coney Island in 1882, but now he would be wedded to the green jacket and white belt for much of the 1884 season. There is no way Corrigan could have known that by offering Isaac such a lucrative contract, he would help accelerate the inevitable changes taking place in horse racing, most of which were already unfolding in the Northeast.

Indicating the changing culture of horse racing, an editorial in the January 1, 1884, issue of the *Springfield Republican* warned that the influence of "crooked men" could ruin the potentially honorable careers of promising young white jockeys. Similarly, horse farmers were beginning to demand white boys as riders for their stables, relegating black jockeys to positions as grooms or stable boys based on the belief that "though handy about horses, [black boys] are as a rule too ignorant to learn anything but the merest handiwork."[82] This attitude, along with Grover Cleveland's election as the first Democratic president since the end of the Civil War, represented significant changes. Horse racing and the horse industry had traditionally depended on black labor, but what had been considered "nigger work" less than a decade ago was now attracting white boys and men who wanted to ride the prized Thoroughbreds in high-stakes races.[83] The mass immigration of Irish into the United States, especially New York, significantly increased the number of white jockeys; poverty and degradation made these men hungry for any opportunity to work. Their whiteness helped European immigrants construct an American identity; they forged relationships with other identifiable whites to deny racial "others" access to power. At the same time, relationships were being forged between white capital and white labor to deny blacks access to traditional occupations. Indeed, jobs that had been African Americans' primary sources of income and identity were now tied to the expanding marketplace and the burgeoning consumerism developing in the late nineteenth century. Isaac's contract with Corrigan and the high salary he was able to command, although a reflection of his abilities as a jockey and a signifier of his character as a man, would eventually lead to black jockeys' exclusion from the sport they had helped build into a billion-dollar business.

As winter turned to spring and Isaac began to prepare for the upcoming season, the popular jockey found himself in somewhat of a bind. Married life had been good to him, and his swollen figure was an indicator of his embrace of leisure and domesticity. Thus, Isaac's main concern was how to make the lighter weights endorsed by the American Jockey Club at the end of the 1883 season. To lose the twenty to thirty pounds he had gained before the season opened in Nashville in May, he created his own training and conditioning program. In an 1885 interview Isaac discussed his "rigorous course of training" and noted that most people "would hardly think it, the best riders in the country—men who earn from $5000 to $10,000 every summer—frequently go to bed hungry every night for weeks." Murphy described the toll the process of "reducing his flesh" took on the mind and body, describing it as "a constant feeling of weakness and sickness which never leaves one except during sleep."[84] During the early spring, his daily routine included taking three- to five-mile walks dressed in layers of clothing to shed pounds through perspiration. His diet was limited to fruit and small bits of meat. This regimen had an adverse effect on his immune system, making him vulnerable. Like most jockeys, Isaac was engaged in a constant fight against his body's natural inclination to grow and mature. Yet Isaac was a professional, and considering that a year earlier, in preparation for a race in Chicago, he had reduced "from 124 pounds to 111 pounds in 36 hours,"[85] Murphy no doubt had his weight under 115 pounds by the beginning of the 1884 season.

In March 1884, in the *Rocky Mountain News*, Corrigan revealed some of his reasons for hiring Murphy:

> I have engaged Isaac Murphy to ride for me because I have found out by experience that it is of very little use to have good or fair horses without having skill and honesty in the saddle. I believe I was punished by riders last season as much as any man in the country, and I don't intend to suffer in the same way again if I can help it. Good riders are scarce and high priced, but I made up my mind to get a good one, and got one of the best—some people think the best. My opinion is that I have as good a rider as anybody. I have my stable heavily engaged for the entire season.[86]

This was proof that honesty and hard work could pay off. Still, it was the amount of money Corrigan was willing to pay Murphy that would become an issue for the white boys looking to compete against him.

The same issue became a source of contention in professional baseball. In 1883 the Toledo Blue Stockings' black catcher Moses Fleetwood Walker was reportedly earning $2,000 per season (about $43,000 in today's dollars). This displeased a number of fans and players, who felt a white ballplayer would be more deserving of that salary. One of the most outspoken against black competition in the league was the manager of the Chicago White Stockings, Adrian "Cap" Anson. Anson's first attempt to draw the color line in baseball fizzled when his own salary from the gate receipts was threatened after he refused to play against the Toledo team on August 10, 1883. Anson eventually allowed his team to play, but he vowed not to play against any team with "a nigger in."[87] Despite his reputation in sporting circles as a seasoned professional who was "magnificent" behind the plate, Walker became the focus of the Southern media's assault on black labor and businesses that took good money away from capable white boys—who, in baseball, were mostly immigrants or poor whites from the margins of society.[88] Walker even received death threats; he was warned that if he played in a scheduled game against the Richmond, Virginia, team, he would suffer at the hands of "75 determined men who have sworn to mob" him if he insisted on playing with white men.[89] It should come as no surprise that the manager of the Toledo team eventually succumbed to the pressure: at the end of the 1884 season, Walker was released from the team. He would eventually find work with other teams, but by the end of the 1880s, the door had been shut on black baseball players in the professional leagues. This foreshadowed the situation in horse racing, as black jockeys began to be shut out by the white boys who wanted to claim their salaries.

Some owners of Thoroughbreds, including Corrigan and E. J. Baldwin, were slow to submit to the idea that black jockeys were a detriment to their stables. Therefore, in the spring of 1884, Isaac Murphy was ready to fulfill his contractual obligations to Corrigan and headed to the Nashville meeting, scheduled to begin May 1. The state of Tennessee had enacted a law segregating passenger trains, so it is possible that this affected Isaac and Lucy's journey. The couple's impression of Nashville is unknown, but they likely recognized the city's Fisk University as an important institution for the educational advancement of black people; it had been one of the original schools founded to educate former slaves and their children. The Murphys may have taken a tour of the campus and perhaps heard the famed Fisk Jubilee Singers perform at some point during their stay in the city. In later years, the couple may have crossed paths with a new arrival to the city, a young W. E. B. DuBois, who received a scholarship to attend Fisk in 1885 and, after graduating in 1888, would eventually earn a doctorate in history from Harvard University, the first African American to do so.

At the Nashville meeting, in a field that included his friend John Stoval, Isaac finished second on A. C. Franklin's three-year-old bay filly named Pansy. The next day, in the Fairview Stakes on Corrigan's Pearl Jennings, Isaac beat the field by a length, winning $700 for his employer.[90] He picked up another mount for Walnut Grove Stables and rode Boulevard to a sixth-place finish, failing to collect a portion of the $250 purse. On the fifth day, in his final race at Nashville, Isaac finished second on Pearl Jennings in the Kirkman Stakes, collecting $100. At the end of the meeting, the Murphys climbed aboard the train bound for Lexington, where the Kentucky Association meeting would begin on May 8 and Isaac was scheduled to ride in the Distillers' Stakes on Corrigan's bay gelding Freeland.

The weather was mild and pleasant on the first day of the Lexington races, but the track was muddy after a flurry of rain showers, which no doubt added to the lushness of the foliage surrounding the track. In the second race of the day, Murphy rode Freeland, a horse he would make famous in 1885 by winning against Miss Woodford at Monmouth Park. After a beautiful start, Murphy took Freeland into the lead and maintained control throughout to win by a length and a half. In the third race of the day atop J. and J. Swigert's Silvio, Isaac again demonstrated control of his charge, guiding him over the wire to win the $300 purse by a length. Over the remainder of the meeting, Isaac had two more mounts but no victories, earning somewhere between $60 and $80 for his services. By then, Isaac's mind had to be focused on the high-stakes races waiting for him in Louisville, where winning carried a little more prestige and earning power.

The spring meeting of the Louisville Jockey Club commenced on Friday, May 15, and the central focus was the Kentucky Derby, the race that had become the pride of Kentucky horsemen. The *Kentucky Live Stock Record* reported the growing importance of the race among the Bluegrass elite: "Every year the interest in the Kentucky Derby increases, and the desire to win also increases with breeders and owners, until it is looked upon as a mark of merit for the colt who is fortunate enough to bear off the Blue Ribbon of the Turf. More interest clusters in and about this race than any other in America, and we have heard a number of prominent breeders and turfmen say that they would rather win the Kentucky Derby than any two events upon the American turf."[91] This article could have been merely well-planned boosterism, designed to attract more fans to the spring classic, but clearly, the Louisville Jockey Club's mission to make the Kentucky Derby the premier event in America was beginning to succeed. The race was taking on a life of its own, and anyone associated with a win at the Kentucky Derby was guaranteed a degree of fame and prestige that was presumably unavailable at other association tracks—at least, this was the case in Kentucky.

For the 1884 running of the Kentucky Derby, Isaac had been hired by William Cottrill of Mobile, Alabama, a former captain in the Confederate army. His mount, the three-year-old colt Buchanan, would turn out to be more trouble than anyone anticipated. Isaac had ridden Buchanan before and had been thrown by the fiery horse. Prior to the race, Cottrill's trainer, William "Bill" Bird, had trouble saddling the ill-tempered colt, whose history as a "bad actor" and flat-out rebel was appropriate, considering his owner's history.[92] Bird did everything he could to coax the horse into submission and eventually got the animal bridled and saddled. Reluctant to rile the horse further, Isaac declined to ride Buchanan in the Derby, fearing for his life. Cottrill warned Murphy of the possible consequences of not complying with their agreement, but only after Cottrill complained to the judges and they threatened to suspend him from the entire Louisville meeting did he finally agree to ride.[93] The spirited horse was outfitted with blinkers to reduce the distractions that might cause him to become "fractious" and uncontrollable.[94] Isaac mounted Buchanan and trotted him out to the post, keeping a tight grip on the reins to keep the horse from bolting.

The key to riding a horse like Buchanan, older trainers would say, was to accept that you cannot control an animal with that much spirit. Jockeys sometimes used up too much energy trying to gain control, and the horse used up too much energy trying to resist—a contest for domination that benefited neither. In fact, a horse like Buchanan—one that was so anxious he seemed ready to burst into a million pieces—was exactly the kind of horse a jockey wanted to have under him. The key was to guide the spirited horse in the right direction using the reins like a rudder on a boat. Isaac knew that to ride Buchanan successfully, he would have to guide him in the right direction: straight ahead.

On May 16, 1884, an estimated 15,000 spectators folded into the stands, piled into the infield, and queued around the track to watch the tenth running of the Kentucky Derby. Lucy was watching in the stands, likely with her sister and other jockeys' wives, as Isaac prepared to ride for his future and his life. After three attempts at a start, the field of nine horses got away, with Buchanan trailing the pack. The pace was killing, and the jockeys were anxious to keep their distance from the leader so as to hide their intention to outstrip the front-runner at the end. At the halfway point, Isaac moved up with Buchanan, still under a heavy pull, advancing into striking distance of the leaders. At the one-mile mark, McLaughlin began whipping Bob Miles to press for the lead, and the rest of the field responded by picking up the pace, with Loftin, Audrain, and Buchanan running even. As the group entered the final stretch, Isaac gave Buchanan "his head, and in a half a dozen strides he had cut down Admiral and came home in a big gallop, an easy winner by two lengths."[95] Even after the race had ended, the spirited horse wanted to keep running. Skill, not luck, was responsible for Buchanan's win, as Isaac demonstrated his unparalleled ability to ride horses of various temperaments and dispositions. Murphy had won his first Kentucky Derby, using the knowledge and know-how of a true professional to achieve success under difficult circumstances.

Isaac won six other races at Louisville: the Dixiana Stakes,

Kentucky Oaks, Clark Stakes, Merchant's Stakes, Tennessee Stakes, and Moet and Chandon Champagne Stakes. He also finished second in four races, third in one, and sixth in one. His contract with Corrigan had paid off for both parties: Corrigan's two best horses, Modesty and Freeland, had run like champions, each winning two stakes races, and Isaac had garnered the attention he deserved. The pair would continue their winning ways at Latonia, where Isaac guided Corrigan's Bonnie Australian to a purse race victory and won three other races for three different owners. Then, at St. Louis, Isaac once again shone on Freeland, the star of the Turf Cash Handicap with a two-length victory over T. M. Berry's John Henry. And at the inaugural meeting of the Washington Park Club, Corrigan's Modesty, with Isaac aboard, dominated the competition, winning the American Derby and close to $13,000 in stakes and purse money. This was twice the amount won by E. J. Baldwin, whose Verano generated $5,465 (this was important, because Baldwin and Corrigan competed to employ the best jockeys to ride their prized horses). Isaac also won the Kenwood Stakes, worth $3,855.[96] As a gesture of appreciation for his professionalism and ability, Corrigan renamed his two-year-old colt Harry White after his prized jockey—a rare occurrence, but no doubt an honor Isaac had earned.

Meanwhile, Lucy traveled with her husband and renewed friendships established at earlier meetings from Louisville to St. Louis to Chicago. Chances are that if the Murphys stayed with local families during the various races, Lucy would write letters to their hostesses, thanking them for their hospitality and generosity. This was proper etiquette for nineteenth-century women pursuing a middle-class lifestyle. Lucy would have learned theses lessons in Frankfort, from the white families she worked for or from Meta Hunt-Reynolds during the brief time they lived at Fleetwood Farm. Or Lucy might have read Florence Hartley's *The Ladies Book of Etiquette, and Manual of Politeness* for guidance on how to lead a proper social life, how to throw dinner parties, and how to dress for particular events and occasions. The manual also covered how to conduct oneself on the street or in a ballroom setting, "polite deportment" and good health habits, and how to deal with one's servants.[97] Indeed, such books would have been invaluable to both Isaac and Lucy, who saw themselves as members of the colored elite and took pride in that position and what it entailed.

As the racing season shifted to the Northeast, Isaac continued his winning ways, especially in high-stakes races with thousands of dollars, individual pride, and regional standing on the line. At Saratoga Springs, Isaac rode Corrigan's Pearl Jennings, Modesty, and Freeland to victory in a number of stakes and purse races. He also rode for several other owners. In addition to attracting the attention of horse racing's elite, Isaac was being noticed by other jockeys, some of whom resented his ability to earn more money while riding in fewer races. One of Isaac's main rivals was Ed "Snapper" Garrison, a daring white jockey whose aggressive style of riding included whipping his horses relentlessly. This was the polar opposite of Murphy's polished, reserved, gentlemanly style, which looked effortless to those unaware of the degree of control he had. Though their lives ran parallel for a while, as jockeying developed into a lucrative profession, Murphy's and Garrison's worlds would eventually collide in the social, political, and economic milieu that would characterize the final decade of the nineteenth century and most of the twentieth.

At the end of the 1884 season, Isaac had ridden in 132 races, winning 51. Walter Vosburgh, the dean of horse racing and sports journalism, elevated Murphy to a position rarely held by black jockeys of the day. In the pages of *Spirit of the Times*, Vosburgh wrote dotingly about Isaac, calling him the quintessential jockey and gentleman, "an elegant specimen of manhood" to be recognized and applauded for his example in the saddle and out.[98] The twenty-three-year-old, whose life must have felt somewhat unreal and unfamiliar, continued to blossom. He had become the toast of horse owners, fans of the turf, and an adoring "colored" public from one coast of the country to the other. He commanded a salary that rivaled that of businessmen, lawyers, politicians, and educators, yet he remained modest and humble. He was married to a beautiful woman who seemed to make the young man happy. Isaac certainly could not have imagined the changes the future had to offer.

## The Life of a Jockey: His Habits and Concerns

While Isaac spent the winter months in Lexington recovering from the long but successful 1884 season, he celebrated another birthday and his second year of marriage to Lucy. How the couple observed Isaac's twenty-fourth birthday and how they celebrated their anniversary likely followed the customs and traditions of the day. Lucy may have thrown a small dinner party to celebrate Isaac's birthday, inviting a few select guests, who would have presented him with gifts. Lucy may have given her husband a book from a favorite author, a painting of one of his favorite horses to hang in his library, or perhaps the handmade monogrammed sash Isaac wore in the one of the few photographs we have of him in his early twenties. For their anniversary, the Murphys might have traveled to Louisville, Chicago, or even Nashville to take in the local sights or attend lectures at the black churches, community-sponsored organizations, or the various Negro colleges. In Chicago, Cleveland, and Nashville, the couple could have gone to the theater, dined out at local restaurants, and visited with their growing number of friends. In their travels, issues related to the color line would have been unavoidable. Their mode of transportation, their reception in the cities they visited, and their ability to gain access to places of interest were no doubt impacted by local decisions to segregate blacks from whites in most public facilities. In line with the customs of the day, the Murphys would have chosen their battles carefully, negotiating their surroundings in such a way as to maintain not only their humanity but also their vision of the future they hoped to experience together.

Isaac's focus was on securing future contracts with owners who were willing to pay his asking price. This would enable him to afford the lifestyle he and his wife had become accustomed to, which included Lucy accompanying Isaac to races across the country. Although the 1880s brought a number of new restrictions on African Americans' everyday lives, resulting from the triumph of white supremacy and both legal and extralegal mechanisms to disenfranchise black people wholesale, Isaac was still somewhat protected from discrimination and harassment. The realm of horse racing was still controlled by the elite, who wanted to maintain the traditions and rituals that supported their view of the world and their place in it. However, with the nation's expansion west, a growing number of wealthy white men—some of them immigrants or the children of immigrants, and others who were antiblack and anti-Chinese— became involved in horse breeding and racing as a formal declaration of their wealth and membership in the American oligarchy. It was at this moment in time that Murphy was both fortunate and ill-fated. Between 1885 and 1890, the world in which he lived and worked would change dramatically.

In early February 1885, while the European powers met to carve up Africa and continue to exploit the continent of its resources, the U.S. government advanced legislation aimed at further unraveling the gains made by African Americans after the Civil War and Reconstruction.[99] These gains were reflected in the number of black educators, scholars, businessmen and -women, politicians, lawyers, and inventors; black schools, churches, fraternal organizations, and societies; and an overall sense of enlightenment and achievement. Black newspapers such as the *New York Freeman*, the *Western Appeal*, and the *Cleveland Gazette* reported the achievements of blacks, providing a public accounting of racial progress. Yet for whites bent on resisting black success as an indicator of black humanity and therefore black citizenship, the stories of achievement were worthless, on the one hand, and dangerous, on the other.

Like most blacks in Kentucky, the Murphys socialized with friends and acquaintances on a regular basis but likely anticipated and experienced difficulty outside their own community, especially where whites asserted their authority. Those blacks who attempted to challenge the segregation and discrimination practiced in Kentucky's theaters, public parks, horse tracks, and public transportation were often brutalized or worse. Isaac and Lucy were well aware of the violence taking place in the Bluegrass—it was all around. They may have chosen to stay in Lexington during the off-season to avoid potential confrontations with white ruffians and white men bent on exercising their rights over blacks, especially black women. However, it is just as likely that they chose to stay home to rest and prepare for the upcoming season, since travel was a requirement of Isaac's occupation.

By the spring of 1885, Isaac had trained hard and reduced his winter weight in preparation to ride at 115 pounds. In May he donned the green and white colors of Ed Corrigan's stable to ride at the Kentucky Association meeting on Fifth and Race Streets. For Murphy, it was privilege to ride in front of a hometown crowd. His familiarity with Lexington's white and black communities, the city's combination of old Kentucky and new Kentucky charm, and the liminal sense of progress in the midst of draconian challenges are probably some of the reasons why he chose to make his home there rather than in Frankfort or Louisville. Isaac grounded himself in the familiar surroundings of the city, where he remained close to his roots in Clark County, his youth in Lexington, and his mother's grave.

At the Kentucky Association meeting, which opened on May 6, Murphy, in characteristic form, won the first two races for Corrigan's stable: a $300 purse race on Pearl Jennings, winning by half a length, and the Distillers' Stakes for three-year-olds on Modesty, winning by three-quarters of a length and earning the prize of $1,250. In addition to the retainer paid by Corrigan, Murphy earned $100 for two victories. The next day, riding for Morris and Patton, Murphy won the $1,425 Phoenix Hotel Stakes for three-year-olds on the bay colt Biersan. Isaac would go on to win two additional stakes races, while bringing his weight down to 110 pounds in the process. Murphy's success at his home course could have been seen as a good omen for the 1885 season. Yet nothing was guaranteed in horse racing.

During the races at Lexington and Louisville, Murphy likely enjoyed the company of other black and even white jockeys—men who had come up on the circuit together and maintained a degree of respect for one another. This situation was becoming uncommon in the East and in the Deep South, where highly successful black jockeys were beginning to disappear. Murphy's affable nature may have attracted people to him like moths to a flame, and from the few images available, he seems to have held court with his fellow jockeys on several occasions. His friend John Stoval was the beneficiary of Murphy's professional advice, even though Stoval was the competition, and his losses could have been to Murphy's benefit. But Isaac was a true sportsman who found dignity in honest labor and hard work. To manipulate the outcome of a race to make money from gambling was not work; it negated the satisfaction of accomplishing something from one's own individual efforts.

At the Louisville races, in front of an estimated 30,000 spectators at the eleventh running of the Kentucky Derby, Isaac and Biersan finished second behind J. T. Williams's Joe Cotton. Isaac also rode in seventeen other races over the span of ten days, winning nine times and finishing second five times.[100] From Louisville, he moved on to the Latonia track, where he won the Hindoo Stakes on Biersan; in fact, he was so highly favored to win that Biersan was left out of the betting pools. Murphy and Biersan immediately took command of the race and won by six lengths to claim the $4,230 prize.[101] He would also win two races for Corrigan's stable on Lizzie Dwyer and Swiney and finish in the money in several other races for other owners. After leaving Covington, he traveled with Corrigan to St. Louis and then Kansas City, winning or placing in almost every race he entered. Finally, Isaac moved on to Chicago, where eccentric California millionaire E. J. Baldwin would up the ante.

On June 27, the first day of the races at Chicago's Washington Park, Baldwin leased Murphy's services, paying Corrigan $1,500 and Murphy $1,000 to ride his bay colt Volante in the American Derby. With more than sixty hopeful participants and only eight places available for the start, the American Derby was one of the richest races on record, amounting to a $10,000 stakes race. The previous year, Murphy had won the American Derby on Corrigan's Modesty; this year, the owner had planned to have Murphy ride Irish Pat, but rather than run the race and perhaps win nothing, Corrigan took the $1,500—a sure thing. Besides, the $1,500 would offset some of the money he already owed to Murphy. Isaac was no doubt pleased to have the opportunity to make an extra $1,000.

Prior to the beginning of the race, rain fell on the 10,000 spectators and created a muddy surface on the track, with several ponds as deep as two inches forming.[102] But the enthusiastic crowd had come to see the American Derby, rain or shine. The fact that Murphy was riding in the mile-and-a-half race only added to the heart-pounding excitement. In a letter to the editor of the *New Hampshire Sentinel*, a writer identified as "Flos" described the action:

> On the start "Alf Estel" took the lead and held it to the quarter pole, where she was passed by "Favor." At the half "Favor" led by a length, and at the three quarter pole she still held her lead, closely followed by "Troubadour," "Irish Pat" and "Volante." "Alf Estel" had dropped back and was virtually out of the race. They finished the mile in the same relative positions. At the mile and a quarter "Favor" still led, and her backers were jubilant. The eight horses swept round the curve on to the "home stretch" in a bunch with "Favor" in front and "Troubadour" and "Volante" close behind, and both gaining slightly. The excitement was intense. The thousands in the grand stand rose to their feet as one person, and there was perfect pandemonium. "Favor wins!" "Favor wins!" "Troubadour'll get there!" "Volante's gaining!" and numerous other cries in the air. As the horses came up to the grand stand "Favor" and "Volante" were neck and neck, both straining every nerve, but "Volante" was the fleeter and passed under the wire a length ahead.
>
> The noted jockey, Murphy, rode "Volante," and he received $500 from Baldwin, the owner of the horse, and $500 from "Plunger" Walton, a big winner on the race, for winning it. His handling of the horse was beautiful. It was a bad day for the favorites all through, only one winning.[103]

Flos's account is interesting for its mention of the widely known gambler Plunger Walton and his $500 payoff to Murphy. Under normal circumstances, Murphy generally avoided men of questionable character.

In the end, the victory benefited not only Baldwin but also Murphy, who could use this performance as an advertisement of his ability to handle a Thoroughbred, which could translate into additional contracts for larger sums of money. In fact, on July 11 Baldwin announced that he had offered Murphy a two-year contract worth $5,000 per season.[104] With an annual salary of $5,000, Murphy would be better paid than most politicians, and he knew it.

In a *Chicago Tribune* interview conducted after he signed with Baldwin, Murphy answered a few questions about his life and career as a jockey. The reporter began his article with a description of Lucy Murphy:

> In a street car en route to the Washington Park races the other day sat a beautiful octoroon girl perhaps 20 years of age, and with her were two other women of a darker hue, who were evidently her companions. It was apparent from their conversation that they were well acquainted with the different horses that were to contest the day's races and also with some of the jockeys who were to ride them. The octoroon girl was the wife of Isaac Murphy, the young mulatto who stands to-day at the head of all American jockeys, and whose services as a rider are in constant demand at race meetings.
>
> Arrived at the race track the women took seats in the grand stand, and it was not long before a bright faced, active young man galloped down the homestretch on the back of one of Ed Corrigan's thoroughbreds giving the woman a smile as he passed by, the salutation being returned by the pretty octoroon.

The reporter met with Murphy before the first race of the day in the paddock area, where he asked a series of questions related to the life of a jockey, Isaac's habits and concerns, and his annual earnings from horse racing. Murphy's answers were clear and concise, divulging sufficient details so as not to oversimplify a jockey's job. One exchange revealed what Murphy thought about himself and his ability to earn such an impressive salary:

> "You ride for yourself, don't you—that is, you are not bound to any one man?" "Yes, I am my own master so far as that is concerned, except that Mr. Corrigan has the first call on my

services. That means that whenever he has a horse in a race I am obliged to ride that animal if he wants me to, and it is only when he has nothing starting that I could ride that it is possible for me to accept mounts from other people. Of course one stable can furnish starters for but a small minority of the races run all over the country, and so I get all the outside riding I want to do."[105]

Murphy's desire to depict himself as a man in control of his own destiny may have been unusual for a black man, let alone a jockey. But Murphy saw himself as a businessman and the captain of his own ship. This persona attracted admirers, such as a "Chicago hardware and leather merchant . . . [who] had an expensive saddle and bridle manufactured, which were . . . presented formally, in the judges stand, to the 'colored Archer.'"[106]

The *Chicago Tribune* interview functioned as an open yet unintended challenge to the sordid ideas circulating about African American masculinity and manhood. Black men's character was coming under more frequent attack in American society, especially through publications that used demeaning dialect and images to maintain notions of white superiority. The *Tribune* writer's effort to present Murphy as a well-spoken professional was significant, considering the degree to which some newspapers and advertisers went out of their way to reinforce popular racial stereotypes.

At the end of the Washington Park meeting on July 11, Isaac and Lucy headed east on the Chesapeake and Ohio Railroad, more than likely traveling in a private Pullman car. They wanted to get settled in Saratoga Springs before July 21, when Isaac was scheduled to ride Corrigan's Pearl Jennings in a sweepstakes for all ages and Irish Pat in the Travers Stakes. On July 23, the same day Isaac won the Excelsior Sweepstakes for all ages on Freeland, former president and Union general Ulysses S. Grant died of throat cancer in Mount McGregor, New York. The editor of the *Live Stock Record* wrote glowingly about Grant: "He was a great man and a great general, and the country he served so well, knew him to admire his military genius. If the heartfelt regrets of the living can ever penetrate in to the chill hall of death, America's famous son General Grant should sleep well, conscious that his fellow-countrymen appreciate his worth and would have given much could they have prolonged his life."[107] Grant's death signaled the passing of an American hero from one of the nation's most challenging times. It also marked the end of the era when reform-minded men worked to help African Americans rise above their former station and take their place in the American body politic.

At the Saratoga races, Murphy had more than a dozen mounts from July 21 to August 1, finishing in the money in a majority of them. The rivalries that developed between owners and between individual jockeys created additional excitement on the track. At Monmouth Park, Isaac rode Corrigan's white-faced Freeland against the Dwyer brothers' Miss Woodford (later, the first American Thoroughbred to win more than $100,000) in the Champion Stakes on August 10 and the Special Sweepstakes on August 18. Freeland won both races handily. In fact, he won the latter race so decisively that Phil Dwyer accused his jockey, Jimmy McLaughlin, of pulling Miss Woodford and challenged Corrigan to a match race for $2,500 a side. Historian Betty Borries suggests that the Dwyer brothers were criticized "for running their horses [so] often" and for wagering large sums of money on the outcome, thus forcing others to do the same.[108] Case in point: Corrigan agreed to put Freeland to the test with only two days' rest, a decision Murphy disagreed with. The *New York Herald* published an article with the headline "Crack Racers to Try Again: Freeland and Miss Woodford to Do Battle Once More at Monmouth," which provided details about the previous race between the two horses, the conditions of the match race, and the exciting outcome guaranteed to those spectators fortunate enough to attend.[109] In another article appearing on the same day in the *New York Times*, successful breeder and gentleman of the turf James T. Williams related how the celebrated Isaac Murphy had gotten his start under Williams's care and direction; how America Murphy had brought her son to him when she was dying of tuberculosis; and how the talented jockey was not only the best in America, he was "incorruptible."[110] Murphy had come a long way: he was at the center of the racing industry within ten years of learning how to ride races.

On August 20 at Long Branch, the day was clear and fair for the race that represented the burgeoning rivalry between eastern and western racing factions. In addition to having only two days to recover from Freeland's previous victory over Miss Woodford, Isaac was sick after reducing from "115 to 110 pounds in order to ride Bluewing in the select stakes," and he lay prostrate in the paddock area while Freeland's trainer, J. W. Rodgers, made all the preparations.[111] As McLaughlin and Murphy, both astride their horses, made their way to the starting point, the estimated 12,000 spectators applauded the competitors. Poised for the start, they waited for the flag to drop and then "shot away together" at a heated pace for the mile-and-a-half race. McLaughlin went to the front on Miss Woodford; Murphy trailed within two lengths for the first half of the match but was gaining ground with every stride. At the three-quarter pole, Murphy began to close in on McLaughlin while keeping a steady pull on Freeland, who wanted to open up his stride. As they entered the stretch, Murphy gave Freeland his head and let him run. McLaughlin worked his whip and spurs, which kept Miss Woodford's attention as she continued to reach out toward the finish line. Like a magnet, Freeland kept coming until he was at the "mare's shoulder," but it was too late.[112] Murphy and Freeland lost by a head.

Many believed that if Murphy had not been ill, Freeland would have won the race, which may have been true. However, the astute Murphy claimed otherwise. In an interview after the race, the professional jockey remarked that he "had told them they were running the horse too soon after the other race."[113] It is likely that Murphy and Corrigan had a confrontation over the match race. Murphy thought he knew what was best for Freeland and thus challenged Corrigan's position not only as his employer but also as a white man, perhaps receiving a public rebuke for his audacity. It is also possible that Murphy learned of a scheme to support heavy betting against the tired Freeland, whose prior victories would have increased the betting pool against Miss Woodford. Any of these situations would have angered Murphy, who valued his reputation more than anything. Whatever it was that drove a wedge between Murphy and Corrigan, Isaac decided to solidify his future employment and signed with Baldwin.

Public opinion was against Murphy. One article labeled his decision to leave Corrigan as "a moment of pique [more] than anything else." It described Murphy as "an ignorant fellow, [who] knows very little outside of riding horses, and has an intensely good opinion of himself."[114] The writer seemed to be saying that Isaac knew nothing of the real world and had become uppity due to his success in the saddle. Depicting a black man as irrational, emotional, and uneducated was not unusual for the period, but it was the first time such a description had been applied to the well-paid, highly sought after Isaac Murphy, whose reputation as a proven professional and an "elegant specimen of manhood" resonated with some of horse racing's most important supporters. Later, it would be reported that Freeland's ankles were, in fact, "swollen and somewhat stiff, and no one who saw him in repose would hail him as the champion of the West and the superior in speed of any horse from Canada to the Rio Grande."[115] Isaac may have been right about Freeland's readiness to race, but Corrigan had treated him like an employee whose sole purpose was to ride when and how he was told to—a relationship Murphy wanted no part of.

Because of the controversy surrounding the race, and wanting to prove that their horse was no fluke, the Dwyer brothers challenged Corrigan to another race for $20,000 a side ($435,000 in today's dollars). As soon as the arrangements were agreed on, Corrigan telegraphed Murphy, who had gone to St. Louis to ride at the fall meeting, requesting that he return to New York in time to ride Freeland in the September 14 race.[116] Murphy was still under contract to Corrigan, but he was responsible for paying own expenses for accommodations and transportation. Thus, Isaac could either ride in the race or face the consequences of breaching his contract, which could have led to him being banned from racing altogether.[117] He chose to ride. The race would take place at the Dwyers' home course in Brooklyn, the Brighton Beach Race Track. Historian Steven A. Reiss suggests that in the mid- to late 1880s, Brighton Beach attracted a crowd that could be described as "rag-tag and riff-raff" due to the immigrant, impoverished, and corrupt nature of those "betting all they are worth on every race."[118] Once again, James McLaughlin would ride Miss Woodford against Murphy on Freeland. The two jockeys had developed a healthy professional rivalry over the course of their careers. Murphy had won two of the three races between Freeland and Miss Woodford, and he was clearly the favorite of African Americans because of his success and achievement in the saddle and out. The Irishman McLaughlin was the pride of the swelling immigrant population seeking acceptance and participation in American society.

Fortunately for Murphy, the fourth and final race proved that he was right about the capabilities of a healthy Freeland. The *Times Picayune* described the contest after Miss Woodford and Freeland separated from the competition and made the final turn before the finish line: "And here the real struggle began. Miss Woodford increased her lead to three parts of a length at the three quarters, but Freeland then went to the front without an apparent effort on the part of Murphy. Amidst a mighty roar of applause from the spectators, Freeland moved out and won in a very easy style by four lengths, Miss Woodford second, three lengths in front of Modesty."[119] Murphy's only complaint might have been that Freeland's three out of four wins over Miss Woodford were attributed solely to the quality of the horse and not the intellect of the jockey.

One might think jockeys would be accustomed to being in the background, since the owners took credit when the horses won and blamed the jockeys when they lost. But we can assume that this situation, among others, fed Murphy's desire to create his own stable and be his own man. To do so, however, he would need capital. As far as wins among jockeys, Isaac was well ahead of the curve. In 1885 the top thirty-one jockeys averaged 145.9 mounts with 27.7 wins, for a total winning record of 19 percent. In contrast, Isaac Murphy won 56 of 146 races, or 38 percent, compiling the best record by far. At the end of the 1885 season, he was hoping to secure his future with the help of E. J. Baldwin's vast California empire.

## Into the West and Beyond

In early April 1886 Isaac and Lucy left Lexington and headed for
Kansas City, where they would board a westbound train for California. E. J. Baldwin's Santa Anita farm was situated on more than
20,000 acres of fertile land in the San Gabriel Valley. Up until that
point, the Murphys had ventured only to the cities of the Midwest
and Northeast. The journey to Denver, Colorado, before heading
through the Rocky Mountains and into the Mormon stronghold of
Provo, Utah, must have been exciting for the two Kentucky-born
travelers, who were seeing the open skies of the Far West for the first
time. The trip to the West Coast also opened up other possibilities,
including interactions with people of Chinese, Mexican, and Native
American origins. When they arrived at the Merced train depot in
northern California on April 19, the Murphys were within a day's
journey of the Baldwin ranch in the southern part of the state.[120]

Arriving at their final destination sometime on the afternoon
on the twentieth, Isaac and Lucy might have been met by John Isaac
Wesley Fisher, a black man whom Baldwin had hired to recruit black
labor from the South, especially North Carolina. In January, Fisher
had traveled to the Southeast hoping to entice a variety of workers
to return to California with him and take advantage of the opportunity to labor and live free from Southern race hatred. On the trip
back to Baldwin's ranch, Fisher had sixty men, women, and children
in tow. Baldwin employed the Southern transplants in his stables as
"trainers, jockeys, exercisers, coachmen and laborers" and provided for all their needs. In some ways, the arrangement was no different from sharecropping, although in a more civilized environment,
since the nature of horse racing in the West was an extension of the
wealth and character of the men who had amassed their vast fortunes overnight. This is not to say that Baldwin did not take advantage of his workers, but in California, blacks were less likely to be
abused than Chinese or Mexicans.

Traveling through land owned by Baldwin, who was also a
major shareholder of the Santa Fe Railroad, the Murphys arrived
at the temporary train station being used until the Santa Anita sta-

tion could be completed. Stepping off the train, they could not help but look north and northeast at the Sierra Madres looming over the valley, like a giant reminder of a world still to be explored and understood. Writer Charles E. Blanchett, who visited Baldwin's ranch only weeks before the Murphys arrived, described his arrival:

> A night's ride from San Francisco on the Southern Pacific R.R. brought me to Savannah, a Spanish settlement fourteen miles south of Los Angeles. I found a conveyance waiting for me, and we soon started for the villa. About 200 yards drive brought us to the outskirts of the Lucky Baldwin Ranch, as it is generally called, and it was fully an hour's brisk driving before we reached the main avenue leading up to the palatial residence, the entire ride covering the lands of the California Croesus. This avenue is laid out in the center of an orange grove, stretching across an area of several hundred acres, and this immense, prolific orchard comprises over 14,000 trees, all bearing fruit and most of them so heavily laden they require propping. I was informed that two carloads of the bright golden fruit had been gathered the day before that had fallen to the ground. Of the 26,000 acres comprising this ranch 16,500 is under cultivation. Standing upon the porch overlooking this area, as far as the eye can reach one sees orchards of oranges, lemons, limes, English walnuts and almonds, with a scattering here and there, in uniform rows, of the eucalyptus, pepper and spice trees. Passing around to the other side of the porch one sees, under the shadow of the Sierra Madres, an immense vineyard covering 800 acres.[121]

Blanchett also noted the presence of more than "fifty houses on the ranch, including a large store and warehouse, nine vaults and packing houses, a saw mill, stables for the draught horses, boarding and lodging houses, and a neat and comfortable school house" for the children of employees.[122] Baldwin had created his own town dedicated to his interests in horses, agriculture, and transportation.

Lucy may have befriended some of the women working on the

farm, and she may have even helped teach the children their lessons. She may have talked to them about her travels to other parts of the country: New York, Chicago, Nashville. It is possible that Lucy inspired some of the young girls and women to dream about the world beyond the lush San Gabriel Valley, perhaps sowing seeds of discontent among them. In her own way, she may have encouraged those trapped on the farm to flee as far as the train tracks would carry them.

Besides the acres and acres of fruit and nut trees, Isaac would have been impressed by the "stock raising district" at the western boundary of the farm, with its newly built "one mile track complete in every detail, judges' and grand stand, private boxes, etc."[123] Baldwin's horses—some bred right there at Santa Anita and others imported from farms in the Bluegrass—were distinguished by their pedigrees. The great horse Lexington's blood flowed in some of the animals stamping and snorting on the Santa Anita ranch. And chances are good that Isaac had ridden many of the horses that had sired Baldwin's Thoroughbreds.

In 1874 Baldwin had purchased two Kentucky stallions, Grinstead and Rutherford, both of which became champions. Baldwin was accustomed to buying a dozen horses from the Bluegrass State in a single season and shipping them back to his California base to develop his own quality racehorses for running and breeding. Kentucky farmers, whose coffers were not as deep and whose investments were limited to local land and local horses, could not compete. Jack Chinn, a Kentucky horse farmer, commented that his reason for selling his operation and quitting the Bluegrass tradition was an inability to compete with the "rich fellows from California" who come to Kentucky and buy dozens of colts at a time, not knowing which ones will turn out to be great. According to Chinn, "It's different with us fellows that haven't got millions. We have to buy one, two or three colts, and if they don't turn out good our money is gone."[124] Owners like Baldwin, Corrigan, Lorillard, and the Dwyer brothers overwhelmed, if not eliminated, the competition.

Why Isaac and Lucy made the trip to California is unclear. They could have just met the Baldwin stable in Louisville for the

spring races, where Isaac could have become accustomed to the
horses and their temperaments within a week or so. However, in
line with Baldwin's desire to win and prove his worth in the East, he
was determined to have an edge over the competition, which meant
not only the best horses but also the best jockeys. He may have been
a gambler, but he did not like to throw money away. In addition to
wanting Isaac to get to know his horses, Baldwin probably asked
Murphy to help train apprentice jockeys, who would be available to
ride for Baldwin's stable once Isaac's contract was up. Isaac chose to
"teach E. J.'s stable workers to ride" races following the same techniques used by Eli Jordan and mentor William Walker.[125] Among
the successful jockeys tutored by Isaac who would wear Baldwin's
racing colors of black with a red Maltese cross were Si McClain,
Pike Barnes, and Willie Van Buren. However, it also makes sense
that Baldwin just wanted Isaac to see his impressive ranch and the
opportunities available if he became part of the Baldwin empire.

After only a week or ten days at Santa Anita, the Murphys
headed back to Lexington, where the Kentucky Association meeting
on Isaac's home track was scheduled to begin on May 5. Despite the
short stay, it was apparently long enough for Murphy to familiarize
himself with Baldwin's horses. Getting to know them as individuals, learning how they ran at different times of day or on an empty
stomach, and feeling how they responded to his requests through
the reins and by his body language were all vital to success. It was
equally important for each horse to become accustomed to the jockey's personality, style of riding, whisperings of encouragement, and
occasional spur in the sides. Whatever Murphy accomplished during
his trip to Santa Anita, it paid off, given his successful 1886 season
on Volante, Silver Cloud, Lucky B, and Solid Silver.

For the most part, Isaac rode well at the Kentucky Association meeting, but his debut as Baldwin's contract rider at Louisville
set the tempo for the 1886 season and beyond. Upon their arrival in
Louisville, Isaac and Lucy, along with trainer Abraham Perry and
his wife Clara, were the guests of Mrs. Sadonia Wrightson, who resided at 191 Madison Street near Twelfth Street.[126] One possible connection between the Murphys and the Wrightsons was that Horace

Wrightson, a porter at Von Borries and Company, was a prominent member of Louisville's African American community and an officer of Southern Cross Lodge Number 39 of the Prince Hall Masons. We do not know whether Abe Perry was a member of the Prince Hall Masons, but Isaac was initiated into the Lincoln Lodge Masons in Lexington in 1891. It seems plausible that members of Lexington's elite black community would have provided Isaac, a favorite son, with introductions to men like Wrightson, who were prominent members of their own communities and would happily extend their hospitality to the Murphys. These kinds of relationships were part of an active network maintained by African Americans to uplift the race. Murphy was recognized as a professional man who had achieved success based on his adherence to nineteenth-century notions of manhood connected to muscular Christianity. Murphy's achievements marked the progress of African Americans in "their march toward greater self-esteem and legitimate recognition."[127]

On May 14, the first day of the Louisville meeting, the weather was cloudy and hot, but even the threat of rain could not deter the 10,000 fans from crowding the stands and the infield, which could accommodate both wagons and people on foot. Lucy Murphy and Clara Perry watched anxiously for their husbands to appear with their prized horses. Unfortunately for Isaac Murphy, this year's Kentucky Derby would not go his way. The winning owner would be another Californian, J. B. Haggin, whose Ben Ali ran away with the prize. Isaac finished fifth on Baldwin's bay colt Lijero, most likely because the horse was carrying an extra 6 to 8 pounds due to Murphy's current weight at or near 120 pounds. Because of this hindrance, Isaac probably did not punish the horse for not running well; he simply used the opportunity to gauge the colt's strengths and weaknesses, while pushing him to finish the race. To horse-racing fans and gamblers hoping to double or quadruple their money, Murphy's loss must have been a disappointment. Fortunately, the well-paid jockey (Baldwin was paying him $6,000 for the 1886 season) was able to redeem himself by winning the Dixiana Handicap for three-year-olds on Baldwin's Lucky B, paying $1,765; the Free Handicap Sweepstakes on Volante, for $800; and the Louisville

Cup on Lucky B, for $1,270 in prize money. He would also go on to win the Fleetwood Handicap, named after the farm of J. W. Hunt-Reynolds, which may have been an emotional moment for Isaac, given his relationship with that late gentleman of the turf. Other victories included several purse races for different owners and the Turf Stakes on Corrigan's Modesty.

Historians have overlooked the fact that having Lucy travel with him gave Murphy a stability that added to his success. Indeed, it seems that his strong bond with his wife gave Isaac a grounded approach to everyday situations, allowed him to concentrate on his work, and helped him maintain his identity. Together, they explored the different cities they visited, spending time with old and new friends and with family connected by blood or by history. From Lexington to Kansas City, Chicago to New York, the Murphys experienced the joys and disappointments of a sport that required not only a strong mind and body but also, based on Isaac and Lucy's example, emotional support and companionship. Lucy helped her husband avoid the temptations present at every turn and the adoring fans willing to stroke a winner's ego. Isaac knew that celebrity could ruin a promising career, and for his part, Murphy rarely failed to perform as expected.

It is possible that the turning point in Murphy's career—and therefore in the careers of all black jockeys—happened during the Washington Park meeting in Chicago after he won the mile-and-a-half American Derby on Baldwin's Silver Cloud. The bay colt was not even expected to finish in the money, but Murphy and Silver Cloud won by three lengths over a strong field that included Kentucky Derby winner Ben Ali and the highly capable Blue Wing. According to the *Live Stock Record*, "No part of the race was fast except the first and second quarters," which meant it was a waiting race—exactly the kind of race Murphy usually dominated because he had the patience to look for openings and take advantage of them when other jockeys tended to lose their concentration. Indeed, after the bunched-up field passed the halfway point, Murphy shot away on Silver Cloud and "opened up a gap of three lengths to the head of the stretch," leaving the rest of the field behind.[128]

An overjoyed Baldwin gave Murphy all the credit for winning a seemingly unwinnable race. Isaac had demonstrated that he should never be counted out, even when riding an underdog. On this particular day, Murphy made a champion of Silver Cloud, and as a reward, Baldwin raised his salary to an unprecedented level for a jockey, black or white. This caused a "tremendous stir" in the racing community and among the public in general. As the press reported:

> The announcement that Lucky Baldwin had raised the salary of Isaac Murphy, the jockey from $6,000 to $10,000 a year, and had given him *carte blanche* besides to ride for who he pleased when his employer's mounts were not required, has made something of a sensation in the racing world. Ten thousand a year for a colored *boy*! Mr. Baldwin's further announcement that Murphy might have a second call for whatever he might seek to ask from Corrigan or anybody else, has likewise startled the community. Mr. Corrigan is not likely to pay Murphy less for second call than he did last year, and this means that the colored *boy* will enjoy an income from salary alone of $1,000 per month.[129]

The writer's reference to the jockey as a "colored boy," even though he was arguably the top professional in his field, was a sign of the growing trend toward the denigration of professional black men. Murphy's ability to command a salary that a majority of men could only imagine should have been a testament to his hard work and honesty, but that was not the case.

Chicago's black community was "agog over the Knight of the turf" after Baldwin's announcement that he was increasing Murphy's salary. To celebrate the jockey's windfall, Chicago's "colored society" organized a reception in his honor at the Sherman House, coordinated by Miss Gracie Knighten. Following the reception, attendees enjoyed a performance by acclaimed tragedian Charles Winter Wood, a graduate of Beloit College in Wisconsin, at the Madison Street Theater.[130] How Murphy responded to all this attention is not known, but we can assume that he was respectful and grateful for the honor bestowed on him by the small South Side community. If he had a chance to speak, he probably vowed to continue to be a representative of the race and its values. When a toast was raised on his behalf, it is possible that Isaac even lifted a glass of champagne to participate in the celebration.

It was reported that "belles of the best circles discuss his [Murphy's] name, read of his thrilling pigskin performances, speculate on his probable earnings in the pool room, speak of his magnificent salary with awe and wonder, and dilate on the size of the bank account and real estate investments."[131] Naturally, Lucy would have felt the need to protect her husband from these gold-digging women, and he may have felt the same about the rogues eyeing his fair-skinned beauty. In the midst of Chicago's celebration of the great jockey's brilliant success, horse racing was about to be transformed from an elite leisure activity to one driven solely by greed and the need to win at all costs. This would have a tremendous impact on Murphy's future, and he would unknowingly participate in altering both horse racing and black jockeys' role in it over the next decade.

Within weeks of Murphy's great victory on Silver Cloud, a scandal at Washington Park rocked the horse-racing world. On July 17, in a three-quarter-mile purse race for $400, Corrigan's champion filly Pearl Jennings was the favorite in a field that featured Mamie Hunt, Glen Almond, Wanda, Dudley Oaks, and Skobeloff. Everyone expected Pearl Jennings to dominate the field, and "she was barred in the betting pools."[132] After a capital start, Pearl Jennings grabbed the lead at the post, but by the half, Dudley Oaks had edged up and passed her. Around the turn and down the stretch, Mamie Hunt took the lead, and Dudley Oaks and Pearl Jennings ran second and third, respectively. Glen Almond made a move at the halfway mark and drove Mamie Hunt's jockey to punish her severely with the whip. At the finish, it was Mamie Hunt first, Glen Almond second, and Pearl Jennings third. If this had been a race against the likes of Ben Ali, Volante, or Freeland, everyone would have accepted the outcome, but it was not. Pearl Jennings's loss did not make sense, given her clear superiority over the rest of the field. Corrigan, as well as others who "saw the behavior of the mare," were almost certain she had been drugged, but by whom?

It would take a month, but on August 17 the *New York Times* reported that a credible suspect had been arrested in Chicago for attempting to poison another of Corrigan's horses:

> The arrest of Thomas Redmond, alias "Texas Tom," for alleged complicity in the attempt to poison Ed Corrigan's mare Lizzie Dwyer, is liable to lead to some startling developments. "Texas Tom" now confesses that the report of his meeting the man Charles Price at Englewood was correct, and that Price gave him $400 to bet on Binnette against Lizzie Dwyer. Price had obtained the money through Mamie Hunt defeating Pearl Jennings on July 17, when the latter was a very strong favorite. It is almost certain that Pearl Jennings was drugged and thus prevented from winning. Many who saw the behavior of the mare at the post that day were convinced at the time that something was wrong with the great sprinter.[133]

Even more disturbing was that Corrigan's own stableman and two of his stable boys were involved in the plot to poison Lizzie Dwyer. They were working with a known gambler named Donaldson, who had sent a telegraph giving the go-ahead to bet on Binnette in the race against Lizzie Dwyer. The plan was foiled when a savvy and observant clerk gave the telegram to Corrigan. As a precaution, Corrigan stayed with his valuable mare throughout the night and "put the dispatch in the hands of detectives," who arrested his men and charged them with conspiracy to poison a racehorse.[134] Of course, gambling was nothing new to horse racing, but how the races were being tampered with changed dramatically with the poisoning of horses.

After the Washington Park meeting in Chicago, the racing public, jockeys, and Thoroughbred owners turned their focus toward the Northeast and the meetings at Saratoga and Monmouth Park, where Murphy continued to dominate the competition and cemented his reputation as the most disciplined jockey of his generation. As far away as Australia, the reading public had become interested in the jockey who was called the "best rider in America" and a "thoroughly straight and honorable man."[135] By the end of the season, the Kentucky jockey had racked up 45 wins in 120 starts, including some of the most important derbies and stakes races in the country riding for his primary employer E. J. Baldwin, his secondary employer Ed Corrigan, and a slew of others willing to pay the popular jockey's fee. Murphy's reputation was rivaled only by that of James McLaughlin.

Finally, an exhausted Murphy returned to Lexington to recover from another season of stress and anxiety, excitement and success. Sleep would be Murphy's favorite winter activity—sleep and some quiet time with his loving wife, Lucy.

Between the end of March and the beginning of April 1887, Isaac and Lucy once again traveled to Santa Anita. Under the guidance of trainer Bob Thomas and Isaac, the platoon of jockeys worked Baldwin's stable of horses into shape after wintering in mild Southern California. Champion stakes winners Silver Cloud and Volante prepared for the coming season alongside two promising two-year-olds: Los Angeles, a chestnut filly, and Emperor of Norfolk, a bay colt. Baldwin had confidence that both these two-year-olds were capable of winning in the East. The latter's bloodline was impressive: he was the son of Norfolk, one of three sons by R. A. Alexander's legendary Lexington.

On April 15 E. J. Baldwin announced that he would be moving his stable of twenty-four horses to Louisville in preparation for the 1887 racing season. This would give the horses an opportunity to get settled in the East and recover from the long, rough, sometimes unpredictable ride over the rails before the season began. According to Baldwin:

My horses are all doing well. Indeed, some of them were ever so far advanced on their preparation that we had to ease up on them. I am told by good judges that the stable is the strongest one that has ever left California, and so I believe myself,

as from Volante, 6 years old, down to my last 2 year old, I can
be well represented in all ages. Especially am I pleased with my
2 and 3 year olds that have many valuable engagements in the
stakes in the East. I go first to Louisville. After the Chicago
meeting, I may divide the stable, one contingent going to Saratoga and the other to Monmouth Park, but everything depends
upon the form of my horses shown in the Middle States.[136]

Murphy was the key if Baldwin's horses were going to be successful against those of juggernaut owners such as Pierre Lorillard,
J. B. Haggin, the Dwyer brothers, and Ed Corrigan, who employed
jockeys James McLaughlin, Ed "Snapper" Garrison, the "Flying
Dutchman" Fred Taral, William Howard, and Anthony Hamilton, a newcomer to the turf. Next to McLaughlin, whose salary
had also risen to $10,000, Murphy was at the top of the list of the
most capable jockeys in the country. As noted earlier, some writers had compared Murphy to Englishman Fred Archer, whose success on Lorillard's Iroquois in 1881 marked the first victory by an
American horse in the prestigious Epsom Downs. While many had
dubbed Murphy the "colored Archer," there were those who believed the sobriquet should have been reversed, calling Archer the
"white Murphy."[137]

   Amid rumors (if not outright fabrications) of a net worth estimated at $125,000 and real estate holdings of tremendous val-
ue, including a country villa outside of Lexington, Isaac remained
modest and reserved. However, one outward manifestation of his
success was the home he and Lucy purchased in June: a ten-room
mansion on seven acres near the Kentucky Association racetrack on
Third Street, in the eastern part of Lexington. The $10,000 home
represented more than Murphy's ability to make money: it represented the maturing of Murphy as a man. The house had all the
modern conveniences, plus an observation deck on the roof that allowed the Murphys to watch the horses being trained at the track;
they could even observe the spring and fall meetings from the convenience of their home. They kept the home on Megowan Street as a
rental property for many years and leased it to a black man named

Charles Anderson, who would become Murphy's trainer after he acquired a small string of four horses.

Newspapers such as the *Spirit of the Times*, *Kansas City Star*, *Cleveland Plain Dealer*, and *Thoroughbred Record*, and even international publications such as the *Australian Town and Country Journal*, carried accounts of Murphy's successful rides, interviews, and biographical information, illuminating the life of America's most successful jockey. The popular jockey's likeness also began to appear in print—in Root and Tinke's print "Famous Runner & Jockeys of America" (1885) and W. S. Kimball and Company's "Champions of Games and Sports" (1887). Murphy was recognized as a central figure in what had become America's most popular spectator sport, making him a highly visible celebrity. In fact, over the course of the next two seasons, his success and popularity would continue to rise, as would his income. Gold Coin Chewing tobacco reproduced and printed a lithograph of Murphy on a tobacco card in 1887 to promote its product. Whether he was compensated for the use of his likeness is not clear, but the increased exposure only enhanced his appeal and reputation. With a projected salary of $25,000 for 1887, a growing bank account, a beautiful wife, and real estate holdings in Lexington and Chicago, Murphy was a step above a majority of American men.

This elevation of a black man to such a high level of respectability was unprecedented, especially given the developing racial animosity in the United States, framed by the question: What is to be done about the Negro? Murphy's answer would have been simple: Leave him alone. Unfortunately, Murphy's star status isolated him and made him particularly vulnerable to criticism and resentment by those who believed a person of his race was undeserving of such recognition.

Nevertheless, because of his contract with Baldwin, the Kentucky jockey had power, and he was not afraid to use it. Murphy decided to ride at no less than 115 pounds for the 1887 season, thus dictating the terms of any arrangements he made with other owners wanting his expertise in the saddle.[138] By the time the Washington Park Jockey Club met in August, Murphy had won several stakes races, including the McGrath Stakes at the spring meeting of the Kentucky Association in Lexington, the Merchant's and the Runnymeade Stakes at Louisville, and the Merchant's Stakes at Latonia. Not surprisingly, the assault on the sport by gamblers, bookmakers, and dishonest owners continued to be a problem. On June 11 the *Live Stock Record* exposed the fact that when an expected winner lost a race, the jockey was often unfairly blamed. "Most of the horses are not pulled by the jockeys," claimed the editor, but are "fixed in the stable before being brought out to run."[139] Regardless of whether the owners themselves were involved in drugging, poisoning, or overfeeding their horses with the intent of hindering their performance, the result was that jockeys' reputations were suffering. Murphy would have to be on the lookout for such tampering if he wanted to maintain his status as a quality jockey.

Returning to Chicago for the June 25 running of the American Derby, Murphy was the favorite to win on Baldwin's three-year-old bay colt Goliah. He had won the first three American Derbies, including his genius victory on Silver Cloud the prior year. On the first day of the races, the "track was in splendid order" and the temperature was tolerable; the summertime crowd exceeded expectations, and an estimated 25,000 spectators filled the stands and the infield to capacity.[140] Valued at more than $13,000, the American Derby was the premier competition in the West, and the winning jockey would be considered a conquering hero. Unfortunately for Murphy, his horse was outclassed in a field that featured Fleetwood Farm's Clarion, F. B. Harper's Libretto, Baldwin's Miss Ford, and J. B. Haggin's C. H. Todd. The race began as a test in patience, with the field taking twenty-five minutes to get aligned for the start. According to the *Omaha Daily World*, it was a two-horse race, with Anthony Hamilton on C. H. Todd and the jockey West on Miss Ford; in the last "one hundred yards [they] had the race to themselves."[141] Hamilton brought home the chestnut colt for his first American Derby victory; Murphy was never a contender.

Although the loss may not have fazed the near-perfect jockey, Hamilton's victory should have been a sign that Murphy was losing his edge in the competition by not riding as often as he had in the past. Had he become less inclined to take chances on horses of questionable character because he was being well paid to run better horses in stakes competitions? Hamilton, in contrast, was a young jockey who was hungry to establish a reputation as a winner; he was willing to ride as many races as necessary to build his resumé and gain access to the higher stakes races and better mounts, which would lead to more money for wins. Hamilton's success against Murphy, his mentor and friend, would increase his opportunities and therefore his earning potential, especially in the East for owners like August Belmont, the Dwyer brothers, and Pierre Lorillard. By July, the *Cleveland Gazette* counted Hamilton among the "colored jockeys" commanding one of the better salaries in America.

In the popular media, Hamilton was described as a "pure type of the Southern negro of to-day, thick set, undersized and with a skin of the blackest hue. In speech he is reserved even to sullenness, almost invariably giving none but monosyllabic answer to questions asked to him."[142] (It is possible that because of his lack of a formal education, Hamilton was self-conscious about speaking in public and chose his words carefully.) Born in Columbia, South Carolina, on July 5, 1866, Tony Hamilton started out as a stable boy, working in a number of stables around his hometown. In the spring of 1884 he made his debut as a bona fide jockey and eventually moved to the Northeast, where he rode for William "Billy" Lakeland at Brighton Beach. Hamilton's success riding for Lakeland drew the attention of J. B. Haggin, who was looking for "a good heavy weight rider" to carry his orange and blue colors, and he found one in the serious Southern-born jockey.[143] By the fall of 1886, Hamilton was training at Rancho Del Paso near Sacramento, California, preparing for his spring 1887 debut. Haggin had agreed to pay him $3,000 per season and allow him to ride for other owners. In an interview with a *New York Herald* reporter, Hamilton is quoted extensively:

I don't think racing is conducted as fairly and squarely now as it used to be, although I believe that the growing interest in turf events will soon provide an effectual remedy for all crookedness. In the West the popularity of racing is increasing far more rapidly than in the East, and in my opinion it will not be many years before the West will regularly defeat the East in running contests. What sort of times do we jockeys have? Well, I think we have pretty good times, at least I do. Plenty to eat, good clothes to wear, money to spend, and that is not altogether hard. I don't have to stand as much training as some of the others, so I have easier times. I keep fit from the beginning to the end of the season, and I never have to make any special preparation for a day's work. My lowest riding weight is 105 pounds, although I could train down to 100 pounds, if occasion demanded. But there is no necessity for that, as the stable has a good light weight in Fred Littlefield.[144]

This was hardly a monosyllabic response. Hamilton was actually very articulate (unless the reporter edited the conversation to fit his own needs for clarity, which is doubtful). In any case, over the course of a few seasons, Hamilton became one of Murphy's prime sources of competition, as well as one of his best friends.

By August 1887, Murphy and the Baldwin stable were back east competing at Saratoga Springs and Monmouth Park. Baldwin's earnings from the Washington Park meeting had exceeded $21,000, with Emperor of Norfolk's success under Murphy's guidance, and he no doubt anticipated making that much or more between these two meetings, especially in the high-stakes races where thousands of dollars could be won.[145] At Saratoga, Murphy rode for Baldwin in the Travers, California, Iroquois, United States Hotel, Tennessee, and Kentucky Stakes; of seventeen races started, he won seven and finished second in six others. Monmouth Park was a different story. Riding Emperor of Norfolk, the favorite in the Select Stakes, Murphy finished out of the money and in sixth place. A *New York Herald* columnist described his poor showing as "out of form."[146] Then Murphy failed to win the fourth race atop Baldwin's Estrella, even though the "mare was believed by every owner and trainer on the track to have a 'sure thing,' so far did she outclass the other starters." According to the *Daily Inter-Ocean*, "Murphy simply pitched the race into the mud through the most criminal carelessness," resulting in a disgraceful finish and a rumor that he "drank enough champagne before the race to affect his riding."[147] That Murphy drank alcohol before the race, perhaps to stave off hunger pains, or that he was prone to drink at all times of the days seems unlikely but not impossible. However, based on his performances on the same horses at Saratoga Springs, where he won twice on Emperor of Norfolk, and given the increasingly common practice of tampering with horses to affect the outcomes of races, it would not be surprising if this is what happened at Monmouth Park, a gambler's haven. If Murphy had been drinking, the judges would have disqualified him once he reached the stands and weighed out. But that did not happen.

In *Spirit of the Times*, Murphy's failed ride on Emperor of Norfolk was openly discussed:

> The very signal defeat of Emperor of Norfolk at the last week at Monmouth, has not ceased to be the subject of no end of talk and various reasons have been assigned. An undue importance has been attached to Isaac Murphy having drank champagne, but this is hardly fair, as the jockey was not under its influence. The colt seemed beaten after he had gone half a mile. But that does not satisfy many who lost money on him, and they seem never done talking about it. Mr. McCullough, who is connected with Green Morris' stable and is a man of very excellent judgment, said before the race that he thought Sir Dixon would win. "But what about Emperor of Norfolk?" he was asked. "I don't think he's himself," he replied.[148]

Clearly, there was more to the story than previously discussed. But the idea that Emperor of Norfolk had been drugged before the race was not elaborated on in the media.

At the Coney Island Jockey Club meeting at Sheepshead Bay, Murphy redeemed himself by winning on Emperor of Norfolk in the Autumn Stakes on September 3 and in the Turf Handicap on Baldwin's Mollie McCarthy's Last three days later, beating Ed Garrison on Lancaster. However, the seed of doubt had been planted in the minds of spectators: Had the honest and reliable ambassador of the sport of kings been corrupted by his success? Had he lost the self-control required to maintain focus on his work in the saddle? Murphy, like Tony Hamilton and Moses Fleetwood Walker, was being put in his place by members of the press who recognized that they had the power to change the fortunes of successful black athletes.

By the end of the season, Isaac was reassured of Baldwin's confidence in him when the owner extended his contract and agreed to pay him $12,500. Baldwin also asked Murphy to ride at 112 pounds, owing to the death of Fred West, Baldwin's other prized employee, who had died "in the mad rush of two year-olds at Saratoga."[149] Unfortunately, at some point, Isaac would begin to suffer from the demands placed on his mind and body and the pressures imposed on him from all directions.

Between seasons, the Murphys took refuge at their new home on East Third Street. Once they had some time to recover from their travels, friends such as Henry Scroggins, Abe and Clara Perry, Dudley Allen and his wife Maggie, Jordan and Belle Jackson, and Reverend Bell would have visited. Their conversations would have been pleasant, including an exchange of information—the Murphys telling their guests about events taking place outside of the Bluegrass, and the Lexingtonians informing Isaac and Lucy about changes in the city, especially with regard to race relations.

It is possible that the Murphys read one or two of the black weeklies and dailies in circulation and, on occasion, used the articles as a basis for conversations related to the position of the Negro in American society and how to respond to attacks on their humanity and citizenship. Reading columns by Thomas Fortune, Iona (Ida B. Wells), and Frederick Douglass; books by historians George Washington Williams, William Still, and the Reverend William J. Simmons; poems by Phillis Wheatley; and the novels of William Wells Brown would have expanded not only their knowledge of things social, political, and economic but also their understanding of the need for education and examples of achievement and success. Reading columns in the *Cleveland Gazette*, *New York Age*, and *Indianapolis Freeman* would have exposed them to the radical ideas being formulated and implemented around the country, especially in the urban areas of the North, where African Americans wielded more influence than in the post-Reconstruction South. Discussions of power, privilege, and purpose would have been filtered through one-on-one conversations and discussions in community settings such as churches, fraternal organizations, or social gatherings where leaders could inform their neighbors about events taking place in cities like Chicago, Cincinnati, and Indianapolis. Murphy's thoughts about the politics of the day are not known.

In February 1888 Benjamin Bruce, editor of the *Live Stock Record*, published an article in response to one circulating about Murphy that tried to diminish his importance to horse racing, depicting him as just another black jockey:

From an article of over a column in length which has been going the rounds of the papers, I clip the following:

"Another jockey who is considered a coming man, and who kept himself in the public gaze during the last season was Isaac Murphy, who, in spite of his name, is neither Irish not Hebrew, but a darky. He has made a good deal of income, something under $5000, and is a successful rider."

The above makes such [a] display of the writer's ignorance of malice, and contains so much untruth that it deserves some notice. Most of the article from which it is clipped is used for the laudation of McLaughlin and Garrison, both of which are too worthy of it to require that another should be depreciated that they might shine.

It is no secret that [in] 1887 Isaac Murphy received a retainer of $10,000 for his services from April 1st to November 1st, with additional pay for his mounts, and the privilege of riding for whom he pleased when not riding for his employer. It is true also that had he chosen to change employers he could have received even a larger sum.

Now the records for the last six years will show by the only true list, the proportion of winning mounts, to the whole number, that Murphy stands at the head of American jockeys.[150]

By 1888, Murphy had won more than 38 percent of his races, while McLaughlin's and Garrison's numbers hovered around 35 and 31 percent, respectively. Yet all three were premier jockeys and were in high demand from coast to coast. Importantly, Murphy had significantly fewer mounts, by choice. Because of his success in stakes races, he was able to dictate the terms of his contracts and ride less than most other jockeys. Stable owners chose Murphy to ride their prized horses quite simply because he was the best pilot of horseflesh available. Bruce concluded his article:

> As "the record speaks" it will show that Murphy's career as a jockey from the time he had his first mount to the end of last season is unrivaled in America.
>
> This is written, it is needless almost to say, without Murphy's knowledge but in a simple justice to one who has ever been unassuming generous to other jockeys, faithful to his employers and the public, which has even trusted him; and who has never by any display of rivalry "blown his own horn."[151]

Bruce's acknowledgment of Murphy's modesty and humility and his unimpeachable success as a jockey was a celebration of the man who lived his life with a purpose.

Unfortunately, deteriorating race relations in American society, evidenced by episodes of brutality in the form of lynching and rape and use of the legal system against the innocent, overlapped and intersected with the increasing popularity of horse racing. Those in control of the sport, especially in the East, attempted to exclude blacks from the saddle so that white jockeys might shine. The depreciation of Murphy's abilities not only took the spotlight off the most successful jockey of his generation but also tried to erase the long history of blacks' contributions to the development of horse racing in America. For Murphy, this was only the start of what would be a coordinated effort to assail his character and damage his reputation as a dependable and trustworthy jockey.

Murphy no doubt appreciated Bruce's public expression of confidence and support. However, the hostility directed toward him and other black jockeys was part of a coordinated assault against black labor throughout the country. Indeed, the collusion between capital and labor to exclude blacks was linked to American social Darwinism and the mythology of white supremacy. In response to the growth of black social, economic, and political power, European immigrants, ethnic minorities, and poor and middle-class whites gravitated toward the only thing that bound them together: fear of black competition. This, as well as a fear of black domination, was at the core of the growing violence against blacks in the 1880s and throughout the 1890s. This assault on African Americans in general and black men in particular was how white men responded when black masculinity threatened their self-conscious ideas about manhood.

Seemingly unaffected by these tensions in society and in the horse-racing world, Isaac continued to plan his future as an owner-trainer. According to the *Washington Critic*, in the spring of 1888 Murphy purchased a small farm near Lexington for $5,000, where he built a stable to house his string of two-year-olds. The article speculated that if all went according to plan, the successful jockey would race his string "this year if they prove to be good for anything."[152] As noted earlier, Murphy hired Charles Anderson, his Megowan Street tenant, to train and care for his four promising colts: Fabulous, Barrister, Nugent, and Champagne Charley. As an aspiring lord of the turf, Isaac had learned a lot working with and for owners such as James T. Williams, J. W. Hunt-Reynolds, Ed Corrigan, L. P. Tarleton, and E. J. Baldwin, and he borrowed freely from their collective knowledge of the industry. His first venture was buying and selling quality horses for a profit, beginning with Barrister, who was sold for $4,000 to Green B. Morris, a successful horse trainer from Kentucky.

Sometime in March, Murphy claimed his stable's racing colors: "black jacket, red cuffs and white belt, red cap with green tassel."[153] Why he chose these particular colors is not known, but it is interesting that a similar color scheme of red, black, and green would be central to the 1960s Black Power movement in the United States. Essentially, Murphy's assertion of his power as a jockey, owner, and

trainer in the world of horse racing—a realm traditionally dominated by white men—signified the development of black power in
horse racing and, by extension, American society. As an empowered
black man seeking to assert his identity and economic power, Isaac
might have intended his color choices to represent black success and
achievement.

Before leaving Kentucky and heading west, Murphy would
have instructed his trainer, Anderson, how to proceed until he called
for his string to travel west to the races in Kansas City and Chicago. Murphy reached Santa Anita by April 1 and began working
with Baldwin's new trainer, R. W. Thomas. For Murphy, going to
California was like going to training camp; his work there would
help him focus, get fit (and perhaps lose weight), and prepare for the
long, grueling season ahead. Isaac may have made the trip alone this
time, leaving Lucy home to supervise their assets and manage their
properties. It is also possible that Lucy's sister, Susan Osborne, had
moved into their Lexington home, in which case Lucy could have
gone west with her husband, entrusting Susan to handle their affairs
in their absence.

The success of the Santa Anita stables in the 1888 season rode
squarely on Isaac's shoulders. How he responded to this pressure remained to be seen. The season began at the annual Nashville Jockey
Club meeting, which opened on April 30.[154] Between Nashville and
Louisville, Isaac experienced only marginal success, finishing second or third in most of his races on Volante and Emperor of Norfolk. However, after a majority of Baldwin's horses shifted to New
York to run in the big-money Brooklyn, American, and Coney Island Jockey Club races, Murphy began to heat up. He won five out
of five races on Emperor of Norfolk and placed first on Volante
in one race and second in three others. One race in particular, the
Brooklyn Cup on May 26, is worth noting.

In a field that included Jimmy McLaughlin on the Dwyer brothers' Hanover and William Howard on A. J. Cassatt's The Bard, Murphy on Volante was considered a contender if the horse could keep
up with the pace expected to be set by Howard. A week earlier, under cold and rainy conditions and on a slow, muddy track, the same

three horses had met in the Brooklyn Jockey Club Handicap, worth $8,460, in front of 10,000 fans huddled in the grandstand. The Bard won, with Hanover finishing a close second; Volante struggled to finish in fifth position. By the time the horses met again on the twenty-sixth for the mile-and-a-half race, the rematch between Howard and McLaughlin and their respective horses was the primary focus of the 20,000 spectators. At the start of the race, McLaughlin took the lead on Hanover, with Murphy in second position on Volante and jockey Martin on Fenelon in third. The Bard was dead last when the flag fell, some "two or three lengths behind the others."[155] Howard soon caught up to the pack, however, and after the three-quarter pole, The Bard lapped and then passed the field, separated by two lengths after a furlong. McLaughlin started to run after Howard, who was only two lengths away at the end of a mile, but Hanover was done; there was no way he could catch The Bard. Realizing he had no chance to win, McLaughlin eased up on Hanover, but he failed to see that Murphy had been waiting to make his move. Without hesitation, Murphy urged Volante to continue the contest and passed a surprised McLaughlin, who tried to ignite Hanover to finish, without luck. Crossing the line to take the $500 prize for second place, Murphy set in motion a series of events that can best be described as both opportunistic and repugnant.

Leaving New York, Murphy arrived in Chicago with Baldwin's stable for the Washington Park meeting, set to begin June 23. He was fully expected to win on the peaking Emperor of Norfolk, and most bookmakers refused to take odds on the speedy colt. Most gamblers knew they would lose money betting against the jockey who had won three of the previous four American Derbies. Another reason not to open the pools to the American Derby was the number of horses available to bet on in other races. The summer races had become so popular among owners that there were more than 2,400 horses in the city for the scheduled events, and stables were in short supply. To accommodate all the animals, park authorities secured "everything that was shaped like a barn within a mile" of the track.[156] This predicament overjoyed the locals, who happily leased their stable space to the out-of-town turfmen.

If Isaac and Lucy were not staying with friends in the city, they could have found accommodations at the Sheridan or the Grand Pacific Hotel, both of which were friendly toward African Americans. Making his way to the track sometime before noon, Isaac would have been greeted by fans hoping to get a look at the horses and their jockeys preparing to compete for the day's cash prizes. On this first day of the summer meeting, a light rain fell; it was barely noticed by those situated in the grandstand and the clubhouse, but spectators in the infield and around the betting ring got a little wet. In the first event of the day, a purse race for $450, Murphy finished second on Volante, a full length behind F. B. Harper's Valuable, ridden by the outstanding Isaac Lewis.

The second race of the day, the American Derby, was valued at $16,000. Baldwin's Emperor of Norfolk was the hands-down favorite, based on Murphy's previous victories on the speedy colt, whose current six-race winning streak excited spectators. To make it a match, however, his stablemate Los Angeles, ridden by Armstrong, and Haggin's Falcon, ridden by Anthony Hamilton, were entered as well. The *Chicago Horseman* conceded that the favorite was obvious:

> The bell now rang for the great event of the day, and though all experienced turfman knew that by every law of public form the Emperor of Norfolk must win, a ripple of excitement thrilled through the vast crowd. The field has dwindled down to seven, and so strong was the public faith in the Santa Anita candidates that 2 and 1 to 1 was placed on the pair, Los Angeles and the Emperor of Norfolk. Los Angeles is an exceedingly handsome and blood-like filly, and the Emperor of Norfolk looks every inch the king he really is.[157]

Maintaining his reputation for not pushing or punishing his mounts unnecessarily, Murphy rode Emperor of Norfolk circumspectly until they were within a dash of the finish, when he gave the horse its head. Emperor of Norfolk won by a length, despite Hamilton's steady punishment of Falcon to the wire. Hardly ever credited in white newspapers with winning based on his intelligence and his understanding of his horse's capabilities, Murphy was even accused of having a penchant for grandstanding. But the evidence indicates that he rode to win—that was all.

After his successful Washington Park showing, where he won a total of four races on Emperor of Norfolk and Volante worth more than $20,000, Isaac and Lucy returned to New York, where he continued to ride for Baldwin at Monmouth Park and Saratoga Springs. In August the Dwyer brothers approached Murphy about engaging his services, as they had become dissatisfied with Jimmy McLaughlin, their primary jockey for the past twelve years. On the surface, the break between the Dwyers and McLaughlin had been amicable and cordial. However, according to the *Live Stock Record*, the Dwyers' decision was the result of McLaughlin's diminishing riding form and his lack of commitment to compete to win every race. "The ill feeling which has existed for some time between the Dwyers and their jockey Jas. McLaughlin has at length ended in a separation between them after twelve years." Furthermore, the "ill feeling began early in the season, and has grown ever since, as the Dwyers think they have lost races which they should have won."[158] One of those races, no doubt, was the one in which McLaughlin virtually gave second place to Murphy. At the time the article was published, a successor had not been picked. However, the following day it was announced that Murphy had agreed to ride for the Dwyers for the rest of the season and would consider signing a contract for 1889.[159] We do not know how McLaughlin felt about being replaced by Murphy, but we can imagine that some whites saw it as another white boy losing a valuable job to an undeserving "nigger."

Murphy's comportment as a professional had earned him the respect and admiration of some of his fellow jockeys, patrons of the turf, and owners. Described as a jockey who "sits his horse with ease" and maintains "little flourish to his finish," Isaac was still in demand by owners who wanted a jockey who would fight to win every race.[160] Although he achieved only 37 victories out of 117 starts during the 1888 season—which was extremely low, compared with Pike Barnes's 626 mounts and 206 wins—Murphy could be depended on to win the high-stakes races. At the end of the season, Murphy debated whether to ride in 1889. It seems that his limited success as an owner-trainer had made him eager to complete the transition to a life outside the rails, where his own reliable jockeys would ride his horses to victory wearing the colors of his stable.

In early November delegates from the western and eastern jockey clubs met in New York to decide the future of horse racing in America and the fate of its jockeys, including Murphy, who, over the last decade, had helped elevate the sport as the "leading amusement" and attraction of the American people.[161] The western committee of the "Turf Congress" consisted of Colonel M. Lewis Clark of Louisville, General J. F. Robinson of the Lexington Association, and J. E. Brewster, secretary of the Washington Park Association. The eastern representatives were John Hunter, president of the American Jockey Club; Philip J. Dwyer, president of the Brooklyn Club; and J. G. K. Lawrence, secretary of the Coney Island Jockey Club. Central to the conversation were issues related to "racing rules, weights and forfeits." Prior to the 4:00 meeting at the St. James Hotel, the delegates met at Lawrence's office to discuss their respective clubs' needs.[162] Three hours later, all the delegates met at the hotel to discuss what changes, if any, should be adopted. Besides discussions of how to improve racing, make rules more uniform, and regulate betting pools, the delegates were most concerned about weight requirements for jockeys. They feared losing quality jockeys who were getting older and thus had increasing difficulty keeping their weight under control. For instance, jockeys like Murphy, McLaughlin, Taral, and Donohue had to take extreme measures to lose weight, which weakened them considerably. As a result, the Turf Congress amended the weight requirements for jockeys (adding four pounds to the 1885 weight standards), based on the horse's age, distance of the race, and month of the year, with no allowance for geldings (see table 7.1).[163] These changes made at the end of the 1888 season would have a positive effect on Murphy's career, and perhaps they played a part in his decision to ride in 1889.

Isaac Murphy was unique among jockeys, both black and white. On quality horses, he dominated and won a majority of rac-

**Table 7.1.** U.S. Weight Standards (in pounds) for Jockeys, November 1888

| Two-Year-Olds | | | | | | |
|---|---|---|---|---|---|---|
| | May | June | July | August | September | October |
| Half mile | 84 | 86 | 89 | 93 | 96 | 99 |
| Three-quarter mile | 80 | 81 | 84 | 88 | 91 | 94 |
| One mile | 79 | 79 | 79 | 81 | 85 | 87 |
| **Three-Year-Olds** | | | | | | |
| | May | June | July | August | September | October |
| Half mile | 110 | 111 | 113 | 115 | 116 | 117 |
| Three-quarter mile | 110 | 111 | 113 | 115 | 116 | 117 |
| One mile | 106 | 107 | 109 | 111 | 112 | 113 |
| Mile and a half | 104 | 105 | 107 | 109 | 110 | 111 |
| Two miles | 102 | 103 | 105 | 107 | 108 | 109 |
| **Four-Year-Olds** | | | | | | |
| | May | June | July | August | September | October |
| All distances | 122 | 122 | 122 | 122 | 122 | 122 |
| **Five-Year-Olds** | | | | | | |
| | May | June | July | August | September | October |
| Half mile | 125 | 124 | 122 | 122 | 122 | 122 |
| Three-quarter mile | 124 | 124 | 124 | 122 | 122 | 122 |
| One mile | 126 | 126 | 124 | 124 | 122 | 122 |
| Mile and a half | 127 | 126 | 125 | 124 | 124 | 124 |
| Two miles | 128 | 127 | 126 | 125 | 124 | 124 |
| **Six-Year-Olds and Older** | | | | | | |
| | May | June | July | August | September | October |
| Half mile | 125 | 124 | 122 | 122 | 122 | 122 |
| Three-quarter mile | 124 | 124 | 124 | 122 | 122 | 122 |
| One mile | 126 | 126 | 124 | 124 | 122 | 122 |
| Mile and a half | 128 | 127 | 126 | 125 | 125 | 125 |
| Two miles | 129 | 128 | 127 | 126 | 125 | 125 |

es; on average horses, he pushed them to their limits and helped them reach their full potential. A consummate professional, Murphy commanded respect not only from his fellow jockeys but also from the owners, who generally dictated how races should be run. On occasion, Murphy was allowed to run a race as he saw fit, based on his ability to judge the competition and place his horse in the right position. And although he worked in close proximity to the gambling set, he maintained his integrity and his reputation as an honest jockey and a man of exceptional morals, whose work ethic and intent to win could not be questioned. Friends like John Stoval, Anthony Hamilton, and young Pike Barnes looked to the seasoned jockey as an example of the kind of professional they aspired to be. When asked to name the best jockey in America, Hamilton commented, "I think that Isaac Murphy is the king of all of them. He is a wonderful judge of pace, and is always good at the finish." Unfortunately, Hamilton's opinion of Murphy's ability in the saddle was overshadowed by the reporter's fascination with his interviewee's complexion, which he noted was "as black as the ace of spades."[164] As odd as it sounds, this was a common digression among white reporters seeking to denigrate the most educated and successful African Americans by forcing them into the canned definitions of blackness accepted by whites.

Murphy understood the power of the written word and the clout wielded by the newspapermen who controlled the stories that appeared in print. It is possible that newspaper articles comparing the salaries of black and white jockeys created a rift between the two groups. Although we cannot be sure of the extent of Murphy's relationships with white rivals such as McLaughlin, Garrison, and Howard, we do know that they maintained a professional decorum that allowed them to compete on the racetrack without resorting to violence. Whether they socialized outside of the track or encouraged their colleagues in races in which they were not competing with one another is absent from nineteenth-century narratives of horse racing. White jockeys from the West were probably more amenable to working with black jockeys, who may have taught them how to ride or how to judge a horse's quality. In the Northeast, where ethnic tensions and racial hatred were more prevalent, white boys training to become jockeys were conditioned to be aggressive and not lose to colored boys. One of the most successful trainers was the abusive William "Father Bill" Daly, who was responsible for the careers of McLaughlin and Garrison. Under the guidance of Daly, they lived with the constant fear of being beaten if they failed to ride as instructed. In his book *Black Maestro*, Joe Drape suggests that Daly was a racist, which would certainly influence how the boys he trained felt about competing alongside black jockeys.[165] How McLaughlin and Garrison felt about Murphy is not known, but there had to be an awareness that losing to the black jockey reduced their standing in Daly's eyes.

With the changes initiated by the Turf Congress in November, which included improving the parks to satisfy the needs of the public and implementing a uniform set of rules for all clubs to adhere to, the 1889 season looked promising. In March, Isaac sat down for an interview with a correspondent from the *New York Herald* at his home in Lexington. The serious but candid jockey observed, "It is pleasant for me to recall the past. Its months and years, no matter what the future may have in store for me, will always be the happiest of my life. I look back to them with delightful memories and keen enjoyment. I would gladly live over the old days, as they were filled with the sunshine of success, in which few shadows ever fell."[166] Plainly, Isaac was shaping the story of his life as he wanted it recalled, without the ugly scars of slavery, abject poverty, death, and the insecurity of being alone in the world. Murphy's public persona was a deeply contemplative individual who was sure of himself and his purpose. There is no doubt that he was all this and more. However, only he and those who had known him since childhood understood the scope of his accomplishments over the course of his fourteen-year career. Toward the end of the interview, Isaac expressed some fondness for his humble beginnings, calling himself "a poor lad" and stating that "the money I earned by my riding was all I had to live on." He continued:

Since that time I have learned year after year, and my salary has been as much as that of a member of President Harrison's Cabinet. Outside of my salary Mr. Baldwin has given me $1,000 extra every time I have won the American Derby for him, and my extra mounts each year bring me on an average as much as my salary.

I believe my percentage of wins to the number of mounts is the best on record in this country, as since my first race in 1875, I have ridden in 1,087 races, 411 of which I have won. The value of the stakes and purses I have no way to estimate, but as I have scored victories in almost every nook and corner of America and my name appears in all the lists of important races I know it must be an enormous sum.

I am as proud of my calling as I am of my record, and I believe my life will be recorded as a success, though the reputation I enjoy was in the stable and in the saddle. It is a great honor to be classed as one of America's greatest jockeys.[167]

Throughout the 1889 season, Murphy's legacy as one of the nation's greatest jockeys would be tested and substantiated in race after race. Between May and October, from St. Louis to New York, the "colored Archer" claimed dramatic victories riding for Baldwin, the Dwyer brothers, and others. In the one-mile Kentucky Handicap for a $3,078 purse, Murphy rode McClelland and Roche's Badge and won by a "short head" over Isaac Lewis on the Labold brothers' Montrose.[168] At the Washington Park meeting, he failed to win the American Derby on Milton's Young's Once Again but copped two wins and a portion of the money in six other races. Coincidentally, black Australian prizefighter Peter Jackson was in Chicago during the Washington Park meeting and was registered at the Grand Pacific Hotel. It is unknown whether Jackson and Murphy crossed paths, but in an interview a month later, Jackson mentioned the jockey in response to a question about prejudice against "boxers of his color in this country":

I have been kindly treated thus far in this country, particularly by the California Athletic Club, which is certainly as square an organization as exists anywhere in the world. John L. Sullivan has spoken unkindly of me several times, but I have never paid any attention to his remarks. He has said that he would not meet me because of my color. I have never challenged him. I challenge nobody. If a white man declines to meet me before he is asked, why, it's none of my business. I consider Sullivan a great fighter and he probably has no peer, but he is unjust in abusing me. Color does not rub off, and I am sure that any of these fighters would not hesitate to go against a black man if he thought he could win. A fighter has no reason to refuse to meet another, even if his color is not the same. Why don't McLaughlin or Garrison refuse to ride in a race because Isaac Murphy has a mount in it? They have as much right to bar color as have the fighters. I am an athlete, and try to be a square man, but these fighters who are afraid to meet "niggers" make me very tired.[169]

Jackson's commentary indicates an awareness of American race relations, whereby white men refused to compete with blacks for fear of losing in a head-to-head competition with an equally talented and determined black man. Jackson's observation was prophetic of the changing racial dynamics in American culture and the rise of Jim Crow segregation, which, in essence, served to save white masculinity and manhood from the perceived damage done by the accelerated achievements of African Americans. Individually and collectively, in the country that had enslaved their ancestors for more than 300 years, black men and women were living and prospering and, in fact, defining what it meant to be American. This was what Isaac Murphy did each time he stepped onto the racetrack.

On July 8 J. B. Haggin telegraphed Murphy, who was still in Chicago, to request the jockey's presence at Monmouth Park, in New Jersey, to ride his chestnut colt Salvator in the Lorillard Stakes the next day. To entice Murphy to say yes, Haggin offered him $2,000 if he were victorious in the high-stakes race. The opportunity to ride for Haggin could lead to additional engagements to ride in other high-stakes races, so Murphy agreed and left Chicago on the midnight train.[170] But why did Haggin want Murphy in the saddle when

Salvator was already the favorite with James McLaughlin scheduled to ride him? Obviously, Haggin wanted to ensure victory, win the $18,000 purse, and beat the Dwyer brothers and other eastern owners, but there may have been another motivation.[171]

The field in the Lorillard Stakes for three-year-olds included the Dwyer brothers' Longstreet, D. D. Withers's Sensation and Faverdale, G. M. Rye's Long Dance, C. Littlefield's Jubal, A. J. Cassatt's Eric, D. J. McCarthy's Sorrento, and Haggin's two colts Kern and Salvator. The *Daily Inter-Ocean* reported on the controversial event:

> It is extremely unfortunate for the best interests of the turf that the race for the Lorillard Stakes to-day at Monmouth Park, won by Salvator, should have been run and won under circumstances so entirely distasteful to every one's idea of fair play. In the first place, more than one habitually conservative turfman kept asking all day long when they saw Kern's name as a probable starter for the Lorillard Stake: "What is Mr. Haggin's idea in starting him? What chance has he got? What is he in for?" And in the course of the race all these questions seemed assured, for at the end of the mile furlong, after lunging all over the course, Kern was deliberately taken by his rider Brant, diagonally across the track, cutting off as he did so Jubal, Eric, and Longstreet, causing all three to pull up so as to lose at least a dozen lengths, while it was said that Eric was cut on one of his legs. All this happened when Kern's stable companion, Salvator, was second, with clear going, and the object of it in many people's opinion was to make sure that none of the contending horses behind Salvator should have a chance to race up to him. Now this is not merely the view of the average $5 better, but is the actual beliefs of dozens of cold blooded horsemen.[172]

Newspapers across the country reported only the results of the race, claiming that the California horse Salvator had conquered the East and that J. B. Haggin had won the Lorillard Stakes and the prize of $18,000. Few outside of New York and New Jersey had any idea what had actually transpired. Haggin's recruitment of Murphy thus made sense: the jockey's reputation for honesty somewhat guaranteed that nothing dishonest was going on, plus he had just arrived at the racetrack on the morning of the race.

Taking advantage of the new weight standards implemented by the Turf Congress and the Dwyer brothers' demand that he ride more frequently in the Northeast, Murphy posted his greatest number of mounts in 1889, with 195. And although he won only 58 races, he was in the money in more than half of the remaining 137 races. For Murphy, who was hoping to extend his career a few more years, the future looked promising. However, within one year, everything would begin to unravel, and he would watch powerlessly as the life he had worked so hard to attain was taken away.

# 8

# In This Peculiar Country

## *1890–1895*

In January 1890 most blacks in Kentucky, as well as in the rest of the nation, were aware of the growing tensions between blacks and whites over the so-called Negro question. The *Kentucky Leader* carried a front-page article explaining the reasoning behind a Senate bill proposing that blacks be forced to emigrate to Africa. Essentially, the bill's sponsor, Senator Mathew Butler, believed that blacks had become the political "foot-ball of contending factions and been made to suffer enough between the upper and nether millstones of opposing forces"—that is, white people. As a group, blacks could never find justice in the United States, according to Butler, because whites would never accept them as equals. In response, Republican senator George Frisbie Hoar of Massachusetts stood up for the rights of African Americans who had been born in the United States, had earned the rights and privileges of citizenship, and were not deserving of banishment to the "dark region of the dark continent," as proposed by radical Democrats. Hoar continued:

It was not, therefore, that the colored race could not be made fit for freedom that this proposition was made; but simply on the ground that the nature of things, or the nature of man, was such that, men of different races (and especially different colors) could not live together, in harmony and peace and freedom and honor under the laws of this Republic. If that was true, then the declaration of independence was a lie; then the Constitution of the United States and the Constitution of every American State rested on rottenness; then the Christian religion, which taught humanity, equality, and that "God made of one blood all the nations of the earth," but a solemn mockery, a solemn falsehood.[1]

Senator Hoar's response was no doubt applauded by the African American community and its leaders, but the black press needed to speak out against schemes to disenfranchise blacks any further.

Within the week, *New York Age* editor Timothy Thomas Fortune called for a national conference and convention in Chicago to galvanize black leadership into a singular body capable of challenging the dizzying effects of white supremacy. On January 25, 140 delegates representing twenty-one states and territories converged on Chicago to decide how to challenge the argument to send blacks out of the United States.[2] In his address to the convention, Fortune stressed the need for individuals to commit to the program and inspire their communities to adhere to the aims espoused by the National Afro-American League. With a sense of urgency, Fortune argued:

If we are true to ourselves, if we are true to our posterity, if we are true to our country, which has never been true to us, if we are true to the sublime truths of Christianity, we shall succeed—we cannot fail.

We shall fight under the banner of truth. We shall fight under the banner of justice. We shall fight under the banner of the Federal Constitution. And we shall fight under the banner of honest manhood. Planting ourselves firmly upon these truths, immutable and as fixed in the frame works of social and political progress as the stars in the heavens, we shall eventually fight down opposition, drive caste intolerance to the wall, crush out mob and lynch law, throttle individual insolence and arrogance, vindicate the right of our women to the decent respect of lawless rowdies, and achieve at last the victory which crowns the labors of the patient, resourceful, and the uncompromising warrior.[3]

Isaac Murphy was no doubt aware of the Chicago convention and the position taken by black leaders with regard to elevating "Afro-Americans" through organization, agitation, and acts of dissent in the tradition of Crispus Attucks, Toussaint-Louverture, and Nat Turner. How he felt about these events can probably best be understood by his actions and choices. But it is important to remember that Lexington's black community was in many respects a community of achievers who were still somewhat protected from the growing racial animosities and institutional denials beginning to influence the outside world.

By February 1890, Isaac was still contemplating whether to end his career in the saddle and make the natural transition to owner and trainer. Given his reputation as a man who was intelligent, hardworking, brave, honest, and modest, Isaac may have seemed out of place in jockeying, which had become rife with unrefined boys and a cartel of rough-and-tumble men. Isaac was more of a gentleman rider who had earned his fortune as a jockey. This was unusual in America, where the owners of Thoroughbred racehorses generally started out wealthy. Few, if any, of the wealthiest of owners had ever raced horses competitively, riding only as a form of transportation or on the occasional foxhunt.

Yet there was such a thing as a gentleman jockey in American equine sports. Most of them were wealthy, athletic, adventuresome types who participated in trotting and steeplechase races, seeking the pleasures of riding a horse as a leisure activity and as a class-oriented form of masculine performance. In comparison, in the earliest accounts of equine sports in England, gentlemen jockeys were considered a disgrace to the upper classes; riding for money was not only uncouth but also beneath a man's station as part of the elite.

A jockey was considered a laborer whose value was in his ability to guide a horse around a track in pursuit of victory (and monetary rewards) against his peers and the stopwatch. There were exceptions, of course, Fred Archer being a primary example of a jockey whose success in the saddle translated into other opportunities. Individual jockeys rarely interacted with their employers outside the liminal space of the racetrack. And though both were a part of the masculine ritual, they represented two separate groups, identities, and modes of existence.

Depending on one's perspective, Isaac's persona as a gentleman jockey was both a contradiction of the supposed differences between the two types of riders and an example of what blacks were capable of achieving in Western civilization. An American capitalist himself, Isaac used his knowledge of horses and of the ins and outs of racing as capital to be invested in the labor of horses. His understanding of American race relations also informed his decision to combine the two categories of gentleman rider and gentleman jockey, which seemed to contradict each other.[4] But in American society, where the ongoing anxiety attached to race, work, and masculinity continued to inform the growing animosity between blacks and whites, he was on point.

From December to March, as he wrestled with his decision whether to retire from the saddle, Isaac's weight hovered between 130 and 140 pounds. If he wanted to ride quality mounts in the Louisville stakes races, he would have to get down to 115 pounds. Meanwhile, Isaac and Lucy spent a considerable amount of time together, enjoying the quiet and calm of the off-season, away from the helter-skelter demands of horse racing. They likely settled into their own routines of enjoyment and repose. Besides riding his horses to keep fit, Isaac pursued other, more manly endeavors, as noted by a *Kentucky Leader* writer reporting on the goings-on around Lexington and the upcoming season at the Kentucky Association racecourse:

> Isaac Murphy, the celebrated jockey, is spending his winter quietly at his fine home in this city. He rarely comes down to town,

and spends most of his time hunting, of which sport he is not only very fond, but he is also a crack shot with either rifle or shotgun. He has a passion for guns and has a choice collection of all kinds of rifles and shotguns. A few nights ago Isaac was initiated into a local colored lodge of Masons, and he is, therefore, probably the only jockey in this country to become a member of the ancient Order.[5]

Murphy's desire for social acceptance was validated with his admittance to the Lincoln Lodge Masons, affirming his status in the black community of Lexington, throughout the Bluegrass region, and quite possibly throughout the country.[6]

Generally composed of professional men—doctors, lawyers, educators, barbers, and ministers—Freemasonry had become a central part of African American community life by 1890.[7] In Kentucky, black Freemasonry had existed since 1880; early members included Louisville's Horace Morris and Lexington's Henry King, M. T. Clay, and Jordan C. Jackson. In Lexington, the officers of Lincoln Lodge Number 10 included Henry Tandy, a well-respected brick mason and building contractor; H. J. Jackson, a partner in Jackson and Wilson, furniture manufacturers; Joe Bradley, who worked for the Chesapeake and Ohio Railroad; Ed Chennault, a past president of the Colored Fair Association and member of the Republican Committee of Fayette County; Charles Mitchell, a barber; James Ellis, a tailor; S. P. Young, the pastor of First Baptist Church; and Albert Johnson, a partner in Mullen and Johnson, carriage makers. Isaac had to relish being part of a brotherhood that included so many community leaders, some of whom had helped guide him through the early years of his life.

Murphy's initiation into the Freemasons not only honored his personal accomplishments and unwavering character but also legitimized his profession. Becoming a Mason put Isaac on a par with some of the well-heeled owners of Thoroughbred farms, who shared the bonds of fraternity but probably did not affiliate with their "colored" brethren. In fact, Isaac's initiation into the Order may have perturbed them. His confirmation as a member of the Knights Templars, a "higher or warrior class" of Freemason,[8] and his designation as the Keeper of Values recognized his commitment to honor and integrity.

In keeping with Victorian traditions of womanhood, Lucy would have gravitated toward leisure activities with friends and acquaintances of the same sex who shared similar interests. Their conversations would have revolved around their respective roles in their families, their community activities, and their relationships with one another. Because of Isaac's membership in the Freemasons, Lucy likely joined the women's auxiliary organization, the Order of the Eastern Stars. Historian Martha S. Jones notes that the role of African American women in the organization was reflected in the greater roles they assumed in shaping their communities' religious activities and their challenges to "gendered conventions of fraternal orders by speaking at their gatherings and questioning their marginal standing" in the community.[9] As a member, Lucy would have been expected to participate in all the rituals of the Order and to learn the opening ode, "Just Before the Battle, Mother":

> Here around the altar meeting,
> Where the sons of light combine
> Mingled with our friendly greeting,
> Is the glow of love divine
> For the Hall to virtue given.
>
> Keep in view the Lodge supernal
> And our emblems on the wall,
> Life is love enthroned in Heav'n
> Point us to the Lodge in Heaven
> Where the true light never wavers
> And the Master of us all
> And our mortal sins for-given.
>
> In the bonds of Mason's duty
> Seek we now the Mason's light,
> Forms of Wisdom, Strength and Beauty

Teach us what is good and right;
Far be every sinful passion,
Near be every gentle grace;
And so at last this holy mission
Shall reveal our Master's face.

Keep in view the Lodge supernal
Life is love enthroned in Heaven
Where the true light never wavers
And our mortal sins for-given.[10]

The Order of the Eastern Stars would convene in members' homes and churches to work on projects related to education, poverty, and the housing of orphaned children. In addition to participating in these meetings, Lucy would have attended lectures and discussed with other middle- and upper-class black women the various issues concerning Lexington's close-knit black community. As the wife of Isaac Murphy, a favorite son of black Lexington, Lucy would have worked to maintain her sense of purpose, while assisting her husband in his development as a community leader.

Both Lucy and Isaac were at home in Lexington, where their membership in the community was confirmed by their many friendships and acquaintances. Almost certainly, the Murphys could be counted among the most prominent Negro men and women in Kentucky, if not in all of America.

## The Prince of Jockeys

While rumors circulated about Isaac's ability to continue to win races and his employment prospects for the spring, his positive qualities were confirmed by the Dwyer brothers' trainer, Frank McCabe. Asked what he thought of the Kentucky jockey's riding during the previous season, McCabe answered:

"First rate. It couldn't have been better," returned Mr. McCabe warmly, "and both the Messrs. Dwyer were more than satisfied with his work for us in the saddle. What nonsense people talk about Murphy not being able to ride any more. I tell you he is a grand horseman, and when you take such a horseman as McLaughlin, Murphy, Howard and Fitzpatrick out of the ranks you leave a great big hole in the list of great American riders. You remember how they talked about Murphy after the race for the Omnibus. I think you were about the only turf writer in New York who came out and said that he rode Proctor Knott a good race. Well, he did. I consider he rode him a grand race. I like Isaac Murphy. He is a model young man to have any dealings with."[11]

Among most knowledgeable trainers and owners, Murphy was still revered; however, by late April, he was still unattached to a stable. It is entirely possible that this was by choice. Murphy had apparently been negotiating quietly with Ed Corrigan to ride his bay colt Riley in the Kentucky Derby, but this was not known until a few weeks before the opening day of the Louisville races.

As planned, Murphy stayed at his Lexington home until after the Kentucky Association meeting, held May 6 to 13. Whether he attended the races in person, sitting in the grandstand, or watched from his own observation deck is not known. Either way, he could not help but notice several of the young, up-and-coming jockeys who would be his competition should he decide to ride during the 1890 season. Especially impressive was the young Lexingtonian Tom Britton, who won six races over the seven-day meeting. The lightweight jockey's daring—whether the result of special talent or raw stupidity—caught the attention of seasoned veterans of the turf who remembered a young Ed Brown, a young William Walker, Isaac Lewis, and numerous others who have since disappeared from the annals of horse-racing history.

Isaac was very introspective about his decision whether to continue riding, processing his thoughts in the quiet of his home. He had not yet settled on who he would ride for after the Kentucky Derby, if anyone, but it was good to have options. The Dwyer brothers, J. B. Haggin, Ed Corrigan, and E. J. Baldwin were all interested. Lucy, no doubt, had some influence over her husband, and feared for his life each time he took to the saddle. However, Isaac was a professional, and he always took all the proper precautions, checking his equipment to make sure his saddle, stirrups, and bridle were properly fitted and secure, and even checking the course the morning before a race, looking for low and muddy spots to help him plan his moves.

By the time the Louisville Jockey Club meeting opened on May 15, everyone knew that Isaac had signed to ride in the Kentucky Derby for Ed Corrigan. On the day of the race, Isaac took an early-morning train from Lexington to a rainy Louisville and reported to the track where Riley was stabled. In an interview in the *Lexington Leader*, Isaac revealed Corrigan's instructions:

> As soon as I got to the track I went to the stable for my colors. Riley was locked up in his stall. The boy in charge asked me if I wanted to see the horse. I told him no; I would see [him] when I came to ride him. I went back to the track, and there was Mr. Corrigan. I asked him what kind of horse he had, and which I had to go against. You see, it was reported that Robespierre had beaten him in his work. Mr. Corrigan said Robespierre had perhaps more speed than Riley, "but there's the horse, and ride him to suit yourself, and use your own judgment."[12]

When the horses were called to the track, Isaac brought Riley from the paddock area and guided him to the post, where they waited for the start of the race. The weather, though not ideal, could have been worse for the spectators in the grandstand. The grounds were wet from rain earlier in the day, but all the fans were excited to see the Derby and hopeful that their particular horse would come away the winner. As a precaution against fatigue, Isaac chose not to gallop Riley around the track to warm him up for the race. Instead, both horse and rider waited patiently at the post, calm and composed.

Taking his cue from Corrigan, Isaac chose a waiting race to conserve Riley's energy. The brown colt Robespierre was in excellent shape, and Isaac expected him to be a challenge from the outset. After a fairly even start, Isaac let the jockey Francis set the pace

on Robespierre for the first mile, watching from third position behind Fleetwood's bay colt Outlook. Keeping a constant pull on Riley, who was "running easy," Isaac and the other jockeys were in no
hurry to pick up the pace in the mud, which meant the race was not
going to break any records.[13] As Bill Letcher moved up to second position, Robespierre kept his pace, and Isaac kept waiting. As the field
rounded the turn into the backstretch, events unfolded as Murphy
had anticipated. Robespierre had spent himself running through the
mud, and Bill Letcher had tried to take the lead too soon. Turning
into the stretch, Isaac let Riley go, and the horse surged ahead unchallenged, winning by three lengths. The victory netted Corrigan
$5,460, and Murphy was paid $1,000 for his services.[14]

When he told his story to a reporter for the *Kentucky Leader*,
Murphy failed to mention how he knew that the fast horse would
wear himself out in the mud or how he knew that Francis would
base his riding strategy on Robespierre's performance under ideal
conditions on a fair track. This knowledge gave him an edge. *Spirit
of the Times* noted that "Murphy had Riley under a gentle pull, and
it was evident that he could send his mount to the front whenever
the latter was called on."[15] Isaac knew that a fast horse wants to run
fast all the time, and on a muddy track he would just waste his energy going nowhere fast. Pace and control mattered, especially in races run under less than ideal conditions. Murphy's calculated victory
on Riley was his second in the Kentucky Derby—his first coming on
Buchanan six years earlier in 1884.

Murphy was able to go home to Lexington after the Derby, returning to Louisville four days later to ride Riley again in the Clark
Stakes. For the second time, the talented veteran jockey guided Corrigan's mighty three-year-old to victory, winning handily by four
lengths over a field that included his two rivals from the Kentucky
Derby, Robespierre and Bill Letcher.[16]

Sometime between Louisville and Latonia, Murphy signed a
$15,000 contract to ride for J. B. Haggin for the 1890 season.[17] This
meant he and Lucy would be relocating to New York for the rest of
the year, racing at Saratoga, Monmouth Park, Brooklyn, and Coney Island. These tracks had been the sites of some of Isaac's most

important and dramatic victories on horses such as Vera Cruz, Falsetto, Freeland, Emperor of Norfolk, and Salvator. Riding against jockeys such as Jimmy McLaughlin, Ed Garrison, Fred Taral, and William Howard, Isaac had easily won hundreds of thousands of dollars for his employers over his fifteen-year career. In New York, he had also created a name for himself among horse-racing enthusiasts who had won small and large sums of money betting on his success in the saddle. Most important, African Americans in the Northeast valued Isaac's success as an indicator of racial progress and achievement in all things, even though some people did not consider jockeying a respectable profession.

There is no doubt that Isaac fully understood the importance of maintaining the confidence of the people who made horse racing possible—the owners as well as the spectators, most of whom had complete faith in his intent to win each race he entered. Like most owners, Haggin knew the advantages of having the best jockey, but he also knew the value of having an incorruptible jockey in the saddle, one whose sole purpose was to compete to win and in whom he could have complete trust and confidence.

Before venturing east to meet Haggin's stable, Isaac had one more obligation to fulfill in the West: riding Corrigan's Riley in the annual Spring Derby at Latonia on May 24. As he had at the Kentucky Association meeting, young Tom Britton excelled at Latonia, capturing seven victories, five second-place finishes, and five third-place finishes. Murphy, in contrast, did not do so well. *Spirit of the Times* reported his loss on Riley, the favorite, in a three-horse race with Kentucky Derby rival Bill Letcher and J. K. Megibben's Avondale: "The three were sent away at the first attempt, and it was at once seen that each jockey was intent on making a waiting race of it. The pace was so slow, however, that Murphy—something he rarely ever does—went to the front and led the other pair by over a length before they had gone a quarter. Likely enough that, with the top weight he would have preferred to remain in the rear, but the others would not let him do so, and so to the front he went."[18] Similar to the Kentucky Derby and the Clark Stakes, Isaac was allowed to run the race as he saw fit. Unfortunately, the other two jockeys, Monk

Overton and Alonzo Allen, had learned something from watching the veteran. They let Isaac go to the front and set the pace, drafting behind him. After three-quarters of a mile, neither would allow Riley to get behind them. In the end, Isaac would be outsmarted by Allen on Bill Letcher.

Commenting on the loss, Isaac stated that the "race was run and won on its merits, anybody could see that. . . . When it came to real racing I gave Riley both whip and spur, but it was no use. I couldn't possibly hold stall off that rush of Letcher's, who had the most speed, and the race was all over at the eight pole."[19] Murphy had been beaten at his own game, and he knew it. A few weeks prior, he had schooled Allen in how to run a waiting race, only to have his hand forced and his own strategy used against him. Whether this was a sign of Murphy's diminishing abilities or the rising level of talent among jockeys in general is not clear. What is clear is that changes were taking place in horse racing that Isaac would be linked to, as well as the victim of. Soon after his race at Latonia, at the request of Matt Byrnes, Haggin's trainer for Salvator and Firenzi, Isaac and Lucy traveled to New York.

Arriving by train sometime before the end of May, the Murphys likely took up residence in the Brooklyn Heights area, in one of the many apartments available to "respectable colored families" in the middle-class urban hamlet of class-cognizant African Americans. Brooklyn was home to some of the most progressive and forward-thinking blacks. Numbering a little over 10,000 by 1890, Brooklyn's black community was filled with energetic, self-reliant people who were openly and outwardly enjoying the benefits of progress through education, religious conviction, and social mobility. A mixture of transplanted Southerners (most of them from Florida), native working-class folks, and the striving elite (many of whom maintained social clubs and owned businesses), Brooklyn was a place of possibilities for blacks. The Murphys likely chose to live in Brooklyn because it was close to the activities they enjoyed in their leisure time and provided easy access to transportation to the horse parks. In addition, they might have been attracted to what historian Carla L. Peterson calls "Black Gotham," with its professionals, entertainments,

and attractions and the opportunity to socialize with the most influential African American men and women in the city.[20]

On June 2 Murphy reported to Morris Park, where he raced
in two sweepstakes for two different owners. In the third race, a
sweepstakes worth $950 for maiden two-year-olds, Isaac took the
second-place prize of $100 on M. Daly's Gold Dollar. In the fifth
race, a sweepstakes for three-year-olds and older, he came in second
on J. B. Haggin's Fitzjames. A few days later he rode Gold Dollar in
the Juvenile Stakes for two-year-olds, placing third behind Marty
Bergan on J. Hunter's Hoodlum and Anthony Hamilton, on August
Belmont's St. Charles.

Writers such as Broad Church recognized that Hamilton and
other "prominent jockeys in the West" were having a tremendous
impact on horse racing and looked to dominate the eastern competition.[21] Other newspapers took notice of black jockeys' success as
professionals:

> The first question a betting man asks about to select a horse to
> carry his money is, "Who has the mount?" If it is a jockey of
> ability, such as Barnes, Garrison or Murphy, he will probably
> be satisfied to risk his dust on his selection, but if it is a mere
> stable lad who holds the reins he will fight shy perhaps. Thus it
> is seen that three little rugged, tanned and wizened bits of hu-
> manity are to a great extent autocrats of the turf. Pikey Barnes,
> Isaac Murphy and George Anderson are three such cracks.
> They are "black and tans," in other words negroes; but how
> they can ride! And honest riders they are too. They know that
> in the skill of their hands and in the alertness of their brains
> and eyes rest many a time the fate of fortunes, and they seldom
> abuse the confidence placed in them.[22]

That the writer commented on the jockeys' blackness is not surprising, given the racial animosity instigated by weary whites posing the
race question and anxious immigrants seeking to eliminate black
competition from the marketplace. The writer may have been ignorant of the fact that blacks had been a part of horse racing in the

United States since its beginning. Only recently had jockeys' work become more prestigious, based solely on the amount of money they could earn and the amount of money made by winning owners in stakes races, such as the American Derby, the Kenner and Travers Stakes, and the Suburban, and in match races, where tens of thousands of dollars could be won or lost. Black jockeys' earning capacity and public prominence would soon cause a firestorm of jealousy.

The problem with horse racing, as Isaac soon learned, was not caused by old money and the men who carried on the genteel tradition of horse ownership in his home state of Kentucky as a matter of prestige and pride. The problem was the men who sought to profit from horse racing by any means, both legal and illegal. The old way, based on Southern traditions of honor and gentlemanly decorum (and connected to the abuses of slavery), was fading into memory. The new era, based on the Northern industrial environment and the conflicts between capital and labor, was opportunistic and fraught with corruption, especially in New York. This dishonesty would consume the spectator sport and eventually cause its downfall.

For Isaac, however, New York was where he had to be for the spring racing season. He would not score a victory at Morris Park until June 12, riding (at 122 pounds) the Hough brothers' Come to Taw in the mile-and-a-half sweepstakes. His second victory came on the same day in the Trial Stakes for three-year-olds on another of the Hough brothers' horses, Burlington. Compared with some of the other jockeys—both up-and-comers and veterans—Isaac had fewer mounts, but his winning ratio was unmatched, especially in the big stakes races.

Haggin hired Murphy to ride in several important races, including the Suburban Handicap scheduled for June 17 at the Coney Island Jockey Club at Sheepshead Bay. On the day of the race, the grounds were overflowing with a multitude of individuals described as "an incongruous, motley mixture" from every station in American life. "Down through the yawing gate the crowd rushed, ran the gauntlet of blind beggars and brazen-lunged touts, and spread without stem into the grand stand, the betting ring, and the paddock," where the horses and stable boys were showcased as they prepared for the race.[23] Among the 30,000 spectators were politicians, men of the turf, and the very wealthy mingling with working-class commoners and the misfits of society who were barely scraping by—all anticipating a battle between well-bred animals and talented jockeys. Of the nine horses in the race, only one would be crowned champion, and only one jockey would be draped with a floral horseshoe and carried off on the shoulders of envious stable boys amid the cheering of spectators and the playing of "Hail to the Chief."

Sometime before the race, Isaac would have studied the track at Sheepshead Bay, analyzing its turns and straightaways, before retrieving his silks and dressing in the jockeys' room. If he was a little heavy, he might have gone for a long walk, hoping to shed a pound or two, or maybe he just sat in the jockeys' room awaiting the call to the post. Despite the pressure to win big races like the Suburban, Isaac rarely showed that stress in his body or on his face. His stoic demeanor could have been interpreted as self-assurance, which he transferred to the horse. Nothing could have been more indicative of a man in total control of his destiny than Murphy in the saddle before a race. Everything about him exuded confidence—or arrogance, depending on one's perspective.

Under threatening gray skies, racing fans continued to fill the horse park. A portion of the crowd gravitated toward the betting ring, where they exchanged thousands of dollars for the chance to attain instant wealth based on the outcome of the race featuring Raceland, Salvator, Firenzi, and Tenny. According to the *St. Louis Post-Dispatch*, "the track is in perfect condition, and if the stories told in the paddock are true the record for a mile and a quarter may be broken."[24] The paper reported that Salvator was a favorite among the trainers who had seen him run his trials on Sunday afternoon, but it failed to mention that the jockey riding Salvator was Isaac Murphy. It was not unusual for the popular media to omit the accomplishments of black men and women in an attempt to protect whites from the pain of seeing former slaves rise above their circumstances. Black success did not bolster the argument that the Negro was doomed to be ignorant, savage, and servile and therefore in need of white guidance and deserving of white brutality. The more unbiased *New York Times* recognized Murphy as a talented individual who had added considerable value to the national pastime.[25] Indeed, he was a hero to whites as well as blacks, especially those who appreciated masterful riding and horsemanship and enjoyed winning money.

When Isaac guided Salvator out of the paddock and past the grandstand and the railbirds, "there was an outbreak of applause and cheers" as the pair worked their way to the starting post. After several false starts, the race began with Murphy toward the rear of the group. The pace was set by Cassius, who got away quickly and, after the "first eighth of a mile," started to pull away from the pack. Salvator, Tenny, and Firenzi were near the rear of the bunch until after the first turn, when Tenny's rider Garrison swung wide in an effort to claim the front and quicken the pace. Fans in the stands and the infield shouted for their favorites: "Cassius wins! They'll never catch him!" "Come on, my Tenny. Oh! Come on!" "Where is Raceland? I can't find him!" "Damn Longstreet."[26]

As the horses approached the homestretch, the crowd continued to cheer. According to the *Brooklyn Eagle*, Murphy used his "calm sense of superiority, to edge to the inside rail and work his way up to Cassius until they were running stride for stride.[27] Then, when Taral swung wide on Cassius, Isaac shot through the opening. Isaac maintained control of his horse until the end, when, with just a little encouragement, Salvator extended half a length ahead of Cassius and three lengths ahead of Tenny. Believing that Murphy had a penchant for close finishes, the media criticized him for cutting the race too close to show off for the grandstand—something he was often accused of.[28] But the public came to see fast-moving animals being steered around the track by daredevils in the saddle; they were less interested in strategists calculating when to move against their opponents.

The *Brooklyn Eagle* attributed the win largely to Salvator himself:

Owners and backers of the Suburban winner were fortunate in the excellent training Salvator has received, in the wide experience and marvelous skill of Isaac Murphy, his rider and more than all else, in the vast reserve powers of speed and endurance in the animal himself. The big chestnut colt bore the brunt of the battle without quaking. For him steel and catgut had no terrors. He carried, like a valiant soldier, the heat and burden of the day and he won for himself, not only a high place on the tablets of terrestrial fame but an ultimate retreat in the higher sphere to which the good horses go when they die.[29]

But Murphy had proved time and time again that breeding alone did not guarantee victory. It took great skill to train a horse and prepare it for success. Although owners and trainers certainly wanted to assume that a horse could win regardless of the jockey, they could not deny that the jockey had to know where to put the horse during a race. Murphy knew how to get the best out of a horse, how to use its innate talent, how much to push, and how much to save for future contests. Isaac was a professional through and through. Regardless of whether he used close finishes to his advantage, he would maintain under cross-examination that he rode to win—no more, no less.

The day after the race, David Pulsifer, Tenny's owner, proposed a rematch with Salvator and Cassius at $5,000 a side; the Coney Island Jockey Club offered an additional $5,000, making the prize a staggering $20,000. Haggin agreed to a race but did not want to include Cassius. He preferred to match Salvator and Tenny at the Sheepshead Bay course for a winner-take-all prize of $15,000. The Coney Island Jockey Club agreed to host the match race, recognizing the contest's appeal to "race goers all over the country."[30] As it turned out, this would be one of the most important races in the career of Salvator, the four-year-old believed to be without peer, and one of the most important races in the career of Isaac Murphy, his jockey.

On June 25, under a hot sun and with a soft breeze coming from the west, 12,000 to 15,000 spectators turned out to see the match race between Tenny and Salvator at Sheepshead Bay. The race promised to set the record straight on several fronts: which was the better horse; who was the better breeder, Pulsifer or Haggin; and who was the better jockey, Isaac Murphy or Ed "Snapper" Garrison. Clearly, in late-nineteenth-century America, and in New York in particular—where immigrants and native whites aggressively and without shame or remorse excluded blacks from American life—the race between Salvator and Tenny had racial implications. The fear of losing to someone who was considered inferior in every way was a threat to the "authentic" definition of American manhood and manliness. Athletes like John L. Sullivan and Adrian "Cap" Anson, both of whom refused to compete against "niggers," were praised by white men who advocated exclusion as a means to protect their income-earning ability as well as their identity.[31] Was this fear on the mind of Ed Garrison or on the minds of those white men who came to see him compete in this head-to-head contest? If Murphy beat him, what would that say about Garrison's masculinity and about blacks in general?

Thanks in part to artists such as Thomas Nast and publishers such as Currier and Ives, there is no doubt that representations of African Americans had become more caricature than truth. Isaac Murphy was a living, breathing embodiment of the contradictions inherent in racial stereotypes, yet popular advertisements of black jockeys with big wide eyes and huge red lips prevailed. It is not clear whether Isaac understood the full implications of the race, but it can be assumed there were people in the stands, both black and white, who did. Indeed, both sides would come to understand that in the fight for racial destiny, every public social, political, and economic victory counted. What seemed to be only a horse race was in fact a very serious contest.

With the grandstand and the grounds abuzz and the betting public wagering on the outcome, Garrison and Murphy took to the track with their capable horses beneath them. The *Louisville Courier-Journal* reported that Garrison "appears to be confident in winning, for he nods and smiles in a satisfied way at some of his admirers," whereas the serious Murphy galloped past the grandstand toward the starting post, looking "neither to the right or left" with a "do or die expression on his face." Right before the race, a heckler shouted to Isaac, "No grand stand finish today, Isaac: the Snapper's a hard one when it comes to a fight." Apparently, Isaac limited his response to a stoic smile and a sphinxlike gaze out onto the track as he awaited the starter's instructions.[32]

At the sight of the red flash emanating from the hand of the starter, Mr. Caldwell, both jockeys got away evenly on the first attempt. In a thunderous chorus, the crowd shouted the customary, "They're off!" Taking the inside first, Garrison tried to keep Tenny in the perfect position for the race, but the swaybacked horse could not maintain the lead after the first turn. Isaac charged forward at trainer Matt Byrnes's signal, opening a gap of as much as three lengths. The calculated dash put Salvator in front and helped him secure the inside rail, which he held for the entire race. Even as Garrison gave chase around the second turn and into the straight, Murphy knew exactly where the competition was at all times, anticipating his moves like a chess master. Keeping Salvator where he needed him, the Kentucky jockey outrode and outsmarted his white counterpart, at one point leading by four lengths.

As the horses entered the homestretch, Isaac remained cool and composed while Garrison began to beat Tenny frantically, trying to gain the lead. With spurs and catgut working on the sides and hindquarters of his horse, Garrison closed the gap and looked to pass Salvator. As they approached the wire, shouts went up, "Tenny wins, Tenny wins," "Dead heat, dead heat." Without flash or flurry, Isaac continued to ride straight as a dart through the finish line, with only a few inches determining winner and loser and "the disposition of . . . vast sums of money." With the exception of Murphy and the judges, very few were sure of the outcome until the name of the horse, the jockey, and the official time were posted on the board: Salvator; Murphy; 2:05.[33] That was a new record for the mile and a quarter, knocking 1.5 seconds off the time set by the Dwyer brothers' Kingston, which Isaac had ridden to several victories the previous season.

One observer who could judge the outcome with pinpoint accuracy was the official photographer of the Coney Island Jockey Club, John C. Hemment. Using a "#2 Beck Lens with an open stop," Hemment captured the horses in stride as they reached the finish line; Murphy was still upright and relaxed, while Garrison leaned forward over Tenny's neck, riding like the devil in heat.[34] In what historian Ed Hotaling identifies as horse racing's first photo finish, it is clear that Murphy's masterful riding culminated in Salvator's victory over Tenny. Unfortunately, fans of the Tenny-Garrison combination lost tens of thousands of dollars. Plunger Dave Johnson lost an estimated $25,000 betting on Tenny over a series of races, and Kentucky horseman Green B. Morris was another big loser. After the race, Morris chastised Garrison for letting Murphy have the inside rail: "You had no business giving him anything. The horse that gets anything from one of my horses in a match has got to fight for it." Garrison explained that he was only following the trainer's instructions, and Morris was "shaken with rage" when he heard that. "If you rode to orders," he exclaimed, "all I've got to say is they were damned bad orders."[35] There was additional criticism of Garrison's riding:

> Henry Clay Ditmas, who is abundantly able to do all he says, remarked, after the race: "I'm willing to put up $10,000 on Tenny for another match with Salvator, to be run in the next two weeks. I think Tenny, properly ridden, can beat him. . . . Said a Salvator man: "if the race had been ridden from 'end to end,' as Colonel Harper used to say, Tenny would have won to a moral certainty. Garrison should have made the race up the back stretch holding the rail and keeping Salvator on the outside. To give Salvator the rail voluntarily was suicidal. I never saw a more fatal mistake."[36]

This was not the first time Murphy had won based on his knowledge of the habits of horses and other jockeys. In the end, Murphy's intelligence along with Salvator's talent won the race, but few could admit that. Most newspapers downplayed Murphy's part in the victory, attributing it solely to Salvator's ability: "Salvator is indeed king of the American turf. Wednesday afternoon at Sheepshead Bay he beat Tenny in the great $10,000 match, and made a new record at a mile and a quarter, running the distance in 2:05, cutting one and a half seconds off Kingston's record. In the Suburban he gave Tenny one pound in weight. Yesterday they ran at even weight, and the result demonstrates not only that the best horse won the Suburban, but that Salvator is probably the greatest racehorse that America has ever produced."[37] Obviously, Murphy had something to do with Salvator's success, just as Garrison had something to do with Tenny's failure, but in keeping with the tradition of sportswriting—a craft in its infancy—most writers refused to acknowledge the skill it took to ride a Thoroughbred in a high-pressure stakes race. Murphy's masterful control over the race from start to finish was omitted from the majority of articles, and despite the photo finish, he was again accused of arrogance and grandstanding for the crowd.

On July 3 the *Chicago Horseman* (the same publication that had called Murphy one of the best to ever ride a Thoroughbred after his American Derby win on Emperor of Norfolk in 1889) published the deprecating "Isaac Murphy's Little Joke":

Murphy's passionate craze for a close finish has given more than one of his backers the heartache. Once upon a time it gave "Lucky" Baldwin, his employer, an ache of another sort. Two years ago Baldwin's horse Volante was to run one day at Saratoga, and Baldwin, calling Murphy up to the grand-stand, said:

"Now, look here, Murphy, I don't want any monkeying about this race—none of your sensational finishes. You just cut the old horse loose and send him along from the fall of the flag to the finish. I've got a lot of money on this race, and I don't want to be worried about the result."

Murphy showed his white teeth in a smile of acquiescence, and then in a low tone informed the ladies in Baldwin's party that he would "make the old man faint away." When the flag fell Murphy pulled Volante back to fourth place, and held him steady around the first turn; down the back-stretch the leaders flew, with Murphy trailing along quietly on Volante as though he was out for a pleasure ride. Baldwin began to kick, and bit off a big chuck of tobacco and began to chew at a tremendous rate. As the horses rounded the lower turn and entered the stretch Murphy began moving up inch by inch, but it seemed an impossibility for him to reach the leaders, but he did, and one by one they surrendered until when within one hundred feet of the wire Volante had disposed of all but one. Then with a magnificent exhibition of horsemanship Murphy fairly lifted his mount up to even terms and in the last bound landed Volante a winner by a nose, or as the sporting fraternity term it, "by an eye lash." Before the jockeys dismounted, Baldwin turned to a member of the party and said: "George, I wish you would get these Volante tickets cashed and bring the money down to the hotel for me. I'm going home right away; I don't feel well. Some fellow swallowed a chew of tobacco which I had in my mouth when that black devil made that close finish."[38]

The only truth in this exaggerated exchange was Murphy's command of Volante in the 1886 Saratoga Cup.

In contrast, the black press could not say enough about Murphy's dominating performance at Sheepshead Bay. According to the *Cleveland Gazette*, those who had declared that "Isaac Murphy could not ride a little bit are those who, since he rode Salvator in the Suburban and the match race with Tenny, are saying that he is the greatest living artist in the pigskin."[39] And *New York Age*'s T. Thomas Fortune used Murphy's dominance over Garrison in the match race to prove a point:

> It was the greatest horse race ever run on any course, but it was Murphy's race from start to finish. He rode the best horse on the turf, and he is the best jockey that ever bestraddled a race horse. I verily believe he could have won by a half a length as easily as by a head.
>
> After the race Mr. Murphy joined his wife on the grand stand; and so modest and unassuming is the Prince of Jockeys that few people around him knew him or paid him any attention. Truly here is an idol of thousands of people who wears his honors lightly.
>
> Counselor Stewart, who had been introduced to Mr. Murphy after the race, introduced Counselor Dickerson and myself to him

and his charming wife. He received the introductions with the ease and grace of the polished gentleman. And such he is.

"Did you ride to break the record?" I asked.

"No," replied Mr. Murphy, "I rode to win."

"Was Garrison in it at any stage of the race?"

"I would rather not answer that question," said Murphy with deliberate firmness.

"Was the incident reproduced in *The Age* last week from the St. Louis *Globe Democrat* [*sic*] about that close finish, and Mr. Haggin's chew of tobacco getting into his throat in consequence of it, correct?"

"Yes, with modifications. It was a mighty close finish," said Mr. Murphy.

"You like close finishes, don't you?"

Mr. Murphy eyed me a moment, and an innocent smile danced over the smooth surface of his pleasant face as he replied: "I ride to win."[40]

Throughout the article, Fortune reminded his readers that Murphy earned $15,000 a season riding for Haggin and maintained the privilege of riding for other stables when doing so did not conflict with his principal employer's demands. But Fortune also emphasized Murphy's character and his role as a man and a husband:

Mr. Murphy has a fine home at Lexington, KY. He neither gambles nor drinks, nor associates with the tough characters who follow the same business as he does. Mrs. Murphy accompanies her husband in all his rounds of the racing season, and no spectator watches with more breathless interest than she does when her husband is up. When the event is over, when the terrible anxiety is passed, when the flyers dash under the wire, those who know say that she wipes the tears from her eyes and heaves a sigh of unutterable relief.[41]

The day after the match race, June 26, Isaac won the mile-and-a-half Coney Island Cup worth $1,500 on Haggin's prized fil-

ly Firenzi, beating a field that included Beverwyck Stable's bay colt
Cassius, with Taral riding, and W. Lakeland's chestnut gelding Tea
Tray, ridden by Hamilton. Two days later he again took Firenzi
across the wire in first place in the Knickerbocker Handicap, best-
ing Marty Bergan by four lengths riding Longstreet for the Dwyer
brothers. If there was any doubt about Firenzi's ability to run under
Murphy's guidance, these races surely erased that doubt: she was a
favorite to win whenever the great black jockey was her rider.

With the track at Monmouth Park undergoing improvements
and scheduled to reopen for the Fourth of July, Isaac and Lucy had
some time to themselves. They had made the acquaintance of publisher Thomas Fortune and attorney T. McCants Stewart, widening their
circle of friends in Brooklyn. The couple likely received invitations to
several social events, and *New York Age* advertised any number of
concerts and lectures hosted by local churches and other organizations, including the African Methodist Episcopal Zion Church, the
Brooklyn Afro-American League, and the Freemasons. Thus, Isaac
and Lucy had their pick of entertainments and opportunities for educational enlightenment. During this time, the Afro-American League
of New York came under fire when its president, John H. Deyo, admitted using his office for political gain. In the eyes of his former
colleagues, Deyo's actions undermined the noble intention of the
Afro-American League, "whose success depended upon strict integrity and the fearless discharge of duty" by its officers and members.
Deyo not only lost his honor but also was labeled a race traitor.[42]

*New York Age* cited the achievements of African Americans in
various occupations of note: "In the pulpit, in the schools and the colleges, in journalism, in the law, on the turf, in the prize ring, in all the
life of our civilization, the Afro-American is acquitting himself as a
man and a brother."[43] Unlike Deyo, these African Americans represented the racial progress made since the end of slavery. For Fortune
and the Afro-American League, these examples of qualified citizenship bolstered their argument. Likewise, Murphy's popularity among
both black and white horse-racing fans provided an opportunity to
question the policies of exclusion in social settings where blacks and
whites should be able to mingle freely as human beings.

Meanwhile, a writer in the *Indianapolis Freeman* commended Murphy and the black Australian prizefighter Peter Jackson for their success, their manly personae, and their acceptance by their white colleagues. However, the writer went on to question "why colored ministers are shunned and spurned by white ones, although both are followers of the meek and lowly Nazarene." Again, the use of interracial sports competitions as metaphors for everyday life were illuminating the existence of racial prejudice. In the realm of sports, Murphy and Jackson were "honored and applauded everywhere by the class who mingle with them, and their color is rarely brought into question—they excel all who contend against them."[44]

Murphy did not exactly excel on August 3. After losing 6 pounds to make his weight requirement of 114 pounds, a weakened Murphy rode Firenzi in the Eatontown Stakes at Monmouth Park against a field that included Garrison atop Tenny, Anthony Covington atop Chesapeake, and Alonzo Clayton atop Soho. Isaac was able to keep up the pace until the end of the mile straightaway sprint; in the end, he just edged out Covington for the second prize of $500. The following morning Isaac rose before 6:00, intending to go for his customary long, brisk walk to make his weight for an important afternoon race for Haggin. Soon after leaving, he became sick and was compelled to return home. Isaac consulted Dr. Smallwood of Forty-Seventh Street, who treated him for two days for severe vomiting and pain that failed to subside. Dr. Miller of Thirty-Second Street was then called in, and he treated Isaac for ten days for the same stomach ailment.[45]

On August 12 a somewhat recovered Isaac toured the new and improved Monmouth Park in preparation for his two races that day. Tired or not, the professional jockey maintained his race-day routine. He galloped around the track on horseback, noting all the soft and muddy places, testing the firmness of the course, and looking for any divots or holes; he examined the contours of the track, studied the turns, and tried to get a feel for the angles. He studied the course in detail and memorized whatever could be an advantage or a disadvantage, depending on the circumstances. All this would help him determine how to attack in different positions coming out of the backstretch toward the finish line. This knowledge, as well as that acquired by watching the other horses warm up and knowing the habits of his fellow jockeys, prepared Isaac for his races.

With Lucy among the estimated 20,000 fans in the stands, Isaac took to the field for the Junior Champion Stakes atop the Kentucky-bred bay gelding Strathmeath, who was everything owner Green Morris had promised: fast. Isaac won the terrific race and more than $28,000 for Morris; Murphy probably received at least $1,000 for his services.[46] After that first race, Isaac experienced some nausea in the paddock area, but fortunately, he managed to recover in time to ride Salvator in the Champion Stakes.

Everyone expected the Champion Stakes to be a great match between Murphy and Garrison, who was intending to apply "different tactics" against Isaac, although it is unclear what those tactics were.[47] But based on the outcome, Garrison never stood a chance. Murphy was in what modern athletes call "the zone." He was like a chess master who could see five moves ahead of the competition because he knew their habits better than they knew themselves. In the homestretch, Isaac let Salvator run free to the wire, leaving his rival behind and leaving no question as to who was the better jockey. At the end of the contest, Isaac trotted Salvator back to the paddock, where he performed the ritual of asking permission to dismount before weighing out and eventually making his way to the stands to meet his beloved Lucy.

The Champion Stakes confirmed what a majority of horse-racing fans in the West had known for years. *Spirit of the Times* called Murphy a "consummate horseman" who had guided one of the best four-year-olds in the country to victory, proving the superiority of the record-setting Salvator. For Murphy, it was the "supreme climax of a grand career."[48]

## A Great Fall from the Mighty Steed of Celebrity

On the morning of August 24, the feeling of accomplishment must have been surreal for Isaac—not that anything in his disposition had changed. Still, to be so widely recognized as the best jockey in America must have been overwhelming. His career had covered three separate decades of horse racing, and he had won all the great races at the most popular tracks in the country atop the likes of Vera Cruz, Falsetto, Volante, Buchanan, Emperor of Norfolk, and Salvator. In addition to the wealth and prestige resulting from those accomplishments, Isaac had become a hero to African Americans who were proud of him and lived vicariously through his successes. In the days following his triumph on Salvator, he was no doubt approached by men, women, and children who recognized the great jockey and knew of his daring feats in the saddle. His serious exterior on the racetrack could not help but be softened by the compliments extended by these strangers and well-wishers.

In Brooklyn, the Murphys were probably the guests of honor in the homes of some of the social elite, who saw the great jockey's celebrity as important to the overall program of racial uplift and self-determination. Recognizing the significance of Isaac's achievements, the *Chicago Horseman* noted: "The negro jockeys are outriding their white rivals in [the] race for great turf prizes this season. McLaughlin is the only white jockey that ever rode the winner of the Champion and Junior Champion in the same year. This year Murphy rode the winner of the Suburban, the Champion and Junior Champion."[49] In black newspapers, Isaac and other contemporary sports figures such as Peter Jackson and George Dixon were recognized for improving the "opinion of the race" among white society not only through their chosen sports but also through their gentlemanly decorum in public.[50] To many people, Isaac was the quintessential gentleman and athlete. In a word, Isaac Murphy represented excellence.

In honor of his recent achievements at Coney Island and Monmouth Park, Isaac was invited to a clambake at the home of Matt Byrnes, J. B. Haggin's trainer. Under Byrnes's supervision, Salvator had reportedly won more than $113,000 in stakes and purses in 1890, and the up-and-coming filly Firenzi had won an impressive $102,000.[51] Isaac took the train to Byrnes's home at Chestnut Grove near Eatontown, New Jersey, and was greeted by members of the Salvator Club, backers of the great three-year-old. According to the

*New York Times*, the evening's events included a presentation by the club to the trainer and jockey who had made the festivities possible. Byrnes was presented with "a magnificent diamond pin, and to Isaac Murphy . . . they gave a fine silver mounted whip."[52]

The rest of the evening was filled with the usual manly entertainments accompanying such affairs. Interestingly, the *Times* article suggested that while Byrnes kept a clear head, Murphy indulged in the festivities quite liberally, taking part in the drinking and toasting. A photograph of the event shows him sitting on a fence rail with other attendees of the clambake, dressed in his finest attire—a "derby, a velvet-collard chesterfield coat, and his fashionable pointy boots."[53] Based on this image—the look of his eyes and the smile on his face—one might assume that he had been drinking. Another explanation is that he was tired and weak from preparing for his upcoming race on Firenzi, or perhaps he was still sick with his stomach ailment. In any case, this photograph would be used as evidence, if not corroborating proof, that the once honorable jockey had become too big for himself and was, in fact, the champagne jockey many suspected him to be.

On Tuesday, August 26, two days after the Salvator Club's celebration, Isaac drank his customary milk punch—a concoction of sweet milk, Kentucky bourbon, vanilla, and sugar—before leaving for the track. Still somewhat "shaken up from being thrown from his carriage the day before," Isaac arrived at Monmouth Park early to take his usual tour of the track.[54] The weather was clear, and as the racing fans filtered through the gates, everyone was expecting a good day of racing. Because his race did not begin until much later, Isaac had time to relax before dressing. At some point he would report to Matt Byrnes to get his instructions for riding Firenzi in the Monmouth Handicap, and they would discuss the proper strategy and who to keep an eye on.

After retreating to the jockeys' dressing room and changing into Haggin's orange and blue silks, Isaac met Lucy and his personal valet at the end of the grandstand in an area generally "set apart for the families of owners and trainers."[55] Isaac and Lucy ordered a bottle of imported Apollinaris mineral water from the café, which the waiter brought to their table, opened, and poured into their respective glasses. Before leaving for the paddock area, Isaac ordered a bottle of ginger ale to share with Lucy, which the waiter also opened and poured for them. The grand treatment the Murphys enjoyed in New York may have caused them to question leaving Brooklyn, where the fashionable elite gravitated toward the crowned prince of jockeys and his princess. The possibilities of life in the Northeast must have crossed their minds on numerous occasions. Then again, the appeal of Kentucky's wide-open spaces and fresh air, and the sense of groundedness provided by Lexington's black community, kept them from falling into the traps of celebrity.

When the time came, Isaac and his valet left Lucy in the grandstand area to meet Secretary Crickmore and weigh in for the handicap race. Isaac was ushered onto the scale, where it was determined that he weighed 128 pounds. To make the proper weight, he had to exchange his lead pads, which apparently caused a noticeable delay. While waiting for the process to be completed, Crickmore brought up a forfeited entry that Isaac supposedly owed at Washington Park, and he asked the jockey when he was going to pay it. Isaac replied that he "didn't think he owed it." However, after a brief discussion, the dignified jockey agreed to pay the fee to close the matter.[56] After making all the necessary adjustments, Isaac was allowed to retreat to the jockeys' dressing area to wait for the start of the race.

With fifteen minutes to spare before the official call to the post, Isaac probably intended to use the time to clear his mind. During these quiet moments, he might have visualized how he would run the race, thought about the pace he needed to maintain, and recalled the various rough areas on the track. Alternatively, Isaac might have been contemplating his retirement from the turf and savoring what could be one of his last rides as the premier jockey of the age. He might have been thinking about the opportunities that lay ahead as a trainer; in that regard, he might have considered following the lead of James McLaughlin, setting up a relationship with an owner who wanted to maintain a stud in the Bluegrass.[57] Or Isaac might have imagined starting a school for jockeys, where he could teach boys how to ride and share his knowledge of pace, tempo, and awareness of the horse. Rather than indulging in any of these daydreams, Isaac might have used the time to simply pray for clarity and protection.

Meanwhile, the betting on Firenzi had all but stopped, with tens of thousands of dollars being wagered by her supporters at "6 to 5 and even odds."[58] Since she was the presumed favorite, most bookmakers had stopped accepting bets; however, a few continued to offer odds against Firenzi, which raised some suspicions but did not overly concern officials.[59] Prince Royal with Hamilton aboard was a 4:1 shot; William Lakeland's Tea Tray was 10:1 and 8:1, and 2½:1 to place. Oddly enough, Tea Tray, with a stable boy named Moore in the saddle, was a popular bet among plungers like Dave Johnson (the same gambler who had lost $25,000 on Tenny), who supposedly wagered a large sum on the long shot to win it all.

When the time came for the field of seven to report to the post, each jockey moved to the paddock area, climbed aboard his horse, and headed toward the track. As the jockeys positioned their horses and awaited Mr. Caldwell's signal to charge the track, Isaac began to feel unwell. After a false start by Pike Barnes, Isaac asked permission to dismount and rearrange his saddle girths, which a nearby stableman helped him with.[60] It is unclear why his saddle would have been loose at this point. However, after readjusting his equipment, Isaac remounted Firenzi, with some assistance. According to several reports, Isaac's face was swollen, his eyes glazed over, and his body slumped in the saddle. Something was terribly wrong.

Nevertheless, the race started, and Isaac and Firenzi got away first, followed by E. J. Baldwin's Los Angeles. The pace was fast as the horses pounded past the grandstand to the cheers of the spectators. After the field had gone only a quarter mile, Murphy seemed to be slowing Firenzi on purpose, allowing the other horses to pass as he attempted to maintain some control over the spirited horse, pulling her head left and right, clinging to the saddle and trying unsuccessfully to guide her movements. Rather than risk death if he fell off his horse in the path of the thundering pack, the quick-thinking Murphy pulled Firenzi to the rear, where he could try to gather his wits and finish the race that had already been lost.

At the finish, the long shot Tea Tray outsprinted Rhono and Lavinia Belle to win the Monmouth Handicap. Still clinging to Firenzi, Isaac passed the judges' stand, traveled another hundred yards, and then fell into a heap on the ground. Mr. Caldwell's assistant, "Polo Jim," caught Firenzi and helped Isaac back into the saddle. According to the *New York Times*, the "helpless jockey was assisted into the saddle and managed to keep his seat until the paddock was reached. Then he forgot to ask the permission of the judge to dismount, and his friends had to put him on Firenzi's back again. He was then conducted to the scale and weighed in, after which he was almost carried to the jockeys' room" by his valet and his friends.[61] As quickly as possible, Isaac was hurried away from Monmouth Park.

After Murphy left the scene, the questions began to hum loudly. Was this the same Isaac Murphy who had weighed in only fifteen minutes prior to the start of the race, seemingly sober and in complete control? Secretary Crickmore had even spoken with Murphy and surely would have noticed if he had been drinking. Did Murphy get drunk in the jockeys' dressing room? If so, why hadn't the attendant reported him to the judges? What about Matt Byrnes? He had seen Murphy in the paddock area and had no reason to believe the race was in jeopardy because of Isaac's state; in fact, Byrnes had bet $50,000 on Firenzi to win. All was lost, including a reputation that had been built over a stellar career.

The Executive Committee, led by Mr. Withers, suspended Murphy, pending an investigation. Withers conducted interviews with a multitude of people who had come into contact with Murphy, as well as with Isaac himself the day after the incident. Isaac claimed that he must have been drugged because he did not drink any alcohol before the race; he had consumed only water and ginger ale from the grandstand café. He could recall everything that had occurred before the start of the race, including his conversation with Crickmore. He told Withers his "head swam and hummed and felt like a vacuum from the moment . . . he dismounted at the starting post to have his saddle adjusted till he passed the scales after the race." Isaac also defended himself against rumors that he was the "champagne jockey" and that his insatiable thirst for the expensive beverage had been the cause of his behavior during the Monmouth Handicap. "No one that knows me," Murphy exclaimed, "would charge me with drinking champagne. I don't drink it because I don't like it."[62]

After considering all the facts and listening to all the parties involved, Withers and the Executive Committee concluded that Murphy had not been drunk. "The evidence is conclusive," he stated, "that [Murphy] drank no intoxicating liquor while here." As to the rumor that Isaac had been drugged, Withers would only say that he took "no stock in that" theory. He explained that Murphy "drank his milk punches at home, and the Apollinaris and ginger ale that he drank here were in sealed bottles, opened before his eyes. If that ginger ale was drugged, it was drugged in Belfast."[63] Several newspapers attributed Murphy's behavior to his supposed intoxication at the clambake two days before the race. The *New York Times* claimed he had overindulged in "champagne, a habit which has in the past gotten the better of him, but never to lead to quite so sad an exhibition of himself as he made at the track yesterday."[64] The *Chicago Horseman* reported that Murphy "disgraced himself in the most shameful manner. . . . He was so drunk that he reeled and rolled in the saddle. He jerked Firenzi all about the track in this wild lurching and tumbling about on her back, ruined all of her chances of winning or getting a place."[65] The question is, what really happened? And if someone did drug Isaac, why?

Rumors spread that bookmakers who had inside knowledge about the outcome of the race and had taken bets on Firenzi at 6:5 and even odds had walked away with thousands. The *Times Picayune* reported that several well-known plungers "won big money on Tea Tray,"[66] including Dave Johnson, who was "credited with winning $20,000 on the race."[67] If a gambling ring wanted to change the outcome of a race without using the traditional means of drugging a horse or paying jockeys to throw the race, drugging the jockey riding the favorite made sense. But there is an alternative theory that is more in line with all the evidence: someone planned to kill Isaac.

In addition to reeling from the effects of some kind of drug, Isaac's equipment had been tampered with. Someone had loosened his saddle after it was placed on Firenzi in the paddock, and someone had administered the drug sometime between the time he left Lucy in the grandstand and the time he mounted his horse in the paddock area before the race. If he had not noticed the loose saddle and adjusted it, who knows what could have happened? Surely he would have fallen from Firenzi at some point in the race, potentially dying from the fall or from being trampled by the other horses. This possibility was never mentioned in the white press.

After the incident at Monmouth Park, the white press continued to make Isaac a pariah. In his defense, the *Cleveland Gazette* ran the following column:

> The greatest of American jockeys has made his greatest mistake, or rather has been caused to do so. The supposition is that something he drank just prior to his mounting Firenzi in the Monmouth handicap at New York City Tuesday was drugged, causing him to reel and roll in the saddle, jerking the Queen of the turf all about the track and causing a sure winner to lose a great race. Neither Salvator nor Tenny were in the race and in consequence Firenzi, with Murphy her rider, was the favorite. Thousands of dollars were placed on her and of course lost. When lifted from the saddle his general appearance, his swollen face, glassy eyes and utter stupefaction, made all firmer in the belief that he had been drugged. The leading New York dailies claim that Jockey Murphy has always possessed a great love for champagne and that some person in whom he had confidence, and who had bet heavily on other horses in the race, took advantage of him, placing a drug in his liquor. He has been suspended pending an investigation. We hope that it will result in his being honorably acquitted, and the punishment of the scoundrel who committed the crime, for we believe that Murphy was drugged. He has ridden too many years and handled too many leading horses to be guilty of making such a blunder. While it is true he has much of this world's goods, we know by long years of experience in the saddle is dearer to him than anything perhaps life.[68]

On September 6 the Executive Committee of Monmouth Park concluded that Isaac "wasn't and couldn't have been drunk, but suspended him for 'the condition he was in.'"[69] The duration of the
suspension was thirty days. To be sure, this outcome did not sit
well with Isaac, nor did it sit well with his powerful employers and
friends, who vouched for his character and requested a further
investigation.

On October 1 a well-rested Isaac returned to the track amid
cheers and applause from the spectators attending the first day of
races at the New York Jockey Club's fall meeting at Morris Park.[70]
Riding in the Manhattan Handicap at 119 pounds aboard Haggin's
mare Firenzi, Isaac finished second to his friend Anthony Hamilton
riding August Belmont's Raceland. The Times Picayune acknowledged the difficulty of returning to peak performance after being
"laid on the shelf for a month or more," which has an effect on an
athlete's "muscle agility and mental balance."[71] Unfortunately, during his suspension Isaac remained ill and in bad shape from the effects of his previous stomach problems, compounded by whatever
caused his state of disorientation on August 26. Around this time,
likely at the suggestion of Thomas Fortune, the Murphys moved to
Red Bank, New Jersey, to a cottage near the Shrewsbury River. It
was quiet there, and Isaac could get some well-deserved rest.

On October 9, a little over a week after his return to the saddle, Murphy was stricken with "pneumonia and inflammation of
the bowels."[72] He had been on a strict regimen of steam baths and
starvation, which caused severe dehydration, in an effort to make
the lower weights demanded by Haggin. At one point he thought he
was well enough to meet with his employer, but "while in the act of
dressing, he suddenly reeled and fell with a crash to the floor." At
first, Lucy believed her husband was dead, as all her attempts to re-
vive him were unsuccessful. Finally, "Dr. Thompson of West For-
ty-Seventh Street was sent for," and he determined that the famous
jockey was suffering from inward spasms, better known as ulcers.[73]
After attending to Isaac for close to a week, Dr. Thompson concluded that he had been poisoned. The doctor told the nurse caring
for Isaac that he might never fully recover, quite possibly because

he was suffering from something internal that could not be treated effectively by nineteenth-century medicine. After a series of treatments, Isaac and Lucy returned to Lexington, where he could convalesce in the quiet of their home and their community.

When the news circulated that Isaac had returned home and was still suffering from the effects of being poisoned in August, Benjamin Bruce of the *Live Stock Record* called for an investigation into the poisoning, and he suggested that the Monmouth Park Racing Association, and Mr. Withers in particular, make "reparation" to Isaac for the "stigma under which he has suffered since his suspension and disgrace."[74] On November 14 the *Philadelphia Inquirer* published a special report regarding the investigation:

A secret investigation was instituted and it has resulted in a full confirmation of the poisoning story. From facts gathered at the time and since convincing proofs have been collected that go to show that a conspiracy was formed to down Murphy by several persons whose names are withheld. The certificates of four responsible physicians have been obtained and with them other indisputable evidence, proving beyond a doubt; that poison and not liquor caused Murphy's downfall. This intelligence will create a sensation in turf circles, especially when it is announced that the guilty persons are to be prosecuted. The developments are awaited with eagerness by the public.[75]

Although the perpetrators were never identified publicly, the inquiry corroborated what Murphy's supporters had maintained all along.

At home in Lexington, a pallid and emaciated Murphy rested. He was still weak from being unable to eat regularly, and his inflamed stomach was kept wrapped with a "wide bandage on it all the time" to prevent excessive swelling; the slightest "jarring" of his body caused considerable pain.[76] However, having returned to his comfortable home in Lexington, he was sleeping better at night, likely the result of Dr. Thompson's prescription. Reporters called on the celebrated jockey to inquire about his future in horse racing. Isaac answered, "Unless I get very much better than I am I shall nev-

er ride again. Still, I dislike to have the stigma of expulsion resting
on me which I feel that I am wholly innocent of being drunk when
I rode Firenzi."[77] Although he had fallen from the great steed of celebrity, the question remained: Would he recover?

## A Question of Destiny

That one race at Monmouth Park marked a transition for Isaac
Murphy. The once flawless professional jockey had become a pariah to whites. Because of his color, white working-class and poor
men loathed him; they would neither empathize with the treachery
of the situation nor endorse an investigation into the facts. Reaction
to the episode at Monmouth Park was a sign of deteriorating race
relations throughout American society and the aggressive and often
violent denial of opportunities for blacks. African Americans were
being deprived of their rights and privileges as citizens of the United
States, especially in the South, where the "Afro-American was being
disenfranchised by State laws as well as by force, fraud and intimidation," all in an effort to return blacks to their former state of ignorance and servility.[78]

For Murphy in particular, and for African Americans in general, the decade would be marked by expulsion, alienation, exclusion,
and the increased stigmatization of black masculinity as corrupt and
inherently menacing. This would lead to a dramatic increase in the
ritual practice of lynching by whites in an effort to rid society of its
"bad niggers" and threats to white ideas of social order. Throughout
the winter and into the spring, in addition to dealing with the sickness that was eating away at his stomach, Isaac would have to contend with the rumors about his degenerate manly character, which
were eating away at his soul. He must have been worried about the
effects on his ability to gain employment, and he would discover
that he had reason to be concerned. Some of his previous employers,
many of whom knew him very well, began to shy away from the talented jockey who once could do no wrong.

Although not fully recovered, Isaac was well enough to travel. In late December he and James Ware, a fellow member of the

Lincoln Lodge Masons, ventured to Cincinnati, Ohio, to visit John Thomas, who was probably a Mason as well.[79] The purpose of their meeting is unknown, but we can speculate that it had something to do with Isaac's position as one of the senior officers of the lodge: he was the senior warden, and Ware was the senior deputy.[80] The men probably attended an official meeting in Cincinnati and were Thomas's guests at his home on Cherry Street. While in Cincinnati, Isaac was no doubt asked about his health and the particulars of the race at Monmouth Park. Based on what we know about Isaac, he likely answered honestly and directly, retelling the story without any fanfare or embellishment. After returning to Lexington, Isaac and Ware would have reported any pertinent information from the Cincinnati meeting to their own lodge members.

At the Masons' lodge, at Pleasant Valley Baptist Church, and elsewhere in the Lexington community, where he was among his peers, Isaac would have felt at home, having no need for the barriers he maintained when engaged with the outside world. Despite the embarrassing and potentially isolating situation, Isaac embraced his community of kinfolk, and they showered him with love and generosity. While he was recovering, well-wishers may have dropped off notes and offered prayers for his speedy recovery. Fans of the great black jockey may have sent telegrams and gifts to help lift his mood. But it is also possible that the prince of jockeys received hate mail from whites who wished his enemies had succeeded in removing him from the racetrack permanently. (The twentieth-century equivalent would be Hank Aaron receiving hate mail for making $100,000 a season playing baseball, leaving some more deserving white boy without a job.) How Isaac handled such criticism is not known, but we can imagine that he dismissed most of it. Locally, of course, Isaac's mentors would have reassured him that they had not lost faith in him; they understood that Isaac's reputation was more important than life itself, and he would seek to right the wrong perpetrated against him. For Isaac, the spring could not come fast enough: he had something to prove.

By the beginning of 1891, despite the obvious disappointments and near tragedy, Isaac had reason to celebrate. On January 6 he turned thirty years old. As part of the birthday celebration, Isaac and Lucy went ice skating. Lucy (who was always a worrier when it came to her husband's health and safety) probably had mixed feelings about this excursion: on the one hand, she wanted Isaac to celebrate his birthday doing something he enjoyed; on the other hand, she was concerned about him going out in the cold, given his recent illness. And, in fact, the ill-advised excursion on the ice sent him back to bed.

Among the Murphys' many friends in Lexington were elder members of the community such as Jordan C. Jackson and his wife Belle and Benjamin and Susan Franklin. Both men were Civil War veterans, and their wives had been significant contributors to the Lexington community. Belle Mitchell Jackson was a teacher and had helped the local churches educate the community's children. Since Isaac had lost both his parents, the Jacksons and the Franklins were like surrogate families and helped him develop a sense of groundedness in Lexington.

Sometime in December Anthony Hamilton announced his engagement to St. Louis native Annie L. Messley, the stepdaughter of Frank Estell, the wealthy and well-known superintendent of the Laclede Building. Isaac and Lucy invited Anthony and his fiancée to Lexington for a reception in their honor. According to the *Lexington Transcript*, the party at the mansion on East Third Street was the social event of the year:

> Saturday, Jan. 14, 1891 at the residence of the premiere jockey, Isaac Murphy, Mr. Anthony Hamilton, the "Black Demon" and his bonny bride, were given one of the grandest receptions that ever came off in Lexington. Dinner was served at 12 o'clock and the luncheon was continued till the large attendance was summoned again to the festive board, when a magnificent repast was discussed to the repletion of all present. Between heats champagne corks were kept flying from parlor to dining room [and the] library in Murphy's private Sanctum till 8 o'clock when the bell ringed to saddle up and come to the post, and when Starter Waxey cried "Go!" the world-renowned Terpsichore Sweepstakes commenced and it

was 11:30 when the race was decided. John Clay was judge, Isaac Lewis was timer, and after honest consultation it was decided that Isaac Murphy got to the "wire first" and Anthony Hamilton "got a place."[81]

The "delightful all-day shower for the jockey Tony Hamilton and his bride" proved to be the most attractive event in Lexington's black community.[82] It is likely that the groom and his hosts invited friends from as far away as California and New York. From the *Lexington Herald*, we know that jockeys William Walker, Isaac Lewis, and Tom Britton attended with their companions, as did members of Lexington's black society, including members from the Sardis and Lincoln Lodges.

The Murphys threw such parties from time to time. For instance, in 1893 Isaac and Lucy celebrated their ten years together by renewing their vows in front of a select number of friends and family invited to the special occasion. The January 31 issue of the *Kentucky Leader* described the occasion:

Isaac Murphy, the premier jockey, probably entertains more elaborately than any other colored man in the South, if not the whole country, and the hospitality he dispenses is regarded as almost princely among *his* people, with whom he and his wife are very popular. On the occasion of his tenth wedding anniversary he exceeded all formal bounds, and favored his friends with a most lavish entertainment.

Murphy has by his deeds of prowess in the saddle won for himself the highest rank among jockies, a handsome fortune and the esteem of his race. As there is but one Isaac Murphy, and his fame extends wherever the thoroughbred horse is known, a description of this anniversary celebration will be of interest to many.

Murphy's comfortable home on East Third street was gaily lighted and decorated for the occasion. At 9 o'clock the famous jockey and his wife entered the parlor in wedding fashion, and in the presence of a large gathering of friends renewed their

marriage vows before Rev. S. P. Young, pastor of the First Colored Baptist Church.

At the conclusion of the ceremony the company sat down to
enjoy the following elaborate menu:

Quails, with Champignons and Claret

Roman Punch

Salted Almonds

Olives

Buldons, with Saratoga Chips

Oyster Patties

Turkey, with Chestnut Dressing

Coffee

Croquettes, with French Peas

Champagne

Chicken Salad

Ices and Cakes

Fruit

During supper Waxey's band played sweet music, and later
the company danced merrily for several hours.

Mrs. Murphy, the hostess, was dressed in white silk,
trimmed with pearls and white lace, and wore ornaments of di-
amonds and gold. She carried a bouquet of Marchiel Niel roses and lilies. She was assisted by Mrs. Sallie Brown and Mrs.
Lizzie Anderson and Katie Hardin and Maria Williams.

At this late day *The Leader* cannot give space to a complete
list of those who attended or of the numerous presents in tin
presented to the famous jockey and his wife.[83]

Such elegance was unprecedented, but it seemed that each celebration of success and achievement brought the couple closer.

After the reception for Hamilton and his fiancée, Isaac stayed
in bed for a week. In fact, his continued debilitated state prevented him from traveling to St. Louis to act as best man at Hamilton's January 22 wedding. Jockey Isaac Lewis stood in for him, and

Isaac and Lucy sent their gift of a silver fruit stand. By the end of January 1891, several newspapers were still claiming that Isaac was "seriously ill" and might not survive to the spring. According to the *Cleveland Plaindealer*, the prognosis was bleak: "Isaac Murphy, the celebrated jockey is seriously ill in Louisville. The doctors fear that his disease will develop into pneumonia and express little hope of his recoup."[84] Similarly, Harry Smith's *Cleveland Gazette* described Isaac as "seriously ill at this home having taken a violent cold while skating Saturday. He has never been a well man since the peculiar sickness the day he rode the notorious Firenzi race."[85] And the *Grand Forks Herald* reported, "The account of the present condition of Isaac Murphy is extremely bad. Reports speak of him looking like a man who is going to die and that before long."[86] With the exception of an occasional interview with the man himself, most of these accounts about Isaac's illness were recycled from previously published articles that were days if not weeks old and embellished with unsubstantiated but tantalizing elements.

By the end of February, Isaac had reportedly recovered from his sickness, "barring a little rheumatism" resulting from lying in bed for long periods.[87] Though well enough to begin preparations for the upcoming racing season, Isaac began training slowly, not wanting to damage his chances of being healthy come spring. Yet he must have felt somewhat insecure, not knowing how much the August incident had damaged his reputation. It seemed to Isaac that the only way to stop the firestorm of negative publicity was to get back into the arena to disprove the lies. But could he, in fact, still be confident about his calling and his abilities, given what had happened to him? How did he feel, knowing that people he worked intimately with may have plotted his downfall or even his demise? He may have experienced a range of emotions from fear and anguish to resentment and a sense of betrayal. Even if he were reinstated and an apology were extended, Isaac's character had been sullied by the mere implication that he had been drunk in the saddle during an important race. The media had reduced the once honored and revered Murphy into a caricature of black manhood: effete, scheming, uncouth, brutal.

For the 1891 horse-racing season, the new National Jockey

Club hoped to increase attendance at courses throughout the country, which would increase the amount of money to be made by owners and investors. But if the 1891 season could match the previous season's 6,000-plus races with an average of 15,000 spectators, racetracks as a whole would be profitable. The *Dallas Morning News* estimated that the horse-racing industry employed upward of 500,000 men and boys in the stables, tracks, fields, betting rings, and poolrooms where legal betting was allowed.[88] Millions of dollars were wagered.

One of the new rules was that each trainer and jockey had to apply for a license annually. Primarily, the intent was to create a uniform set of rules throughout the national racing circuit. Always the consummate professional, Isaac registered with the National Jockey Club and paid his license fee sometime before the beginning of the Kentucky Association meeting on April 28. By then, Isaac had secured a number of horses to ride during the meeting. He had also found a kindred spirit in one of the few African American trainer-owners who shared his sense of independence and racial pride: fellow Lexingtonian Dudley Allen of Jacobin Stables. Allen's choice to connect his business venture in a white-dominated industry with black destiny was truly revolutionary. That Allen named his stable after French revolutionaries is intriguing and illustrates his knowledge of the world. It is possible that he and his fellow African Americans living in Lexington had knowledge of the African Diaspora and of Haitian revolutionary Toussaint-Louverture, the black Jacobin who defeated Napoleon. Allen was making a statement about who he was and what he intended to do. To have Isaac in the saddle completed the cabal of talented individuals who knew horses and knew how to win races. Clearly, if a horse from Jacobin Stables could win, black identity would be the beneficiary. For the 1891 season, Jacobin's premier horse would be Kingman, of which Allen was part owner.

By April 28, Isaac was fit and ready to begin the season, having trained virtually in his own backyard at the Kentucky Association track, where he stabled his horses. To lose weight, Isaac would continue the regimen that had been successful in the past: layering himself with sweaters and taking three- to five-mile walks each morning. As Isaac well knew, a jockey's hunger pains were rarely satisfied. He ate very little food in the morning and even smaller portions at dinner. But if he wanted to get back to where he had been before the incident at Monmouth Park, there could be no shortcuts. In addition to Kingman, Isaac rode Ed Corrigan's Riley, W. E. Applegate's Prince of Darkness, and Fleetwood's Missal. He even rode Estelle, one of the horses owned by his own firm, Murphy and Holloway, to a second-place finish in a purse race. However, Kingman would make the season an early success for Isaac.

At the Kentucky Association meeting, Isaac and Kingman began one of the most impressive runs of the season. With his riding weight down to 114 pounds, Isaac won two races on Kingman, including the Phoenix Hotel Stakes for a purse of more than $3,000. From Lexington, the Jacobin Stables traveled to Louisville, where Isaac and Kingman were scheduled to participate in the seventeenth running of the Kentucky Derby against a field of three other horses: T. J. Clay's Balgowan, Eastin and Larable's High Tariff, and Bashford Manor's Hart Wallace. On the morning of May 13, Derby Day, the skies were cloudy and hazy, but by early afternoon, a pleasant spring breeze and warm temperatures brightened the day considerably. At the start of the race, "Kingman came out first, ridden by Isaac Murphy, and the recognition of the horse and rider was followed by cheers that the surrounding knobs and hill tops took up and echoed back again."[89] Clearly, Isaac had not lost his appeal among Derby fans, who declared their support with rousing applause and cheers. In front of the estimated 40,000 in attendance—including Lucy, somewhere in the grandstand—Isaac was riding for pride as well as a paycheck. On the slow, dusty track, Isaac elevated his star when he took control of the race, turning a "big exercising gallop" into a real race and riding "Kingman hard to win by a length" over the great Monk Overton.[90] In what would be known as the "Funeral Procession Derby" (because of the slow pace), Isaac became the first jockey to win three Kentucky Derbies, and Dudley Allen became the first black owner of a Derby winner. With his back-to-back victories in major stakes races, Isaac was diluting the stain on his name, but he had not yet traveled back to the East, where the dirty deed had happened and major challenges to his career and his well-being still awaited him.

From Louisville, Jacobin Stables went to Covington, Kentucky, and the Latonia racecourse. The day of the race dawned cloudy and cool, with a threat of rain. The previous evening's rain had made the track heavy and slow, but Murphy and Allen knew that Kingman, the favorite, was at home in the mud. As expected, Isaac and the magnificent Kingman took the Latonia Derby; the win earned Isaac an additional $1,000 and the top spot among the year's stakes winners. A lesser known incident at Latonia involved Isaac the businessman. He was racing a number of horses from his own stable, including his brown filly Estelle, who was entered in a selling race for $600. There was some sort of disagreement about the price of the horse with the buyers, the Scroggan brothers out of Louisville, and a "row" had to be averted.[91] Whether Isaac was directly involved is not known, but it is interesting to imagine he was ready to throw a punch if necessary.

Back east, Isaac started out at Morris Park, winning a tough race on Empire Stables' Lyceum in which he outrode the phenomenal Willie Simms and veteran James McLaughlin. According to the *New York Times*, the betting pools supported Murphy: "The handicappers and the players of sure things had all decided that Uno Grande of the McLewee string with Jimmy McLaughlin in the saddle must surely win the dash. The Monmouth contingent thought differently, however, and they played Lyceum, who was trained at the Branch, and on whom Isaac Murphy had the mount."[92] Isaac won the six-furlong race for maiden three-year-olds by a neck, hugging the rail and edging out Simms on J.B. Interestingly, although the spectators recognized Simms and McLaughlin as quality jockeys, they still trusted Murphy in the clutch. More important, Isaac's victory on Lyceum would influence his future in ways he did not expect.

The *New York Times* reported on June 12 that "Isaac Murphy is to ride for F. C. McLewee during the remainder of the season in place of McLaughlin."[93] Apparently, J. A. and A. H. Morris were dissatisfied with McLaughlin's performance and sought to be released from their $3,000 contract, offering the veteran rider $500. McLaughlin refused to settle for less than $1,000, which closed the matter, but it led to his release by McLewee, who was also dissatisfied with his riding. The press did not report how Isaac felt about replacing his rival, but surely he could understand his colleague's shock at not being appreciated. This incident demonstrates the changing culture of horse racing and how owners dealt with jockeys. The confrontations between labor and capital, which were so much a part of American mining and building practices, had filtered into the once genteel sport of kings.

Gentlemen with tremendous wealth and a desire to invest in the leisure activities of their friends were no longer at the center of America's pastime. The new masters of the turf were capitalists whose clear objective was to invest a minimal amount of capital in a horse's ability to win and turn a profit. As a consequence, nonwinning jockeys became a liability that could not be afforded or, in the case of McLaughlin and others, tolerated. It was not good enough to win second- and third-place prize money. The new men of the turf sought to maximize profits and profitability, period. The culture cultivated and nurtured by gentlemen of the turf over the preceding 100 years was all but gone in the East. Whatever vestiges remained would soon be dissolved or absorbed into the well-dressed cesspools called racetracks, which would spawn organized crime in the early twentieth century.[94]

For Isaac, this kind of treatment by owners would eventually become the tipping point. But at the time, although his winning percentage had dipped significantly from previous years, he was still a dependable rider in stakes races. On August 18 at the crowded Morris Park, eleven of the country's top three-year-olds were waiting for Mr. Caldwell to start the Omnibus Stakes. At the flash of the red flag, the field was off to a thunderous start. Taking a page from the past, Isaac rode a waiting race on the bay colt Rey del Rey (son of Norfolk), getting a feel for the other horses and the skills of the other jockeys. The veteran jockey watched as horse after horse fell off, waiting patiently for someone to make a mistake. Then, at the last furlong pole, there it was: a gap opened up between the two leaders, and Isaac shot through it and into the rail. "So swift did he come that people looked at him for an instant as if thunder struck," wrote the *New York Times*.[95] In what could be considered a victory of wisdom and artistry over youthful daring and vigor, Isaac won on Rey del Rey and claimed the $28,000 in prize money for McLewee. This answered any lingering questions about his ability to ride and win in spectacular fashion. He was as sharp as ever.

In the Nursery Stakes on October 10 at Morris Park, Murphy would prove himself again, guiding McLewee's Yorkville Belle across the finish line for a first prize of $14,000.[96] By the end of the 1891 season, Isaac would record 32 wins in 114 races, for a winning percentage of 28.1—his second lowest in his seventeen years as a jockey (his winning percentage in 1878 had been 22.6). Despite his expertise, proven ability, and overall success in the saddle, Isaac's relevance in horse racing was slowly diminishing.

For Isaac, horse racing and jockeyship, especially in the East, had become less about skill and mastery and more about winning at all costs. For the first time in his adult life, he felt that his control of his own destiny was slipping away. But there was no way to stop the winds of change in American society. The best solution for Isaac, it seemed, was to navigate the rough patches and seek shelter if the gusts got too strong. Yet even in the comfort and shelter of his beloved Lexington, he could no longer avoid what was becoming an inevitable reality.

## Wade in the Water

With an annual salary ranging from $15,000 to $25,000, Isaac Murphy enjoyed a degree of independence and social mobility that was uncommon among black Americans and, for that matter, white Kentuckians. Isaac's early experiences with white men such as J. W. Hunt-Reynolds, Ed Corrigan, and E. J. Baldwin, and later with his lawyer L. P. Tarleton, helped shape and validate his feelings of masculine power: These men recognized his unique abilities on a horse and paid him well for his services. But for a majority of white men, this was not the case.

In Kentucky and throughout the country, a successful black man was a slap in the face to a majority of whites. In this peculiar country, the last thing white working-class men wanted to see was an educated, hardworking, well-to-do Negro living a comfortable, honest life. Black success was perceived as a detriment to white identity in general and to white manhood in particular, especially when the white yeoman farmer and his city-dwelling cousins were struggling just to secure a crust of bread for their dinner or shoes for their children's feet. More precisely, if a black man could raise himself from the depths of slavery into a position where he had gained a significant foothold in American society, what did that say about an impoverished white man who had never been enslaved or methodically abused? One could only conclude that something must be wrong with the white man. In essence, the white man was not the black man's equal; there was no viable excuse for his failures or inability to provide for his family.

As a result, Isaac Murphy and other black men had to contend with white men whose sense of self-worth came not from their ability to work and be productive but from what they had failed to achieve. To combat the insecurity and anxiety created by the success of African Americans, whites used various means to bar any and all expressions of black achievement. Further, through social clubs, unions, and trade organizations, white men attempted to limit black access to well-paying jobs, which translated into male power in a patriarchal society. Notwithstanding the hurdles, traps, and coercions intended to devalue public displays of manliness by African American men, questions related to maintaining an ideal manhood continued to trouble white men. This tension would, in fact, feed fears related to the blackening of America through miscegenation and lead to the attempt to control white women's sexuality. The ultimate question was, who would be the representative of American manhood and masculinity?

By January 1892, Isaac and Lucy had settled into their usual routines in Lexington, having spent the last three months reacquainting themselves with their surroundings, their neighbors, and their circle of friends. To facilitate his projected transition from jockey to owner-trainer, Isaac spent the winter visiting stables throughout the Bluegrass in search of horses to purchase. Believing he had found a good prospect on John T. Clay's stud farm, Isaac paid $2,000 for the chestnut colt The Hero, foaled in 1889, hoping to win stakes races worth ten times the purchase price.[97]

At the nearby Kentucky Association stables, where Isaac housed his string of horses, the master jockey would have worked with his assistant trainer, grooms, and stable boys to keep all his horses in top condition through the winter in preparation for the spring races. Horses were a pricey investment, so the gentleman jockey had to be hoping he had a potential champion among his Thoroughbreds. He also began to receive offers for contract work for the next season from Frank Ehret's Hellgate Stable, F. C. McLewee, James Bradley, and R. T. Holloway. Additionally, Hellgate Stable commissioned him to "purchase one or two good colts in Kentucky, that promise to do well this year in their three year old form."[98] With this commission, Isaac could add horse trader to his growing list of occupations.

While Isaac planned his personal training schedule, worked out his stable's entries for the season (nearly four months away), and coordinated his contracts with various employers, Lucy made plans to celebrate her husband's thirty-first birthday and their wedding anniversary. Over the course of their marriage, Isaac and Lucy were rarely apart. They seemed to enjoy traveling together and participating in the culture, entertainment, and society life of the various cities they visited, from Los Angeles to Chicago to New York. The reason for their childless state is unknown. Perhaps there were fertility issues, or maybe they simply wanted to wait until Isaac's riding years were over and he did not have to travel so frequently. Said differently, children might have been an inconvenience to the young couple caught up in their upper-middle-class lifestyle.

A few weeks after Isaac and Lucy celebrated their ninth wedding anniversary, the *Indianapolis Freeman* published an account of the public meeting between delegates of the Anti–Separate Coach State Convention and the Joint Railroad Committee. They were listening to arguments related to a December 1891 bill sponsored by state senator Tipton Miller, a Democrat from Calloway County. The bill proposed to legally separate blacks and whites on passenger trains operating in and traveling through the state of Kentucky with a "wooden partition, with a door therein . . . and shall bear in some conspicuous place appropriate words in plain letters indicating the race it is set apart for."[99] Essentially, the bill had originated at the request of constituents from rural Kentucky, mostly farmers and poor whites who never traveled by railroad themselves but "were offended that blacks were even on the trains, and even more so at the thought that some of them might be traveling first class."[100] At the state capital, John H. Jackson, a black representative elected by the Anti–Separate Coach State Convention delegates, argued that such a law was harmful not only to blacks but also to the future of the state and its development:

> Professor John H. Jackson, of the State Normal school, was the first to take the floor. He explained how the Negroes of Kentucky were opposed to the separate coach bill and told why they protested against its passage. There were differences in social and mental conditions among colored people, as well as among whites. Some were low and depraved and unfit to associate with the decent. Others were ambitious and enterprising, who loved their country, respected themselves and wanted to be near the better class of whites because of the refining and civilizing teaching such association imparted. He closed by offering as a substitute from all the pending measures a bill which made first and second class divisions of passengers, to apply to whites and blacks alike. Not color, but condition was to form the dividing line. He wanted the colored people to be made to feel that they were fellow-citizens in deed and in fact.[101]

As the state senate debated the bill, with both Republicans and Democrats challenging its validity, African Americans continued to make their thoughts known and their voices heard. On April 19 Lexington-born educator and community leader Mary Britton cri-

tiqued the civility of the state's best citizens for allowing the desires
of the self-conscious masses of ignorant folks to cause trouble for a
vulnerable population of law-abiding and peaceful citizens. In the
*Kentucky Leader*, Britton wrote: "We are aware that the Assembly has the power to inflict such a law, but is it right? While we no
longer chill the blood of our friends by talking of branding irons,
chains, whips, blood hounds and to the many physical wrongs and
abominations of slavery, this foe of American prejudice renders our
lives insecure, our homes unhappy, and crushes out the very sinew
of existence—freedom and citizenship."[102] The African American
community's response to the separate coach bill, which the railroad
companies also opposed, was important in the long history of dissent and active agitation against the wrongs advanced by white supremacy as the natural state of things.[103]

Black Kentuckians were shocked to learn on May 24, 1892,
that Governor Brown had signed the separate coach bill into law,
after it had passed the house by a vote of sixty-five to twenty-five
and the senate by a vote of eighteen to ten.[104] Thus began the process of formalizing the concept of racial segregation, which would
spread like a cancer to the "other states of the late Confederacy in
excluding colored people from public places, such as hotels, theaters, passenger coaches, etc."[105] Regardless of their social, political, and economic status as a race, whites understood that they
possessed cultural capital that could be converted into political
power. Even the unsophisticated who lacked wealth could claim
their whiteness as collateral, which became a form of currency to
be used in the maintenance of white power over blacks and other
racial minorities.

Isaac was likely concerned that the new separate car law would
hinder his ability to travel and pursue his occupation. However, because he was scheduled to ride in the East for a majority of the 1892
season, the initial effect would be minimal. Although we cannot
know for sure, it is possible that Isaac and Lucy supported efforts
to test the law in the same fashion that Homer Plessy tested Louisiana's separate car law. They could afford the financial commitment
required to pursue a lawsuit, and given their position as leaders in

the Lexington community, they might have been expected to do so. More immediately pressing, though, was how this national movement of exclusion would affect Isaac's interactions with white owners, jockeys, and horse-racing officials around the country. Would the color line be drawn on the track, as it was in the boxing ring and on the baseball field?

After winning the Phoenix Stakes on R. T. Holloway's Wadsworth in characteristic style, "never showing in front until the half was reached," Isaac headed east to begin the racing season with the confederation of stables composed of McLewee, Ehret, and Allen.[106] The Murphys might have returned to Red Bank, New Jersey, to the cottage they had resided in the previous August. In any case, Isaac was there to race at the New York Jockey Club's spring meeting at Morris Park. On May 30, in the first race of the day, Isaac rode Barrick and Withrow's chestnut colt Dr. Hasbrouck to victory, defeating Fred Littlefield riding Correction. Dr. Hasbrouck easily carried Isaac's 122 pounds, winning the five-furlong race in a record time of fifty-nine seconds, which drew applause from the appreciative crowd.[107] On June 3 Isaac repeated his winning ways, taking the Ladies Stakes on Ehret's chestnut filly Yorkville Belle over a field that included jockeys Willie Simms and Anthony Hamilton. Three days later, having dropped 10 pounds to ride at 107 pounds in the Withers Stakes on Yorkville Belle, Murphy finished third and in the money, but he was exhausted. Seeing Isaac suffer in the effort to keep his weight down must have been agonizing for Lucy.

Surviving his drastic weight loss, the determined professional had a few days to rest before the Great Eclipse Stakes, worth $20,000 to the winning stable. In his cottage at Red Bank, Isaac would have slept to regain his strength, but he would not alter his other routines: his customary five- to ten-mile walk layered in sweaters to promote perspiration, and his minuscule meals consisting of a little fruit and small bits of meat for protein. For the Great Eclipse Stakes, Isaac was scheduled to ride Ehret's Don Alonzo, a two-year-old bay colt with a ton of potential. On the day of the race, Morris Park was swollen with spectators milling around the grandstands and the grass that framed the straightaway. In addition to Isaac riding the favorite, the field of eleven starters included Fred Taral aboard Sir Walter, Ed Garrison on Shelley Tuttle, and William Fitz-patrick on Dr. Rice. In Isaac's view, these three sure-handed jockeys were the ones to beat.

After a bit of drama at the starting line—three jockeys were thrown, including Garrison, whose horse literally laid down on the ground to unseat him—the start came off all right. In a great race between two highly capable horses, Sir Walter and Don Alonzo, Taral edged Murphy by a head at the finish. The two horses had met previously in the Great American Stakes in Brooklyn, where Garrison had ridden Sir Walter to victory. From the beginning, Murphy had played his waiting race as the three front-runners ran "stride for stride" down the straightaway toward the finish. Although the *New York Times* recognized that the winner did not have an "easy victory of it," it criticized Murphy's "weak finish that beat" Don Alonzo.[108] This critique of Isaac's riding would continue throughout the meeting. In the *New York Herald-Tribune*, an anonymous writer had this to say:

People who apologize for Murphy's riding forget that in 1890 he was so drunk in an important race when he rode Firenzi that he fell off the mare's back, and was suspended for thirty days by the racing authorities. He has never been of any real value as a jockey since and his wretched riding on Don Alonzo, York-ville Belle and other horses has cost the Ehret Stables this year at least $50,000, which they would have won with a compe-tent jockey on its horses. Never was the riding of a jockey more thoroughly exposed than was that of Murphy by Don Alonzo's extremely easy success in the Sapling Stakes in fast time. With Murphy up, this colt has been beaten in stake after stake by a head in slow time. With Taral up, Don Alonzo won Sapling Stakes under double pull in fast time. The inference is easy. But there is not the slightest danger of the Board of Control com-prehending the situation. That remarkable body needs a stroke of lightning to electrify its sessions. Nothing else will ever illu-minate its scant intelligence.[109]

How Isaac took this criticism is not known, but he likely pointed out that most of the writer's points were false. Murphy had been publicly exonerated of any wrongdoing in the 1890 incident; he had won both the Kentucky and the Latonia Derbies in 1891; and since the New York Jockey Club meeting, he had not only won on Yorkville Belle but also placed on Don Alonzo.

What is most telling about the writer of this critique is the language he used to describe the difference between how Murphy rode (slow) and how jockeys were supposed to ride (fast), indicating no appreciation of the time when gamesmanship, strategy, and sportsmanship were part of horse racing. Clearly, the writer had no sense of history and Murphy's role in the development of the sport in America. But that was Isaac's problem: those times were gone. In addition, he no longer had two- and four-mile races to pace himself and test the field. In the context of the changing significance of sports, Isaac was becoming obsolete, and owners and spectators no longer appreciated the vast knowledge and experience a master jockey brought to the sport of horse racing.

Within three days of the article being published, the Ehret-McLewee-Allen combination informed Isaac that his services were no longer needed. The partners offered to settle his contract by paying him only $3,000 of the $10,000 agreed on. Of course, Isaac refused to accept their less than generous offer, and the *New York Times* reported that "he will have all that is due to him and . . . will report for duty daily so long as he is required to by the terms of his contract and claim full pay for his services." The veteran jockey refused to back down, and his response to the criticism was simply that "he was unfairly treated." The *Times* noted, "Saturday last when he was set down and Taral was secured to ride Don Alonzo for the stable, . . . the fact that Taral won the stake with the colt is no proof that he [Murphy] could not have done so, particularly as the horse had nothing to beat in the race while he has always had a hard lot to beat when Murphy has had the mount on him, and been beaten by the very narrowest of margins."[110]

Within days, Isaac's relationship with the Ehret-McLewee-Allen firm was severed, and he was given his full salary. However,

he could not ride for any other owners without the permission of
the firm. When another owner wanted Murphy to ride Morello in
the $65,000 Futurity Stakes, which guaranteed a $7,000 purse to the
winning jockey, McLewee refused to allow him to take the mount,
noting that Murphy "was getting a rather large salary for doing nothing and that he thought he had better continue to earn it by sitting in
the grand stand and watch the race from that spot instead of Morello's back."[111] Morello won the Futurity with William Howard up, and
a few jockeys, including Murphy, were jealous, angry, or both.

At the end of the season, Isaac and Lucy returned to Lexington
without any fanfare. Isaac lacked the major victories that used to
put him in the spotlight. In fact, his 1892 totals were an abysmal six
wins out of forty-two starts. This is understandable, considering his
contract dispute with Ehret, McLewee, and Allen and their control
over him. Besides the contract issues that prevented him from taking more mounts, the other major obstacle for Isaac was the changing nature of horse racing. Gone were the prominent owners who
strategized against each other like chess masters playing a rook for a
pawn. The game was now all about speed, straightaway racing, and
running as many horses as possible. The pastoral had been replaced
by the industrial model of productivity: constant movement equals
profitability.

Having had his season come to a close in such an unprecedented fashion, Isaac became more aware of the potential challenges
ahead. He understood that his career and everything he had worked
for were in jeopardy each time he was denied a mount or passed
over for a white jockey. What he thought about the changes in the
sport and the new breed of owners he shared only with his closest friends and, of course, with Lucy. Over the winter of 1892 and
into the spring of 1893, he sought answers to questions related to
his future as a jockey. Would he choose the path of his mentor, Eli
Jordan, and become a trainer for the wealthiest owners? Would he
maintain his own stable with quality horses and engage jockeys to
wear his colors, competing for purses and power at the jockey clubs
in the East and the West? Could he retire from the track altogether
and find a new occupation that would provide the same comforts he

and Lucy had become accustomed to? What did the future hold for Isaac Burns Murphy?

At their Lexington residence, Isaac and Lucy undoubtedly discussed their future, daydreaming about the possibility of regaining what had been lost after his poisoning at Monmouth Park in 1890 and the subsequent allegations and negative publicity. If not for that event, it is possible that the contract dispute with the Ehret-McLewee-Allen firm would not have occurred; that he would not have lost the opportunity for additional mounts and the revenue they could generate; and that the catcalls from the white boys and men in the stands, trying to put Isaac in his place, would not have been so cutting. But the attempt on his life *did* occur, and Isaac could not help but remember that each time he raced. Worst of all, when the quiet hours between dusk and dawn allowed for deep contemplation, Isaac could not help but turn over in his mind the fact that he was a black man in a country that was becoming exceedingly hostile to people of African descent. He was a black man competing for the same opportunities as white men, who despised him because of his success.

A few weeks after Lucy and Isaac celebrated their tenth wedding anniversary by hosting more than a dozen friends and relatives at their home, Isaac announced his plan to continue in the saddle while making the transition to a full-time owner-trainer. Like Ansel Williamson, Ed Brown, Dudley Allen, and William Walker, Isaac would use his experience and his knowledge of horses and racing to author the rest of his life's story. If anyone could develop winners, surely he could. Echoing his announcement, the *New York Times* ran with the story: "Jockey Isaac Murphy has decided to ride this season for his own stable, when he can make weight. He will personally superintend the training and preparation of his horses for stake events, and has collected quite a string of runners."[112] What better way to respond to the challenge of being denied a chance to earn a living in an occupation he had helped revolutionize?

In mid-February an article appeared in the *Live Stock Record* that may have been a boost to the still somewhat dejected Murphy. Under the pen name "Longfellow," the author wrote:

A majority of the turfmen, at Churchill Downs, are disposed to stick to Isaac Murphy as the premier jockey of America. He was so long the acknowledged head and front of his profession, that it is no easy matter for his admirers to concede that there is now any one superior to him in the saddle. They claim that Murphy did not have a fair showing in the East last year, and that what riding he did compared favorably with that of Garrison, or any other jockey. I talked with an experienced trainer on this subject, and he said that he watched Murphy's work in the saddle very closely, and saw him do as fine riding as he ever did in his life. The same trainer says that Murphy will be able to ride this year at 110 pounds or perhaps less. It has been reported that he is negotiating with Mr. Foxhall Keene with the view of signing with him, this year, as head jockey, but the report has not yet been substantiated. It looks like Murphy was preparing to have a stable of this own, as he has recently purchased several promising two-year olds, and already owned a few in the older divisions. With his large experience with horses, it looks like Murphy ought to make a success of a stable of his own.[113]

This article must have come as a great surprise to Isaac, who was no doubt preparing for the 1893 season with some apprehension. In fact, it may have changed his mind about riding for himself, given the expense of running a stable and chasing prizes at racecourses across the country. There is little evidence that Isaac actually entered a horse under his colors in any meeting during the 1893 season.

By late February, it was reported that Murphy had agreed to ride for Gideon and Daly for the season, taking the "heavy weight riding for their stable."[114] Along with Monk Overton, Isaac gave the Gideon and Daly stable coverage in the weight categories that would net the most return for their investment in horseflesh as well as talent in the saddle. Other black jockeys also took advantage of the opportunity to ride as "heavyweights"; Tom Britton signed with Captain S. S. Brown out of Mobile, Alabama.[115] If Murphy, Overton, and Britton could maintain their weight at less than 118 pounds, they could get big races and earn a portion of the large purses. Isaac thus guaranteed himself a salary.

From March to May, Isaac trained for his opening race in Lexington at the Kentucky Association meeting. Whether or not he wanted to admit it, the older he got, the harder it was to lose weight through the routine of wasting and purging. The five- and ten-mile walks in heavy sweaters and the long rides on horseback without the proper diet could be dangerous. A dehydrated body was vulnerable to fatigue, as well as kidney failure and other chronic illnesses. Nevertheless, with his weight under 115 pounds by the first of May, Isaac was able to fulfill his contract with Gideon and Daly; he also rode for Kentucky distiller James E. Pepper.

On the second day of the meeting, in his first race of the season, Isaac took Pepper's La Joya to victory on the muddy track. According to the *Live Stock Record*, Isaac showed a flash of his past brilliance as he sat on the "game little Hindoo filly and rode home a comparatively easy winner" in the Melbourne Stud Stakes.[116] The *Cleveland Gazette* recognized that "his riding was superb and was characterized by one of his old time finishes."[117] In his three races, Isaac placed first in two and second in one, helping Pepper's stable collect $6,410 in winnings. For all who paid attention, this was the Isaac Murphy they knew—beating back the challengers with a calm consistency that was the ultimate sign of confidence. If the Lexington races represented the first act of his final play, surely Churchill Downs was the second act, which promised high drama and suspense.

Isaac and Lucy traveled by train through the familiar Kentucky countryside to Louisville. Unlike Lexington, the weather in Louisville was "delightful," and the crowd was as attractive as ever.[118] The nineteenth running of the Kentucky Derby on May 10 was on the minds of everyone on the grounds, including Isaac, who was scheduled to ride Pepper's Mirage.[119] Unfortunately, three days of rain put the track in bad condition, making it heavy and sloppy. This would be Isaac's eleventh Kentucky Derby. In his last outing in 1891, on Dudley Allen's Kingman, he had claimed his third victory and the prestige of being the first to do so. All in attendance knew that the proven veteran of the turf should not be taken lightly, even though Pepper's chestnut three-year-old colt did not impress the spectators. But with only five other horses entered, Isaac had a chance, albeit one the oddsmakers put at 12:1.[120]

An estimated 30,000 people filled the stands and the infield at Churchill Downs. It was a clear day, and a bouquet of colorful hats worn by the women in attendance looked like a festival of spring flowers. Lucy was no doubt present in the stands. This had been the scene of many glorious wins for her husband. In the infield, wagons, carts, and buggies jammed the space, where there were lively activities in between races: games for children and music to satisfy the restless. When the time came, all eyes focused on the track, anticipating the beginning of the Derby.[121]

Carrying an extra seven pounds, Isaac mounted Mirage in the paddock area and was guided to the track, where he galloped to the starting line to await the beginning of the race. Anxiety was high among both horses and jockeys, but Mirage was less anxious than the impatient Lookout, the favorite. As the jockeys and horses lined up, the eyes of the spectators turned toward the starter, Pettingill, who watched the field closely before dropping the flag. The six competitors flew down the straightaway and into the first turn, with Lookout and Linger taking the lead and Mirage a close third. After the first mile, Lookout took command of the race, and Linger dropped out of contention. Working on an outclassed Mirage, Isaac slipped from third to fifth behind Plutus, Boundless, and Buck McCann. As the field entered the final quarter, the order remained the same. Isaac claimed an inglorious fifth place, beating only Linger to the wire. There would be no fourth Derby victory for Isaac.

During the Louisville meeting, Isaac took additional mounts, including a May 11 start in the Hurstbourne Stakes for two-year-olds on W. O. Scully's bay filly Philopena. One week later, on May 18, he rode J. Hannigan and Company's bay colt King Charley in a purse race worth $500. He had reduced to 113 pounds, dropping 5 pounds since his second-place finish on Philopena. On King Charley, he also finished in the money, taking third place. This would be his last appearance as a jockey at Churchill Downs.

From Louisville, Isaac traveled to Covington and the Latonia Jockey Club meeting, where he was scheduled to ride for W. H. Landeman in the Ripple Stakes. Isaac had had some memorable wins at Latonia, including the Hindoo Stakes for three-year-olds on Leonatus in 1883. On May 27, on a heavy track and riding against less experienced jockeys, Isaac took first prize on Landeman's chestnut colt Walnut.[122] There was no doubt that he could still ride. The difference was that other jockeys—some of whom Murphy had coached—had caught up to his ability.

Isaac then traveled by train from Covington to St. Louis, Missouri, where he and Lucy had a chance to visit with friends and acquaintances. The St. Louis Jockey Club meeting provided Isaac an opportunity to ride John Cooper, a crowd favorite, in two races. In the first one, they finished fourth in a field of nine, to the disappointment of the spectators. Two days later, on June 15, they had a chance to redeem themselves. In the second race of the day (worth $400), Isaac (weighing in at 113 pounds) brought John Cooper to the line again. After a fair start, the horses and their jockeys seemed determined to make a race of it. For four furlongs they challenged for control. Down the stretch, Isaac took the lead and willed John Cooper over the finish line, edging out Eling David for first place.[123] Five days later, on June 20, he took the first prize of $1,000 in the St. Louis Brewing Association Stakes, winning easily on St. Joe.[124] His St. Louis trip had been a success.

After leaving St. Louis a few days later, Isaac and Lucy arrived in Chicago to prepare for the annual Washington Park meeting beginning on June 24. As they had done on previous occasions, the Murphys either stayed with friends in the city or found accommodations at the Sheridan or Grand Pacific Hotel. Surprisingly, despite winning four American Derbies, Isaac was not the favorite in the race. Instead, that honor went to his rival Ed "Snapper" Garrison, who would be riding J. E. Cushing's impressive brown colt Boundless. For Isaac, who would be riding the unproven St. Croix, the $50,000 race had important financial incentives: he would receive $8,000 for a win, $7,000 for finishing in second place, or $3,000 for finishing in third.

On the day of the race, the *Live Stock Record* reported that H. P. McGrath's Aristides, the great "Little Red Horse," had died in St. Louis at the age of twenty-one.[125] Under the guidance of the great black jockey Oliver Lewis and the great black trainer Ansel Williamson, Aristides had won the inaugural Kentucky Derby in 1875. Fourteen-year-old Isaac had attended that meeting with his mentor Eli Jordan. Chances are that Isaac thought about Aristides and his fine qualities that day and remembered the chestnut colt's run in the first Kentucky Derby.

On the day of the American Derby, Isaac's former employer Ed Corrigan disrupted the routine weigh-in session when he had Monk Overton arrested for breach of contract, claiming the jockey had not honored his commitment to ride for Corrigan should he have a horse for the Derby. According to several newspaper accounts, Overton had promised to ride Ramapo for Gideon and Daly, either forgetting or disregarding his legally binding agreement with Corrigan. Unfortunately, he was removed from the Washington Park grounds and suspended from the meeting. With Overton unavailable, Dave Gideon offered the mount to Charley Thorpe, an up-and-coming jockey that the Scroggan brothers employed.[126]

After weighing in, Isaac and St. Croix made their way to the track, where 75,000 fans crowded the stands and the infield. As the field of competitors crossed in front of the grandstand, cheers and applause went up. After dozens of attempts to start the race, the frustrated Pettingill stepped down from his stand and confronted the jockeys on the field. In a fit of absolute frustration, he identified four jockeys—Lambley, Garrison, Taral, and Dogget—whose persistent efforts to jump-start the race were causing the problem. He fined them each $250 and warned them against any further disruption of the Derby.[127]

By the time the flag finally dropped, it was six o'clock in the evening, and the crowd was restless and tense.[128] Taking the lead, Ingomar and Don Alonzo sprinted to the inside rail. Behind them and still trying to gain position were G. W. Johnson, Chorister, Aldebaran, Ramapo, and Oporto. In the final group of eight horses bunched up in the rear were Murphy on St. Croix, along with Garrison on Boundless. For much of the race, both Murphy and Garrison laid back, waiting for an opportunity to charge into the lead. After a mile, the field shifted dramatically, with St. Leonards taking the lead in front of Clifford. By the time the horses entered the final turn, the jockeys had their horses ready to close the gap at a devil's pace. But before Isaac could get St. Croix out of the bunch, Garrison broke away from the group into the middle of the track and began to work his whip on Boundless. At the eighth pole, Garrison had gained two lengths on the field and was striding Boundless home to an eight-length victory. Isaac never got St. Croix out of the pack and finished in ninth place. In a postrace interview, he expressed his disappointment: "I thought [for] sure I could get St. Croix up one, two, [or] three. . . . It galled me terribly. I was to get $8,000 if I won."[129] We don't know for sure whether the other jockeys conspired to keep Murphy from finishing in the money, but it's a possibility.

Years after Murphy's death, an article appeared in *Abbott's Monthly* that might explain what kept him from victory. Describing a race in which he and Murphy had been the focus of foul play, a former jockey revealed how Murphy could have been prevented from making a run for the grand prize:

I was a much younger rider than he was, and he seemed to take a liking to me. Might have been because I told him of times when other jockeys were trying to frame the race against him.

You see, Murphy would never agree to pull a horse or enter into a deal to throw a race; nobody can ever say that about him. So finally, some jockeys would get together and plan to shut him out entirely in a race.

On the way to the paddock one day, I muttered to Murphy that something was about to happen in that race. It was a big field, and the time was well-chosen for any trick.

Following his usual custom, Murphy laid off the pace. Going into the backstretch he had a good position in the outside about half-length behind me, and I was laying the same distance back of the first horse. Behind us were twelve others bunched closely.

. . . As we come near the three quarter pole, Murphy be-
gins to move forward, but just when he is passing me, two more
horses come up on the outside and start bearing him in. The
jockey inside me pulls out a little ahead.

In a flash Murphy catches the drift and swings his right
foot quickly into the neck of the horse closing him in. This
throws the horse off stride back into the other one, and in that
instant we went on out of the jam.

. . . They had picked the right spot where the judges couldn't
get a clear view, but the funniest part was the boy never reported his horse being kicked by Murphy.[130]

These kinds of narratives help explain how white jockeys colluded
to keep black jockeys from winning the big purses and thus denied
them future opportunities to sign lucrative contracts.

After the Washington Park meeting, rumors spread that Isaac
would be offered the opportunity to ride Boundless in the Realization Stakes at Sheepshead Bay, because Garrison had had a falling out with Cushing.[131] Garrison was unhappy that he hadn't been
paid more for the American Derby win; he received whatever had
been agreed to before the race. Perhaps Garrison had promised a
few jockeys a portion of his winnings (for their help in tying up
Murphy), and the payoffs cost him more than expected. As it turned
out, Isaac didn't ride in the Realization Stakes. Instead of heading to
New York, he stayed in Chicago, taking mounts from the Flash Stables and Ed Corrigan and finishing second and third, respectively,
over a three-day period.[132] After collecting his earnings and paying
his debts, Isaac and Lucy boarded the eastbound train to New York
for engagements at Monmouth Park and Saratoga.

From July 7 to August 8, Isaac raced at Monmouth Park, Saratoga, and the Brooklyn Jockey Club, showing in five races and finishing out of the money in a dozen others. Not until he returned
west to Chicago for the Hawthorne Park fall meeting in October
would his number of mounts increase, as well as his income. From
October to December, Isaac finished in the money nineteen times:
two first-place, ten second-place, and seven third-place finishes. By

year's end, it was clear he had experienced a sharp reduction in the number of races run and in the number of big stakes victories.

Whether by coincidence or as a result of the growing animosity between white and black jockeys, there was a surge in the number of images depicting black jockeys as stereotypical Sambos and coons, especially by printmakers Nathaniel Currier and James Merritt Ives. Their Darktown series of lithographs perpetuated the common stereotypes associated with African Americans—in particular, the unsavory and uncivilized representations of African American athletes and politicians. There is no doubt that the purpose of these lithographs and other artistic representations was to humiliate and to erase any sense of humanity, manhood, and pride that black men derived from their occupations. More important, the images helped white men cope with the fact that the myth of white supremacy was jeopardized each time a black man succeeded. Unfortunately, the series of lithographs and dozens of advertisements lampooned black jockeys as idiotic buffoons, incapable of achieving anything that could be considered significant or important. These images influenced how black jockeys were later depicted in American history—as inconsequential footnotes to the sport of horse racing.

Trainers were also considered fair game. In the July 22, 1893, edition of the *Live Stock Record*, Albert Cooper was depicted as a hapless Negro who lacked the capacity to be a celebrated trainer of Thoroughbred horses:

When Albert Cooper . . . was training for E. J. Baldwin, some years back he asked the latter along in the fall for a balancing of accounts. Cooper had, of course, drawn money on account, and needed the balance due him. Baldwin acquiesced, and taking out his memorandum book and pencil began to figure. After some minutes he said: "Well, Albert, there was so much due you, and you have drawn so much. Difference in my favor, $82 overdraft. In other words, you owe me $82." Cooper's face was a study at this. He figured that there were several hundred dollars due him, and here he was in debt $82? Finally he said to Baldwin: "Gib me de book and pencil, boss." Taking

THE PRINCE OF JOCKEYS

them he imitated Baldwin's motions of addition and subtraction, pored over them for awhile and handed them back with: "Dat's all right boss. Aught for aught, figger for a figger, all for the white man; nuffin for [the] nigger." As Cooper can neither read nor write, the humorous aspect of the episode and its mirthful echoes have not died away yet.[133]

From all accounts, Cooper was as shrewd a trainer as he was a businessman. The fact that Baldwin was known to underpay his farm and stable workers was likely the origin of the story, embellished to denigrate Cooper. Besides being another example of the media's perpetuation of stereotypes, the story undermined Cooper's history as a successful trainer for owners such as Theodore Winters and J. B. Haggin.[134] Cooper eventually developed his own public stable, where he trained horses for several owners, as well as his own stable of Thoroughbreds, some of which cost him upward of $15,000.[135] Clearly, Cooper (like Isaac and many others) was no buffoon, but that did not stop the caricatures and iconography that removed all humanity from black subjects. Something more ominous was happening to horse racing that neither Cooper nor Murphy could have anticipated.

On December 18, less than two weeks after Isaac and Lucy returned to their home in Lexington, the *Baltimore Sun* reported that he had announced his intent to retire as a professional rider. The article speculated on the reason for this decision: that Isaac had "become fat in the last two years, and any attempted reduction in flesh would be a menace to health and even life. Being independent in fortune, he feels like retiring and spending the remainder of his days in ease."[136] Whether Isaac had alluded to his retirement in Chicago or whether the story was fabricated to elicit a response from him is not known. However, we do know that the *Live Stock Record* refuted both Isaac's retirement and his weight problem: "Murphy is now at his home in this city and his health is greatly improved." What is more, Isaac is "lighter than he has been for several years. He will most likely ride in the East next season."[137] If he had planned to retire from racing before the *Baltimore Sun* article appeared, Isaac's sense of pride and dignity may have caused him to change his mind. He was his own man, and he would retire when he was ready to do so.

On January 4, 1894, the most "prominent horsemen in the East" gathered at the Hoffman House in New York City to begin the process of establishing a National Jockey Club to regulate Thoroughbred racing.[138] Led by Dr. James Robert Keene, the new organization would be run by powerful men of "industry, finance, politics and sports" whose real interest was the integrity of horse racing and the enforcement of uniform rules throughout the United States.[139] However, it was not without controversy. The National Jockey Club used intimidation to force other jockey clubs to join the organization; if they refused, their races would be boycotted by the most influential stables in America. The club also implemented an application process for trainers and jockeys in an effort to regulate who could be employed. Along with these changes, the *Live Stock Record* reported the invention of a new starting device to prevent "dishonest jockeys" from having an unfair advantage.[140] The canvas and wood contraption was said to be able to start a race within five minutes' time, reducing the degree of jockeying for position and making horse racing more consistent. The game was evolving at a rapid pace to meet the needs of the owners and the spectators, especially those in the East.

Isaac, who was not naïve by any means, was well aware of what was happening to horse racing. He recognized that many of the changes were influenced by those who wanted to ensure the sport's honesty and provide good entertainment to spectators. However, he also knew that white jockeys and owners were likely colluding to reduce the number of mounts available to black jockeys, and if he wanted to remain relevant, he would have to find a place in horse racing's future. In the media he was very clear about his intentions for the 1894 season: "I am just as well now as I ever was and I cannot understand the report started that I had retired from the saddle. My present weight is about 115 pounds. So you see I am in pretty good shape. To keep my flesh hard I have a small gymnasium at home, where I punch the bag, swing clubs, etc. I can ride as light now as I could several years ago."[141] A man of his times, Isaac understood the value of physical fitness and year-round training to keep his body ready for the next grueling season. With regard to his contract situation, Isaac explained that he planned to ride in the "East, but as yet I have not made arrangements to ride for any particular stable. I will have a few horses in training myself that will race in the west."[142]

By March, Murphy had not registered his colors with the American Turf Congress, a good indication that his stable was not active; however, he had reportedly been working with a promising three-year-old filly.[143] Most important, Isaac had received several offers to ride but had not signed with a stable for the coming season.[144] There could have been a number of reasons for this, including a waning desire to expose himself to the exceedingly hostile environment at the tracks; too little money offered for his services, given the expenses he incurred as an independent contractor; and a reluctance to commit to the brutal routine required to make weight for another season.

The *Live Stock Record* reported Murphy's thoughts about how modern jockeyship had changed: "Many promising boys were ruined with instruction usually given to them in sprinting races 'get off in front and die there.' They are not given the opportunities to develop the faculty of judging pace, which he considers the prime pre-requisite in a jockey. He laid particular stress upon the point that the horse generally had more to do with winning the race than the jockey, although he said poor jockeys had beaten many a good horse."[145] For the seasoned veteran, new challenges threatened to make a mockery of him and his success.

At the end of March, Isaac decided not to go away without a fight. He officially registered and paid the necessary fees to secure his licenses as a jockey, trainer, and owner, all of which were granted by the National Jockey Club.[146] On April 14 he registered four horses from his stable: a chestnut colt named Valliant, a bay colt named Norvin, a brown filly named Enid, and an unnamed bay gelding. He registered his colors as blue with orange sleeves, and he named his operation Netherland Stables.[147] Clearly, he was attempting to make a point, naming his stable after a country involved in the slave trade and claiming the Princevlag colors (absent white) as a signifier of that historical fact. His horses' names were also distinctly European: Valliant, after Villiars the Valiant or Simon the Valiant from the British tales of King Arthur; Norvin, which means "friend of the north" in German; and Enid, which means "soul" in Welsh. (Perhaps the nameless bay gelding represented black jockeys.) Isaac thus demonstrated not only his knowledge of British literature but also his knowledge of history, culture, and language.

By the end of the Lexington spring meeting, Isaac had started in six races, finishing out of the money in five and taking a second-place finish on Valliant on May 10, earning $50 for Netherland Stables.[148] One week later, Isaac had his stable in Louisville ready to participate in the Louisville Jockey Club meeting and demonstrate his ability as an owner and trainer in the venue where he had become famous as a winning jockey. On May 16, in a purse race for $400, Isaac's Valliant won first prize.[149] Three days later, Valliant, ridden by Alonzo Clayton, took second place.[150] At Latonia on May 31, Valliant took the $500 first prize in the second race of the day, with Henry Williams aboard.[151] On June 8, Valliant took another first prize worth $400.[152] Overall, Netherland Stables finished with $730 in profits from the two victories by Valliant, but for whatever reason, the operation was dissolved.

In early June Isaac was offered a chance to participate in the stage production of *The Derby Winner*, which featured a cast of forty-two actors and six real racehorses, including the retired Freeland. Written by Al Spink of the *Sporting News*, the play was performed in October in midwestern cities such as Omaha and Lincoln, Nebraska, and St. Louis and Kansas City, Missouri. Among the many reviewers, writer Willa Cather was so critical of the play that she would not publish the names of the actors, for fear it would ruin their future opportunities.[153] Isaac was a businessman, and if the play could provide him with an income, he was willing to sign on. He was not the only professional athlete to take to the stage. In 1893 the great black Australian prizefighter Peter Jackson had played the role of Tom in Charles E. Davies's "spectacular production" of Harriet Beecher Stowe's *Uncle Tom's Cabin*.[154] In an almost voyeuristic way, the spectacle was enhanced by Jackson's presence, and he drew people to the theater whose real interest was seeing the "black prince" of boxing.

In December *Spirit of the Times* ran a story announcing that the once highly revered jockey Isaac Murphy was the "drawing card" for the play *The Derby Winner*. The spectator aspects of the production would no doubt appeal to horse-racing fans interested in seeing living history.[155] Isaac, who played himself riding Freeland, was an attraction to theatergoers and basically served as a prop or an artifact from a historical moment. Many saw Murphy's willingness to participate in the campy production as an indicator of his demise as a jockey. The *New York Times* seized the opportunity to point this out:

> Isaac Murphy, the colored jockey, who up to the time of his performance on Firenzi at Monmouth Park, three years ago, was considered one of the best riders of the turf, is in hard luck. Since his drunken exhibition referred to, he has not been able to secure much employment. He has always been extravagant in his habits, with a marvelous capacity for champagne. "The Smoked Archer," as he was called is now riding the famous old gelding Freeland in a play called "The Derby Winner," which is being performed in the West. He wears Ed Corrigan's colors, just as he did when he rode Freeland in this great race against Miss Woodford at the Brighton Beach track ten years ago.[156]

Four years after Isaac had been exonerated of any wrongdoing at Monmouth, the *New York Times* was still suggesting that his fall from grace had been the result of high living. These kinds of stories appealed to whites who were threatened by black competition. They were signs of a changing American landscape where the social, economic, and political aspects of everyday life were interconnected, and whiteness had to be defended as relevant. The one way Isaac knew how to quiet his critics (and there were many) was to win, and 1895 presented another season and another opportunity to do so.

On March 14, 1895, Isaac left the Fayette County courthouse with his fourteen-year-old apprentice, James Frazer, in tow. Judge Bullock had just appointed him Frazer's guardian. The boy had been living in the countryside just outside Lexington when his mother died. How he became a ward of the county and apprenticed to Isaac is not known, but his grandmother, Charlotte Frazer, was not happy about the judge's ruling. Under the law, Isaac was required to "pay the boy or his father, grandmother or whoever claimed it $5 per month and clothe and feed the lad until he becomes of age."[157] Mrs. Frazer sought counsel to help her remove her grandson from the Murphy home, but the judge would not reverse his ruling, and the grandmother vowed to "get even with Mr. Murphy."[158] Just how she intended to do so, she didn't say. Isaac was interested in training the boy to be a jockey and shaping his character in a positive way. Perhaps Isaac and Lucy thought of young James as the child they always wanted.

Since the beginning of February, Isaac had been training for the 1895 season and the possibility of returning to the East, where there was plenty of money to be made riding quality mounts in large stakes races. He had known the glory of winning at Saratoga and at Monmouth Park. And he knew that if he wanted to get back on top, he would have to prove he was the same reliable jockey of old—the one who could take fans' breath away as he finished a close race by a head or a nose. By April, the *Kansas City Times* was reporting that Isaac had trained down to 112 pounds and was in "better shape to ride than in years."[159]

Traveling to Tennessee to ride in the new Memphis Jockey Club races, Isaac no doubt wanted to show well after being somewhat absent for a year. It's not clear whether he had any mounts before April 15, but we do know he rode to a third-place finish that day on Caracas, son of his old friend Emperor of Norfolk, owned by E. J. Baldwin.[160] While Isaac was in Tennessee making a comeback bid, his friend and protégé Willie Simms was in England winning praise at

New Market after his victory in the Crawford Stakes on Utica, the three-year-old owned by Philip Dwyer and Richard Croker.[161] Prior to leaving for England, Willie had consulted with Isaac about racing in Europe. Young jockeys like Simms, Hamilton, Overton, and Clayton considered Isaac a mentor and a model of professionalism and success, as well as a friend and adviser. Although Simms could not have known it, Isaac's career was coming to a close as his own was about take off.

On April 26, the opening day of the Lexington spring meeting, Isaac finished in the money in two events—taking third in the inaugural Scramble worth $25, and claiming the $275 first-place prize for T. C. McDowell in the fifth race of the day.[162] Riding in front of his hometown crowd, Isaac had every reason to believe he was poised to reclaim his status as a champion jockey. With Lucy watching from the stands, Isaac had the support of the one person who knew him better than he knew himself.

When the western meetings ended, the bulk of participants (owners, trainers, grooms, and jockeys) shifted their focus and resources to the East, where the money was good—even great—in the better contests. In early May, Isaac and Lucy were in New York (and later in Red Bank, New Jersey), where several good mounts and good money awaited.

On May 15 an early-morning shower made the air cold and crisp at the track at Gravesend. The rain had formed puddles, revealing the lowest spots in the track and indicating that the evening races would be slow and muddy.[163] Some horses would be more affected than others by the rain-soaked track. For the Brooklyn Handicap, the bookmakers' favorites Dr. Rice and Ramapo were evenly matched in a field of competitors that included J. R. and F. P. Keene's Hornpipe, ridden by Anthony Hamilton, and Erie Stables' Lazzarone, ridden by Isaac Murphy. By noon, the sun had come out from behind the clouds, and with it some hope for a drier race.

After the preliminary races, Isaac and the other eleven jockeys weighed in for the Brooklyn Handicap. Because of the track conditions, Isaac would have to use all his skill and know-how to keep the 20:1 underdog Lazzarone in contention. The same was true of Hamilton on the lightweight colt Hornpipe, which the bookmakers predicted would be swallowed up by the field of proven winners. By four o'clock in the afternoon, the stands were crowded with young and old racing fans eager to place their bets and hoping for a windfall.

As the horses appeared on the track, cheers went up from the stands. Splendid specimens of horseflesh snorted at the ground and in the air, their muscles relaxed yet firm to the naked eye. Isaac galloped past the stands on the "large muscular thoroughbred" Lazzarone.[164] Backers of the great horses watched as their pilots jockeyed for position at the post. When the flag fell at 4:45 PM, a dozen horses and their jockeys dashed to take the rail and set the pace. Isaac got out quickly on Lazzarone but was caught up in a mass of horseflesh and knocked back to the eighth position in front of Hamilton on Hornpipe. After six furlongs, several horses dropped out of contention, but Isaac had just begun to ride. Into the stretch, Sir Walter had the lead, and his jockey was pressing him to pull away. Using his whip to urge Lazzarone on, Isaac gained ground inch by inch until he passed Sir Walter and took the lead. At the finish, however, Hamilton, who had been at Isaac's hip, got Hornpipe over the finish line a head in front of his friend and mentor to collect the $10,000 prize.[165] The race was won in unforgettable fashion, with both Murphy and Hamilton using their intelligence and their horses' ability to beat the odds. For the old-time race goers, it was a thing of beauty, reminiscent of the early days when the game was unsullied by bookmakers, politicians, and crooked jockeys out to make a buck.

Although he didn't win, Isaac proved he could still compete against some of the best jockeys. The *New York Herald* credited Isaac for keeping Lazzarone in contention: "Had Lazzarone won a big coup would have been pulled off. Donohue had given him a long, steady 'prep,' and the fact that he had done scarcely any fast work put most people off. Murphy rode a splendid race and deserves every commendation."[166] A few weeks later, Isaac rode Lazzarone to a third-place finish in the Brookdale Handicap, earning $200 for Erie Stables. His next big race on the colt would be the Suburban Handicap at Coney Island on Saturday, June 15, for a first prize of $5,000 and a chance to obtain more mounts.

In preparation for the race, Isaac suggested to Lazzarone's trainer, William Donohue, that they use blinkers to keep the horse from wandering and getting knocked off stride. At Gravesend, Isaac had observed that Lazzarone was sluggish and sulked at the start of the race. He believed blinkers would keep the horse focused straight ahead and encourage him to respond to his guidance without a struggle. In the last workout, Isaac was proved right, as the colt was "much better than the horse had previously shown."[167] For the Suburban Handicap, Lazzarone would wear blinkers.

But on June 15, the day of the race, Donohue replaced Isaac with Anthony Hamilton. For whatever reason, and without any warning, the decision to change jockeys had been made by the trainer and the owners, J. R. and F. D. Beard. Why they chose to do this, and why they waited until the day of race to do so, is a mystery. Frustrated, Isaac watched from the stands as Lazzarone ran a flawless race, outdistancing the field for the win.

After the race, a dejected Murphy commented to the media: Erie Stables had engaged him "to ride Lazzarone, and prevailed on me to stay over here to ride him . . . and then when he wins I have to stand on the ground while Hamilton gets the mount. I reduced so as to make weight, and never knew until this morning Hamilton would ride." Noting that the horse had run with blinkers on, Isaac felt he had been treated "very shabbily" and had been unfairly deprived of a winning mount after riding Lazzarone so successfully in the Brooklyn Handicap.[168] Clearly, the Beard brothers wanted to have the two best jockeys under their control to narrow the competition and ensure victory for Erie Stables. They didn't care about the long-standing friendship between Murphy and Hamilton: it was about winning. Isaac likely felt torn—angry with his friend for taking the mount, and angry with the Beard brothers for treating him with disrespect.

Between July and August, Isaac was offered very few mounts. After a few more forgettable races in the East and accusations that his failure to win or place was the result of being drunk in the saddle, Isaac returned home to Lexington, without any fanfare, to race in the Kentucky Association's fall engagement. By September 14, his record was abysmal: one first-place, one second-place, and seven third-place finishes and ten unplaced mounts. Of all active jockeys, Murphy was at the bottom of the list in wins, winning percentage, and mounts. Back in Lexington, he at least had the comfort of being at home, even though his mind was surely racked with confusion, disappointment, and anger at the unsavory changes in the industry and his lack of success.

On November 13, aboard the Bradley brothers' Tupto, Isaac won in the hands-down fashion the hometown crowd was accustomed to. This was only his second win of the year, and he probably thought it would be perfect to end the season on a high note. Then again, if there was money to be made, who was he to walk away from the opportunity? Six days later, riding Athenian, Isaac finished last in a field of eleven.[169] The irony may have been lost on the spectators, but the great black jockey whose life had followed all the twists and turns of America's struggle to accept African Americans as citizens rode his last race on a horse whose name was representative of the origin of modern democracy. Based on the outcome of this particular race, democracy was dead. Isaac Murphy was done.

Quite plainly, Isaac Murphy's time had passed. Exactly when that happened is anyone's guess. Perhaps it was before the mysterious sickness that sullied his reputation and seriously injured his career. Maybe it happened when he decided to go east rather than west to California, where the millionaire miners would have welcomed talented jockeys like Isaac to teach them about horse racing's traditions. Whenever or wherever it happened, Isaac was caught in a changing society that villainized black people and in a changing industry that he had helped grow but now dismissed him. In the end, it was not a lack of talent or diminishing skills that caused Isaac Murphy to fade from the racecourses he had once dominated; it was the changing times and a new politics of the turf influenced by urbanization, capitalism, industrialization, and racism. He was a throwback to a time that promised dignity and honor for the patient and obedient, based on the mythological pretense of Republicanism.

# 9

# A Pageantry of Woe

## *1896*

On the morning of Sunday, February 16, 1896, a veil of dread descended on the stylish two-story, red-brick Victorian home at 419 East Third Street in Lexington, Kentucky. Four days prior, in the liminal hours between night and day, Lucy Murphy wept as her husband, Isaac Burns Murphy, the famed jockey and hero of the turf, struggled to take his last breath and then died. He had been sick for more than two weeks with a flulike illness, but the possibility of death had not been entertained—at least not publicly. The overcast February morning was not unusual for the time of year, and the cool, crisp air was characteristic of central Kentucky winters. Yet on this particular morning, the grayness of the day lent to the sullen mood. The funeral notices had gone out the day after his death, informing select friends and family that the services would begin at three o'clock at the Murphy residence. As expected, a dozen or so acquaintances arrived early to help ensure that all went as planned. The Reverend Spencer P. Young of Lexington's First Baptist Church would lead the services, followed by a selection of songs by the Lexington Choral Club; time permitting, those closest to the

family would offer condolences. The body would then be escorted
by a procession of the Lincoln and Sardis Lodge of Colored Masons
and the Bethany Commandery of the Knights Templar to African
Cemetery Number 2—the final resting place for thousands of former slaves and free blacks from the Lexington area.

One of the early arrivals was a fifteen-year-old white girl
named Nannie Atchison. Prior to Murphy's death, Nannie had visited the home on numerous occasions to buy milk, butter, and eggs
from Lucy's sister, Susan Osborne. In 1893 Nannie's father, William
Atchison, had moved the family to their new home—a one-story
wood-frame house at 398 Third Street, not far from the Murphys.
Nannie had been raised around horses and horse racing. Her father
worked for Murphy at the Lexington racetrack that backed up to
the Murphys' ten-acre lot, and she sometimes went along to watch.
She knew of Isaac's importance as a jockey and had listened to her
father and other men defend him when he was accused of being
drunk in 1890 at Monmouth Park. She had heard the rumor that he
had been drugged because of his unwillingness to throw races and
the speculation that he had become a target of powerful white men
in the East.

Isaac's success on the oval track had been the pride of Lexington. He would say: "I am as proud of my calling as I am of my
record, and I believe my life will be recorded a success, though the
reputation I enjoy was earned in the stable and in the saddle. It is
a great honor to be classed as one of America's greatest jockeys."[1]
His three Kentucky Derby victories (in 1884, 1890, and 1891) and
hundreds of wins in Nashville, Louisville, St. Louis, Chicago, Saratoga, and New York made fans and enthusiasts of the turf rich and
brought positive attention to the thriving horse industry, which employed thousands from central Kentucky. Like royalty, the Murphys
moved in and out of various social circles, befriending influential
black and white doctors, lawyers, and business owners from one
coast to the other. Many recalled the Murphys' home in Lexington
as the scene of lively parties and joyous celebrations. As a popular
hero to many, Isaac Murphy worked to balance his responsibilities
as a community leader, a husband, and the most successful jockey of

his generation. He was a conduit between the black community and the powerful white elite of Lexington.

Nannie entered the Murphy home, where the air was thick with the perfume of the floral arrangements, wreaths, and bouquets of exotic flowers sent by Murphy's friends and contemporaries. In the parlor, next to the casket, was a large display of lilies of the valley, sent by three of the owners Murphy had ridden for: Ed Corrigan, L. P. Tarleton, and Ed Brown. These gestures of condolence, remembrance, and appreciation were touching, to say the least.

Also in attendance were the great black jockeys Anthony Hamilton and James "Soup" Perkins, who had benefited greatly from their friendship with Murphy. Hamilton was a personal friend, and Perkins, the winner of two Kentucky Derbies, had learned how to judge the pace of a horse from Murphy. Isaac frequently discussed his racing philosophy with anyone who showed an interest in his approach to riding and to life. To Nannie Atchison and the hundreds of mourners lining up in the cold to pay their respects, Murphy was a paragon of virtue. She ventured into the parlor to view Murphy's small, lifeless body dressed in black and the traditional white gloves and apron of a Mason. He was resting in a beautiful copper casket covered in purple crushed velvet with silver trimmings, a replica of President Ulysses S. Grant's coffin. Nannie would remember Isaac as a "nice, neatly dressed, very clean and very pleasant person" with a gentle disposition.[2]

The mood throughout Lexington was heavy with sorrow, reminiscent of the passing of a great leader. Very early that Sunday morning, the Murphy residence came alive with activity. In the early afternoon, after wading through the thick crowd of mourners, Reverend Young greeted those invited to attend the private ceremony. A member of the Prince Hall Masons, Young had counseled Isaac and Lucy on matters of faith and virtue and had officiated when they renewed their wedding vows in 1893 in front of family and friends. On this day, however, those gathered in the densely packed rooms adjoining the parlor listened as Young eulogized the man who had risen from slavery to become a beacon of light among the colored and white peoples of Lexington. He reminded the mourners of Murphy's early life as the son of slaves, the death of his father while serving as a Union soldier during the Civil War, and his determined mother, who worked as a washerwoman, laundress, and housekeeper to ensure her son's future. Those gathered in the Murphy home recalled the oppression of slavery and the stories handed down and across generations about Africa and about black men like Samuel Oldham, who had claimed his freedom and thrived as a businessman in Lexington. They remembered the human trains leaving the slave market at Cheapside, heading south to Mississippi and Louisiana, a death sentence for most. They recalled children being traded for plows and livestock, families being separated without remorse, and the failed attempts to claim freedom by running away.

Reverend Young described how blessed Murphy had been to be brought up in a Negro community that valued education, religion, and moral uprightness. And Murphy had demonstrated his appreciation by staying close to home, contributing to the growth of his community, and by being an example to the colored children and adults of Lexington. In addition to Isaac's mother and father, he spoke of Eli Jordan, the outstanding trainer who had been like a father to Isaac when he needed guidance and direction. He then turned and looked at each of the jockeys in the room, noting how Murphy had influenced their careers and encouraged them to maintain their integrity in a sport where money and vice threatened to destroy the fiber of the soul.

Reverend Young recognized the fellowship and brotherhood Murphy had enjoyed as a member of the Lincoln Lodge Masons, as well as the support and friendship of men like John C. Jackson, H. A. Tandy, Dr. Perry Robinson, Dr. John Hunter, and Dudley Allen, to name but a few. Finally, Young turned to Lucy Murphy, the widow of the great black jockey, consoling her with the knowledge that she had been a good and faithful wife and that her nurturing of her husband's soul had benefited all who loved and cherished him. She need not worry about him, for he was now with his maker and with his mother and father, and together they were rejoicing among the angels in heaven.

At the conclusion of the eulogy, the Lexington Choral Club, led by Henry Tandy, solidified the mood with selections that reminded those in attendance of their religious faith and their shared past. Even in this late Victorian age, Negro spirituals uplifted those who had grown up in slavery and then flourished in freedom. Singing a familiar Negro spiritual, Dr. Robinson's deep baritone invoked memories of the past, and the words could be heard by those waiting patiently on the frozen lawn in front of the Murphy residence:

Wade in the water
Wade in the water, children,
Wade in the water
God's a-going to trouble the water

See that host all dressed in white
God's a-going to trouble the water
The leader looks like the Israelite
God's a-going to trouble the water
See that band all dressed in red
God's a-going to trouble the water
Looks like the band that Moses led
God's a-going to trouble the water

Look over yonder, what do you see?
God's a-going to trouble the water
The Holy Ghost a-coming on me
God's a-going to trouble the water

If you don't believe I've been redeemed
God's a-going to trouble the water
Just follow me down to the Jordan's stream
God's a-going to trouble the water

After Robinson's moving rendition, the entire chorus sang "Down by the Riverside," which brought the gathering to their feet, rocking and swaying, serving as a temporary elixir to ease their collective unhappiness. Even so, Lucy felt the hurt and emptiness of the loss of her best friend and lover.

Throughout their thirteen years of marriage, Lucy and Isaac had rarely been apart. Lucy had married Isaac for love and security; Isaac had married Lucy for love and companionship. He had protected her from the vulnerabilities and abuses other black women experienced in the marketplace; he had secured her future as a middle-class woman. She had helped him build his professional career as a jockey and a businessman, encouraging him to shed his introverted nature and pushing him to enjoy the benefits of his hard work. Isaac's marriage to Lucy was the key to his consistency as an athlete. He found comfort and purpose in their collaboration. Suffice it to say, Lucy's destiny was inextricably linked to Isaac's: if he was hurt, she too suffered.

The Murphys were upper middle class, respectable, and religious, and with Isaac's death, Lucy felt a responsibility to properly honor and memorialize his good name and noble character. Moreover, there was a certain etiquette that Lucy had to adhere to, paying particular attention to her appearance and her performance at the funeral. To ensure that her husband retained his dignity, even in death, she employed the services of Porter and Jackson Undertakers, owned and operated by William Jackson and John C. Jackson, two prominent leaders of Lexington's black community. The undertakers made arrangements for the embalming of Murphy's body, ordered the replica of President Grant's casket, and helped coordinate the day's program with Reverend Young. Lucy's sister Susan helped draft the funeral announcement and answered many of the inquiries directed at Lucy. She too was aware of the need to keep up appearances and ensured that Lucy was properly attired in a stylish black mourning dress and black gloves.

As the front door of the Murphy residence opened, the 500 or so people still gathered outside cleared a path to the hearse waiting to take the prince of jockeys to his final resting place. In full regalia, members of the Bethany Commandery Knights Templar, directed by Marshall T. Clay, formed two columns leading from the interior of the home to the hearse parked on the street. Pallbearers Scott Williams, John T. Clay, Henry Mack, Lee Christy, Howard Williams, Ed Brown, William Walker, and Henry S. Walker carried Murphy's remains to the waiting vehicle. Gently they placed the copper casket through the rear opening and slowly pushed it forward until it rolled to a stop; the undertakers then secured the casket inside the vehicle. Members of the Lincoln and Sardis Lodges and Bethany Commandery then moved into position in front of the hearse driven by David Samuels, a neighbor of the Murphys. After Lucy was inside her carriage and everyone was in place, Commander Clay signaled the beginning of the procession. Hundreds of people dressed in black funeral wear settled in the carriages lined up side by side, and they slowly moved westward on Third Street in a familiar "pageantry of woe." As a final show of respect, Lexington's citizens lined the streets to watch. Black and white families stood in awe at the spectacle of Murphy's funeral procession. Most recognized the significance of the moment and paused to mark the occasion.[3]

As the carriages neared Limestone Street, the hearse driver saw hundreds of people waiting at the intersection—the curious wanting to know what was happening, and the reverent wanting one final look at the famous jockey. The various classes and races present in the crowd were a clear indicator of Murphy's impact on the larger Lexington community. Moving up Limestone, crossing Fourth, Fifth, and Sixth Streets, then finally making a right turn onto Seventh Street, the procession edged closer to the cemetery. As the first part of the procession reached the gates of the black burial grounds, snow began to fall. With military precision, the Masons and Bethany Commandery formed two lines on either side of the casket as it was carried to the rectangular hollow that would receive Murphy's remains. After all were gathered around, the Masonic rites were bestowed on the deceased, and Reverend Young offered the benediction, perhaps from Genesis 3:16: "And the Lord said, 'In the sweat of thy face shalt thou eat bread, till thou return unto the ground; for out of it wast thou taken: for dust thou art, and unto dust shalt thou return.'" Amid the sobs and tears of the mourners, the casket was lowered into the cold, hard ground. The final ritual was left to the men handling the shovels, still clumped with dirt from their morning chore of preparing the ground. The grief-stricken masses watched as the men spilled earth down over the casket and filled in the void. As the snow began to cover the cemetery in a blanket of white, the final shovel of dirt was passed over the mound, and the wooden marker was hammered into the ground, indicating the final resting place of the prince of jockeys.

# Epilogue

Putting a life into perspective in a way that is not only meaningful but also revealing of the choices and decisions made in the context of events, intended or otherwise, can be a difficult proposition. This is especially true when there are no personal papers or archives to consult. In this case, gathering the threads, shards, and jagged pieces of a life can be a painstaking task. Biography involves the exploration and clarification of the past in ways that may not fit traditional means of writing historical narratives. Revealing the world into which a person is born, lives, and eventually dies requires an interdisciplinary approach that utilizes various sources and analytical methods to draw conclusions. Invariably, the intent is to explore and understand the multitude of factors responsible for shaping the individual the biographer has deemed captivating and worthy of a commitment of time, resources, and energy. The biographer's mandate is to leave little doubt in the minds of readers.

The life of Isaac Burns Murphy followed the contours of American history. He was born during slavery and died at the beginning of Jim Crow segregation, one of the many crossroads in America's social, economic, and political development. He was raised in a community that took seriously the promises of the Declaration of Independence, and Isaac's achievements were a testament to black Lexington's commitment to its future, as demonstrated by its commitment to its children. Through the efforts of teachers, ministers, and common folk, Isaac understood that his own achievement was a sign of the community's progress and advancement. Isaac knew that he represented the people he came from, and he honored his past by remaining a part of the Lexington community.

Lucy Murphy became an example of black womanhood that challenged many popular notions of who could claim to be a "lady." Educated, beautiful, and a key component of Isaac's success, Lucy helped shape the man who would be identified as an elegant specimen of manhood. Both Isaac and Lucy were instrumental in elevating the black professional jockey to an occupation that was considered the equal of a doctor or lawyer. It is clear that they had a great impact on both their friends and outside observers who viewed Murphy as the quintessential jockey whose legendary status grew with every victory, every quote published, and every dignified likeness produced for public consumption.

After the death of her husband, Lucy still had her sister Susan and Lexington's black community for support. However, nothing could minimize the loss of her beloved Isaac. For a long time, she kept flowers on his grave. Records show that Lucy continued to live at the Third Street home until around 1903, when she sold the property and moved with Susan to 347 North Limestone Street. Lucy apparently exhausted her savings and the money left to her in Isaac's will,[1] because at some point she began to work as a housekeeper in Lexington to support herself. On February 24, 1910, Lucy died of pneumonia at her home, shortly after the fourteenth anniversary of her husband's death. The lone photograph of Lucy is in the T. T. Wendell Collection at the Kentucky Historical Society. She was beautiful.

More than 100 years after Isaac's death, there is growing interest in the history of black jockeys and their impact on the sport of kings. Previously, depictions of black jockeys were limited to lawn statues, the caricatures used in advertisements for horse liniments, and the Sambo-like figures in the lithographs made popular by Currier and Ives. Clearly, these did not reflect the contributions of black jockeys to the greatness of the sport. Unfortunately for African Americans, the emphasis has not been on the totality of a life lived during the tumultuous period between the Civil War and the end of the nineteenth century, or on the achievements in all things among that first generation born at the end of slavery. For most, the success of black jockeys in the nineteenth century is seen as some form of racial superiority connected to their athleticism. The history of black jockeys is not understood as an extension of the institution of slavery, which evolved into a critical example of agency in the context of horse racing during Reconstruction and the decade that followed.

Initially, horse racing was primarily a leisure activity of the wealthy, upper-class elite, and participation as a horse owner required a certain birthright. For a brief time, black jockeys were lionized as "artists of the pigskin" and "heroes of the turf," but then their significance dissolved into nothingness. Yet it always surprises me when people say with disbelief, "There were black jockeys?" The history of horse racing is directly linked to the South and gentlemen farmers, so I often respond by pointing out that someone had to clear the land, cultivate the fields, and raise the crops; someone had to build the barns and fences to maintain the livestock; and someone had to care for those animals, which required early-morning feedings as well as the grooming and training of horses. Presidents George Washington and Andrew Jackson and some of the wealthiest men in America had horses on their estates, and a majority of them owned slaves. Without a doubt, enslaved African Americans were responsible for taking care of these animals, so it was natural that they developed into outstanding jockeys. They were always there, in the background and foreground, both directly and indirectly, maintaining the façade of white supremacy.

Isaac Murphy's rise as the premier jockey of his day coincided with the many opportunities that opened up for blacks in the postbellum period, especially during Reconstruction. The fact that he was able to read and write from an early age, gain access to the wealthiest Americans (who paid him well for his services), and use his purchasing power as a capitalist made him a model for resistance to popular notions of black inferiority. He was a modern black man who would defend his integrity when challenged, using his words not only sparingly but also strategically. If the notion of black manhood was stained by past ideas related to polygenesis or a religious understanding of who had been made to serve whom, his success and public civility contributed to the unraveling of racist ideas with an eloquence that was both disarming and maddening to rabid white supremacists.

Murphy's example of what African Americans could achieve when competing on a level playing field became the focus of black leaders such as T. Thomas Fortune, who recognized that public spectacles like horse racing could provide metaphors for American race relations. For Fortune, the question of identity was not that much of a concern for blacks, who were in the process of developing a new sense of themselves as first-class citizens through their striving and development; in contrast, whites' ideas about civilization and their place in it were unraveling quickly because most whites believed the myth of black inferiority. The public success of black men and women caused whites to question who they were, how these changes in society would shape their futures, and, ultimately, what they could do to make it stop.

The realization that blacks could rise above their previous station based on their pursuit of education, gainful employment, and power as consumers undermined whites' sense of racial superiority. In the spring of 1896, three months after Isaac's death, the Supreme Court's decision in *Plessy v. Ferguson* heralded the beginning of Jim Crow segregation. The "separate but equal" policy adopted by the U.S. government unleashed hell on earth for African Americans, who became the focus of retribution by whites jealous of their success. Subjected to public humiliation, harassment, and even lynching, African Americans were forced to fight back, leave their homes, or learn to negotiate the changing times using the skills honed during slavery.

Murphy's death also marked the demise of the black jockey in American horse racing. By the end of the century, only a handful of quality black jockeys could be found on American racetracks. Great riders like Anthony Hamilton (1866–1904), Willie Simms (1870–1927), and Jimmy Winkfield (1882–1974), the last black jockey to win the Kentucky Derby, were shut out by a system that favored white jockeys and wanted to rid the tracks of black competition. Eventually, all three would leave the United States to race in Europe.

In 1895 Simms became the first American jockey to win a race at Newmarket in England, riding an American Thoroughbred named Eau Gallie. Simms's style of riding on the neck of his horse was ridiculed by the English elite, until he won the Crawford Plate at Newmarket.[2] His success helped change how the English thought about horse racing and jockeyship. In 1901 Simms traveled to France and raced at the Jockey Club in Paris. After retiring, Simms made a name for himself as a capable trainer, using his expertise to teach young riders about jockeyship. He later developed an interest in steeplechase racing and helped shape the sport with his style of riding. Simms would die in 1927, outliving Murphy by nearly thirty years.

The same year Murphy died, his close friend Anthony Hamilton became the focus of a scheme to purge horse racing of its most visible and successful black riders. Accused of pulling a horse at Brighton Beach on July 23, 1896, Hamilton was suspended and brought before Jockey Club officials. After a meeting with the stewards, who questioned him about his "peculiar rides on Hornpipe," he was allowed to return to racing.[3] Despite the stewards' findings and the lack of evidence that Hamilton had done anything wrong, like Murphy, he too became the focus of racial taunts and slurs. On the track, white jockeys colluded to keep him from winning major races by boxing him in, which would eventually limit the number of mounts he was offered and the amount of money he could make. Like Simms, Hamilton would eventually leave America for Europe. In 1901 he was contracted to ride for J. Metcalf, who owned one of the most important stables in Austria-Hungary. Later that year Hamilton applied for a passport to St. Petersburg, Russia, where he would race Russian-bred horses for wealthy breeders in Warsaw. Hamilton's success in Europe would end with his untimely death in Italy in 1904.

Following the death of Hamilton, Jimmy Winkfield also left the United States for Europe, where he earned a living racing horses for wealthy owners in Russia and Austria-Hungary. With back-to-back Kentucky Derby victories (1901 and 1902), Winkfield had been one of the top jockeys in the United States, but like Hamilton, he chose to leave because of the hostile environment. European jock eying paid well, and it was attracting talent from several countries. In the "Land of the Czars," Winkfield became the premier jockey for General Michael Lazareu, whose wealth and love of horses made the duo a lethal combination on Russian tracks, especially in the Warsaw Derby. Over a ten-year period, Winkfield would earn hundreds of thousands of dollars, marry interracially, move to France, and live like no other American jockey could have imagined. Winkfield was the last of the great black jockeys, and with his death in 1974, the era came to a close. The memories associated with them also began to fade into obscurity.

In 1955, the year Isaac Murphy became the first black jockey inducted into the National Museum of Racing's Hall of Fame in Saratoga, New York, controversy erupted over where he had been buried. The *Lexington Herald* carried the erroneous wire story from Mobile, Alabama:

> There are perhaps still a few around who recall the tragic death some 58 years ago in a spill at the old Lexington track where some 15 horses trampled him [Isaac Murphy] to death. But even fewer probably recall that his body was shipped to Mobile, Alabama, and buried in a white cemetery.
>
> It was the wish of Willie Cottrill, owner of Buchanan, Murphy's first Derby winner, that the jockey be buried in the family plot. The owner and breeder, one of the wealthy men of his time, died before Murphy, but his wish was carried out. A head marker once designated the jockey's grave, but it has long since disappeared.[4]

Clearly, the paternalistic tone of this editorial harks back to a time when white men could lay claim to black bodies as property, in life and in death. Joe Thomas, a reporter for the *Lexington Herald*, wrote a the response that would begin the search for Isaac Murphy. "Faux pas," Thomas began his June 28, 1955, column:

> Isaac Murphy was not killed in a spill at the old Lexington track. He is buried in Lexington and it was very unlikely that

his body was ever sent to Mobile, Alabama, for internment in the family plot of Willie Cottrill, owner of Buchanan, Murphy's first Kentucky Derby winner.

This department apparently was the victim of some Alabama folklore, which is now taken for fact. The source of the information in Sunday's Turf Topics was a Mobile newspaper.

Actually, the great Negro rider died in his bed of pneumonia February 12, 1896. He had last ridden at the previous fall at the local track and had won on his last mount. Obituary accounts written at the time make no mention of his burial anywhere but Lexington.[5]

Thomas's column would motivate newspaperman Frank Borries (1914–1968) to look for Murphy's grave and validate the Hall of Fame jockey's final resting place.

Unfortunately, by 1955, African Cemetery Number 2 had been neglected for decades. Overgrown "weeds, briers and brambles" consumed the sacred space and covered the overturned grave markers and headstones. With the help of Gene Webster (the son of Richard Webster, a contemporary of Murphy's), Borries located the burial site of the great jockey from Lexington.[6] All that remained was a four-foot-tall concrete marker, erected in 1909 by a group of men from the community who wanted to honor Murphy's memory. The discovery of the whereabouts of Murphy's grave led to a controversial attempt to honor his memory.

In January 1967 the vice president of the Kentucky Club Tobacco Company, Stuart F. Bloch, saw an opportunity to both gain publicity for his company and honor the memory of Isaac Burns Murphy. The idea was for the tobacco company to create a monument to Murphy and rebury him at Man o' War Park in Lexington, Kentucky. By May, a committee had been formed that included Judge Joe Johnson, Mayor Fred Fugazzi, and Hall of Fame jockey Eddie Arcaro as acting chairman. Apparently, no one discussed the proposal with Lexington's African American community, which would be losing one of its symbols of achievement and success. In addition, this plan would take Isaac away from, Lucy, who had been buried next to him, and separate him from the generations of African Americans buried in the sacred space. Rather than taking Murphy from his community and using his likeness as a commodity, a better course of action would have been to clean up the cemetery and provide funding for its maintenance, but that would have involved a public acknowledgment of past wrongs.

In the years following, Frank Borries began research for a biography on Murphy. Although he was unable to complete it, the project was taken up by his wife, Betty (1915–2006). Her *Isaac Murphy: Kentucky's Record Jockey* (1988) was the first to offer a glimpse of the man who was considered one of the most important jockeys in American horse racing. In subsequent years, sports historians have recognized Murphy's significance as a jockey, but few have depicted him as a man who knew his place in the world. Few have attempted to understand the rootedness provided by African American communities and the sense of agency instilled in their children. The legacy of Isaac Burns Murphy is one of complex origins, a sense of purpose, and an extraordinary degree of intelligence. Lexington, Kentucky, is fortunate to have him as a model of the best kind of nobility: humble, dignified, human.

# Acknowledgments

This project began soon after I completed my doctoral studies at Emory University in 2007. I had never heard of Isaac Burns Murphy until I began researching the importance of sports to African Americans during the mid- to late nineteenth century. Though Murphy's life and career were the focus of the first chapter of my dissertation, the story was far from complete. After consulting with my mentors—the late Rudolph P. Byrd and emeritus professor of urban studies at Emory University, Dana White—I decided to pursue a more in-depth biography of Murphy. Several grants and fellowships allowed me to travel to archives, repositories, and special collections across the country, including a National Endowment for the Humanities Fellowship in American Studies, a John H. Daniels Fellowship at the National Sporting Library for the Study of Horse and Field Sports, a University of Missouri Research Board Grant, a Faculty Research Grant from the University of Missouri–Kansas City, and several Emory University Travel Grants.

I owe tremendous thanks to the archivists and staff members at the numerous repositories I visited over the last ten years. In fact, since the time I started this project, the amount of information available has more than quadrupled. I used both traditional means of researching in the archives, painstakingly reading every newspaper, letter, and diary in the various collections, as well as digital technology, whereby I was able to photograph documents, images, and obscure publications and consult them at my convenience. Still, in my opinion, the sense of discovery one feels among the actual books and collections can never be replaced by technology. I am thankful for all the research librarians and archivists who still get excited about old card catalogs that contain useful information for researchers interested in knowing the price of hemp in 1850 or what kinds of licorice were sold at the general stores in Louisville.

I am a firm believer that the archives and research libraries are essential to understanding the course of human history from a local, national, and global perspective. These include the Keeneland Research Library and Repository; the University of Kentucky Special Collections; the Kentucky Historical Society; the Kentucky State University African American Center for Excellence; the Filson Society; the Churchill Downs Museum; Berea College; the Transylvania University Archives; the Lexington Public Library; the Camp Nelson Foundation; the Camp Nelson National Cemetery; the Alexander Gumby Collection at Columbia University; the Chicago History Museum; the African American Civil War Museum; the Arcadia Public Library; the Bancroft Special Collections at the University of California at Berkeley; Emory University Manuscript, Archives, and Rare Books Library; the Library of Congress; and the Schomburg Center for Research in Black Culture.

While I was on leave from the University of Missouri–Kansas City, I was supported by provost Gayle Hackett, chair of the History Department Gary Ebersole, and colleagues Jesse Choo, Mary Ann Wynkoop, John Herron, Diane Mutti-Burke, Lou Potts, and Drew Bergerson. In Lexington, I was welcomed by Professor Gerald Smith at the University of Kentucky, and in Frankfort, by Professor Anne Butler at Kentucky State University.

I also owe a debt of gratitude to previous researchers and writers, whose collective work on the history of black jockeys has been invaluable. I begin with Frank Borries, whose early research on Murphy became the foundation for the biography *Isaac Murphy: Kentucky's Record Jockey* (1988), completed by his wife Betty after Frank's death. Ed Hotaling's *Great Black Jockeys* (1999) accounts for the role of African Americans in the development of horse racing. The husband-and-wife team of Monica Renae and James Robert Saunders published an excellent work titled *Black Winning Jockeys of the Kentucky Derby* (2003). Maryjean Wall's *How Kentucky Became Southern* (2010) is important to an understanding Kentucky's evolution as a center for horse development.

I must extend a heartfelt thank you to the University Press of Kentucky for allowing me the space and flexibility to tell the story of Isaac Burns Murphy in a unique way. If I have learned anything from reading biographies—and I have read my share—it is that every life is different and therefore cannot be approached through a universal formula or a single template. A special thank you to Linda Lotz, whose critical eyes and ears helped shape and polish this very important work.

To Paige Knight and Julie Newton, colleagues specializing in preservation and digitization at Emory University, thank you for your assistance in attaining the photographs for this book.

Finally, I want to express my thanks and appreciation to the people in my life who were most patient, supportive, and understanding of the time and effort required to create such a volume: my wife, Navvab; my son, Ellington; and my daughter, Sofia.

The result is a glimpse of a life that had previously been taken for granted. It is my hope that this contribution will encourage the meaningful work of others who share an interest in the prince of jockeys: Isaac Burns Murphy.

# Chronology

| | |
|---|---|
| 1861 | Isaac Burns Murphy is born on David Tanner's farm in Clark County, Kentucky. |
| 1868 | Lucy Carr is born in Frankfort, Kentucky. |
| 1874 | Isaac begins as an apprentice with James T. Williams and Richard Owings after his mother loses her money in the Lexington branch of the Freedmen's Bank. |
| 1875 | Isaac has a mount in the final race of the Louisville Jockey Club meeting on May 22, 1875. In his first taste of the big time, he rides J. T. Williams's Lady Greenfield to a last-place finish. |
| 1876 | Before the fall meeting of the Louisville Jockey Club, Isaac changes his last name from Burns to Murphy, at the request of his mother to honor his grandfather. |
| 1877 | Isaac rides for J. W. Hunt-Reynolds for the first time at the Nashville Blood Horse Association meeting. |
| 1878 | Isaac is suspended in Cincinnati after being accused of slashing another jockey with his whip. |
| 1879 | Isaac wins the Louisville Cup on Hunt-Reynolds's Fortuna, the Tobacco Stakes on Churchill and Johnson's Little Ruffin, the Clark Stakes for three-year-olds on Hunt-Reynolds's Falsetto, the Tennessee Stakes for two-year-olds on G. W. Bowen and Company's Wallenstein, and the Merchant's Stakes on Hunt-Reynolds's Blue Eyes. America Murphy dies of cancer. |

| 1880 | J. W. Hunt-Reynolds dies on September 22 at the Westfeldt family reunion in North Carolina. |
|------|---|
| 1881 | Isaac wins the Grand Prize of Saratoga on J. T. Williams's Checkmate. |
| 1882 | Isaac rides at the Coney Island Jockey Club on Ed Corrigan's Pearl Jennings. |
| 1883 | Isaac marries Lucy Carr in Frankfort and purchases a home on Megowan Street in Lexington. He advertises his services in the *Kentucky Live Stock Record* and signs a contract to ride for California millionaire Elias J. Baldwin. |
| 1884 | Isaac wins his first Kentucky Derby on William Cottrill's Buchanan. He wins the first American Derby at Chicago's Washington Park on Corrigan's Modesty. |
| 1885 | Isaac wins his second American Derby on E. J. Baldwin's Volante. |
| 1886 | Isaac wins his third American Derby on E. J. Baldwin's Silver Cloud. |
| 1887 | Isaac appears on three different tobacco cards produced by manufacturers W. S. Kimball Company, Goodwin and D. Buchner, and the Kinney Brothers. |
| 1888 | Murphy claims his own colors: black jacket, red cuffs, white belt, and red cap with a green tassel. Isaac wins his fourth American Derby on E. J. Baldwin's Emperor of Norfolk. |
| 1889 | A biographical sketch of Murphy appears in the *Kentucky Leader* on March 20. |
| 1890 | Isaac wins his second Kentucky Derby on Ed Corrigan's Riley. Riding J. B. Haggin's Salvator, Isaac beats Ed Garrison on Tenny in a match race at the Suburban. At Monmouth Park, he is accused of being drunk but is later exonerated, and a plot to poison him is exposed. |

| | |
|---|---|
| 1891 | Isaac wins his third Kentucky Derby on Kingman. Jockey William Walker marries Hannah Estill at the Murphys' home. |
| 1892 | Jockey Anthony Hamilton and his bride, the former Annie L. Messley, attend an engagement party in their honor at the Murphys' home in Lexington. Isaac is released from his contract with the firm of Ehret, McLewee, and Allen but receives his full salary of $10,000. |
| 1893 | The Murphys celebrate their tenth wedding anniversary by renewing their vows and throwing a party at their Lexington home, attended by their friends from around the country, including the top black jockeys in America. |
| 1894 | Murphy signs to ride for the McClellands. Isaac appears in A. H. Spink's stage play *The Derby Winner*. |
| 1895 | Isaac rides in twenty races and wins only two. |
| 1896 | Murphy dies at home. His funeral is attended by more than 500 people, and he is buried in African Cemetery Number 2. |
| 1910 | Lucy dies of pneumonia at home in Lexington. She is buried next to her husband. |

# Notes

## Introduction

1. Philip Foner, ed., *Frederick Douglass: Selected Speeches and Writings* (Chicago: Lawrence Hill Books, 1999), 375.

2. See Gary B. Nash, *The Forgotten Fifth: African Americans in the Age of Revolution* (Cambridge, MA: Harvard University Press, 2006), 98–105.

3. See Ira Berlin, *Many Thousands Gone: The First Two Centuries of Slavery in North America* (Cambridge, MA: Belknap Press of Harvard University Press, 1998), for an in-depth discussion of the establishment and emergence of slavery in North America and in the European colonies.

4. See John Hope Franklin, *From Slavery to Freedom: A History of African Americans* (New York: Alfred A. Knopf, 1967), 126–44; David Waldstreicher, *Slavery's Constitution: From Revolution to Ratification* (New York: Hill and Wang, 2010).

5. Quoted from the constitution of the Kentucky Abolition Society in Lowell H. Harrison, *The Antislavery Movement in Kentucky* (Lexington: University of Kentucky Press, 1978), 18–37.

6. Henry Clay, *Speech of the Hon. Henry Clay before the American Colonization Society, in the Hall of the House of Representatives, January 20, 1827* (Washington, DC: American Colonization Society, 1827), 7–8.

7. See David Walker and Peter Hinks, eds., *David Walker's Appeal to the Colored Citizens of the World* [1831] (University Park: Pennsylvania State University, 2000).

8. George Moses Horton, *The Hope of Liberty: Containing a Number of Poetical Pieces* (Raleigh, NC: Gales and Son, 1829), 8–9. http://docsouth.unc.edu/southlit/horton/horton.html.

9. Delany argues that the founding fathers chose to place people of African descent at the bottom of the political hierarchy because that group was identifiably different from those of European ancestry:

> The United States, untrue to her trust and unfaithful to her professed principles of republican equality, has also pursued a policy of political degradation to a large portion of her native born countrymen, and that class is the Colored People. Denied equality not only of political but of natural rights,

in common with the rest of our fellow citizens, there is no species of degradation to which we are not subject.

Reduced to abject slavery is not enough, the very thought of which should awaken every sensibility of our common nature; but those of their descendants who are freemen even in the non-slaveholding States, occupy the very same position politically, religiously, civilly and socially, (with but few exceptions,) as the bondman occupies in the slave States.

In those States, the bondman is disfranchised, and for the most part so are we. He is denied all civil, religious, and social privileges, except such as he gets by mere sufferance, and so are we. They have no part nor lot in the government of the country, neither have we. They are ruled and governed without representation, existing as mere nonentities among the citizens, and excrescences on the body politic—a mere dreg in community, and so are we. Where then is our political superiority to the enslaved? None, neither are we superior in any other relation to society, except that we are de facto masters of ourselves and joint rulers of our own domestic household, while the bondman's self is claimed by another, and his relation to his family denied him. What the unfortunate classes are in Europe, such are we in the United States, which is folly to deny, insanity not to understand, blindness not to see, and surely now full time that our eyes were opened to these startling truths, which for ages have stared us full in the face.

Martin Delany, *The Condition, Elevation, Emigration and Destiny of the Colored People of the United States*, ed. Toyin Falola (1852; reprint, New York: Humanity Books, 2004), 44–45.

10. Orlando Patterson, *Slavery and Social Death: A Comparative Study* (Cambridge, MA: Harvard University Press, 1985).

11. Joy Degruy, *Post Traumatic Slave Syndrome: America's Legacy of Enduring Injury and Healing* (Milwaukee: Uptone Press, 2005).

12. See Ed Hotaling, *The Great Black Jockeys: The Lives and Times of the Men Who Dominated America's First National Sport* (Rocklin, CA: Forum Prima Publishing, 1999).

13. See the following texts for discussions of notions of black inferiority and imagined racial destiny: W. E. B. DuBois, *The Souls of Black Folk* (Chicago: A. C. McClurg, 1903); David R. Roediger, *The Wages of Whiteness: Race and the Making of the American Working Class* (London: Verso, 2002); George Lipsitz, *The Possessive Investment in Whiteness: How White People Profit from Identity Politics* (Philadelphia: Temple University Press, 1998); George M. Fredrickson, *The Black Image in the White Mind: The Debate on Afro-American Character and Racial Destiny, 1817–1914* (Middletown, CT: Wesleyan University Press, 1971); Eric Lott, *Love and Theft: Blackface Minstrelsy and the American Working Class* (New York: Oxford University Press, 1995); Orlando Patterson, *Rituals of Blood: Consequences of Slavery in Two American Centuries* (New York: Basic Civitas, 1998); and Maurice O. Wallace, *Constructing the Black Masculine: Identity and Ideality in African American Men's Literature and Culture, 1775–1995* (Durham, NC: Duke University Press, 2002).

14. Frederick Douglass, "Oration in Memory of Abraham Lincoln, Delivered at the Unveiling of the Freedmen's Monument in Memory of Abraham Lincoln, in Lincoln Park, Washington, D.C., April 14, 1876," in Foner, *Frederick Douglass: Selected Speeches and Writings*, 619–20.

## 1. Into the Bluegrass

1. For an in-depth examination of the numerous slave rebellions and revolts throughout American history, see Herbert Aptheker, *American Negro Slave Revolts* (New York: International Publishers, 1970), 86–87; Charles Johnson and Patricia Smith, *Africans in America: America's Journey through Slavery* (New York: Harcourt, Brace, 1998), 94–96; John Hope Franklin, *From Slavery to Freedom: A History of African Americans* (New York: Alfred A. Knopf, 1967), 77–78.

2. See Kenneth P. Bailey, *The Ohio Company of Virginia and the Westward Movement, 1748–1792: A Chapter in the History of the Colonial Frontier* (Glendale, CA: Arthur H. Clark, 1939).

3. See Marion B. Lucas, *A History of Blacks in Kentucky: From Slavery to Segregation, 1760–1891* (Frankfort: Kentucky Historical Society, 2003), xi; Richard H. Collins, *Annals of Kentucky or Important Events in the History of Kentucky, 1539–1874* (Covington, KY, 1874), 15. Gist's survey and his contact with the Indians on behalf of the Ohio Land Company would be one of the root causes of the French and Indian War (1756–1763). The French believed, correctly, that the English were attempting to claim the territory and disrupt their relationship with the Ohio Valley Indians.

4. See William E. Foley, *Wilderness Journey: The Life of William Clark* (Columbia: University of Missouri Press, 2004); Landon Y. Jones, *William Clark and the Shaping of the West* (New York: Hill and Wang, 2004); Robert B. Betts, *In Search of York: The Slave Who Went to the Pacific with Lewis and Clark* (Boulder: Colorado Associated University Press, 1985).

5. Clark mentions York in his journal, but the entries are not related to what York observes, feels, fears, or dreams. However, based on Clark's records, we can deduce that York was a very capable man. Poet Frank X Walker has written an imaginative account of the life of York in his book *Buffalo Dance: The Journey of York* (Lexington: University Press of Kentucky, 2004).

6. This style of hunting took hunting parties away for weeks or months at a time. Thomas D. Clark explains: "A party of forty hunters from the Yadikin Valley in North Carolina . . . were called 'Long Hunters' because of their long stay in the Kentucky wilderness." Thomas D. Clark, *A History of Kentucky* (Ashland, KY: Jesse Stuart Foundation, 1988), 31–34.

7. Benjamin Quarles, *The Negro in the American Revolution* (Chapel Hill: University of North Carolina Press, 1961), 8. Also see Michael Lee Lanning, *African Americans in the Revolutionary War* (New York: Citadel Press Books, 2000), 32; Franklin, *From Slavery to Freedom*, 131.

8. Edward Braddock to Robert Napier quoted in Quarles, *The Negro in the American Revolution*, 8.

9. Benjamin Quarles, "The Colonial Militia and Negro Manpower," *Mississippi Valley Historical Review* 45, no. 4 (March 1959): 644.

10. Steven Channing, *Kentucky: A History* (New York: W. W. Norton, 1977), 8–9.

11. See Stephen Aron, *How the West Was Lost: The Transformation of Kentucky from Daniel Boone to Henry Clay* (Baltimore: Johns Hopkins University Press, 1996), for an in-depth discussion of how Kentucky changed.

12. According to historians, it was future president George Washington who set the land rush in motion in 1770, with his land claim in the Big Sandy Valley.

13. Clark, *History of Kentucky*, 33–40; Aron, *How the West Was Lost*, 64–70; Channing, *Kentucky*, 9–16.

14. Aron, *How the West Was Lost*, 25.

15. The father of future U.S. Supreme Court justice John Marshall Harlan was one of the explorers in Harrod's party. James Harlan, along with his brother Silas, traveled with Harrod and settled near the Salt River, where the brothers constructed a house from the local stone. See Loren P. Beth, *John Marshall Harlan: The Last Whig Justice* (Lexington: University Press of Kentucky, 1992), 8–9.

16. Zachariah F. Smith, *The History of Kentucky* (Louisville: Courier Journal Job Printing Company, 1886), 29. See also Clark, *History of Kentucky*, 34–38; Channing, *Kentucky*, 16; John E. Kleber, ed., *The Kentucky Encyclopedia* (Lexington: University Press of Kentucky, 1992), 413–15.

17. Virgil A. Lewis, *History of the Battle of Point Pleasant* (Charleston: Tribune Printing Company, 1909).

18. Quarles, *The Negro in the American Revolution*, 8.

19. Philip Foner, ed., *The Complete Writings of Thomas Paine* (New York: Citadel Press, 1945), 2:15–19.

20. The Intolerable Acts have been defined as the laws implemented by England to pay for its wars with Spain, France, and the native peoples of North America.

21. W. B. Hartgrove, "The Negro Soldier in the American Revolution," *Journal of Negro History* 1, no. 2 (April 1916): 119.

22. See Gary B. Nash, *The Forgotten Fifth: African Americans in the Age of Revolution* (Cambridge, MA: Harvard University Press, 2006), 35–48.

23. Channing, *Kentucky*, 6.

24. Clark, *History of Kentucky*, 42.

25. See C. W. Webber, *Romance of Natural History; or, Wild Scenes and Wild Hunters* (Philadelphia: Lippincott and Grambo, 1852), 213–47; Lewis, *History of the Battle of Point Pleasant*, 118–19.

26. See J. Winston Coleman, *Slavery Time in Kentucky* (Chapel Hill: University of North Carolina Press, 1940), and Lucas, *History of Blacks in Kentucky*, for a discussion of the Captain John Cowan's census of the settlers at Fort Harrod, which found ten slaves over the age of ten and seven Negro children younger than ten years old.

27. George Washington Ranck, *Boonesborough: Its Founding, Pioneer Struggles, Indian Experiences, Transylvania Days, and Revolutionary Annals* (Louisville: John P. Morton, 1901), 10–13.

28. Meredith Mason Brown, *Frontiersman: Daniel Boone and the Making of America* (Baton Rouge: Louisiana State University Press, 2008), 55–57.

29. Aron, *How the West Was Lost*, 71.

30. Ibid., 68.

31. Channing, *Kentucky*, 32.

32. David Rice, *Slavery Inconsistent with Justice and Good Policy* (New York: Samuel Wood, 1812), 7.

33. Aron, *How the West Was Lost*, 92; Clark, *History of Kentucky*, 65; Kleber, *Kentucky Encyclopedia*, 116–17; Ellen Eslinger, ed., *Running Mad for Kentucky: Frontier Travel Accounts* (Lexington: University Press of Kentucky, 2004), 36–37.

34. John Catanzarti, ed., *The Papers of Thomas Jefferson* (Princeton, NJ: Princeton University Press, 1997), 27:270–71.

35. Aron, *How the West Was Lost*, 95.

36. See Francis Fredric, *Slave Life in Virginia: A Narrative by Francis Fredric, Escaped Slave* (Baton Rouge: Louisiana State University, 2010), 19–31.

37. Richard C. Wade, *Slavery in the Cities: The South 1820–1860* (London: Oxford University Press, 1968), 3.

38. Henry Clay, *Speech of the Hon. Henry Clay before the American Colonization Society, in the Hall of the House of Representative, January 20, 1827* (Washington, DC: American Colonization Society, 1827), 4.

39. David Walker and Peter Hinks, eds., *David Walker's Appeal to the Colored Citizens of the World* [1831] (University Park: Pennsylvania State University, 2000), 71.

40. Born in slavery to an African mother on Benjamin Turner's farm in Southampton, Virginia, on October 2, 1800, Nat Turner was recognized as a child with a special calling whose life was intended for some great purpose. Throughout his youth, Turner was frequently reminded of his special status by other blacks in his community and even by some whites, who recognized his uncommon intellect and thoughtfulness.

Like a majority of enslaved African Americans, Turner's religion played a significant role in his development as an individual and a community member. Moreover, his recognition and acceptance of the traditions of his community were necessary to the survival of memories of the past connected to Africa, to notions of freedom, and to a life filled with possibilities based on long-held traditions. His acceptance of the rituals and beliefs handed down and across generations allowed Turner to expand his faith in things unseen, which helped him understand how whites used slavery to justify their treatment of African Americans as brutes and human chattel. What is more, his growing knowledge of all things biblical and his increasing awareness of the world around him gave Turner visions of the violence to be committed under his leadership and how his actions would be embedded in the collective memory of both the oppressed and the oppressor. In *The Confessions of Nat Turner* (1831), Turner recalls being divined by his community as a leader:

> It had been said of me in childhood by those by whom I had been taught to pray, both white and black, and in whom I had the greatest confidence, that I had too much sense to be raised, and if I was, I would never be of any use to any one as a slave. Now finding I had arrived to man's estate, and was a slave, and these revelations being made known to me, I began to direct my attention to this great object, to fulfill the purpose for which, by this time, I felt assured I was intended. [Quoted in Scott French, *The Rebellious Slave: Nat Turner in American Memory* (New York: Houghton Mifflin, 2004), 291.]

After a series of visions (and quite possibly a reading of David Walker's *Appeal*), Turner set out to pursue justice for abused and degraded blacks by ridding the world of those he deemed responsible for their torment: whites. On August 21, 1831, Turner and six other men of African descent marched across Southampton, leaving in their wake fifty-five dead white men, women, and children. No one was spared. By the time Turner and his band of self-appointed executioners were captured by the local militia, their numbers had increased to almost sixty. Turner escaped, but after three weeks of hiding in the woods surrounding Southampton, he surrendered without incident to Benjamin Phipps, a local farmer.

At his trial, Turner pled not guilty to charges of "making insurrection, and plotting to take away the lives of divers free white persons & co. on the 22nd of August, 1831." Turner never wavered in his belief that his actions were both right and sane. After a short deliberation, Turner was sentenced to hang by his neck until dead, and that punishment was carried out on November 11. What happened next can only be attributed to the same institution that drove Turner to act in the first place. Local doctors claimed Turner's body and proceeded to dissect and dismember it. After their examination, they sold his skin to artisans, who fashioned it into money purses and wallets; his flesh was processed and sold as grease for various industrial uses; and his skull was displayed and studied as a curiosity.

African American historians would recognize Turner's efforts to avenge past abuses as heroic. He is considered one of America's most important freedom fighters.

41. U.S. census data, 1830.

42. Coleman, *Slave Times in Kentucky*, 142–47.

43. See Franklin, *From Slavery to Freedom*, 177–78; George P. Rawick, *From Sundown to Sunup: The Making of the Black Community* (Westport, CT: Greenwood, 1972), 88; Albert Bushnell Hart, *The American Nation: A History*, vol. 10, *Slavery and Abolition* (New York: Harper and Brothers, 1906), 124.

44. Jennie Holliman, *American Sports 1785–1835* (Durham, NC: Seeman Press, 1931), 107–9.

45. Among the most noteworthy American gentlemen farmers was George Washington, who maintained a stable of quality horses at his Mount Vernon

farm and at his home in Virginia. Prior to the Revolutionary War, Washington was one of many wealthy colonists who had the means to purchase blooded animals and establish a reputation as a breeder of fine stock. During the war, General Washington used his exceptional ability on horseback to lead the colonial forces against the British regulars. After the war, Washington began to improve his stock by purchasing whatever reasonably priced blooded animals he could find. Along with slaves to work his extensive farmlands, Washington needed the muscle of horses and mules to plow his lands, pull wagons and carriages, carry grain and feed to market, move supplies from one location to another, and provide basic transportation. In a letter dated December 30, 1792, Washington addresses the management of his Mount Vernon farm:

> My horses too [in the management of which he professes to have skill] might derive much benefit from a careful attention to them; not only to those which work, but to the young ones, and to the breeding mares: for I have long suspected that Peter, under pretence of riding about the Plantations to look after the Mares, Mules, &ca; is in pursuit of other objects; either of traffic or amusement, more advancive of his own pleasures than my benefit. It is not, otherwise to be conceived, that with the number of Mares I have, five and twenty of which were bought for the express purpose of breeding, though now considerably reduced from that purpose, alone; should produce not more than six or eight Colts a year.

George Washington, *The Writings of George Washington*, vol. 12, *1790–1794*, comp. and ed. Worthington Chaucey Ford (New York: G. P. Putnam's Sons, 1891), 279.

46. South Carolina Jockey Club, *History of the Turf in South Carolina* (Charleston, SC: Russell and Jones, 1857), 16.

47. William Preston Mangum II, *A Kingdom for a Horse: The Legacy of R. A. Alexander and Woodburn Farms* (Louisville: Harmony House, 1999), 8; Dennis Domer, "Inventing the Horse Farm," *Kentucky Humanities*, October 2005, 3–12.

48. Mangum, *Kingdom for a Horse*, 11.

## 2. America Bourne

1. Historians have cited various dates as Isaac Murphy's birthday, including January 1, April 16, and November 10, 1861, but they agree that he was born on David Tanner's farm in Clark County, Kentucky. A majority have quoted directly from Murphy's 1896 obituary written by Llewellyn P. Tarleton, "Isaac Murphy: A Memorial," *Thoroughbred Record*, March 21, 1896, 136 (also published in the *Lexington Herald*). Tarleton mistakenly states that Tanner's farm was located in Fayette County.

The 1850 U.S. census shows Tanner's limited ownership of slave labor. The itemized listing includes three black female slaves (one mulatto), ranging in age from ten to nineteen; a twenty-one-year-old male; and two adults—a male aged fifty and a female aged forty-two. The same census lists the slaves belonging to David's brother, Branch Tanner: three female slaves (two mulattos), ranging in age from twenty-seven to ninety; a thirteen-year-old mulatto male; and a six-year-old black male. I believe that the nineteen-year-old female was America Murphy, Isaac's mother. In examining the document that recorded America's death from rectal cancer, it is clear that she was mulatto and that, based on her age at death, she was born sometime between 1830 and 1835. See Ed Hotaling, *The Great Black Jockeys: The Lives and Times of the Men Who Dominated America's First National Sport* (Rocklin, CA: Forum Prima Publishing, 1999), 239; David Wiggins, *Glory Bound: Black Athlete in a White America* (Syracuse, NY: Syracuse University Press, 1997), 22; Anne S. Butler, "Racing's Buried History: Too Little Known about the Real Lives of 19th Century's Black Jockeys," *Lexington Herald Leader*, April 9, 2001, H1, 4.

2. Due to the nature of slavery, the children born to enslaved black women were considered no more valuable than prized farm animals, with the exception of Kentucky Thoroughbreds, which were actually more valuable owing to their pedigrees and their symbolic representation of mastery over nature. What mattered most to the slave owner was that the offspring was born alive and the mother survived the birthing process, as both represented financial investments. What little knowledge we have about the births of these children comes from former slaves' oral histories, slave owners' records, and the official records of births kept by state and local governments. Although historians and scholars of African American history and life often use oral histories to establish some semblance of a foundation, the experiences of black women throughout the antebellum period have been overgeneralized. What historians and biographers must both explore and incorporate into their work are the gaps in knowledge that cannot be fully accounted for through traditional methods of inquiry. There is more than one way to get to the roots of the questions that perplex and dumbfound us with regard to black life in America prior to the Civil War. We need to be radical, yet responsible. The records in the archives and repositories throughout the state of Kentucky, as well as those hidden in plain sight in local libraries and historical societies, are the best places to uncover the various factors that influenced the life of a boy named Isaac Murphy.

3. Kentucky Birth, Marriage, and Death Records—microfilm (1852–1910), microfilm rolls 994027–994058, Kentucky Department for Libraries and Archives, Frankfort, KY.

4. Judge Andrew P. Napolitano, *Dred Scott's Revenge: A Legal History of Race and Freedom in America* (Nashville: Thomas Nelson, 2009), 60–61.

5. For a description of one of the most horrendous examples of brutality in Kentucky, perpetrated by Lilburn and Isham Lewis, nephews of Thomas Jefferson, see Marion B. Lucas, *A History of Blacks in Kentucky: From Slavery to Segregation, 1760–1891* (Frankfort: Kentucky Historical Society, 2003), 47–48.

6. Frederick Douglass, "Captain John Brown Not Insane," *Douglass*

*Monthly*, November 1859, in *Frederick Douglass: Selected Speeches and Writings*, ed. Philip Foner (Chicago: Lawrence Hill Books, 1999), 375–76.

7. For an examination of how slave societies organized themselves, see Henry Box Brown, *Narrative of the Life of Henry Box Brown* [1851], ed. John Ernest (Chapel Hill: University of North Carolina Press, 2008 ); William Still, *Still's Underground Rail Road Records: With a Life of the Author* (Philadelphia: William Still Publishing, 1886); Wilbur Henry Siebert, *The Underground Railroad from Slavery to Freedom* (New York: Macmillan, 1898); Steven Hahn, *A Nation under Our Feet: Black Political Struggles in the Rural South from Slavery to the Great Migration* (Cambridge, MA: Belknap Press of Harvard University Press, 2003).

8. See Annette Gordon Reed, *The Hemingses of Monticello* (New York: Norton, 2008), 106–7.

9. Eugene Genovese, *Roll, Jordan, Roll: The World the Slaves Made* (New York: Pantheon Books, 1974), 45, argues:

> Slavery as a mode of production creates a market for labor, much as capitalism creates a market for labor power. Both encourage commercial development, which is by no means to be equaled with capitalist development (understood as a system of social relations within which labor-power has become a commodity). . . . Although ancient slavery did not create a market for labor-power, it did, by creating a market for human beings and economic products induce a high level of commercialization that, together with the successful consolidation of a centralized state, combined to bequeath a system of law upon which modern bourgeois society could build.

10. During the middle of the nineteenth century, the infant mortality rate among enslaved African Americans was more than double that among whites. See Kenneth Stampp, *The Peculiar Institution: Slavery in the Ante Bellum South* (New York: Vintage Books, 1956), 314–21.

11. The Supreme Court's 1857 decision in the Dred Scott case made it clear that enslaved and free African Americans could not expect white men to grant them the privileges of full citizenship.

12. I believe that Green Murphy was actually Jeremiah Murphy, a tavern keeper who ran an inn out of his home in Lexington. See J. Winston Coleman, *Stage Coach Days in the Bluegrass* (Lexington: University Press of Kentucky, 1955), 55.

13. See John E. Kleber, ed., *The Kentucky Encyclopedia* (Lexington: University Press of Kentucky, 1992), 314–15; Randolph Hollingsworth, *Lexington: Queen of the Bluegrass* (Charleston, SC: Arcadia Publishing, 2004), 21, 41; John Wilson Townsend, *Lore of the Meadowland: Short Studies in Kentuckiana* (Lexington: Press of J. L. Richardson, 1911), 28–34; Lucas, *History of Blacks in Kentucky*, 122–23.

14. "Ike Murphy's Real Name," *Daily Inter Ocean*, July 28, 1891, 3.

15. *Lexington 1859–60 City Directory* (Lexington: Hitchcock and Searles, 1859), 86.

16. George Washington Ranck, *Boonesborough: Its Founding, Pioneer*

*Struggles, Indian Experiences, Transylvania Days, and Revolutionary Annals* (Louisville: John P. Morton, 1901), 130.

17. See the following for in-depth discussions of interracial sex, power, and African American identity construction: Martha Hodes, *White Women, Black Men: Illicit Sex in the 19th Century South* (New Haven, CT: Yale University Press, 1997), 96; Brenda E. Stevenson, *Life in Black & White: Family and Community in the Slave South* (New York: Oxford University Press, 1996), 180–82; Genovese, *Roll, Jordan, Roll*, 413–31; Winthrop Jordan, *White over Black* (Chapel Hill: University of North Carolina Press, 1968), 167–78.

18. Francis Fredric, *Slave Life in Virginia: A Narrative by Francis Fredric, Escaped Slave* (Baton Rouge: Louisiana State University, 2010), 27–33.

19. Lewis Clarke, *Narrative of the Sufferings of Lewis Clarke* (Boston: David H. Ela, 1845), 9.

20. Kentucky Birth Records, 1852–1910, Ancestry.com; original data from Kentucky Birth, Marriage, and Death Records—microfilm (1852–1910), microfilm rolls 994027–994058, Kentucky Department for Libraries and Archives, Frankfort, KY.

21. Albert Bushnell Hart, *The American Nation: A History*, vol. 16, *Slavery and Abolition, 1831–1841* (New York: Harper and Brothers, 1906), 122.

22. Genovese, *Roll, Jordan, Roll*, 506–8.

23. See ibid., 496–97, for the different ways slave mothers tried to protect their children from lives of servitude.

24. James F. Hopkins, *A History of the Hemp Industry in Kentucky* (Lexington: University Press of Kentucky, 1951), 24. See also Eric Thompson et al., *Economic Impact of Industrial Hemp in Kentucky* (Lexington: Center for Business and Economic Research, University of Kentucky, July 1998); Lowell H. Harrison and James C. Klotter, *New History of Kentucky* (Lexington: University Press of Kentucky, 1997), 292–93.

25. 1850 U.S. census data and listing of free inhabitants in Bourbon County.

26. In chapter 5 of *Narrative of William Wells Brown: A Fugitive Slave, Written by Himself* (Boston: Anti-Slavery Office, 1847), Brown describes being hired out as a slave in various capacities and occupations. While working with Mr. Walker, a St. Louis slave trader, Brown was exposed to the additional cruelties of Southern slavery. In *The Autobiography of the Reverend Josiah Henson* (Reading, PA: Addison-Wesley, 1969), 17, Henson discusses the breakup of his family after his owner died:

> The doctor's death was a great calamity to us, for the estate and the slaves were to be sold and the proceeds divided among the heirs. The first sad announcement that the sale was to be; the knowledge that all ties of the past were to be sundered; the frantic terror at the idea of being sent "down south"; the almost certainty that one member of a family will be torn from another; the anxious scanning of the purchasers' faces; the agony at parting, often of ever, with husband, wife, child—these must be seen and felt to be fully understood.

27. Marriages between slaves from different farms happened frequently, although slave masters tried to discourage the practice. Sudie Duncan Sides argues: "When planters would not sell slaves who wished to be married, the marriages took the form of . . . the slaves living separately and visiting one another on the weekend. In marriages such as these, there was no legal binding contract provided or licenses granted that would obligate the slave owners to provide a guarantee to not sell the children born during the enslavement of the female. In some cases, the slave owner took the liberty to maintain sexual access to the body of his legal property." Philip A. Bruce's revisionist historical examination reluctantly admits that the system of slavery "debased both man and woman by making true marriage impossible." Furthermore, no matter how "faithfully both members of the couple might observe the marital obligations, their union could amount only to a passing arrangement as long as their owner had the power to sell either at any moment that his interests moved him to do so. The possibility of such rupture, followed by a final separation, was enough in itself to weaken, or at least to embitter, the relation, however firmly cemented apparently by affection and the birth of children." Sudie Duncan Sides, "Slave Weddings and Religion: Plantation Life in the Southern States before the American Civil War," *History Today* 24, no. 2 (1974): 87; Philip A. Bruce, *The Plantation Negro as a Freeman: Observations in His Character, Condition, and Prospects in Virginia* (New York: G. P. Putnam's Sons, 1889), 16. See also John Hope Franklin, *From Slavery to Freedom: A History of African Americans* (New York: Alfred A. Knopf, 1967), 172–73.

28. See Herbert Gutman, *The Black Family in Slavery and Freedom, 1750–1925* (New York: Pantheon Books, 1976), 569–70, n. 4.

29. Ibid.

30. In this ritual, one of the best known among slaves, the couple simply stepped over a new broom in the presence of family and community members. These traditions were useful for the preservation of mores and values, but their strength depended on their inheritance (how they were acquired) and their diffusion (how they were carried from one place to another) among those seeking to maintain a sense of communal continuity and social understanding within the context of slavery. Carl Wilhelm von Sydow, "On the Spread of Tradition," in *Selected Papers on Folklore* (Copenhagen: Rosenkilde and Bagger, 1948), 11; Lucas, *History of Blacks in Kentucky*, 18–19.

31. See John Komlos, "Shrinking in a Growing Economy? Mystery of Physical Stature during the Industrial Revolution," *Journal of Economic History* 58, no. 3 (September 1998): 779–802; Michael R. Haines, "Growing Incomes, Shrinking People—Can Economic Development Be Hazardous to Your Health? Historical Evidence for the United States, England, and the Netherlands in the Nineteenth Century," *Social Science History* 28, no. 2 (Summer 2004): 249–70.

32. John W. Blassingame, *The Slave Community: Plantation Life in the Ante-Bellum South* (New York: Oxford University Press, 1972), 95–97.

33. Several slave narratives illuminate the practice of selling children away from their mothers or selling mothers without their newborns, who were placed

in the care of other female slaves. See Charles Elliott, *The Sinfulness of American Slavery* (Cincinnati: L. Swornstedt and J. H. Power, 1850); J. Winston Coleman, *Slavery Time in Kentucky* (Chapel Hill: University of North Carolina Press, 1940), 119–25; James Mellon, ed., *Bullwhip Days: The Slaves Remember: An Oral History* (New York: Avon Books, 1988), 28–29; Walter Johnson, *Soul by Soul: Life Inside the Antebellum Slave Market* (Cambridge, MA: Harvard University Press, 1999), 32–40; Gutman, *The Black Family in Slavery and Freedom,* 148–55.

34. William E. Cain, ed., *William Lloyd Garrison and the Fight against Slavery: Selections from the Liberator "Disunion," June 15, 1855* (Boston: Bedford/St. Martin, 1995), 141–44.

35. Lewis Collins and Richard Henry Collins, *Collins' Historical Sketches of Kentucky*, vol. 1 (Covington, KY: Collins and Company, 1878), 102.

36. Elizabeth Hyde Botume, *First Days amongst the Contrabands* (New York: Arno Press, 1968).

37. Frederick Douglass, "Oration in Memory of Abraham Lincoln, Delivered at the Unveiling of the Freedmen's Monument in Memory of Abraham Lincoln, in Lincoln Park, Washington, D.C., April 14, 1876," in *Frederick Douglass: Selected Speeches and Writings*, ed. Philip Foner (Chicago: Lawrence Hill Books, 1999), 619–20.

## 3. Seizing Freedom

1. The 1854 Kansas-Nebraska Act, which allowed the populations in those two territories to choose whether to support the expansion of slavery within their borders, nullified the Missouri Compromise, which had prevented slavery from expanding beyond the 36°30' line.

2. "Forcing Down the Free Colored People," *Weekly Anglo African*, September 3, 1859, Black Abolitionist Archive, University of Detroit Mercy Libraries, http://research.udmercy.edu/find/special_collections/digital/baa/item.php?record_id=1612&collectionCode=baa.

3. See John Hope Franklin, *From Slavery to Freedom: A History of African Americans* (New York: Alfred A. Knopf, 1967), 266; Frederick Douglass, "Speech on the Dred Scott Decision," in *Negro Social and Political Thought: 1850–1920*, ed. Howard Brotz (New York: Basic Books, 1966), 249. The Compromise of 1850 provided that: (1) California would enter the Union as a free state, (2) the other territories would be organized without slavery as part of the discussion, (3) Texas would cede certain lands to New Mexico with compensation, (4) slaveholders would be guaranteed protection with a firm fugitive slave law, and (5) the District of Columbia would be free from the slave trade.

4. Historians believe the Fugitive Slave Act of 1850 accelerated the rate by which free and enslaved African Americans sought refuge in the North, taking advantage of the Underground Railroad and its network. It has also been acknowledged that the law increased the number of antislavery advocates in the

North because it forced whites to become involved in the lives of Southerners. See Wilbert Siebert, *Underground Railroad: From Slavery to Freedom* (New York: Arno Press, 1968), 209–14; Josiah Henson, *The Life of Josiah Henson, Former-ly a Slave, as Narrated by Himself* (London: Charles Gilpin, Bishopgate With-out, 1851), 17; Marion Gleason McDougall, *Fugitive Slaves, 1619–1865* (Boston: Ginn, 1891), 43.

5. See Robert Clemens Smedley, *History of the Underground Railroad in Chester and the Neighboring Counties* (Lancaster, PA: John A. Hiestand, 1883), 107–30.

6. Frederick Douglass, "No Struggle, No Progress," in *Lift Every Voice: African American Oratory 1787–1900*, ed. Philip S. Foner and Robert James Bran-ham (Tuscaloosa: University of Alabama Press, 1998), 310–11.

7. Leon Litwack, *North of Slavery: The Negro in the Free States, 1790–1860* (Chicago: University of Chicago Press, 1961), 250.

8. Quoted in Douglass, "Speech on the Dred Scott Decision," 247–62.

9. Quoted in Frederick Douglass, "The Dred Scott Decision," May 14, 1857, in *Frederick Douglass: Selected Speeches and Writings*, ed. Philip Foner (Chicago: Lawrence Hill Books, 1999), 347. See also *The Decision of the Supreme Court of the United States and the Opinions of the Judges Thereof in the Case of Dred Scott versus John F. A. Sandford* (Washington, DC: Cornelius Wendall Printer, 1857), 9.

10. *Political Debates between Hon. Abraham Lincoln and Hon. Stephen A. Douglas* (Columbus: Follett, Foster, 1860), 232.

11. The fallout over the Kansas-Nebraska Act created the momentum that helped form the Republican Party.

12. Following the firing on Fort Sumter in April, Arkansas and North Caro-lina seceded in May, and Tennessee followed in June.

13. *Douglass Monthly* 3 (May 1861): 451–52.

14. Editorial, "What of the Night?" *Weekly Anglo African*, April 20, 1861, http://research.udmercy.edu/find/special_collections/digital/baa/item.php?record_id=918&collectionCode=baa.

15. Alfred M. Green, "Let Us Take up the Sword," in Foner and Branham, *Lift Every Voice*, 357–59.

16. Quoted in Richard Leeman, *African American Orators: A Bio-Critical Sourcebook* (Westport, CT: Greenwood Press, 1996), 308.

17. See Kenneth Stamp, ed., *The Causes of the Civil War* (New York: Touchstone Books, 1991); Henry Louis Gates Jr., ed., *Lincoln on Race and Slav-ery* (Princeton, NJ: Princeton University Press, 2009); *Political Debates between Lincoln and Douglas*.

18. Abraham Lincoln, "Address at Cooper Institute," February 27, 1860, in *Abraham Lincoln, Slavery and the Civil War* (Boston: Bedford/St. Martin's, 2001), 83.

19. Peter H. Clark, *The Black Brigade of Cincinnati* (Cincinnati: Jos. B. Boyd, 1864), 4–5.

20. See Christian G. Samito, *Becoming American under Fire: Irish Americans, African Americans, and the Politics of Citizenship during the Civil War* (Ithaca, NY: Cornell University Press, 2009).

21. Martin R. Delany, *Martin R. Delany: A Document Reader* (Chapel Hill: University of North Carolina Press, 2003), 137.

22. Hondon B. Hargrove, *Black Union Soldiers in the Civil War* (Jefferson, NC: McFarland, 1988), xi; Darlene Clark Hine and Earnestine Jenkins, *A Question of Manhood: A Reader in U.S. Black Men's History and Masculinity*, vol. 1 (Bloomington: Indiana University Press, 1999), 46; Marion B. Lucas, *A History of Blacks in Kentucky: From Slavery to Segregation, 1760–1891* (Frankfort: Kentucky Historical Society, 2003), 153.

23. Quoted in Benjamin Quarles, *The Negro in the Civil War* (New York: Da Capo Press, 1989), 167.

24. See James A. Ramage, *John Wesley Hunt: Pioneer Merchant, Manufacturer and Financier* (Lexington: University Press of Kentucky, 2009).

25. Ibid., 41–53; John E. Kleber, ed., *The Kentucky Encyclopedia* (Lexington: University Press of Kentucky, 1992), 447; Lowell H. Harrison and James C. Klotter, *New History of Kentucky* (Lexington: University Press of Kentucky, 1997), 100.

26. Basil Duke, *History of Morgan's Cavalry* (New York: Neale, 1906); James A. Ramage, *Rebel Rider: The Life of General John Hunt Morgan* (Lexington: University Press of Kentucky, 1986).

27. Sarah Parker Remond, "The Negro in the United States of America," in Foner and Branham, *Lift Every Voice*, 380.

28. The impressment of enslaved African Americans was practiced in both the North and the South to obtain the large labor force required to build fortifications. African Americans also dug trenches, built forts, cleared fields, and performed domestic duties for soldiers during the war.

29. Although President Lincoln authorized the use of "black troops" in December 1862, he exempted Kentucky from that federal mandate. The African American soldiers stationed at Camp Nelson before 1864 were recruited from places such as Ohio and New York. Lucas, *History of Blacks in Kentucky*, 151–54.

30. Letter from Smith D. Atkins to a friend in Illinois, November 2, 1862, in *Free at Last: A Documentary History of Slavery, Freedom, and the Civil War*, ed. Ira Berlin et al. (New York: New Press, 1992), 75.

31. Union general Benjamin A. Butler first used the term "contrabands" to describe enslaved African Americans who had been "confiscated" as property by the Federal government. Franklin, *From Slavery to Freedom*, 222; Elizabeth Hyde Botume, *First Days amongst the Contrabands* (New York: Arno Press, 1968), 10.

32. *Douglass Monthly*, January 1863, in Foner, *Frederick Douglass: Selected Speeches and Writings*, 524.

33. Lucas, *History of Blacks in Kentucky*, 154.

34. In a memorandum dated June 12, 1863, Captain Theron E. Hall writes: "Camp near Hickman's Bridge Ky will be called Camp Nelson in honor [of] the

memory of the late Maj. Gen. William Nelson" (cited in Richard D. Sears, *Camp Nelson, Kentucky: A Civil War History* [Lexington: University Press of Kentucky, 2002], 4). At the beginning of the war, Lincoln had tapped Nelson, a former naval officer to recruit loyalists to fight against the Confederacy. Nelson became head of the Army of Kentucky in July 1862. He was a heavy-handed leader and not beloved by his men. On September 29, 1862, the surly Nelson was confronted in the lobby of the Galt House in Louisville by Brigadier General Jefferson Columbus Davis, whom Nelson had removed from field command. After a heated exchange between the two, a humiliated Davis demanded an apology for what he believed to be an attack on his honor. Nelson refused. Davis left the hotel lobby but returned a short time later with a pistol and shot Nelson in the heart. He died less than fifteen minutes later. Despite the murder, Davis was never convicted and continued to serve in the U.S. military. See Collins and Collins, *Collins' Historical Sketches*, 113; Kleber, *Kentucky Encyclopedia*, 676; Donald Clark, *The Notorious "Bull" Nelson: Murdered Union General* (Carbondale: University of Illinois, 2011).

35. Sears, *Camp Nelson*, xxxiv.

36. See Richard D. Sears, *A Utopian Experiment in Kentucky: Integration and Social Equality at Berea, 1866–1904* (Westport, CT: Greenwood Publishers, 1996).

37. Ira Berlin et al., *Freedom: The Destruction of Slavery*, series 1, vol. 1, *1861–1867*, War Department Official Records (Cambridge: Cambridge University Press, 1986), 855–56.

38. Brain R. Eades, *Slaves to Soldiers: A History of the Black Community at Camp Nelson, Jessamine County, Kentucky* (Nicholasville, KY: Camp Nelson Preservation and Restoration Society, 1995), 2.

39. See Peter Bruner, *A Slave's Adventures towards Freedom: Not Fiction, but the True Story of a Struggle* (Oxford, OH: n.p., 1918).

40. See Luis F. Emilio, *A Brave Black Regiment: The History of the 54th Massachusetts, 1863–1865* (New York: Da Capo Press, 1995); Corporal James Henry Gooding, *On the Altar of Freedom: A Black Soldier's Civil War Letters from the Front* (Amherst: University of Massachusetts Press, 1991); James M. McPherson, *The Negro's Civil War: How American Negroes Felt and Acted during the War for the Union* (New York: Pantheon Books, 1965); Andrew Ward, *River Run Red: The Fort Pillow Massacre in the American Civil War* (New York: Penguin Group, 2005); John Cimprich, *Fort Pillow: A Civil War Massacre and Public Memory* (Baton Rouge: Louisiana State University, 2005); Joint Select Committee on the Conduct of the War, *April 21, 1864, Fort Pillow Massacre* (Evansville: Adena, 2005).

41. Letter from Colonel Cicero Maxwell, Commander of U.S. Forces in Southwestern Kentucky, to General J. T. Boyle, Commander of the District of Kentucky, December 5, 1863, in Berlin et al., *Freedom*, 594–95.

42. Ibid.

43. *U.S. Statutes at Large, Treaties, and Proclamations*, vol. 13 (Boston, 1866), 6–11.

44. Berlin et al., *Freedom*, 21.

45. For information on Warren Viley, see William Preston Mangum II, *A Kingdom for a Horse: The Legacy of R. A. Alexander and Woodburn Farms* (Louisville: Harmony House Publishers, 1999), 41.

46. Affidavit of Patsy Leach, March 25, 1865, reproduced in Sears, *Camp Nelson*, 187; Ira Berlin, ed., *Freedom's Soldiers: The Black Military Experience* (Cambridge: Cambridge University Press, 1998), 268–69.

47. Hundreds of recruits, including Jerry Skillman, converged on Camp Nelson in 1864, but it is unclear whether their families followed. However, evidence shows that a majority of men who volunteered to fight brought their families along with them to secure their freedom as well. These women and children, as well as the elderly seeking refuge at the camp, created shortages of food and accommodations. At Camp Nelson, from April to July 1864, an average of three children and one woman died each day as a result of disease and malnutrition. Sears, *Camp Nelson*, iii; Lucas, *History of Blacks in Kentucky*, 160–62.

48. Sears, *Camp Nelson*, 83–86.

49. Ibid., 86.

50. Ibid., 84.

51. Lucas, *History of Blacks in Kentucky*, 154.

52. Sears, *Camp Nelson*, xxxvii.

53. Elijah Marrs, *Life and History of Elijah P. Marrs, First Pastor of Beargrass Baptist Church* (Louisville: Bradley and Gilbert, 1885), 17–18.

54. Hine and Jenkins, *Question of Manhood*, 46.

55. Sears, *Camp Nelson*, 87.

56. Ibid.

57. See Quarles, *The Negro in the Civil War*, 220–24.

58. Quoted in McPherson, *The Negro's Civil War*, 187.

59. See Sears, *Camp Nelson*, 125.

60. See Sears, *Utopian Experiment in Kentucky*, 5.

61. Letter from Fee to Jocelyn, August 8, 1864, in Sears, *Camp Nelson*, 110.

62. Ibid., 116.

63. W. Stephen McBride and Kim A. McBride, *Seizing Freedom: Archaeology of Escaped Slaves at Camp Nelson, Kentucky* (Nicholasville, KY: Camp Nelson Civil War Heritage Park, 2009), 12–15.

64. Sears, *Utopian Experiment in Kentucky*, 10, 12.

65. "From Kentucky: Cruel Treatment of the Wives and Children of U.S. Colored Soldiers," *New York Tribune*, December 2, 1864, 1.

66. Quoted in Sears, *Camp Nelson*, 135–36.

67. Captain Hall to Captain Dickson, November 26, 1864, in Sears, *Camp Nelson*, 136.

68. Dickson to Major General S. G. Burbridge, in Sears, *Camp Nelson*, 137.

69. Several books and essays examine the U.S. military's reluctance to officially acknowledge the impact of African American soldiers on the outcome of numerous battles and the overall victory over the Confederacy. For example, see

William Glenn Robertson's essay in *Black Soldiers in Blue: African American Troops in the Civil War Era*, ed. John David Smith (Chapel Hill: University of North Carolina Press, 2002), 169–99.

70. See U. S. Grant, *Personal Memories of U. S. Grant*, vol. 2 (New York: Charles L. Webster, 1886), 334.

71. "The Casualties and the Incident," *Boston Herald,* October 4, 1864, 2.

72. U. S. Grant to Henry W. Halleck, August 1, 1864, in *War of the Rebellion: Official Records of the Union and Confederate Armies*, vol. 40, pt. 1 (Washington, DC: Government Printing Office, 1892), 17; hereafter cited as *WROR*.

73. Robin Smith and Ron Field, *Uniforms of the Civil War: An Illustrated Guide for Historians, Collectors, and Reenactors* (London: First Lyons Press, 2004), 135.

74. Godfrey Weitzel, *Entry of the United States Forces into Richmond, VA, April 3, 1865: Calling Together of the Virginia Legislature and Revocation of the Same* (Cincinnati: Cincinnati Historical Society, 1965).

75. Ibid., 53.

76. Garland H. White, Chaplin, Twenty-Eighth U.S. Colored Infantry, Richmond, VA, April 12, 1865, in *Congressional Record*, April 22, 1865; Edwin S. Redkey, ed., *A Grand Army of Black Men* (Cambridge: Cambridge University Press, 1992), 175.

77. G. W. to Colonel E. W. Smith, "Swift Creek," April 13, 1865, in *WROR*, series 1, vol. 46, p. 739.

78. "One Petersburg Letter," *Philadelphia Inquirer*, April 20, 1865, 3.

79. For black soldiers' influence over former slaves, see General Order No. 11, April 24, 1865, in *WROR*, series 1, vol. 46, p. 932.

80. John J. Peck to Edward M. Stanton, April 15, 1865, ibid., 782.

81. U. S. Grant to Major General Halleck, April 30, 1865, ibid., 1016.

82. Halleck to Ord, May 1, 1865, ibid., 1062.

83. Weitzel to Lieutenant Colonel T. S. Bowers, May 16, 1865, ibid., 1160.

## 4. From the Silence and the Darkness

1. Charles S. Peirce, "Chronology, Eclipses, and Tides," in *The Atlantic Almanac* (Boston: Tickner and Fields, 1869), 62.

2. "The Eclipse," *Quincy Whig*, August 7, 1869, 4; "The Solar Eclipse," *Public Ledger*, August 7, 1869, 2.

3. Peirce, "Chronology, Eclipses, and Tides," 62.

4. "The Approaching Eclipse," *The Mystic Star: A Monthly Magazine, Devoted to Masonry and Its Literature* (Chicago: Hanna and Billings, 1869), 181; "The Solar Eclipse," *New York Times,* July 6, 1869, 3.

5. Reporting his findings to the Royal Astronomical Society in London, Morton wrote, "Forty-one perfect photographs were taken during the eclipse, and five of these . . . were taken during totality which lasted with us 2m 42s." Quoted by Alfred Mayer, *Proceedings of the American Philosophical Society* 11, no. 82 (1869): 204–8.

Notes to Pages 112–119

6. George W. Ranck, *History of Lexington, Kentucky: Its Early Annals and Recent Progress* (Cincinnati: Robert Clarke, 1872), 402.

7. See John Hope Franklin, *Reconstruction after the Civil War* (Chicago: University of Chicago Press, 1994); Eric Foner, *Forever Free: The Story of Emancipation and Reconstruction* (New York: Vintage Books, 2006); W. E. B. DuBois, *Black Reconstruction in America, 1860–1880* (New York: Free Press, 1992).

8. DuBois, *Black Reconstruction in America*, 671.

9. Ibid.

10. See Victor B. Howard, "The Black Testimony Controversy in Kentucky, 1866–1872," *Journal of Negro History* 58, no. 2 (April 1973): 150; Lowell H. Harrison and James C. Klotter, *New History of Kentucky* (Lexington: University Press of Kentucky, 1997), 218.

11. Brian R. Eades, *Slaves to Soldiers: A History of the Black Community at Camp Nelson, Jessamine County, Kentucky* (Camp Nelson, KY: Camp Nelson Preservation and Restoration Foundation, 1995), 14.

12. See Richard D. Sears, *Camp Nelson, Kentucky: A Civil War History* (Lexington: University Press of Kentucky, 2002), 339–47; Marion B. Lucas, *A History of Blacks in Kentucky: From Slavery to Segregation, 1760–1891* (Frankfort: Kentucky Historical Society, 2003), 193; Victor B. Howard, "The Struggle for Equal Education in Kentucky, 1866–1884," *Journal of Negro History* 46, no. 3 (Summer 1977): 309.

13. See the letter from Abisha Scofield to Rev. Strieby and Whipple, Secretaries of the AMA, December 14, 1866, regarding the violence unleashed on Camp Nelson once Federal troops left the military encampment. Sears, *Camp Nelson*, 354–58.

14. Ronald E. Butchart, *Schooling the Freed People: Teaching, Learning, and the Struggle for Black Freedom, 1861–1876* (Chapel Hill: University of North Carolina Press, 2010), 15.

15. George C. Wright, *Life behind the Veil: Blacks in Louisville, Kentucky 1865–1930* (Baton Rouge: Louisiana State University Press, 1985), 47.

16. 1860 U.S. census data; John Kellogg, "Negro Urban Cluster in the Postbellum South," *Geographical Review* 67, no. 3. (July 1977): 314.

17. James Duane Bolin, *Bossism and Reform in a Southern City: Lexington, Kentucky 1880–1940* (Lexington: University Press of Kentucky, 2000), 4.

18. John D. Wright Jr., *Lexington: Heart of the Bluegrass* (Lexington: Fayette County Historic Commission, 1982), 21.

19. Ibid., 72–73.

20. Ibid., 98; Bolin, *Bossism and Reform*, 7; Herbert A. Thomas Jr., "Victims of Circumstance: Negroes in a Southern Town, 1865–1880," *Register of the Kentucky Historical Society* (July 1973): 256.

21. See the biography of William C. Goodloe in Ranck, *History of Lexington*, 389.

22. Wright, *Lexington: Heart of the Bluegrass*, 98.

23. John Kellogg suggests that the housing created for African Americans outside of Lexington lacked the gathering places found in the city, such as grocery

stores and barbershops. The primary social organizations in these outlying areas were churches: four in 1860, and eleven in 1881. John Kellogg, "The Formation of Black Residential Areas in Lexington, Kentucky, 1865–1887," *Journal of Southern History* 48, no. 1 (February 1982): 49.

24. Steven Hahn, *A Nation under Our Feet: Black Political Struggles in the Rural South from Slavery to the Great Migration* (Cambridge, MA: Belknap Press of Harvard University Press, 2003), 17.

25. The 1870 U.S. census clearly indicates the changes resulting from the Civil War and emancipation, such as the number of African Americans moving from rural areas of Kentucky to cities such as Lexington.

26. Bolin, *Bossism and Reform*, 6.

27. "Ike Murphy's Real Name," *Daily Inter Ocean*, July 28, 1891, 3.

28. Tax records between 1868 and 1869 show one fewer child in the household, and Isaac Murphy's obituary mentions that "America moved with Isaac and a little sister, who died in childhood, into Lexington where [they] lived with her father Green Murphy." Llewellyn P. Tarleton, "Isaac Murphy: A Memorial," *Thoroughbred Record*, March 21, 1896.

29. John W. Blassingame, *The Slave Community: Plantation Life in the Ante-Bellum South* (New York: Oxford University Press, 1972), 60–76.

30. Lucious H. Holsey, "The Colored Methodist Episcopal Church," in *African American Religious History: A Documentary Witness* (Durham, NC: Duke University Press, 1999), 254.

31. Hahn, *Nation under Our Feet*, 41.

32. Rev. C. H. Parrish, ed., *Golden Jubilee of the General Association of Colored Baptists in Kentucky* (Louisville: Mayes Printing Company, 1915), 268–72; John H. Spencer, *A History of Kentucky Baptists from 1769 to 1885* (Cincinnati: J. R. Baumes, 1885), 653–74; Alice Allison Dunnigan, *The Fascinating Story of Black Kentuckians: Their Heritage and Traditions* (Washington, DC: Associated Publishers, 1982), 133–34; L. H. McIntyre, *One Grain of Salt: The First African Baptist Church West of the Allegheny Mountains* (Lexington: L. H. McIntyre, 1986), 1–11; Lucas, *History of Blacks in Kentucky*, 121–22.

33. McIntrye, *One Grain of Salt*, 15–17.

34. *Biography of London Ferrill, Pastor of the First Baptist Church of Colored Persons, Lexington, KY* (Lexington: A. W. Elder, 1854), 7.

35. Ibid., 8. Jeremiah Murphy's history in Lexington began in the early part of the century, around 1803. In 1804 Murphy was granted permission "to keep a tavern at his dwelling house in Lexington, for one year." In 1834 Murphy sold a tract of land to the owners of the Kentucky Association's racetrack and added to the original purchase. J. Winston Coleman Jr., *Stage Coach Days in the Bluegrass* (Lexington: University Press of Kentucky, 1995), 55. Also see Ranck, *History of Lexington*, 131.

36. Spencer, *History of Kentucky Baptists*, 657.

37. "Narrative of the Life of General Leslie Combs of Kentucky," *American Whig Review*, February 1852, 142–55.

38. Wright, *Lexington: Heart of the Bluegrass*, 43–45.

39. Lucas, *History of Blacks in Kentucky*, 123–24.

40. To defend white supremacy and oppose Reconstruction and racial mixing, groups such as the Ku Klux Klan formed to intimidate blacks and their supporters and gain social, political, and economic control of the South. See John Hope Franklin, *Reconstruction after the Civil War* (Chicago: University of Chicago Press, 1994), 150–69; Foner, *Forever Free*, 134–35; George C. Wright, *Racial Violence in Kentucky, 1865–1940* (Baton Rouge: Louisiana State University, 1990), 40–44.

41. On the development of an education system for blacks during Reconstruction and the role of the black church, see Howard, "The Struggle for Equal Education in Kentucky," 305–28.

42. Butchart, *Schooling the Freed People*, 11.

43. See letter from Rev. Edward P. Smith to M. E. Strieby, Secretary of the American Missionary Association, October 4, 1865, in Sears, *Camp Nelson*, 269–71.

44. Ibid.

45. Butchart, *Schooling the Freed People*, 7.

46. See McIntyre, *One Grain of Salt*, 38; Spencer, *History of Kentucky Baptists*, 656.

47. The AMA supported the freedmen in developing black churches and attracting "a better educated and competent ministry" that would be able to meet the demand for enlightened black religious leaders in the latter part of the nineteenth century. American Missionary Association, *The Twenty-Third Annual Report of the American Missionary Association* (New York: American Missionary Association, 1869), 58.

48. Butchart, *Schooling the Freed People*, 17–51.

49. I believe Isaac Murphy may have attended school at First African Baptist Church for two reasons: first, he lived in Jordan's Row in downtown Lexington, near where First African Baptist was located; second, Murphy's ten-year-anniversary wedding ceremony in 1893 was presided over by the Reverend S. P. Young, minister of First African Baptist, who would also officiate at Murphy's funeral in 1896.

50. See letter from Mary Colton to George Whipple, October 10, 1865, in Sears, *Camp Nelson*, 271.

51. Ibid.

52. W. D. Johnson, *Biographical Sketches of Prominent Negro Men and Women of Kentucky* (Lexington: Standard Print, 1897), 18–19. The Brittons lived on Mill Street between Second and Third sometime between 1859 and 1866. *Lexington 1859–60 City Directory* (Lexington: Hitchcock and Searles, 1859), 37.

53. Johnson mentions that Henry Britton was a member of the Colored Fair Association's inaugural board of directors and was elected secretary. However, the official ledger containing the board's minutes and a list of officers does not mention Britton. This can probably be attributed to the absence of the August 11, 1869,

minutes. Shortly after the association's creation, Henry Scroggins took over as secretary and remained in the position until 1875. Johnson, *Biographical Sketches of Prominent Negro Men and Women of Kentucky*, 75–89.

54. See Richard D. Sears, *A Utopian Experiment in Kentucky: Integration and Social Equality at Berea, 1866–1904* (Westport, CT: Greenwood Publishers, 1996), 77; Harrison and Klotter, *New History of Kentucky*, 57; James T. Haley, *Afro-American Encyclopedia; Or Thoughts, Doings, and Sayings of the Race, Embracing Lectures, Biographical Sketches, Sermons, Poems, Names of Universities, Colleges, Seminaries, Newspapers, Books, and a History of the Denominations, Giving the Numerical Strength of Each* (Nashville: Haley and Florida, 1895), 563.

55. Colton to Whipple, October 10, 1865.

56. Parrish, *Golden Jubilee*, 83–85.

57. Lucas, *History of Blacks in Kentucky*, 239.

58. Marjorie H. Parker, "Some Educational Activities of the Freedmen's Bureau," *Journal of Negro History* 23, no. 1 (Winter 1954): 10.

59. See DuBois, *Black Reconstruction in America*, 645–48.

60. One example of whites' response to the changing legal status of blacks was reported in "Freedmen's Affairs," *Cincinnati Daily Gazette*, January 8, 1866, 3. An officer from the Freedmen's Bureau wrote:

> Although much opposition is manifested towards the free labor system, as a general rule men of intelligence in [South Carolina and Georgia] express their determination to cooperate with the Freedmen's Bureau in its efforts to elevate the condition of the Negro, and preserving harmony between the races. In Florida, however, the same good feeling does not seem to exist, a number of whites having notified General Foster by letter that unless they were allowed to whip and shoot Negroes whenever it suited their fancy, they would leave the State. Their request not being acceded to, large numbers of the planters are immigrating to Texas, where they hope to enjoy unrestricted liberty in the exercising of the harmonizing efforts in behalf of the African.

61. In *Black Reconstruction in America*, DuBois discusses the conflicting ideas whites had to process about human nature and self-discovery. In the foreword he writes:

> It would be only fair to the reader to say frankly in advance that the attitude of any person toward this story will be distinctly influenced by his theories of the Negro race. If he believes that the Negro in America and in general is an average and ordinary human being who under a given environment develops like other human beings, then he will read this story and judge it by the facts adduced. If, however, he regards the Negro as a distinctly inferior creation, who can never successfully take part in modern civilization and whose emancipation and enfranchisement were gestures against nature, then he will need something more than the sort of facts that I have set down. But this latter person, I am not trying to convince. I am simply pointing out these two points of view, so obvious to Americans, and then without further ado, I am assuming the truth in the first.

In fine, I am going to tell this story as though Negroes were ordinary human beings, realizing that this attitude will from the first seriously curtail my audience.

62. John Watson Alvord, *Bureau Refugees, Freedmen and Abandoned Lands 1867: Third Semi-Annual Report of Schools for Freedmen* (Washington, DC: Government Printing Office, 1867), 33.

63. Howard, "The Struggle for Equal Education in Kentucky," 307.

64. See John Cox and LaWanda Cox, "General O. O. Howard and the Misrepresented Bureau," *Journal of Southern History* 19, no. 4 (November 1953): 433–34.

65. Ibid., 436.

66. In February 1866 a distinguished group of black men met with President Johnson in the White House: George T. Downing, William E. Mathews, John Jones, John F. Cook, Joseph E. Otis, A. W. Ross, William Whipper, John M. Brown, Alexander Dunlap, Frederick Douglass, and Douglass's son Lewis. Among other pressing matters, the delegation asked the president about his policy regarding black suffrage. Johnson explained that, in his opinion, giving the black man the vote would create the perfect conditions for a race war. Frederick Douglass responded with a question: "You enfranchise your enemies and disenfranchise your friends?" He continued: "My own impression is that the very thing that your Excellency would avoid in the Southern states can only be avoided by the very measure that we proposed. . . . I would like to say a word or so in regard to that matter of enfranchisement of the blacks as a means of preventing the very thing which your Excellency seems to apprehend—that is a conflict of races." Quoted in DuBois, *Black Reconstruction in America*, 298–99.

67. John Hope Franklin, *From Slavery to Freedom: A History of African Americans* (New York: Alfred A. Knopf, 1967), 304–6.

68. Howard, "Struggle for Equal Education in Kentucky," 307.

69. In *A History of Blacks in Kentucky*, Lucas accounts for the cost of purchasing Ladies Hall and reveals that one of the key figures in securing the building was James Turner, a plasterer. Turner was also a board member of the Colored Fair Association.

70. See Lucas, *History of Blacks in Kentucky*, 239–41; American Missionary Association, *Twenty-Third Annual Report*, 44.

71. "Report of Schools; State of Kentucky, from Month of September, 1866," Records of the Field Officers for the State of Kentucky, Bureau of Refugees, Freedmen, and Abandoned Lands, 1865–1872, roll 49, Monthly and Other School Reports, Kentucky, April 1866–July 1870, National Archives and Records Administration, Washington, DC.

72. Joe M. Richardson, "Francis L. Cardozo: Black Educator during Reconstruction," *Journal of Negro History* 48, no. 1 (Winter 1979): 78.

73. S. C. Hale, "Kentucky: Howard School Lexington," *American Missionary* (September 1867): 198–99.

74. T. K. Noble to J. W. Alvord, January 13, 1869, and T. K. Noble to J. W. Alvord, July 1, 1868, Records of the Education Division of the Bureau of Refugees,

Freedmen, and Abandoned Lands, 1865–1871, roll 21, Monthly and Other School Reports, Kentucky, April 1866–July 1879, National Archives and Records Administration, Washington, DC.

75. "The Hottest Day of the Season," *Cincinnati Daily Enquirer*, July 14, 1869, 1; "Speakers for the Colored Educational Convention," *Cincinnati Commercial Tribune*, July 13, 1869, 1.

76. In his personal reports to the Freedmen's Bureau, Runkle includes his observations of the Colored Educational Convention: "The Convention proved satisfactorily that the colored man know[s] how [to] transact business and demonstrate[d] that there are colored men whose oratorical powers compare favorably with any of the white race, and Kentucky, who boasts of her orators, has seldom had within her borders men who speak more sensibly and more effectively that Peter Clark or John Mercer Langston." B. P. Runkle, "Narration Report of Schools for Six-Months Ending July 1st, 1870," Freedmen's Bureau papers.

77. "Colored Educational Convention," *Courier Journal*, July 15, 1869, 1.

78. "Second Day's Proceedings of Their Educational Convention," *Courier Journal*, July 16, 1869, 1.

79. "The Colored Educational Convention in Louisville," *Baltimore Sun*, July 20, 1869, 4.

80. Johnson, *Biographical Sketches of Prominent Negro Men and Women*, 77; Lucas, *History of Blacks in Kentucky*, 288–89.

81. Johnson, *Biographical Sketches of Prominent Negro Men and Women*, 77.

82. The Colored Fair Association's ledger, which records board attendance, financial decisions, and revenues, is missing information from the initial planning meeting. For additional information about the Colored Fair Association, see Lucas, *History of Blacks in Kentucky*, 289.

83. "The Great Colored Fair," *Indianapolis Freeman*, October 3, 1891, 3.

84. R. C. O. Benjamin, *Negro Business Directory Fair Souvenir for Lexington, KY, 1899* (Lexington: Standard Printing Company, 1899), 1.

85. The living accommodations at 17 Jordan's Row have been identified as the place Isaac Murphy lived with his grandfather, Green Murphy.

86. Online database, Civil War Pension Index: General Index to Pension Files, 1861–1934, Ancestry.com; original data from General Index to Pension Files, 1861–1934, T288, National Archives and Records Administration, Washington, DC.

87. Huntley Dupre, *Rafinescue in Lexington, 1819–1826* (Lexington: Bur Press, 1945), 53.

88. For a discussion of Jeremiah Murphy's early business life in Lexington, see Charles R. Staples, *The History of Pioneer Lexington* (Lexington: University Press of Kentucky, 1996), 288. According to Staples, Jeremiah Murphy's first job was as custodian of the first courthouse constructed in 1788. See also Epes Sargent, *The Life and Public Services of Henry Clay* (New York: Greenley and McElrath, 1844), 23; Evert Augustus Duyckinck, *Portrait Gallery of Eminent Men and Women of Europe and America* (New York: Johnson, Wilson, 1873), 235.

89. Ranck, *History of Lexington*, 130–31.

90. *Lexington 1859–60 Directory*. http://www.rootsweb.ancestry .com/~kyfayett/1859_directory.htm.

91. Kellogg, "Formation of Black Residential Areas in Lexington," 49.

92. Ibid.

## 5. The New Order of Things

1. Lewis Collins and Richard Henry Collins, *Collins' Historical Sketches of Kentucky*, vol. 1 (Covington, KY: Collins and Company 1878), 199.

2. The visible occurrence caused magnetic disturbances and disrupted telegraph transmissions for more than sixteen hours. Scientists at the Kew Observatory witnessed eruptions on the surface of the sun; some were rather large in diameter and grouped with others. These sunspots, scientists later correlated, precede solar flares that eject massive amounts of radioactive material. Carried by the solar winds, this material travels at more than a million miles per hour, and the earth is in its direct path. Fortunately, the earth's magnetic poles act as a force field, diverting much of the radioactive material around the planet. The relatively little that gets through is trapped at the North and South Poles, where the combination of magnetism and charged particles causes the sky to glow bluish green or red.

3. George W. Ranck, *History of Lexington, Kentucky: Its Early Annals and Recent Progress* (Cincinnati: Robert Clarke, 1872), 130.

4. Ibid., 131–32.

5. Thomas D. Clark, *A History of Kentucky* (Ashland, KY: Jesse Stuart Foundation, 1988), 186.

6. Suzanne Marshall, *Violence in the Black Patch of Kentucky and Tennessee* (Columbia: University of Missouri Press, 1994), 60.

7. Frederick Douglass, "Appeal to Congress for Impartial Suffrage," 1867, in *Selected Addresses of Frederick Douglass: An African American Heritage Book* (Radford, VA: Wilder Publications, 2008), 31–37.

8. On January 24 the African American community of Frankfort, Kentucky, called a meeting to discuss the best way to motivate the "colored people" of the state to take responsibility for their political interests and contest the Democrats' claim that they were "ignorant and incapable of self-government." Instead, the black leadership of Frankfort proposed a state convention "to discuss and prosecute means appertaining to the political issues of the day, and to the vital interest of our race throughout the State." In the convention's preamble, the Committee of Arrangements stated: "Whereas, We, the colored people of the State of Kentucky, as in other States, as a class, since the organization of the government, have been unjustly deprived of our natural born rights, we now do hail with profound gratitude to God the new order of things appertaining to our status and inevitable approachment of our enfranchisement manhood by the enactment and ratification of the Fifteenth Constitutional Amendment." *Kentucky Statesman*, February 1, 1870, 3.

9. John Kellogg provides an excellent description of Lexington as a distinctly Southern city: "Although located in what is generally considered a border state, Lexington itself, as well as the surrounding Bluegrass Region, was distinctly southern in terms of racial composition, antebellum extent of slaveholding, and attitude of the white population towards Negroes and their place in society. The Bluegrass was a traditional stronghold of slaveholding interests in the state, and Lexington itself was an important slave market." John Kellogg, "The Formation of Black Residential Areas in Lexington, Kentucky, 1865–1887," *Journal of Southern History* 48, no. 1 (February 1982): 25.

10. Kellogg discusses the establishment of the Lower Street cluster of homes as happening as early as 1844. Ibid.

11. Rev. C. H. Parrish, ed., *Golden Jubilee of the General Association of Colored Baptists in Kentucky* (Louisville: Mayes Printing Company, 1915), 249–52; Marion B. Lucas, *A History of Blacks in Kentucky: From Slavery to Segregation, 1760–1891* (Frankfort: Kentucky Historical Society, 2003), 239.

12. Advertisement for the Lexington branch of the National Savings Bank and Trust Company, *Kentucky Statesman*, November 8, 1870, 3.

13. After Bush was convicted and sentenced to death, Tarleton argued that his client had not received fair treatment because the jury did not represent a body of his peers: Kentucky law excluded "colored men" from serving on juries, which, Tarleton claimed, violated the Fourteenth Amendment. The initial guilty verdict was overturned by the U.S. Circuit Court, only to have that decision overturned in the Kentucky Court of Appeals. Finally, on January 29, 1883, Tarleton won his appeal before the U.S. Supreme Court, in an opinion written by Justice John Marshall Harlan. However, the Kentucky court ignored the high court's opinion, convicted Bush of murder, and hanged him on November 21, 1884. See "Color Line in Juries," *Columbus Daily Enquirer*, February 2, 1883, 1; "John Bush, after Six Years in Prison and Four Tedious Trials, Appeals, etc., Is Hanged—Was He Guilty?" *Daily Evening Bulletin*, November 22, 1884, 1.

14. Lisa Materson discusses black women's power both before and after ratification of the Fifteenth Amendment: "At community rallies, women voted on issues and expressed their opinions, sometimes shouting them from the crowd. They made their politics known in other ways. In 1868, for instance, white employers in Mississippi were alarmed when cooks and maids showed up for work wearing campaign buttons with images of the Republican presidential candidate Ulysses S. Grant." Lisa Materson, *For the Freedom of Her Race: Black Women and Electoral Politics in Illinois, 1877–1932* (Chapel Hill: University of North Carolina Press, 2009), 4.

15. Elsa Barkley Brown discusses the power black women wielded in and over their Southern communities, especially with regard to voting Republican. She suggests that African American women were not averse to using force to ensure that their "men folk" did their duty as major stakeholders in their communities. A black man who decided to vote Democratic would be subjected to the ire of the whole black community, especially the women. Elsa Barkley Brown, "To Catch

the Vision of Freedom," in *African American Women and the Vote, 1837–1965* (Amherst: University of Massachusetts Press, 1997), 66–99.

16. An article in the *Kentucky Statesman* reported some of the difficulties experienced by black Republicans: "On the morning of the election in Lexington at one of the precincts the polls were not opened till a late hour, and the poor excuse offered that the appointed clerk, Capt. Lindsay, had failed to come and must be waited for. Again, the polls were closed an hour or two for breakfast, then about two hours for dinner, and all through the day the work 'dragged its slow length along,' with disgusting tardiness." "The Election," *Kentucky Statesman*, August 5, 1870, 3. See also "Our County Democrats and the Negroes," *Kentucky Statesman*, July 14, 1870, 2.

17. "Colored Meeting in Lexington," *Kentucky Statesman*, February 18, 1870, 3.

18. Kellogg's compelling article "The Formation of Black Residential Areas in Lexington" clearly describes the various neighborhood dynamics, based on who lived where. Directly south of the central district of Lexington was the black business district on Vine Street, which was also known as Hunt's Row, named after the John Wesley Hunt's son.

19. "Colored Schools," *Kentucky Statesman*, January 7, 1870, 3.

20. "Colored Schools," *Kentucky Statesman*, January 28, 1870, 3.

21. *Maydwell's 1867 Directory of Lexington* (Cincinnati: Miami Print and Publishing Company, 1867).

22. "The Great Colored Fair," *Indianapolis Freedman*, October 3, 1891, 3.

23. Kevin Gaines, *Uplifting the Race: Black Leadership, Politics, and Culture in the Twentieth Century* (Chapel Hill: University of North Carolina Press, 1996), 19.

24. The October 21, 1870, issue of the *Kentucky Statesman* broke down U.S. census data into categories based on gender, race, and location in the city's four wards. In the First Ward, where America lived, black women outnumbered black males almost three to two.

25. Deed No. 89, Fayette County Deed Book 49, County Court April 1870–Oct. 1871, 640.

26. Robinson would run for office as the Democratic Party's "colored" candidate in 1871. He was supported by other black leaders such as George Scroggins and Erasmus Wells, both of whom believed the Republicans were not sincere about advancing black men into power. The election of two blacks in 1870—Hiram Revels of Mississippi to the Senate on January 20 and Joseph Rainey to the House of Representatives on December 12—symbolized the dramatic changes taking place across the South. Robinson and colleagues recognized that the time was right for black men to claim the political power available through public office.

27. Application No. 174.318 and Certificate No. 137.891, issued as confirmation of a valid claim to the pension of Jerry Burns, Civil War Pension Index: General Index to Pension Files, 1861–1934, Ancestry.com; original data from General Index to Pension Files, 1861–1934, T288, National Archives and Records Administration, Washington, DC.

28. Patricia Hill Collins, *Fighting Words: Black Women and the Search for Justice* (Minneapolis: University of Minnesota Press, 1998), 5.

29. W. E. B. DuBois, *Black Reconstruction in America, 1860–1880* (New York: Free Press, 1992), 671.

30. DuBois's chapter "Back towards Slavery" in *Black Reconstruction in America* is an excellent study of how whites in the South responded to Reconstruction and the advancement of blacks as socially, economically, and politically viable individuals. For specific accounts of violence in Kentucky during Reconstruction, see George C. Wright, *Racial Violence in Kentucky, 1865–1940: Lynchings, Mob Rule and "Legal Lynchings"* (Baton Rouge: Louisiana State University, 1990).

31. John Hope Franklin, *Reconstruction after the Civil War* (Chicago: University of Chicago Press, 1994), 150–69.

32. Wright, *Racial Violence in Kentucky*, 39.

33. "The Ku Klux: Greeley's Men at Work in Kentucky—They Hang a Man, His Wife and His Daughter to a Tree," *New York Times*, November 5, 1870, 1.

34. See Wright's account of this lynching in *Racial Violence in Kentucky*, 51.

35. Alexander Keyssar, *The Right to Vote: The Contested History of Democracy in the United States* (New York: Basic Books, 2000), 76.

36. Spencer Talbott, Freedman's Bank Records, 1865–1871, Ancestry.com; original data from Registers of Signatures of Depositors in Branches of the Freedman's Savings and Trust Company, 1865–1874, micropublication M816, National Archives and Records Administration, Washington, DC.

37. "Bank Book and Circulars," in *Documentary History of Reconstruction: Political, Military, Social, Religious, Educational & Industrial 1865 to the Present Time* (Cleveland: Arthur H. Clark, 1906), 384.

38. "Freedmen's Savings and Trust Company," House of Representatives, Report No. 58, 43rd Congress, 2nd session, January 25, 1875, 5.

39. America Burns is listed as owning "one city lot" worth $400 in the Fayette County tax records.

40. "Freedmen's Bank," House of Representatives, Report No. 502, 44rd Congress, 1st session, May 19, 1876, 3.

41. DuBois, *Black Reconstruction in America*, 599; Carl Osthaus, *Freedmen, Philanthropy, and Fraud* (Urbana: University of Chicago, 1976), 1.

42. See Osthaus, *Freedmen, Philanthropy, and Fraud*, 1–20; DuBois, *Black Reconstruction in America*, 599–600; John Hope Franklin, *From Slavery to Freedom: A History of African Americans* (New York: Alfred A. Knopf, 1967), 314–15; Eric Foner, *Forever Free: The Story of Emancipation and Reconstruction* (New York: Vintage Books, 2006), 193–94; Franklin, *Reconstruction after the Civil War*, 181–82.

43. Advertisement for the Lexington branch of the National Savings Bank and Trust Company, *Kentucky Statesman*, November 8, 1870, 3.

44. DuBois would argue that the Freedmen's Bank was a failure largely because of the lack of Federal regulation of the bank's controllers. DuBois, *Black Reconstruction in America*, 599–600.

45. Osthaus, *Freedmen, Philanthropy, and Fraud*, 52.

46. Ibid., 50.

47. Advertisement for the Lexington branch of the National Savings Bank and Trust Company," *Kentucky Statesman*, November 8, 1870, 3.

48. DuBois, *Black Reconstruction in America*, 599–600; America Burns, Record No. 1479, Freemen's Bank Ledger.

49. According to Osthaus, *Freedmen, Philanthropy, and Fraud*, 100–101, the actual "amount due to whites was quite substantial at New Orleans and New York, and perhaps great at Beaufort and Jacksonville," where whites had invested heavily in the bank to take advantage of the interests rates. This was problematic, as the Freedmen's Bank was intended to be a savings bank for blacks only.

50. DuBois, *Black Reconstruction in America*, 599.

51. "Freeland's Famous Jockey: Joe Cotton's Owner Tells How He First Taught the Boy to Ride," *New York Times*, August 20, 1885, 3.

52. Historians have suggested that Green Murphy may have been involved in the decision to apprentice his grandson to the Williams and Owings stable, but I have been unable to locate Green Murphy in any of the 1870–1890 census data for Lexington. In fact, as noted previously, neither of the males listed as living in America and Isaac's First Ward home was Green Murphy. David Wiggins, *Glory Bound: Black Athletes in a White America* (Syracuse, NY: Syracuse University Press, 1997), 22; Ed Hotaling, *The Great Black Jockeys: The Lives and Times of the Men Who Dominated America's First National Sport* (Rocklin, CA: Forum Prima Publishing, 1999), 239.

53. Theodore Ayrault Dodge, *Riders of Many Lands* (New York: Harper and Brothers, 1894), 171–75.

54. Ranck, *History of Lexington*, 136.

55. David Roediger, *The Wages of Whiteness: Race and the Making of the American Working Class* (London: Verso, 2002), 144–45.

56. James Weldon Johnson, *Black Manhattan* (New York: Arno Press and the *New York Times*, 1968), 61.

57. Frank Talamadge Phelps, "The Nearest Perfect Jockey," *Thoroughbred Record*, May 13, 1967, 1247.

58. Herbert Gutman suggests that both during and after slavery, African Americans maintained a sense of community through the use of "fictive, or quasi" kinship names such as "uncle" and "aunt." We also know from history that whites utilized the prefix of uncle and aunt to mark older African American men and women as subordinate. This naming would evolve into the twentieth century phenomenon of white men calling black men George, and black men responding antagonistically to the label calling white men Mr. Charley. Herbert Gutman, *The Black Family in Slavery and Freedom, 1750–1925* (New York: Pantheon Books, 1976), 220–22.

59. "Freeland's Famous Jockey," 3.

60. "Isaac Murphy Was One of the Greatest Men that Ever Rode," transcript of a telephone interview conducted with Nate Cantrell by Pamela Douglas,

March 15, 1976, Betty Borries Collection, Keeneland Research Library, Lexington, KY.

61. Ibid.

62. In his short story "The Man Who Was a Horse," African American folklorist Julius Lester gives us a glimpse of what Murphy would eventually feel while riding one of his mounts:

> The longer he was with the herd, the less he thought. His mind slowly emptied itself of anything relating to his other life and refilled with sky, plain, grass, water and shrubs. At these times he was more aware of the full-bodied animal beneath him. His own body seemed to take on a new life and he was aware of the wind against his chest, of the taut muscles in his arms, which felt to him like the forelegs of his horses. The only thing he didn't feel he had was tail to float in the wind behind him.

Julius Lester, *Long Journey Home: Stories from Black History* (New York: Dell, 1972), 88.

63. John H. Davis calls Isaac Murphy "one of the best judges of pace on the American turf." According to Davis, Murphy "could tell to almost the fraction of a second just how fast a horse under him was going." John H. Davis, *The American Turf: History of the Thoroughbred, Together with Personal Reminiscences by the Author, Who, in Turn, Has Been Jockey, Trainer and Owner* (New York: John Polhemus, 1907), 88.

## 6. Learning to Ride and Taking Flight

1. "King of the Pigskin Artists: The Successful Career of Isaac Murphy, the Colored Archer of America," *New York Herald*, March 17, 1889, 24.

2. Lewellyn P. Tarleton, "Isaac Murphy: A Memorial," *Thoroughbred Record*, March 21, 1896, 136.

3. *American Slavery as It Is: Testimony of a Thousand Witnesses* (New York: American Anti-Slavery Society, 1839), 186–87.

4. *American Racing Colors: Colors of the Owners of Racing Horses as Worn by Their Jockeys at the Meetings of the American Jockey Club* (New York: Thomas K. Miller, 1884).

5. "Freeland's Famous Jockey," *New York Times*, August 20, 1885, 3.

6. There is a wonderful section on the traditional purpose of apprenticeships for stable boys who wanted to become jockeys in C. R. Acton, *Silk and Spur* (New York: Charles Scribner's Sons, 1936), 58–70.

7. Will Ogilvie, "Aintree Calls," *Bailey's Magazine of Sports and Pastimes* 101, no. 650 (April 1914): 199.

8. "The Spring Campaign," *Kentucky Live Stock Record* 1, no. 3 (February 19, 1875): 38.

9. "Stock Gossip," *Kentucky Live Stock Record* 1, no. 4 (February 26, 1875): 54.

10. "King of the Pigskin Artists," 24; Betty Borries, *Isaac Murphy: Kentucky's Record Jockey* (Berea: Kentucke Imprints, 1988), 23.

11. According to Thomas Clark, "Crab Orchard was selected for the meeting place because it was at the forks of the Louisville and Lexington branches of the Wilderness Road." Thomas D. Clark, *A History of Kentucky* (Ashland, KY: Jesse Stuart Foundation, 1988), 77. Being that this was the location of Isaac Murphy's first professional race, it is appropriate that was at a kind of crossroads between old and new, past and present. See also Lincoln County Historical Society, *Lincoln County, Kentucky* (Stanford, KY: Turner Publishing, 2002), 34.

12. "King of the Pigskin Artists," 24; Borries, *Isaac Murphy*, 23.

13. "King of the Pigskin Artists," 24.

14. Borries, *Isaac Murphy*, 54.

15. "King of the Pigskin Artists"; R. Gerald Alvey, *Kentucky Bluegrass Country* (Jackson: University Press of Mississippi, 1992), 135–36.

16. John E. Kleber, ed., *The Kentucky Encyclopedia* (Lexington: University Press of Kentucky, 1992), 496–97; Alvey, *Kentucky Bluegrass Country*, 188–89; Matt Winn, *Down the Stretch: The Story of Colonel Matt J. Winn as Told to Frank G. Menke* (New York: Smith and Durrell, 1945), 3; Lynn S. Renau, *Racing around Kentucky* (Louisville: Lynn S. Renau Antiques Consultant, 1995), 43–57.

17. Acton, *Silk and Spur*, 11.

18. Henry Custance, *Riding Recollections and Turf Stories* (London: Edward Arnold, 1894), 13–17; "Mr. Richard Ten Broeck," *Bailey's Monthly Sporting Magazine of Sports and Pastimes* 8, no. 51 (1864): 55–57.

19. Robert Black, *The Jockey Club and Its Founders in Three Periods* (London: Smith, Elder, 1891), 332.

20. Jim Bolus, *Run for the Roses: 100 Years at the Kentucky Derby* (New York: Hawthorne Books, 1974), 7; Winn, *Down the Stretch*, 26–27.

21. Bolus, *Run for the Roses*, 9.

22. Winn, *Down the Stretch*, 3.

23. Bolus, *Run for the Roses*, 11.

24. Renau, *Racing around Kentucky*, 47.

25. Bureau of the Census, "1870: Population," in *Ninth Census of the United States* (Washington, DC: Government Printing Office, 1872), 1:150.

26. *Kentucky Live Stock Record* 1, no. 16 (May 14, 1875): 231.

27. "A Riverside Farmer at Lexington," *Cincinnati Daily Gazette*, May 22, 1877, 2.

28. Bolus, *Run for the Roses*, 10; "The Inaugural of the Louisville Jockey Club," *Kentucky Live Stock Record*, reprinted in *Hoofprints of the Century* (Lexington: Thoroughbred Record, 1975), 16.

29. Bolus, *Run for the Roses*, 11.

30. In *New History of Kentucky* (Lexington: University Press of Kentucky, 1997), 136, Lowell Harrison and James Klotter identify Robert Scott as a farmer and breeder of blood animals. Whether Williams and Owings trained and raced Lady Greenfield for Scott is unclear. However, other than 1875, she does not show up as a racehorse of any significance.

31. "Racing Record for 1875," in *Spirit of the Times* (New York: Spirit of the Times, 1876), 31.

32. Philip St. Laurent, "The Negro in World History," *Tuesday Magazine* 3, no. 11 (July 1968): 16.

33. Orlando Patterson, *Slavery and Social Death: A Comparative Study* (Cambridge, MA: Harvard University Press, 1982), 249.

34. Philip A. Bruce, *The Plantation Negro as a Freeman: Observation on His Character, Condition, and Prospects in Virginia* (New York: G. P. Putnam's Sons, 1889), 243–44.

35. George M. Fredrickson, *The Black Image in the White Mind: The Debate on Afro-American Character and Racial Destiny, 1817–1914* (Middletown, CT: Wesleyan University Press, 1971), 245.

36. Tarleton, "Isaac Murphy: A Memorial," 136.

37. *Kentucky Live Stock Record* 3, no. 21 (May 22, 1876): 330.

38. "The Turf," *New Orleans Times*, December 28, 1875, 3.

39. "Cincinnati Railroad," *Cincinnati Commercial Tribune*, October 26, 1875, 4; "Railway Matters," *Cincinnati Daily Gazette*, January 1, 1878, 7; "Chester Park," *Cincinnati Commercial Tribune*, July 3, 1878, 8.

40. "Queen City Jockey Club," *Cincinnati Commercial Tribune*, January 23, 1878, 8.

41. He finished fourth on T. J. Megibben's Eaglet on the third day in the first race and again on Eaglet on the fourth day in the third race. "The Turf," *Kentucky Live Stock Record* 3, no. 23 (June 3, 1875): 360–61.

42. "The Kentucky Association," *Kentucky Live Stock Record* 4, no. 13 (September 23, 1876): 196.

43. "The Turf: Louisville Jockey Club: Second Day—Springbranch, Whisper, Redding and Eva Shirley the Winners," *Kentucky Live Stock Record* 4, no. 14 (September 30, 1876): 210.

44. W. E. B. DuBois, *Black Reconstruction in America, 1860–1880* (New York: Free Press, 1992), 691–92.

45. *Cincinnati Daily Gazette*, October 30, 1876.

46. DuBois, *Black Reconstruction in America*, 694.

47. Douglas A. Blackmon, *Slavery by Another Name: The Re-enslavement of Black Americans from the Civil War to World War II* (New York: Doubleday, 2008), 56.

48. Frederick Douglass, "Convict Lease System," 1895, 36, Frederick Douglass Papers, Library of Congress, Washington, DC.

49. Blackmon, *Slavery by Another Name*, 53.

50. "Stock Gossip: Messrs. Williams & Owings' Stable," *Kentucky Live Stock Record* 5, no. 15 (April 14, 1877): 228.

51. "The Turf," *Kentucky Live Stock Record* 5, no. 19 (May 12, 1877): 291.

52. "The Louisville Spring Meeting," *Kentucky Live Stock Record* 5, no. 20 (May 19, 1877): 312.

53. "Louisville Jockey Club, Tuesday, May 22d—the Derby Day," *Kentucky Live Stock Record* 5, no. 21 (May 26, 1877): 323.

54. Ibid.

55. "Sixth Day," *Kentucky Live Stock Record* 5, no. 22 (June 2, 1877): 340.

56. "King of the Pigskin Artists," 24.

57. "Louisville Races," *Wheeling Register*, May 25, 1877, 1; "Sixth Day," *Kentucky Live Stock Record* 5, no. 22 (June 2, 1877): 340.

58. "Ten Broeck's Great Race," *Wheeling Register*, May 30, 1877, 1; "Ten Broeck Cuts Down the Fastest Two Mile Record Three Seconds," *New Orleans Times*, May 30, 1877, 1; "A Glorious Event," *Plain Dealer*, May 26, 1877, 1.

59. For compelling examinations of the genesis of horse racing in the East, see Steven Reiss, *The Sport of Kings and the Kings of Crime: Horse Racing, Politics and Organized Crime in New York, 1865–1913* (Syracuse, NY: Syracuse University Press, 2011); Kimberly Gatto, *Saratoga Race Course: The August Place to Be* (Charleston, SC: History Press, 2011); Ed Hotaling, *They're Off! Horse Racing at Saratoga* (Syracuse, NY: Syracuse University Press, 1995).

60. Reiss, *Sport of Kings*, 17.

61. Hotaling, *They're Off!* 88.

62. Reiss, *Sport of Kings*, 21.

63. "Saratoga: A Festival Week, a Genteel Affair, Hotel Life, the Weather, an Interesting Scene, a Splendid Picture," *New York Times*, July 19, 1865, 2.

64. Myra B. Young Armstead, *Lord, Please Don't Take Me in August: African Americans in Newport and Saratoga Springs, 1870–1930* (Urbana: University of Illinois Press, 1999), 39.

65. Hotaling, *They're Off!* 72; Reiss, *Sport of Kings*, 22.

66. "Saratoga: A Festival Week," 2. This was most likely the African Methodist Episcopal Zion Church discussed by Armstead in *Lord, Please Don't Take Me*, 115; Mount Olivet Baptist Church was not built until after 1870.

67. In a letter to his mother, Walt Whitman described the chaos in New York after the conscription law was passed:

> So the mob has risen at last in New York—I have been expecting it, but as the day for the draft had arrived & every thing was so quiet, I supposed all might go on smoothly—but it seems the passions of the people were only sleeping, & have burst forth with terrible fury, & they have destroyed life & property, the enrolment buildings &c as we hear—the accounts we get are a good deal in a muddle, but it seems bad enough—the feeling here is savage & hot as fire against New York, (the mob—"copperhead mob" the papers here call it,) & I hear nothing in all directions but threats of ordering up the gunboats, cannonading the city, shooting down the mob, hanging them in a body, &c &c—meantime I remain silent, partly amused, partly scornful, or occasionally put a dry remark, which only adds fuel to the flame—I do not feel it in my heart to abuse the poor people, or call for rope or bullets for them, but that is all the talk here, even in the hospitals.

"Correspondence," July 19, 1863, Walt Whitman Archive, Charles E. Feinberg Collection of Walt Whitman, 1839–1919, Library of Congress, http://whitmanarchive.org/biography/correspondence/cw/tei/loc.00777.html.

68. Theodore Corbett, *The Making of American Resorts: Saratoga Springs, Ballston Spa, Lake George* (New Brunswick, NJ: Rutgers University Press, 2001), 155.

69. John Morris [pseud.], *Wanderings of a Vagabond: An Autobiography* (New York: John O'Connor, 1873), 197–261.

70. "Saratoga Association," *Kentucky Live Stock Record* 5, no. 24 (June 16, 1877): 376.

71. See Hotaling, *They're Off!* 118; Reiss, *Sport of Kings*, 34–35.

72. "The Season at Saratoga: All the Hotels Are Ready," *New York Times*, June 17, 1878, 1; Hotaling, *They're Off!* 117–18.

73. "The Turf: Saratoga Races," *Kentucky Live Stock Record* 6, no. 6 (August 4, 1877): 82.

74. Ibid., 83.

75. "Third Day of Second Meeting—A Dead Heat for the Grinstead Stakes between Duke of Magenta and Spartan," *Kentucky Live Stock Record* 6, no. 8 (August 25, 1877): 115.

76. Rev. C. H. Parrish, ed., *Golden Jubilee of the General Association of Colored Baptists in Kentucky* (Louisville: Mayes Printing Company, 1915), 249–52; Marion B. Lucas, *A History of Blacks in Kentucky: From Slavery to Segregation, 1760–1891* (Frankfort: Kentucky Historical Society, 2003), 239.

77. See Kevin Gaines, *Uplifting the Race: Black Leadership, Politics, and Culture in the Twentieth Century* (Chapel Hill: University of North Carolina Press, 1996).

78. Nicodemus Town Company, broadside, circa 1877, Kansas Historical Society, reproduction in Photograph Collection E185.1877*1.

79. "Colored Emigrants: Their Departure Yesterday Evening for Kansas," *Lexington Press*, September 6, 1877, 4.

80. Nell Irvin Painter, *Exodusters: Black Migration to Kansas after Reconstruction* (New York: Alfred A. Knopf, 1977), 149–53.

81. George C. Wright, *Racial Violence in Kentucky, 1865–1940: Lynchings, Mob Rule, and "Legal Lynchings"* (Baton Rouge: Louisiana State University, 1990), 1.

82. "King of the Pigskin Artists," 24.

83. "The Louisville Race," *Kentucky Live Stock Record* 6, no. 14 (October 6, 1877): 212.

84. "Baltimore Races," *Kentucky Live Stock Record* 6, no. 18 (November 3, 1877): 278.

85. "Obituary—Death of Creedmoor," *Kentucky Live Stock Record* 6, no. 20 (November 17, 1877): 308.

86. "Kentucky Association," *Kentucky Live Stock Record* 7, no. 20 (May 18, 1878): 307.

87. "King of the Pigskin Artists," 24.

88. Ibid.

89. Ibid.

90. Catherine Thom-Bartlett, *"My Dear Brother": A Confederate Chronicle* (Richmond: Dietz Press, 1952), 88.

91. "Death of Col. J. W. Hunt-Reynolds," *Tri-Weekly Yeoman*, September 25, 1880; Thom-Bartlett, *"My Dear Brother,"* 89.

92. "Fleetwood Stock Farm," *Kentucky Live Stock Record* 3, no. 5 (January 29, 1876): 65.

93. "Death of Col. J. W. Hunt-Reynolds"; *Journal of Proceedings of the Forty Eighth Annual Convention of the Protestant Episcopal Church in the Diocese of Kentucky* (Louisville: John P. Morton, 1876), 17–20; Charles F. Hinds, *Ascension Episcopal Church: Frankfort, Kentucky, 1836–1996* (Frankfort: HAE, 1996), 53–57.

94. "Death of Col. J. W. Hunt-Reynolds"; Thom-Bartlett, *"My Dear Brother,"* 89. In 1867 J. W. Hunt-Reynolds sent $1,000 to Columbus, Georgia, to support the widows and children of Confederate soldiers killed in the Civil War. "A Wealthy Young Kentuckian," *Memphis Daily Avalanche*, February 1, 1867, 1.

95. Tax Commissioner's Book, Franklin County, KY, 1875, 42.

96. "Kentucky Association Races: Third Day," *Kentucky Live Stock Record* 8, no. 11 (September 14, 1878): 165.

97. Ibid.

98. "Louisville Jockey Club—Fall Meeting," *Kentucky Live Stock Record* 8, no. 14 (October 5, 1878): 213.

99. "An Interview with F. B. Harper—Some Inconsistencies Worth Noting," *Kentucky Live Stock Record* 8, no. 5 (August 3, 1878): 72.

100. Maryjean Wall, *How Kentucky Became Southern* (Lexington: University Press of Kentucky, 2010), 127.

101. Orlando Patterson, *Rituals of Blood: Consequences of Slavery in Two American Centuries* (New York: Basic Civitas, 1998), 27.

102. "Seventh (Extra) Day," *Kentucky Live Stock Record* 8, no. 14 (October 5, 1878): 213.

103. Ed Hotaling, *The Great Black Jockeys: The Lives and Times of the Men Who Dominated America's First National Sport* (Rocklin, CA: Forum Prima Publishing, 1999), 242.

104. See Gayle Bederman, *Manliness and Civilization: A Cultural History of Gender and Race in the United States, 1880–1917* (Chicago: University of Chicago Press, 1996).

105. Laura Hillenbrand, *Seabiscuit: An American Legend* (New York: Ballantine Books, 2001), 69.

106. "Jockey Ike Murphy: Methods of Training and Riding," *Kansas City Star*, July 11, 1885, 4.

107. Ibid.

108. "Kentucky Association: First Day," *Kentucky Live Stock Record* 9, no. 20 (May 17, 1879): 306.

109. "Louisville Jockey Club," *Kentucky Live Stock Record* 9, no. 21 (May 24, 1879): 324.

110. "Coming Races at Detroit," *Kentucky Live Stock Record* 9, no. 26 (June 28, 1879): 405.

111. "Isaac Murphy: Biographical Sketch of the Great Lexington Jockey," *Kentucky Leader*, March 20, 1889, 3.

112. Michelle Wallace, *Righteous Disposition: African Americans and the Politics of Racial Destiny after Reconstruction* (Chapel Hill: University of North Carolina Press, 2004), 9.

113. "Race Horses at Saratoga," *New York Herald*, June 18, 1879, 5.

114. Hotaling, *They're Off!* 135.

115. "Colored Jockey," *Macon Telegram*, November 25, 1879, 2.

116. "Saratoga," *Spirit of the Times* 97, no. 20 (July 26, 1879): 624.

117. Ibid.

118. Tarleton, "Isaac Murphy: A Memorial," 136.

119. Census Year: 1880, Census Location: Lexington, Fayette, Kentucky, p. 294, l. 6, Archive Roll 18, Archive Collection T655, National Archives and Records Administration, Washington, DC.

120. Walter Harrison Cripps, *Cancer of the Rectum: Its Pathology, Diagnosis, and Treatment* (London: J. and A. Churchill, 1880), 173.

121. The University of Kentucky archives contain a wonderful narrative of the Spencer family history, including the story of Benjamin Franklin Spencer, a Frankfort resident who became a shoemaker. Spencer lived in Frankfort at the same time as Isaac Murphy, so they may have known each other, and Spencer may have made Murphy a pair of boots.

122. "Negro Emigration from Kentucky," *Kentucky Live Stock Record* 11, no. 11 (March 13, 1880): 169.

123. "Funeral of Colonel J. W. Hunt Reynolds," *Lexington Weekly Press*, October 6, 1880, 2.

## 7. An Elegant Specimen of Manhood

1. Ed Hotaling, *The Great Black Jockeys: The Lives and Times of the Men Who Dominated America's First National Sport* (Rocklin, CA: Forum Prima Publishing, 1999), 249.

2. Laura Hillenbrand discusses the activities of jockeys in Tijuana, Mexico, where they "lived high and hard, riding by day, roaming the town in dense, noisy scrums by night, pouring into Molino Rojo, then the Turf Club saloon, then on to wild exploits in town, chasing giggling girls buck naked down motel corridors, stealing all the room keys to the town's biggest hotel." Laura Hillenbrand, *Seabiscuit: An American Legend* (New York: Ballantine Books, 2001), 84.

3. For more on how jockey clubs participated in the sex industry, see Alain Corbin and Alan Sheridan, *Women for Hire: Prostitution and Sexuality in France after 1850* (Cambridge, MA: Fellows of Harvard College, 1990); Walter J. Fraser, *Savannah in the Old South* (Athens: University of Georgia Press, 2003), 165.

4. See Eric Lott's discussion of the "White Negro" in *Love and Theft* (New York: Oxford University Press, 1995), 49–55.

5. Myra B. Young Armstead, *Lord, Please Don't Take Me in August* (Urbana: University of Illinois Press, 1999).

6. Hotaling, *Great Black Jockeys*, 242.

7. Ibid.

8. "State and Suburban," *Cincinnati Daily Gazette*, October 29, 1880, 3.

9. "Names Claimed," *Kentucky Live Stock Record* 13, no. 16 (April 16, 1881): 251; "Turf Talk," *Cincinnati Commercial Tribune*, April 18, 1881, 2.

10. "Immigration," *Kentucky Live Stock Record* 13, no. 20 (May 14, 1881): 305; George F. Seward, "Mongolian Immigration," *North American Review* 134, no. 307 (June 1882): 565.

11. Anna Pegler-Gordon, *In Sight of America: Photography and the Development of U.S. Immigration Policy* (Berkeley: University of California Press, 2009), 2–3; Kerry Abrams, "Polygamy, Prostitution, and the Federalization of Immigration Law," *Columbia Law Review* 105, no. 3 (April 2005): 641–716.

12. Sarah Barringer Gordon, "The Liberty of Self-Degradation: Polygamy, Woman Suffrage, and Consent in Nineteenth-Century America," *Journal of American History* 83, no. 3 (December 1996): 819.

13. Alexander Crummell, "The Dignity of Labour," in *Civilization and Black Progress: Selected Writings of Alexander Crummell on the South*, ed. J. R. Oldfield (Charlottesville: University Press of Virginia, 1995), 69.

14. Seward, "Mongolian Immigration," 567.

15. Abby Ferber, *White Man Falling: Race, Gender, and White Supremacy* (New York: Rowman and Littlefield, 1998), 4.

16. For a discussion of the representation of black men as jockeys, see Maryjean Wall, "Kentucky's Isaac Murphy: A Legacy Interrupted" (MA thesis, University of Kentucky, 2003), 81–88.

17. Frederick Douglass, "The Color Line," *North American Review* 132, no. 295 (June 1881): 568.

18. Ibid., 575.

19. "Fleetwood Farm," *Kentucky Live Stock Record* 13, no. 16 (April 16, 1881): 249.

20. Ibid., 250.

21. "The Turf," *Daily Inter-Ocean*, May 6, 1881, 5.

22. "Kentucky Association," *Kentucky Live Stock Record* 13, no. 20 (May 14, 1881): 307.

23. "Louisville Jockey Club Spring Meeting," *Kentucky Live Stock Record* 13, no. 22 (May 28, 1881): 340.

24. Ibid., 342.

25. "Louisville Spring Meeting," *Kentucky Live Stock Record* 13, no. 23 (June 4, 1881): 361.

26. Ibid., 345.

27. "St. Louis Jockey Club," *Kentucky Live Stock Record* 13, no. 25 (June 18, 1881): 388.

28. Ibid.

29. "Death of Ansel Williamson," *Kentucky Live Stock Record* 13, no. 26 (June 25, 1881): 409.

30. Annette Gordon Reed, *The Hemingses of Monticello* (New York: W. W. Norton, 2008), 44.

31. Ansel Williamson, jockey Ed Brown (later known as "Brown Dick"), and an unidentified groom are depicted in an oil painting of R. A. Alexander's most prized horse, Asteroid. It took artist Edward Troye three months to complete the painting, which is signed and dated December 11, 1864. Whether Troye's intent was to record the lives of these three black men, or whether his goal was simply to capture Asteroid's greatness, the painting illustrates that these men were more than human chattel. Indeed, Williamson and Brown were considered two of the top black horseman of the era and have been recognized as significant contributors to the sport of horse racing both during and after slavery.

32. Marcy S. Sacks, *Before Harlem: The Black Experience in New York City before World War I* (Philadelphia: University of Pennsylvania, 2006), 6–7.

33. James Weldon Johnson, *Black Manhattan* (New York: Da Capo Press, 1991), 58.

34. Ibid., 74.

35. Ibid., 64.

36. Ralph E. Luker, "Missions, Institutional Churches, and Settlement Houses: The Black Experience, 1885–1910," *Journal of Negro History* 69, no. 3–4 (Summer–Autumn 1984): 105–6.

37. In Robert Dowling's discussion of works by African Americans refuting white outsiders' commentary on black life, he references the work of Anna Julia Cooper. In *A Voice from the South*, Cooper responds to William Dean Howell's novel *An Imperative Duty*, which, according to Dowling, paints a narrow picture of black life. Robert Dowling, *Slumming in New York: From the Waterfront to Mythic Harlem* (Urbana: University of Illinois Press, 2007), 82–83.

38. "Editor's Historical Record," *Harper's Magazine*, November 1881, 956; Ira Rutkow, *James A. Garfield* (New York: Times Books, 2006), 1–3; Justus D. Doenecke, *The Presidencies of James A. Garfield & Chester A. Arthur* (Lawrence: Regents Press of Kansas, 1981), 95–96.

39. "The Great Need of Kentucky," *Kentucky Live Stock Record* 14, no. 4 (July 23, 1881): 56.

40. "Ed Corrigan and Some Incidents of His Picturesque Career," *Muskegan News Chronicle*, August 10, 1912, 10.

41. These numbers were derived by estimating how much Murphy received in riding fees plus 10 percent of the winnings in purse races and 20 percent in stakes races. He was responsible for his own travel costs, accommodations, and food.

42. C. J. Foster, "Isaac Murphy, Colored Jockey," *New York Sportsman* 14, no. 3 (January 20, 1883): 34.

43. "Isaac Murphy, the Noted Jockey," *Frankfort Roundabout*, January 27, 1883, 2.

44. Michelle Wallace, *Righteous Disposition: African Americans and the Politics of Racial Destiny after Reconstruction* (Chapel Hill: University of North Carolina Press, 2004), 9.

45. The only known photograph of Lucy Carr Murphy is in the T. T. Wendell Collection at the Kentucky Historical Society in Frankfort. From the image, it is apparent that she was a beautiful woman.

46. Douglas A. Boyd, *Crawfish Bottom: Recovering a Lost Kentucky Community* (Lexington: University Press of Kentucky, 2011), 19.

47. "Convention of Colored Men at Frankfort, February 23rd," *Kentucky Statesman*, March 1, 1870, 4.

48. See Victor Howard, *Black Liberation in Kentucky: Emancipation and Freedom, 1862–1884* (Lexington: University Press of Kentucky, 1983), 160–76.

49. Victor B. Howard, "The Struggle for Equal Education in Kentucky, 1866–1884," *Journal of Negro Education* 46, no. 3 (Summer 1977): 320.

50. Boyd, *Crawfish Bottom*, 19.

51. "First Class Jockey," *Kentucky Live Stock Record* 17, no. 11 (March 17, 1883): 170.

52. "Stock Gossip," *Kentucky Live Stock Record* 17, no. 12 (March 24, 1883): 180.

53. Emma Lou Thornbrough, *T. Thomas Fortune: Militant Journalist* (Chicago: University of Chicago Press, 1972), 44.

54. Irvine Garland Penn, *The Afro-American Press and Its Editors* (Springfield, MA: Willey, 1891), 483.

55. "The Prince of Jockeys: Isaac Murphy of Kentucky in and out of the Saddle," *New York Age* 3, no. 40 (July 5, 1890): 1.

56. "Sentiment and Doings of Our People," *New York Globe*, January 27, 1883, 2.

57. Darlene Clark Hine, "Rape and the Inner Lives of Black Women in the Middle West: Preliminary Thoughts on the Culture of Dissemblance," *Signs* 14, no. 4 (Summer 1989): 912–13.

58. Ibid., 915.

59. Lexington had paved streets before 1893, but the city had to use a vitrified brick to maintain the stability of major roads and streets. *Brick Roadways: Interstate Vitrified Brick and Paving Company* (Philadelphia: Press of Allen, Lane and Scott, 1894), 110.

60. "Kentucky Association," *Kentucky Live Stock Record* 17, no. 19 (March 12, 1883): 292.

61. James C. Claypool, *The Tradition Continues: The Story of Old Latonia, Latonia, and Turfway Racecources* (Fort Mitchell, KY: T. I. Hayes, 1997), 3.

62. "Latonia Jockey Club," *Kentucky Live Stock Record* 17, no. 23 (June 9, 1883): 360.

63. Claypool, *The Tradition Continues*, 5.

64. "The Three Cities' Course Opened with Great Success," *Cincinnati Commercial Tribune*, June 10, 1883, 1.

65. St. Clair Drake and Horace A. Cayton, *Black Metropolis: A Study of Negro Life in a Northern City* (Chicago: University of Chicago Press, 1993), 48; Christopher Robert Reed, *Black Chicago's First Century*, vol. 1, *1833–1900* (Columbia: University of Missouri Press, 2005), 238.

66. Reed, *Black Chicago's First Century*, 232.

67. "Social Gossip," *New York Globe*, August 18, 1883, 3.

68. "Saratoga Letter," *New York Globe*, August 18, 1883, 4.

69. At its core, democratic capitalism is a Marxist formulation that benefits workers.

70. "The Civil Rights Decision," *New York Globe*, October 20, 1883, 2.

71. Abraham L. Davis and Barbara Luck Graham, *The Supreme Court, Race, and Civil Rights* (Thousand Oaks, CA: Sage Publications, 1995), 46–48; Loren P. Beth, *John Marshall Harlan: The Last Whig Justice* (Lexington: University Press of Kentucky, 1992), 222–39; Douglas A. Blackmon, *Slavery by Another Name: The Re-enslavement of Black Americans from the Civil War to World War II* (New York: Doubleday, 2008), 93.

72. Deed from Green Clay Goodloe and Betty B. Goodloe to Isaac Murphy, Deed Book 68, p. 525, Fayette County Court, November 5, 1883.

73. Hotaling, *Great Black Jockeys*, 249.

74. Daniel Carter is listed in the *1883–84 Townsend's Lexington City Directory* (Lexington: Transylvania Printing Company, 1884), 40, as one of several paper hangers. Freedmen's Bank documents (Freedmen's Bank Records, 1865–1871, Ancestry.com; original data from Registers of Signatures of Depositors in Branches of the Freedmen's Savings and Trust Company, 1865–1874, micropublication M816, National Archives and Records Administration, Washington, DC) list a painter named Daniel Carter who was married to Mary Belle and had a daughter named Winnie. This could be the same individual. By employing black labor, Murphy had a positive impact on his community.

75. "Rain at the Race Track: Interferes with the Race Track, But Improves the Course," *Kentucky Leader*, January 19, 1890, 3. I would like to thank Anne Butler, PhD, of Kentucky State University for insight into Murphy's role in the Lincoln Lodge Masons.

76. See Joseph Mason Andrew Cox, *Great Black Men of Masonry 1723–1982* (New York: Blue Diamond Press, 1982); Loretta J. Williams, *Black Freemasonry and Middle Class Realities* (Columbia: University of Missouri Press, 1980); Edward Nelson Palmer, "Negro Secret Societies," *Social Forces* 23, no. 2. (December 1944): 207–12; Mary Ann Clawson, "Fraternal Orders and Class Formation in the Nineteenth-Century United States," *Comparative Studies in Society and History* 27, no. 4 (October 1985): 672–95.

77. Buddy Thompson, *Madame Belle Brezing* (Lexington: Buggy Whip Press, 1983), 61.

78. "Ed Corrigan's Career," *Kansas City Times*, July 17, 1885, 2.

79. Joe Drape, *Black Maestro: The Epic Life of an American Legend* (New York: William Morrow, 2006), 36.

80. "Sporting Summary," *New Hampshire Patriot*, December 20, 1883, 8.

81. *Turf, Field and Farm*, December 14, 1883, 2.

82. "Professional Jockeys," *Springfield Republican*, January 1, 1884, 8.

83. David Roediger, *The Wages of Whiteness: Race and the Making of the American Working Class* (London: Verso, 2002), 146.

84. "Isaac Murphy: Methods of Training and Riding," *Kansas City Star*, July 11, 1885, 4.

85. *Boston Herald*, August 1, 1883, 3.

86. "Sprays of Sport," *Rocky Mountain News*, March 24, 1884, 2.

87. Quoted in David W. Zang, *Fleet Walker's Divided Heart: The Life of Baseball's First Black Major Leaguer* (Lincoln: University of Nebraska Press, 1999), 39.

88. *Toledo Blade*, April 27, 1883, 3.

89. *Sporting Life*, September 24, 1883, 3.

90. *Kentucky Live Stock Record* 19, no. 19 (May 10, 1884): 201.

91. "The Turf," *Kentucky Live Stock Record* 19, no. 20 (May 24, 1884): 322.

92. Hotaling, *Great Black Jockeys*, 250.

93. "The Honors of the Turf: The Kentucky Derby Won by Buchanan," *New York Times*, May 17, 1884, 2.

94. Hotaling, *Great Black Jockeys*, 250; Betty Borries, *Isaac Murphy: Kentucky's Record Jockey* (Berea: Kentucke Imprints, 1988), 54; James Robert Saunders and Monica Renae Saunders, *Black Winning Jockeys in the Kentucky Derby* (Jefferson, NC: McFarland, 2003), 56.

95. "Honors of the Turf: Kentucky Derby Won by Buchanan," 2.

96. "Washington Park Races," *Kentucky Live Stock Record* 20, no. 1 (July 5, 1884): 4.

97. Florence Hartley, *The Ladies Book of Etiquette, and Manual of Politeness* (Boston: J. S. Locke, 1876), 75.

98. Quoted in Hotaling, *Great Black Jockeys*, 253.

99. From November 1884 to February 1885, leaders from fourteen European nations met to decide the fate of the African continent as a source of future wealth for the imperial powers. On February 26, 1885, the member nations ratified the General Act of the Berlin Conference in support of carving up the continent into European colonies. The subsequent "scramble for Africa" was a source of continued pain and suffering for Africans, who had experienced the brutality, indignity, and inhumanity of the European slave trade for close to 400 years. See Henry Morton Stanley, *The Congo and the Founding of Its Free State: A Story of Work and Exploration* (Cambridge: Cambridge University Press, 2011); Barbara Harlow and Mia Carter, eds., *Archives of Empire*, vol. 2, *The Scramble for Africa* (Durham, NC: Duke University Press, 2003); Giuseppe Maria Finaldi, *Italian National Identity in the Scramble for Africa:*

*Italy's African Wars in the Era of Nation-Building, 1870–1900* (Bern: International Academic Publishers, 2009).

100. "The Kentucky Derby: Great Excitement over the Event," *Kansas City Star*, May 14, 1885, 1; "A Famous Southern Derby," *New York Herald*, May 15, 1885, 6.

101. "Latonia Jockey Club," *Live Stock Record* 21, no. 22 (May 30, 1885): 340.

102. "The American Derby," *New Hampshire Sentinel*, June 28, 1885, 2.

103. Ibid.

104. "A High Priced Jockey," *New York Times*, July 12, 1885, 2; *Springfield Republican*, July 12, 1885, 1; *Elko Daily Independent*, July 13, 1885, 2; "Engaged by Lucky Baldwin for Two Years," *Kansas City Star*, July 11, 1885, 2; "A Valuable Jockey," *Oregonian*, July 12, 1885, 8.

105. "Jockey Ike Murphy: Methods of Training and Riding," *Kansas City Star*, July 11, 1885, 4 (reprinted from the *Chicago Tribune*).

106. "The Turf: Corrigan's Chicago," *Kansas City Times*, July 13, 1885, 2.

107. "General U. S. Grant," *Live Stock Record* 22, no. 6 (August 8, 1885): 88.

108. Borries, *Isaac Murphy*, 80.

109. "Crack Racers to Try Again: Freeland and Miss Woodford to Do Battle Once More at Monmouth," *New York Herald*, August 20, 1885, 6.

110. "Freeland's Famous Jockey," *New York Times*, August 20, 1885, 3.

111. "Eastern Racing," *San Francisco Bulletin*, August 21, 1885, 3.

112. Ibid.

113. Ibid.

114. "Baldwin Engages Murphy," *San Francisco Bulletin*, August 21, 1885, 3.

115. "The Defeat of Freeland," *New York Herald-Tribune*, August 21, 1885, 4.

116. "Notes of the Turf," *New York Times*, September 14, 1885, 2.

117. In several cases in which jockeys breached their employment contracts, their employers posted notices in the *Kentucky Live Stock Record* to warn other potential employers.

118. Steven A. Reiss, *The Sport of Kings and the Kings of Crime: Horse Racing, Politics, and Organized Crime in New York, 1865–1913* (Syracuse, NY: Syracuse University Press, 2011), 52–53.

119. "The Turf," *Times Picayune*, September 15, 1885, 8.

120. "Passengers Coming," *Los Angeles Herald*, April 20, 1886, 1.

121. "Baldwin's Ranch," *Detroit Free Press*, April 10, 1886, 2.

122. Ibid.

123. Ibid.

124. "Turf Notes," *Daily Inter-Ocean*, December 6, 1886, 6.

125. Sandra Lee Snider, *Elias Jackson "Lucky" Baldwin* (Los Angeles: Stairwell Group, 1987), 28–29.

126. "The Kentucky University," *New York Freeman*, May 29, 1886, 1; *Carson's Directory of the City of Louisville for 1885* (Louisville: C. K. Caron, 1885), 443.

127. Charles H. Wesley, *The History of Prince Hall Grand Lodge of Free and Accepted Masons of the State of Ohio, 1849–1960* (Wilberforce, OH: Central State College Press, 1961), 10.

128. "Washington Park Club," *Live Stock Record* 24, no. 1 (July 3, 1886): 3.

129. "The Pig-Skin Bayard: Isaac Murphy and His $12,000 a Year," *Daily Alta California*, July 23, 1886, 1.

130. Ibid.

131. Ibid.

132. "Washington Park Races," *Live Stock Record* 24, no. 4 (July 24, 1886): 53.

133. "Poison for Horses," *New York Times*, August 17, 1886, 5.

134. "Race Horses Drugged," *Kansas City Times*, August 15, 1886, 1.

135. "Isaac Murphy," *Australian Town and Country Journal*, September 25, 1886, 36.

136. "Lucky Baldwin's Flyers," *New York Times*, April 16, 1885, 1.

137. Hotaling, *Great Black Jockeys*, 256.

138. "Personal Mention," *Weekly Pelican*, April 30, 1887, 2.

139. "Pulling Horses," *Live Stock Record* 25, no. 24 (June 11, 1887): 376.

140. "Chicago Summertime Meeting," *Live Stock Record* 26, no. 1 (July 2, 1887): 3.

141. "A Great Turf Event," *Omaha Daily World*, June 17, 1887, 2.

142. "Jockeys Born and Made," *New York Herald*, June 27, 1887, 2.

143. Ibid.

144. Ibid., 2.

145. "Washington Park Club," *Live Stock Record* 26, no. 4 (July 23, 1887): 56.

146. "Sir Dixon's Triumph," *New York Herald*, August 24, 1887, 6.

147. "Bad Day for Favorites," *Daily Inter-Ocean*, August 24, 1887, 3.

148. "Post and Paddock," *Spirit of the Times*, September 3, 1887, 201.

149. "Track and Stable Talk," *Aberdeen Daily News*, December 28, 1887, 3.

150. "Isaac's Murphy's Position as a Jockey," *Live Stock Record* 27, no. 8 (February 25, 1888): 682.

151. Ibid.

152. "A Jockey's Comfortable Income," *Washington Critic*, February 11, 1888, 5.

153. "Isaac Murphy, the Colored Archer," *Chicago Horseman*, April 26, 1888, 496.

154. "Track Boulevard," *Chicago Horseman*, May 10, 1888, 568.

155. "Must Bow to The Bard," *Daily Inter-Ocean*, May 27, 1888, 2.

156. "Five Races Today," *Daily Inter-Ocean*, June 23, 1888, 3.

157. "Washington Park," *Chicago Horseman*, June 28, 1888, 790.

158. "Personals," *Live Stock Record* 8, no. 9 (September 1, 1888): 137; "Jimmy McLaughlin," *New York Times*, August 29, 1888, 2.

159. "Hankins & Campbell, Owners of the Chicago Stable, Have Engaged Jimmy McLaughlin," *Daily Inter-Ocean*, August 30, 1888, 1.

160. "Ike Murphy, the Colored Archer—Salary $10,000," *Cleveland Gazette*, August 18, 1888, 2.

161. "The American Turf Congress," *Live Stock Record* 28, no. 18 (November 3, 1888): 277.

162. "The Turf Congress: Western Men to Meet with Eastern Racing Authorities To-day," *New York Times*, November 15, 1888, 8.

163. "The New Scale of Weight," *Live Stock Record* 28, no. 21 (November 24, 1888): 327; "New Weights for Racers," *New York Times*, November 22, 1888, 2.

164. "Ike Murphy, the Colored Archer—Salary $10,000," 2.

165. Drape, *Black Maestro*, 54–57.

166. "King of the Pigskin Artists," *New York Herald*, March 17, 1889, 24.

167. Ibid.

168. "Badge by a Head," *New York Herald*, May 19, 1889, 2.

169. "For Lovers of Sport: Peter Jackson's Opinion of Certain Pugilists," *Wheeling Register*, August 18, 1889, 3.

170. "Lorillard Day at Monmouth," *New York Herald*, July 9, 1889, 8.

171. "Haggin's Hoard Increased," *Daily Inter-Ocean*, July 10, 1889, 2; "Isaac Murphy, the Finest Race Rider in the Country," *Indianapolis Freeman*, July 27, 1889, 2.

172. "Won by Foul Riding," *Daily Inter-Ocean*, July 10, 1889, 2.

## 8. In This Peculiar Country

1. "The Race Problem," *Kentucky Leader*, January 17, 1890, 1.

2. "The League a Fact," *New York Age*, January 25, 1890, 2.

3. "Afro-American League Convention Speech, *New York Age*, January 25, 1890, 2.

4. For a good explanation of the differences between a gentleman rider and a gentleman jockey, see "Gentleman Jockeys," *Bailey's Magazine of Sports and Pastimes 5* (November 1862): 218–27.

5. "Rain at the Racetrack," *Kentucky Leader*, January 19, 1890, 3.

6. William H. Ballard, *History of Prince Hall Freemasonry in Kentucky* (Lexington: Prince Hall Free and Accepted Masons, 1950); Martin Delany, *The Origins and Objects of Ancient Freemasonry: Its Introduction into the United States, and Legitimacy among Colored Men* (Pittsburgh: W. S. Haven, 1853); Harry B. Davis, *A History of Freemasonry among Negroes in America* (Detroit: Harlo Press, 1979); Charles Wesley, *The History of Prince Hall Grand Lodge of Free and Accepted Masons of the State of Ohio, 1849–1960* (Wilberforce, OH: Central State College Press, 1961).

7. In 1775 "Prince Hall and fourteen other free men of color were initiated into Masonry in Boston by an army lodge of a British regiment stationed in that city." Davis, *History of Freemasonry among Negroes*, 21.

8. "Knights-Templars vs. Knights-Templar," *Freemasons' Monthly Magazine* 24, no. 10 (August 1, 1865): 289.

9. Martha S. Jones, *All Bound up Together: The Woman Question in African American Public Culture, 1830–1900* (Chapel Hill: University of North Carolina Press, 2007), 169.

10. Dudley Wright, *Women and Freemasonry* (London: William Rider and Son, 1922), 108.

11. "Forty-One Race Horses," *Brooklyn Eagle*, March 2, 1890, 18.

12. "How the Derby Was Won," *Lexington Leader*, May 16, 1890, 1.

13. Ibid.

14. Newspapers like the *Cleveland Gazette* tended to exaggerate Murphy's winnings in an effort to elevate his significance as an iconic figure and an example of success and power. It reported that Ed Corrigan's winnings on Riley amounted to $15,000, almost three times the amount actually won. "The Race's Doings," *Cleveland Gazette*, June 14, 1890, 1.

15. "Louisville: Riley Proves to Be the Best Three Year Thus Far," *Spirit of the Times*, May 24, 1890, 1.

16. "Louisville Jockey Club," *Live Stock Record* 31, no. 21 (May 24, 1890): 324.

17. "Turf Notes," *Philadelphia Inquirer*, May 15, 1890, 6; "Turf Gossip," *Live Stock Record* 31, no. 21 (May 24, 1890): 326; "Personal," *San Francisco Bulletin*, July 25, 1890, 4.

18. "Latonia," *Spirit of the Times*, May 31, 1890, 1.

19. Ibid.

20. Carla L. Peterson, *Black Gotham* (New Haven, CT: Yale University Press, 2011).

21. "Racing in the West," *Spirit of the Times*, June 7, 1890, 1.

22. "Famous Riders: Three Colored Jockeys Who Have Done Wonderful," *Bismarck Tribune*, June 8, 1890, 4.

23. "A Suburban for Salvator: Cassius Second and Tenny Third in America's Greatest Race," *New York Times*, June 21, 1890, 1.

24. "The Big Suburban: Thousands to See the Greatest Race Ever Run in America," *St. Louis Post-Dispatch*, June 17, 1890, 2.

25. "A Suburban for Salvator," 1.

26. Ibid.

27. "A Splendid Turf Triumph," *Brooklyn Eagle*, June 18, 1890, 4.

28. "A Suburban for Salvator," 1.

29. "A Splendid Turf Triumph," 4.

30. "A Challenge," *Brooklyn Eagle*, June 19, 1890, 1; "The Favorites Beaten: A Tame Day's Racing at the Sheepshead Bay Race Track," *New York Times*, June 21, 1890, 8.

31. See David W. Zang, *Fleet Walker's Divided Heart: The Life of Baseball's First Black Major Leaguer* (Lincoln: University of Nebraska Press, 1995); Gail Bederman, *Manliness and Civilization: A Cultural History of Gender and Race in the United States, 1880–1917* (Chicago: University of Chicago, 1995); Colleen Aycock and Mark Scott, eds., *The First Black Boxing Champions: Essays on Fighters of the 1800s to the 1920s* (Jefferson, NC: McFarland, 2011).

32. "King of the Turf: Salvator Meets Tenny," *Louisville Courier-Journal*, June 18, 1890, 2.

33. Ibid.

34. "Instantaneous Photography," *Wilson's Photographic Magazine* 27, no. 382 (November 15, 1890): 699–700. Hemment was one of the first people to recognize the value of photography in sports. His photograph of the finish between Salvator and Tenny initiated a new element in horse racing: the photo finish. "Adventures in Photography," *Delineator*, November 1903, 641–46.

35. "King of the Turf: Salvator Meets Tenny," 2.

36. "Quarterstretch Notes," *New York Herald-Tribune*, June 26, 1890, 3.

37. "Salvator," *Chicago Horseman*, June 26, 1890, 1107.

38. "Isaac Murphy's Little Joke," *Chicago Horseman*, July 3, 1890, 1154.

39. "The Turf," *Cleveland Gazette*, July 12, 1890, 8.

40. "The Prince of Jockeys," *New York Age*, July 5, 1890, 1.

41. Ibid.

42. "A Lively League Meeting," *New York Age*, July 12, 1890, 1.

43. "Prince of Jockeys," 1.

44. "The World and the Church," *Indianapolis Freeman*, July 19, 1890, 7.

45. "His Physician Declares that Isaac Murphy Was Poisoned at Monmouth Park," *Daily Inter-Ocean*, November 17, 1890, 2.

46. "Track and Boulevard," *Chicago Horseman*, August 21, 1890, 1420.

47. "Monmouth Park," *Chicago Horseman*, August 14, 1890, 1379.

48. "Post and Paddock," *Spirit of the Times*, August 16, 1890, 142–43.

49. "Track and Boulevard," *Chicago Horseman*, August 28, 1890, 1462.

50. "In Their Field of Action," *Cleveland Gazette*, August 23, 1890, 2.

51. "Track and Boulevard," *Chicago Horseman*, August 21, 1890, 1420.

52. "A Monmouth Sensation," *New York Times*, August 27, 1890, 3.

53. Ed Hotaling, *The Great Black Jockeys: The Lives and Times of the Men Who Dominated America's First National Sport* (Rocklin, CA: Forum Prima Publishing, 1999), 264–65.

54. "Isaac Murphy Thought to Have Been Drugged," *Times Picayune*, August 29, 1890, 2.

55. "Murphy's Strange Illness," *New York Herald*, August 28, 1890, 7.

56. "The Monmouth Park Meeting," *Chicago Horseman*, September 4, 1890, 1494.

57. James McLaughlin had retired from racing after the Dwyer brothers replaced him with Murphy, and he became a trainer for Pierre Lorillard's Rancocas string of horses. But soon after the Monmouth Park affair, he decided to return to

the saddle for Frank Ehret's Hellgate Stable out of California. "Track and Boulevard," *Chicago Horseman*, September 4, 1890, 1504.

58. "Monmouth Sensation," 3; "Isaac Murphy's Mistake," *Kentucky Leader*, August 27, 1890, 1.

59. "Post and Paddock," *Spirit of the Times*, August 30, 1890, 226; "Isaac Murphy's Mistake," 1; "Monmouth Park Meeting," 1494.

60. "Isaac Murphy's Mistake," 1.

61. "Monmouth Sensation," 3.

62. "Murphy's Strange Illness: Neither Drunk nor Drugged, But in a Very Bad Way," *New York Herald*, August 28, 1890, 2.

63. Ibid.

64. "Monmouth Sensation," 3.

65. "Track and Boulevard," *Chicago Horseman*, September 4, 1890, 1504.

66. "Sporting: The Turf," *Times Picayune*, August 29, 1890, 2.

67. "Isaac Murphy's Mistake," 1.

68. "Isaac Murphy's Fall," *Cleveland Gazette*, August 30, 1890, 2.

69. "The Investigation," *Chicago Horseman*, September 11, 1890, 1543.

70. "The Race's Doings," *Cleveland Gazette*, October 11, 1890, 1.

71. "Sporting: The Turf," *Times Picayune*, October 6, 1890, 2.

72. "Jockey Murphy," *Evening News*, October 9, 1890, 2.

73. "Peace and Good Will," *Daily Inter-Ocean*, November 17, 1890, 2.

74. "Was Isaac Murphy Poisoned," *Live Stock Record* 32, no. 21 (November 22, 1890): 329.

75. "Isaac Murphy Was Poisoned: Proof that the Crack Jockey Was Wrongfully Accused of Drunkenness," *Philadelphia Inquirer*, November 15, 1890, 1.

76. "Isaac Murphy Ill," *Chicago Herald*, November 23, 1890, 1.

77. Ibid.

78. "Pot Calling the Kettle," *Cleveland Gazette*, December 20, 1890, 2.

79. The 1890 city directory has a listing for John Thomas, a brick setter, on Cherry Street north of Chase Street, which is near Race Street. *Williams' Cincinnati Directory* (Cincinnati: Williams and Co., 1890), 1333.

80. Ballard, *History of Prince Hall Freemasonry*, 104.

81. "Grand Reception," *Lexington Transcript*, January 25, 1891, 2.

82. Hotaling, *Great Black Jockeys*, 268.

83. "Won Fame as a Jockey: And He Showers Hospitality on His Friends," *Kentucky Leader*, January 31, 1893, 10.

84. "Sporting News," *Cleveland Plaindealer*, January 9, 1891, 2.

85. "Jockey Murphy Very Ill," *Cleveland Gazette*, January 10, 1891, 2.

86. "Tales of the Turf," *Grand Forks Herald*, January 25, 1891, 3.

87. "Tales of the Turf," *State: South Carolina*, February 26, 1891, 6.

88. "A Great Racing Year: Arrangements for the Greatest Season on the American Turf," *Dallas Morning News*, March 22, 1891, 17.

89. "Kingman Won with Ease," *Salt Lake Tribune*, May 14, 1891, 1.

90. "Louisville Jockey Club," *Live Stock Record* 33, no. 20 (May 16, 1891): 308.

91. "Turf and Track Notes," *New York Herald*, June 4, 1891, 9.

92. "Off Day at Morris Park," *New York Times*, June 4, 1891, 3.

93. "Racing and Trotting Notes," *New York Times*, June 12, 1891, 2.

94. For an excellent study of horse racing, politics, and organized crime in New York, see Steven Reiss, *The Sport of Kings and Kings of Crime: Horse Racing, Politics and Organized Crime in New York: 1865–1913* (Syracuse, NY: Syracuse University Press, 2011).

95. "Rey del Rey the Winner," *New York Times*, August 19, 1891, 2.

96. "Afro American Celebrities," *Indianapolis Freeman*, October 17, 1891, 1.

97. "Sale of The Hero," *Live Stock Record* 35, no. 3 (January 16, 1892): 37.

98. "The Hellgate Stable," *Live Stock Record* 35, no. 4 (January 20, 1892): 59.

99. George C. Wright, *Life behind the Veil: Blacks in Louisville, Kentucky 1865–1930* (Baton Rouge: Louisiana State University Press, 1985), 63.

100. Ibid., 62.

101. "Kentucky's Negro Orators and the 'Separate Coach,'" *Indianapolis Freeman*, February 13, 1892, 3.

102. *Kentucky Leader*, April 19, 1892.

103. "The Color Line in Kentucky," *Bridgeton Evening News*, April 1, 1892, 2.

104. "A Day's Happenings," *Aberdeen Daily News*, April 4, 1892, 3; "The General Assembly," *Semi-Weekly Interior Journal*, May 24, 1892, 3; "Color Line in Kentucky," 2.

105. *Wichita Daily Eagle*, May 25, 1892, 4.

106. "Sporting News," *Detroit Plaindealer*, May 13, 1892, 1.

107. "Pessara Wins the Handicap," *Philadelphia Inquirer*, May 31, 1892, 1.

108. "Sir Walter a Grand Colt," *New York Times*, July 12, 1892, 3.

109. "Don Alonzo's Victory," *New York Herald-Tribune*, July 24, 1892, 1.

110. "Racing Note," *New York Times*, July 27, 1892, 3.

111. "A Futurity for Morello," *New York Times*, August 28, 1892, 3.

112. "Horses and Their Owners," *New York Times*, February 11, 1893, 6.

113. "Out at Churchill Downs," *Live Stock Record* 37, no. 7 (February 18, 1893): 109.

114. "Jockeys Signed—Prominent Riders Who Have Made Contracts for the Year," *Times Picayune*, February 26, 1893, 3.

115. "Local Turf News," *Live Stock Record* 37, no. 12 (March 25, 1893): 207.

116. "Second Day—Track Sloppy, Weather Cloudy," *Live Stock Record* 37, no. 18 (May 6, 1893): 322.

117. "Some Race Doings," *Cleveland Gazette*, May 13, 1893, 1.

118. "The Kentucky Derby: The Nineteenth Renewal of that Classic Event," *Live Stock Record* 37, no. 19 (May 13, 1893): 352.

119. "The Derby Today," *Idaho Statesman*, May 10, 1893, 1.

120. "The Kentucky Derby," *Oregonian*, May 10, 1893, 2.

121. "Lookout Wins: Thirty Thousand People See the Kentucky Derby Run," *Cleveland Plaindealer*, May 11, 1893, 5.

122. "Latonia Jockey Club," *Live Stock Record* 37, no. 22, (June 3, 1893): 403.

123. "Morello Had a Walkover: Mississippi Stakes at St. Louis Taken without Exertion," *Daily Inter-Ocean*, June 16, 1893, 4.

124. "Light Card and Small Crowd: St. Louis Events Nearly Ruined by General Scratching," *Daily Inter-Ocean*, June 21, 1893, 4.

125. "Aristides Dead," *Live Stock Record* 37, no. 25 (June 24, 1893): 453.

126. "Great Day for Sports," *Evansville Courier and Press*, June 25, 1893, 1.

127. Ibid.

128. "A Great Stake for Boundless," *New York Times*, June 25, 1893, 3.

129. "Great Day for Sports," *Evansville Courier and Press*, June 25, 1893, 1.

130. Leon Taylor, "Isaac Murphy, Winner of Fourteen American Derbies," *Abbott's Monthly*, July 1932, 46.

131. *Live Stock Record* 38, no. 1 (July 1, 1893): 8.

132. *Live Stock Record* 38, no. 2 (July 8, 1893): 28.

133. *Live Stock Record* 38, no. 4 (July 22, 1893): 59.

134. *The American Turf: An Historical Account of Racing in the United States, with Biographical Sketches of Turf Celebrities* (New York: Historical Company, 1898), 356.

135. *Live Stock Record* 38, no. 7 (August 12, 1893): 105.

136. "Isaac Murphy May Ride No More," *Baltimore Sun*, December 18, 1893, 7.

137. "Local Turf News," *Live Stock Record* 38, no. 27 (December 30, 1893): 422.

138. "The National Jockey Club," *Live Stock Record* 39, no. 2 (January 13, 1894): 23.

139. William H. P. Robertson, *The History of Thoroughbred Racing in America* (New York: Bonanza Books, 1964), 174–76.

140. "A New Starting Device," *Live Stock Record* 39, no. 2 (January 13, 1894): 42.

141. "Isaac Murphy Will Ride Again," *Live Stock Record* 39, no. 1 (January 6, 1894): 4.

142. Ibid.

143. "Registered Owners' Colors," *Live Stock Record* 39, no. 6 (February 10, 1894): 87.

144. "Local Turf News," *Live Stock Record* 39, no. 9 (March 3, 1894): 134.

145. "Isaac Murphy Will Ride Again," 4.

146. "Jockeys Granted Licenses," *Live Stock Record* 39, no. 14 (April 7, 1894): 211.

147. "Horses in Training," *Live Stock Record* 39, no. 15 (April 14, 1894): 227.

148. "Winning Stables at Lexington," *Live Stock Record* 39, no. 20 (May 19, 1894): 306.

149. "Louisville Jockey Club," *Live Stock Record* 39, no. 20 (May 19, 1894): 306.

150. "Louisville Jockey Club," *Live Stock Record* 39, no. 21 (May 26, 1894): 322.

151. "Latonia Jockey Club," *Live Stock Record* 39, no. 23 (June 9, 1894): 356.

152. "Latonia Jockey Club," *Live Stock Record* 39, no. 24 (June 16, 1894): 373.

153. Willa Cather, "The Derby Winner," *Nebraska State Journal*, October 5, 1894, 6.

154. Robyn R. Warhol, "Ain't I de One Everybody Come to See," in *Hop on Pop: The Politics and Pleasures of Popular Culture*, ed. Henry Jenkins et al. (Durham, NC: Duke University Press, 2002), 665.

155. *Spirit of the Times*, December 1, 1894, 670.

156. "Horses and Their Owners," *New York Times*, December 14, 1894, 7.

157. "She Wants Her Boy," *Morning Herald*, March 15, 1895, 4.

158. Ibid.

159. "Soldiers against Tigers," *Kansas City Times*, April 4, 1895, 5.

160. "New Memphis Jockey Club Races," *Thoroughbred Record*, April 19, 1895, 253.

161. "Talk about Turf Affairs: Sims's Victory over English Jockeys," *New York Herald-Tribune*, April 22, 1895, 3.

162. "The Lexington Meeting," *Thoroughbred Record*, May 4, 1895, 285.

163. "Hornpipe's Handicap," *Dallas Morning News*, May 16, 1895, 3.

164. "Hornpipe's Brooklyn Handicap: The Light Weighted Colt from the Keene's Stable Outfoots a Rare Field in the Big Race at Gravesend," *New York Herald*, May 16, 1895, 4.

165. "Hornpipe Wins: The Great Gravesend Handicap Race Won by Hornpipe," *Grand Forks Herald*, May 16, 1895, 1.

166. Ibid.

167. "Lazzarone Vindicated," *Thoroughbred Record*, June 22, 1895, 392.

168. "To Be Investigated: Stewards of the Meeting Question the Owner and Trainer of Lazzarone," *New York Herald*, June 16, 1895, 3.

169. "Racing at Lexington," *Thoroughbred Record*, November 23, 1895, 243.

# 9. A Pageantry of Woe

1. "Isaac Murphy: Biographical Sketch of the Great Lexington Jockey," *Lexington Leader*, March 20, 1889, 3.

2. Letter dated April 28, 1967, from Frank Borries to Amelia from the Keeneland Library, describing his interview with Mrs. Nancy (Nannie Atchison) Slade. This letter is in the Betty Borries Collection of Isaac Murphy materials, Center of Excellence for the Study of Kentucky African Americans, Kentucky State University.

3. "Noted Jockeys to Act as Pall Bearers at Isaac Murphy's Funeral, *Kentucky Leader*, February 14, 1896, 8.

## Epilogue

1. See "In the Courts," *Morning Herald*, March 10, 1896. Isaac Murphy's will stipulated that his outstanding bills be paid, including his funeral expenses. He named Lucy B. Murphy as his sole executor. His estate was valued at $30,000, which included the property in Lexington and in Chicago.

2. Ed Hotaling, *The Great Black Jockeys: The Lives and Times of the Men Who Dominated America's First National Sport* (Rocklin, CA: Forum Prima Publishing, 1999), 298.

3. "Hamilton Is All Right," *New York Times*, August 1, 1896, 1.

4. Newspaper clipping from the *Lexington Herald*, June 26, 1955, in the Frank and Betty Borries Collection of Isaac Murphy material, Keeneland Library.

5. Joe Thomas, *Lexington Herald*, June 28, 1955.

6. See Frank Borries's notes, articles, and newspaper clippings in the Betty Borries Collection of Isaac Murphy materials, Kentucky State University.

# Index